Justice and the Politics of Difference

3-14

33-65

81-91

~~~~

96-191

234-41

Justice and the Politics of Difference

Iris Marion Young

PRINCETON UNIVERSITY PRESS

PRINCETON, NEW JERSEY

Published by Princeton University Press, 41 William Street,
Princeton, New Jersey 08540
In the United Kingdom: Princeton University Press, Chichester, West Sussex

Library of Congress Cataloging-in-Publication Data
Young, Iris Marion, 1949–
    Justice and the politics of difference / Iris Marion Young.
        p. cm.
    Includes bibliographic references and index.
    ISBN 0-691-07832-7 (alk. paper) — ISBN 0-691-02315-8 (pbk. : alk. paper)
    1. Social justice. 2. Oppression (Psychology) 3. Pluralism (Social
    sciences) 4. Political participation. 5. Social institutions. I. Title.
    JC578.Y68   1990   90-36988
    320′.01′1—dc20

This book has been composed in Linotron Caledonia

Princeton University Press books are printed on acid-free paper, and meet the
guidelines for permanence and durability of the Committee on Production Guidelines
for Book Longevity of the Council on Library Resources

Printed in the United States of America

20 19 18 17 16 15 14 13 12 11

ISBN-13: 978-0-691-02315-1 (pbk.)

ISBN-10: 0-691-02315-8 (pbk.)

For Dave

Contents

Acknowledgments   ix

INTRODUCTION   3

CHAPTER 1
Displacing the Distributive Paradigm   15

The Distributive Paradigm   16
The Distributive Paradigm Presupposes and Obscures
  Institutional Context   18
Overextending the Concept of Distribution   24
Problems with Talk of Distributing Power   30
Defining Injustice as Domination and Oppression   33

CHAPTER 2
Five Faces of Oppression   39

Oppression as a Structural Concept   40
The Concept of a Social Group   42
The Faces of Oppression   48
Applying the Criteria   63

CHAPTER 3
Insurgency and the Welfare Capitalist Society   66

Normative Principles of Welfare Capitalist Society   67
The Depoliticization of Welfare Capitalist Society   70
The Ideological Function of the Distributive Paradigm   74
The Administered Society and New Forms of Domination   76
Insurgency and the Repoliticization of Public Life   81
The Dialectic of Recontainment versus Democracy   88
Democracy as a Condition of Social Justice   91

CHAPTER 4
The Ideal of Impartiality and the Civic Public   96

Postmodernist Critique of the Logic of Identity   98
The Ideal of Impartiality as Denying Difference   99
The Impossibility of Impartiality   102
The Logic of Identity in the Ideal of the Civic Public   107
Ideological Functions of the Ideal of Impartiality   111
Participatory Democracy and the Idea of a Heterogeneous
  Public   116

CHAPTER 5
The Scaling of Bodies and the Politics of Identity 122
The Scaling of Bodies in Modern Discourse 124
Conscious Acceptance, Unconscious Aversion 130
Behavioral Norms of Respectability 136
Xenophobia and Abjection 141
Moral Responsibility and Unintended Action 148
Justice and Cultural Revolution 152

CHAPTER 6
Social Movements and the Politics of Difference 156
Competing Paradigms of Liberation 158
Emancipation through the Politics of Difference 163
Reclaiming the Meaning of Difference 168
Respecting Difference in Policy 173
The Heterogeneous Public and Group Represenation 183

CHAPTER 7
Affirmative Action and the Myth of Merit 192
Affirmative Action and the Principle of Nondiscrimination 193
Affirmative Action Discussion and the Distributive Paradigm 198
The Myth of Merit 200
Education and Testing as Performance Proxies 206
The Politics of Qualifications 210
Oppression and the Social Division of Labor 214
The Democratic Division of Labor 222

CHAPTER 8
City Life and Difference 226
The Opposition between Individualism and Community 227
The Rousseauist Dream 229
Privileging Face-to-Face Relations 232
Undesirable Political Consequences of the Ideal of Community 234
City Life as a Normative Ideal 236
Cities and Social Injustice 241
Empowerment without Autonomy 248

EPILOGUE: INTERNATIONAL JUSTICE 257

References 261
Index 277

Acknowledgments

THE WRITING of this book was supported by a grant from the American Council of Learned Societies and by a sabbatical leave from the Worcester Polytechnic Institute.

Many of the central positions in this book were inspired by the stimulating discussions about gender, race, and class held at meetings of the Radical Philosophers Association from 1985 to 1987.

Many colleagues commented on various portions of the manuscript in various stages of its development. Thanks to Seyla Benhabib, Lawrence Blum, Charles Ellison, Ann Ferguson, Nancy Fraser, Marilyn Friedman, Robert Fullinwider, Roger Gottlieb, Philip Green, Nancy Hartsock, Alison Jaggar, William McBride, Linda Nicholson, Lucius Outlaw, Deborah Rhode, Richard Schmitt, Mary Shanley, James Sterba, and John Trimbur. The ideas in this book have been enriched by many conversations with Martha Minow, Susan Okin, and Thomas Wartenburg.

Thanks to Frank Hunt for a sympathetic and expert editing job.

Most of all, thanks to Dave Alexander, who read several drafts of the manuscript and offered irreplaceable help; who discussed the ideas with me during many evenings, and listened to my complaints and frustrations; who offers more than one could ask in intellectual and emotional companionship.

Portions of this book have appeared elsewhere in different form. I would like to thank the publishers for permission to make use of the following materials:

"Five Faces of Oppression," *Philosophical Forum* 19, no. 4 (Summer 1988), pp. 270–90, revised as Chapter 2.

"Impartially and the Civic Public: Some Implications of Feminist Critiques of Moral and Political Theory," in Seyla Benhabib and Drucilla Cornell, eds., *Feminism as Critique* (Polity Press and University of Minnesota Press, 1987), pp. 56–76, for some material in Chapter 4.

"Polity and Group Difference: A Critique of the Ideal of Universal Citizenship," *Ethics* 99, no. 2 (January 1989), pp. 250–74, and "Difference and Social Policy: Reflections in the Context of Social Movements," *University of Cincinnati Law Review* 56, no. 2 (Fall 1987), pp. 535–50, both for some material in Chapter 6.

"Abjection and Oppression: Unconscious Dynamics of Racism, Sexism and Homophobia," in Arlene Dallery and Charles Scott, eds., *The Crisis in Continental Philosophy* (SUNY Press, 1990), for a portion of Chapter 5.

"The Ideal of Community and the Politics of Difference," *Social Theory and Practice* 12, no. 1 (Spring 1986), pp. 1–26, for a portion of Chapter 8.

Justice and the Politics of Difference

Introduction

WHAT are the implications for political philosophy of the claims of new group-based social movements associated with left politics—such movements as feminism, Black liberation, American Indian movements, and gay and lesbian liberation? What are the implications for political philosophy of postmodern philosophy's challenge to the tradition of Western reason? How can traditional socialist appeals to equality and democracy be deepened and broadened as a result of these developments in late twentieth-century politics and theory? Justice is the primary subject of political philosophy. These questions are thus inseparable from questions about justice. What conceptions of social justice do these new social movements implicitly appeal to, and how do they confront or modify traditional conceptions of justice?

These are some of the questions that propel the inquiry in this book. In addressing them I explore some problems of positivism and reductionism in political theory. The positivism of political theory consists in too often assuming as given institutional structures that ought to be brought under normative evaluation. The reductionism I expose is modern political theory's tendency to reduce political subjects to a unity and to value commonness or sameness over specificity and difference.

I argue that instead of focusing on distribution, a conception of justice should begin with the concepts of domination and oppression. Such a shift brings out issues of decisionmaking, division of labor, and culture that bear on social justice but are often ignored in philosophical discussions. It also exhibits the importance of social group differences in structuring social relations and oppression; typically, philosophical theories of justice have operated with a social ontology that has no room for a concept of social groups. I argue that where social group differences exist and some groups are privileged while others are oppressed, social justice requires explicitly acknowledging and attending to those group differences in order to undermine oppression.

Although I discuss and argue about justice, I do not construct a theory of justice. A theory of justice typically derives fundamental principles of justice that apply to all or most societies, whatever their concrete configuration and social relations, from a few general premises about the nature of human beings, the nature of societies, and the nature of reason. True to the meaning of *theoria*, it wants to see justice. It assumes a point of view outside the social context where issues of justice arise, in order to gain a comprehensive view. The theory of justice is intended to be self-standing, since it exhibits its own foundations. As a discourse it aims to be whole, and to show justice in its unity. It is detemporalized, in that nothing comes before it and future events will not affect its truth or relevance to social life.

Theorists of justice have a good reason for abstracting from the particular circumstances of social life that give rise to concrete claims of justice, to take a position outside social life that rests on reason. Such a self-standing rational theory would be independent of actual social institutions and relations, and for that reason could serve as a reliable and objective normative standard for evaluating those institutions and relations. Without a universal normative theory of justice grounded independently of the experience of a particular society, it is often assumed, philosophers and social actors cannot distinguish legitimate claims of justice from socially specific prejudices or self-interested claims to power.

The attempt to develop a theory of justice that both stands independent of a given social context and yet measures its justice, however, fails in one of two ways. If the theory is truly universal and independent, presupposing no particular social situations, institutions, or practices, then it is simply too abstract to be useful in evaluating actual institutions and practices. In order to be a useful measure of actual justice and injustice, it must contain some substantive premises about social life, which are usually derived, explicitly or implicitly, from the actual social context in which the theorizing takes place. Many have argued that Rawls's theory of justice, for example, must have some substantive premises if it is to ground substantive conclusions, and these premises implicitly derive from experience of people in modern liberal capitalist societies (see Young, 1981; Simpson, 1980; Wolff, 1977, pt. IV).

A theory of justice that claims universality, comprehensiveness, and necessity implicitly conflates moral reflection with scientific knowledge (Williams, 1985, chap. 6). Reflective discourse about justice, however, should not pose as knowledge in the mode of seeing or observing, where the knower is initiator and master of the known. Discourse about justice is not motivated originally by curiosity, a sense of wonder, or the desire to figure out how something works. The sense of justice arises not from looking, but as Jean-François Lyotard says, from listening:

> For us, a language is first and foremost someone talking. But there are language games in which the important thing is to listen, in which the rule deals with audition. Such a game is the game of the just. And in this game, one speaks only inasmuch as one listens, that is, one speaks as a listener, and not as an author. (Lyotard, 1985, pp. 71–72)

While everyday discourse about justice certainly makes claims, these are not theorems to be demonstrated in a self-enclosed system. They are instead calls, pleas, claims *upon* some people by others. Rational reflection on justice begins in a hearing, in heeding a call, rather than in asserting and mastering a state of affairs, however ideal. The call to "be just" is always situated in concrete social and political practices that precede and exceed the philosopher. The traditional effort to transcend that finitude toward a universal theory yields only finite constructs which escape the appearance of contingency usually by recasting the given as necessary.

Rejecting a theory of justice does not entail eschewing rational discourse about justice. Some modes of reflection, analysis, and argument aim not at building a systematic theory, but at clarifying the meaning of concepts and issues, describing and explaining social relations, and articulating and defending ideals and principles. Reflective discourse about justice makes arguments, but these are not intended as definitive demonstrations. They are addressed to others and await their response, in a situated political dialogue. In this book I engage in such situated analysis and argument in the mode of critical theory.

As I understand it, critical theory is a normative reflection that is historically and socially contextualized. Critical theory rejects as illusory the effort to construct a universal normative system insulated from a particular society. Normative reflection must begin from historically specific circumstances because there is nothing but what is, the given, the situated interest in justice, from which to start. Reflecting from within a particular social context, good normative theorizing cannot avoid social and political description and explanation. Without social theory, normative reflection is abstract, empty, and unable to guide criticism with a practical interest in emancipation. Unlike positivist social theory, however, which separates social facts from values, and claims to be value-neutral, critical theory denies that social theory must accede to the given. Social description and explanation must be critical, that is, aim to evaluate the given in normative terms. Without such a critical stance, many questions about what occurs in a society and why, who benefits and who is harmed, will not be asked, and social theory is liable to reaffirm and reify the given social reality.

Critical theory presumes that the normative ideals used to criticize a society are rooted in experience of and reflection on that very society, and that norms can come from nowhere else. But what does this mean, and how is it possible for norms to be both socially based and measures of society? Normative reflection arises from hearing a cry of suffering or distress, or feeling distress oneself. The philosopher is always socially situated, and if the society is divided by oppressions, she either reinforces or struggles against them. With an emancipatory interest, the philosopher apprehends given social circumstances not merely in contemplation but with passion: the given is experienced in relation to desire. Desire, the desire to be happy, creates the distance, the negation, that opens the space for criticism of what is. This critical distance does not occur on the basis of some previously discovered rational ideas of the good and the just. On the contrary, the ideas of the good and the just arise from the desiring negation that action brings to what is given.

Critical theory is a mode of discourse which projects normative possibilities unrealized but felt in a particular given social reality. Each social reality presents its own unrealized possibilities, experienced as lacks and desires. Norms and ideals arise from the yearning that is an expression of freedom: it does not have to be this way, it could be otherwise. Imagination is the faculty of transforming the experience of what is into a projection of what could be, the faculty that frees thought to form ideals and norms.

Herbert Marcuse describes this genesis of ideals from an experience of the possibilities desired but unrealized in the given:

> There are a large class of concepts—we dare say, philosophically relevant concepts—where the quantitative relation between the universal and the particular assumes a qualitative aspect, where the abstract, universal seems to designate potentialities in a concrete, historical sense. However "man," "nature," "justice," "beauty," or "freedom" may be defined, they synthesize experiential contents into ideas which transcend their particular realizations as something to be surpassed, overcome. Thus the concept of beauty comprehends all the beauty not *yet* realized; the conception of freedom all the liberty not *yet* attained. . . .
>
> Such universals thus appear as conceptual instruments for understanding the particular conditions of things in light of their potentialities. They are historical and supra-historical; they conceptualize the stuff of which the experienced world consists, and they conceptualize it with a view of its possibilities, in the light of their actual limitation, suppression, and denial. Neither the experience nor judgment is private. The philosophic concepts are formed and developed in the consciousness of a general condition in a historical continuum; they are elaborated from an individual position within a specific society. The stuff of thought is historical stuff—no matter how abstract, general, or pure it may become in philosophic or scientific theory. (Marcuse, 1964, pp. 214–15)

In his notion of interpretation as social criticism, Michael Walzer endorses a similar approach to moral reflection. The social critic is engaged in and committed to the society he or she criticizes. She does not take a detached point of view toward the society and its institutions, though she does stand apart from its ruling powers. The normative basis for her criticism comes from the ideals and tensions of the society itself, ideals already there in some form, in espoused principles that are violated, for example, or in social movements that challenge hegemonic ideas. The criticism of the social critic "does not require either detachment or enmity, because he finds a warrant for critical engagement in the idealism, even if it is a hypothetical idealism, of the actually existing moral world" (Walzer, 1987, p. 61).

This book has its philosophical starting point in claims about social domination and oppression in the United States. Ideas and experience born in the new left social movements of the 1960s and 1970s continue to inform the thoughts and actions of many individuals and organizations in contemporary American political life: democratic socialist, environmentalist, Black, Chicano, Puerto Rican, and American Indian movements; movements against U.S. military intervention in the Third World; gay and lesbian liberation; movements of the disabled, the old, tenants, and the poor; and the feminist movement. These movements all claim in varying ways that American society contains deep institutional injustices. But they find little kinship with contemporary philosophical theories of justice.

My aim is to express rigorously and reflectively some of the claims about justice and injustice implicit in the politics of these movements, and to explore their meaning and implications. I identify some bases for disparity between contemporary situated claims and theoretical claims about justice in fundamental assumptions of modern Western political philosophy. This project requires both criticism of ideas and institutions and the assertion of positive ideals and principles. I criticize some of the language and principles of justice that dominate in contemporary philosophy and offer alternative principles. I examine a number of policies, institutions, and practices of U.S. society, and show how some of the philosophical principles I criticize are also ideological insofar as they reinforce these institutions and practices. I offer, finally, some alternative visions of ideal social relations.

Though my method is derived from critical theory, I reject some tenets of critical theorists. While I follow Habermas's account of advanced capitalism and his general notion of communicative ethics, for example, I nevertheless criticize his implicit commitment to a homogeneous public. I am also indebted to several other approaches to philosophy and political theory. I extend some contemporary feminist analyses of the male bias implicit in the ideals of rationality, citizenship, and equality central to modern moral and political theory. My inquiry about a positive sense of group difference and a politics that attends to rather than represses difference owes much to discussions of the meaning of difference in such postmodern writers as Derrida, Lyotard, Foucault, and Kristeva. From this postmodern orientation, in which I also include some of the writings of Adorno and Irigaray, I appropriate a critique of unifying discourse to analyze and criticize such concepts as impartiality, the general good, and community.

From the lessons of these critiques I derive an alternative conception of differentiated social relations. The analyses and arguments in this book also draw on analytic moral and political philosophy, Marxism, participatory democratic theory, and Black philosophy.

Recent years have witnessed much discussion about the virtues and vices of each of these theoretical approaches, and many would find them incompatible. A debate about modernism versus postmodernism has recently raged among critical theorists, for example—a debate which has an analogue among feminist theorists. In this book I do not explicitly treat metatheoretical questions about the criteria for evaluating theoretical approaches to social and normative theorizing. When social theorists and social critics focus on such epistemological questions, they often abstract from the social issues that originally gave rise to the disputes and impart an intrinsic value to the epistemological enterprise. Methodological and epistemological issues do arise in the course of this study, but I treat them always as interruptions of the substantive normative and social issues at hand. I do not regard any of the theoretical approaches which I take up as a totality that must be accepted or rejected in its entirety. Each provides useful tools for the analyses and arguments I wish to make.

I begin in Chapter 1 by distinguishing between an approach to social justice that gives primacy to having and one that gives primacy to doing. Contemporary theories of justice are dominated by a distributive paradigm, which tends to focus on the possession of material goods and social positions. This distributive focus, however, obscures other issues of institutional organization at the same time that it often assumes particular institutions and practices as given.

Some distributive theories of justice explicitly seek to take into account issues of justice beyond the distribution of material goods. They extend the distributive paradigm to cover such goods as self-respect, opportunity, power, and honor. Serious conceptual confusion results, however, from attempting to extend the concept of distribution beyond material goods to phenomena such as power and opportunity. The logic of distribution treats nonmaterial goods as identifiable things or bundles distributed in a static pattern among identifiable, separate individuals. The reification, individualism, and pattern orientation assumed in the distributive paradigm, moreover, often obscure issues of domination and oppression, which require a more process-oriented and relational conceptualization.

Distributive issues are certainly important, but the scope of justice extends beyond them to include the political as such, that is, all aspects of institutional organization insofar as they are potentially subject to collective decision. Rather than attempting to stretch distribution to cover these, I argue that the concept of distribution should be limited to material goods, and that other important aspects of justice include decision-making procedures, the social division of labor, and culture. Oppression and domination, I argue, should be the primary terms for conceptualizing injustice.

The concept of oppression is central to the discourse of the contemporary emancipatory social movements whose perspectives inspire the critical questions of this book. Yet there exists no sustained theoretical analysis of the concept of oppression as understood by these movements. Chapter 2 fills this conspicuous gap in social theory by defining oppression. Actually a family of concepts, oppression has five aspects which I explicate: exploitation, marginalization, powerlessness, cultural imperialism, and violence. Distributive injustices may contribute to or result from these forms of oppression, but none is reducible to distribution and all involve social structures and relations beyond distribution.

Oppression happens to social groups. But philosophy and social theory typically lack a viable concept of the social group. Notably in the context of affirmative action debate, some philosophers and policymakers even refuse to acknowledge the reality of social groups, a denial that often reinforces group oppressions. In Chapter 2 I develop a specific concept of the social group. While groups do not exist apart from individuals, they are socially prior to individuals, because people's identities are partly constituted by their group affinities. Social groups reflect ways that people identify themselves and others, which lead them to associate with some people more than others, and to treat others as different. Groups are identified in relation to one another. Their existence is fluid and often shifting, but nevertheless real.

The concept of justice is coextensive with the political. Politics, in Hannah Pitkin's words is "the activity through which relatively large and permanent groups of people determine what they will collectively do, settle how they will live together, and decide their future, to whatever extent this is within their power" (Pitkin, 1981, p. 343). Roberto Unger defines politics as "struggle over the resources and arrangements that set the basic terms of our practical and passionate relations. Preeminent among these arrangements," he observes, "is the formative institutional and imaginative context of social life" (Unger, 1987a, p. 145). Politics in this sense concerns all aspects of institutional organization, public action, social practices and habits, and cultural meanings insofar as they are potentially subject to collective evaluation and decisionmaking. When people say a rule or practice or cultural meaning is wrong and should be changed, they are usually making a claim about social justice. This is a wider understanding of the meaning of politics than that common among most philosophers and policymakers, who tend to identify politics as the activities of government or formal interest-group organizations. Chapter 3 takes up a primary contribution of new left social movements, their continuing effort to politicize vast areas of institutional, social, and cultural life in the face of forces of welfare state liberalism which operate to depoliticize public life.

With many critical theorists and democratic theorists, I criticize welfare capitalist society for depoliticizing the process of public policy formation. Welfare state practices define policy as the province of experts, and confine conflict to bargaining among interest groups about the distribution of social benefits. The distributive paradigm of justice tends to reflect and reinforce this depoliticized public life, by failing to bring issues of decisionmaking power, for example, into explicit public discussion. Democratic decisionmaking processes, I argue, are an important element and condition of social justice.

Some feminist and postmodern writers have suggested that a denial of difference structures Western reason, where difference means particularity, the heterogeneity of the body and affectivity, or the inexhaustibility of linguistic and social relations without a unitary, undifferentiated origin. This book seeks to show how such a denial of difference contributes to social group oppression, and to argue for a politics that recognizes rather than represses difference. Thus Chapter 4 argues that the ideal of impartiality, a keystone of most modern moral theories and theories of justice, denies difference. The ideal of impartiality suggests that all moral situations should be treated according to the same rules. By claiming to provide a standpoint which all subjects can adopt, it denies the difference between subjects. By positing a unified and universal moral point of view, it generates a dichotomy between reason and feeling. Usually expressed in counterfactuals, the ideal of impartiality expresses an impossibility. It serves at least two ideological functions, moreover. First, claims to impartiality feed cultural imperialism by allowing the particular experience and perspective of privileged groups to parade as universal. Second, the conviction that bureaucrats and experts can exercise their decisionmaking power in an impartial manner legitimates authoritarian hierarchy.

Impartiality, I also suggest in Chapter 4, has its political counterpart in the ideal of the civic public. Critical theory and participatory democratic theory share with the liberal theory they challenge a tendency to suppress difference by conceiving the polity as universal and unified. This universalist ideal of the civic public has operated to effectively exclude from citizenship persons identified with the body and feeling—women, Jews, Blacks, American Indians, and so on. A conception of justice which challenges institutionalized domination and oppression should offer a vision of a heterogeneous public that acknowledges and affirms group differences.

One consequence of the ideal of moral reason as impartiality is the theoretical separation of reason from body and feeling. In Chapter 5 I discuss some implications of modern society's denigration of the body. In its identification of some groups with despised or ugly bodies, rationalistic culture contributes to the oppressions of cultural imperialism and violence. The cultural logic that hierarchizes bodies according to a "normative gaze" locates bodies on a single aesthetic scale that constructs some kinds of bodies as ugly, disgusting, or degenerate. Using Kristeva's theory of the abject, I analyze the political importance of feelings of beauty and ugliness, cleanliness and filth, in the interactive dynamics and cultural stereotyping of racism, sexism, homophobia, ageism, and ableism.

In our society aversive or anxious reactions to the bodily presence of others contribute to oppression. Such cultural reactions are usually unconscious, however, often exhibited by liberal-minded people who intend to treat everyone with equal respect. Because moral theories tend to focus on deliberate action for which they seek means of justification, they usually do not bring unintended social sources of oppression under judgment. A conception of justice that fails to notice and seek institutional remedy for these cultural sources of oppression, however, is inadequate. I discuss some remedies in processes of consciousness raising and cultural decision-making.

Such cultural change occurs partly when despised groups seize the means of cultural expression to redefine a positive image of themselves. In the last twenty years feminists, Black liberation activists, American Indians, disabled people, and other groups oppressed by being marked as fearful bodies have asserted such images of positive difference. Such movements of group pride have come to challenge an ideal of liberation as the elimination of group difference from political and institutional life. In Chapter 6 I argue for principles and practices that instead identify liberation with social equality that affirms group difference and fosters the inclusion and participation of all groups in public life.

The principle of equal treatment originally arose as a formal guarantee of fair inclusive treatment. This mechanical interpretation of fairness, however, also suppresses difference. The politics of difference sometimes implies overriding a principle of equal treatment with the principle that group differences should be acknowledged in public policy and in the policies and procedures of economic institutions, in order to reduce actual or potential oppression. Using examples from contemporary legal debate, including debates about equality and difference in women's liberation, bilingual education, and American Indian rights, I argue that sometimes recognizing particular rights for groups is the only way to promote their full participation. Some fear that such differential treatment again stigmatizes these groups. I show how this is true only if we continue to understand difference as opposition—identifying equality with sameness and difference with deviance or devaluation. Recognition of group difference also requires a principle of political decisionmaking that encourages autonomous organization of groups within a public. This entails establishing procedures for ensuring that each group's voice is heard in the public, through institutions of group representation.

Within the context of a general principle that promotes attending to group differences in order to undermine oppression, affirmative action programs do not appear so extraordinary as contemporary rhetoric often makes them seem. In Chapter 7 I support affirmative action programs, not on grounds of compensation for past discrimination, but as important means for undermining oppression, especially oppression that results from unconscious aversions and stereotypes and from the assumption that the point of view of the privileged is neutral. Discussion of affirmative action, however, tends to exhibit the distributive paradigm of justice. Concerned only with the distribution of positions of high reward and prestige among groups, this discussion tends to presuppose institutions and practices whose justice it does not question. I examine two such assumptions in particular: the idea that positions can and should be distributed according to merit criteria, and the hierarchical division of labor that makes some scarce positions highly rewarded and most positions less desirable.

The ideal of merit distribution of positions is an instance of the ideal of impartiality. Criteria of merit assume that there are objective measures and predictors of technical work performance independent of cultural and normative attributes. But I argue that no such measures exist; job allocation is inevitably political in the sense that it involves specific values and norms which cannot be separated from issues of technical competence. If merit distribution of scarce positions is impossible, the legitimacy of those positions themselves is brought into question. A hierarchical division of labor that separates task-defining from task-executing work enacts domination, and produces or reinforces at least three forms of oppression: exploitation, powerlessness, and cultural imperialism. Some of this injustice can be mitigated indirectly by democratizing workplaces. But the division between task-defining and task-executing work must also be attacked directly to eliminate the privileges of specialized training and ensure that all persons have skill-developing work.

Critics of liberalism and welfare bureaucracy often appeal to the ideal of community as an alternative vision of social life. Community represents an ideal of shared public life, of mutual recognition and identification. The concluding chapter argues that the ideal of community also suppresses difference among subjects and groups. The impulse to community often coincides with a desire to preserve identity and in practice excludes others who threaten that sense of identity. I develop another ideal of social relations and politics, which begins from our positive experience of city life. Ideally city life embodies four virtues that represent heterogeneity rather than unity: social differentiaion without exclusion, variety, eroticism, and publicity.

Far short of the ideal, contemporary American cities actually contain many injustices. Capital movement and land use decisions produce and reproduce injustices not well captured by a theory that focuses primarily on patterns of end-state distribution. Additional injustices arise from the separation of functions and segregation of groups produced by zoning and suburbanization. Contrary to many democratic theorists, however, I think that increasing local autonomy would exacerbate these problems. The normative ideal of city life would be better realized through metropolitan regional government founded in representational institutions that begin in neighborhood assemblies. I end the book with a short discussion of how the issues raised in this book may be extended to considerations of international justice.

In pursuit of a systematic theory, much philosophical writing addresses an audience made up abstractly of all reasonable persons from the point of view of any reasonable person. Because I understand critical theory as starting from a specific location in a specific society, I can claim in this writing to be neither impartial nor comprehensive. I claim to speak neither for everyone, to everyone, nor about everything.

My personal political passion begins with feminism, and it is from my participation in the contemporary women's movement that I first learned to identify oppression and develop social and normative theoretical reflection on it. My feminism, however, has always been supplemented by commitment to and participation in movements against military intervention abroad and for systematic restructuring of the social circumstances that keep so many people poor and disadvantaged at home. The interaction of feminism with Marxism and participatory democratic theory and practice accounts for the plural understanding of oppression and domination I present in these pages.

My own reflections on the politics of difference were ignited by discussions in the women's movement of the importance and difficulty of acknowledging differences of class, race, sexuality, age, ability, and culture among women. As women of color, disabled women, old women, and others increasingly voiced their experiences of exclusion, invisibility, or stereotyping by feminist discourse, the assumption that feminism identifies and seeks to change the common position of women became increasingly untenable. I do not at all think this means the end of specifically feminist discourse, because I still experience, as do many other women, the affinity for other women which we have called sisterhood, even across differences. Nevertheless this discussion has compelled me to move out of a focus specifically on women's oppression, to try to understand as well the social position of other oppressed groups.

As a white, heterosexual, middle-class, able-bodied, not old woman, I cannot claim to speak for radical movements of Blacks, Latinos, American Indians, poor people, lesbians, old people, or the disabled. But the political commitment to social justice which motivates my philosophical reflection tells me that I also cannot speak without them. Thus while my personal passion begins with feminism, and I reflect on the experience and ideas of the peace, environmental, and anti-intervention movements in which I have participated, the positions I develop in this book emerge from reflection on the experience and ideas of movements of other oppressed groups, insofar as I can understand that experience by reading and by talking with people in them. Thus while I do not claim here to speak for all reasonable persons, I do aim to speak from multiple positions and on the basis of the experience of several contemporary social movements.

Philosophers acknowledge the partiality of the audience to which their arguments are addressed, it seems to me, often even less than they acknowledge the particularity of the voice of their writing. In this book I make some assumptions that perhaps not all reasonable persons share: that basic equality in life situation for all persons is a moral value; that there are deep injustices in our society that can be rectified only by basic institutional changes; that the groups I have named are oppressed; that structures of domination wrongfully pervade our society. Certainly many intellectuals and policymakers today are sympathetic enough with these assumptions to want to participate in discussion of some of their implications for conceiving and imagining social justice. For those who do not share one or more of these assumptions, I hope the analyses and arguments in this book will nevertheless stimulate a fruitful political dialogue.

CHAPTER 1

Displacing the Distributive Paradigm

> It was in general a mistake to make a fuss about so-called *distribution* and put the principal stress on it. Any distribution whatever of the means of consumption is only a consequence of the distribution of the conditions of production themselves. The latter distribution, however, is a feature of the mode of production itself.
>
> —Karl Marx

THOUSANDS of buses converge on the city, and tens of thousands of people of diverse colors, ages, occupations, and life styles swarm onto the mall around the Washington Monument until the march begins. At midday people move into the streets, chanting, singing, waving wild papier-mâché missiles or effigies of government officials. Many carry signs or banners on which a simple slogan is inscribed: "Peace, Jobs, and Justice."

This scene has occurred many times in Washington, D.C., in the last decade, and many more times in other U.S. cities. What does "justice" mean in this slogan? In this context, as in many other political contexts today, I suggest that social justice means the elimination of institutionalized domination and oppression. Any aspect of social organization and practice relevant to domination and oppression is in principle subject to evaluation by ideals of justice.

Contemporary philosophical theories of justice, however, do not conceive justice so broadly. Instead, philosophical theories of justice tend to restrict the meaning of social justice to the morally proper distribution of benefits and burdens among society's members. In this chapter I define and assess this distributive paradigm. While distributive issues are crucial to a satisfactory conception of justice, it is a mistake to reduce social justice to distribution.

I find two problems with the distributive paradigm. First, it tends to focus thinking about social justice on the allocation of material goods such as things, resources, income, and wealth, or on the distribution of social positions, especially jobs. This focus tends to ignore the social structure and institutional context that often help determine distributive patterns. Of particular importance to the analyses that follow are issues of decision-making power and procedures, division of labor, and culture.

One might agree that defining justice in terms of distribution tends to bias thinking about justice toward issues concerning wealth, income, and other material goods, and that other issues such as decisionmaking power or the structure of the division of labor are as important, and yet argue that distribution need not be restricted to material goods and resources. Theorists frequently consider issues of the distribution of such nonmaterial goods as power, opportunity, or self-respect. But this widening of the concept of distribution exhibits the second problem with the distributive paradigm. When metaphorically extended to nonmaterial social goods, the concept of distribution represents them as though they were static things, instead of a function of social relations and processes.

In criticizing distributively oriented theories I wish neither to reject distribution as unimportant nor to offer a new positive theory to replace the distributive theories. I wish rather to displace talk of justice that regards persons as primarily possessors and consumers of goods to a wider context that also includes action, decisions about action, and provision of the means to develop and exercise capacities. The concept of social justice includes all aspects of institutional rules and relations insofar as they are subject to potential collective decision. The concepts of domination and oppression, rather than the concept of distribution, should be the starting point for a conception of social justice.

THE DISTRIBUTIVE PARADIGM

A distributive paradigm runs through contemporary discourse about justice, spanning diverse ideological positions. By "paradigm" I mean a configuration of elements and practices which define an inquiry: metaphysical presuppositions, unquestioned terminology, characteristic questions, lines of reasoning, specific theories and their typical scope and mode of application. The distributive paradigm defines social justice as the morally proper distribution of social benefits and burdens among society's members. Paramount among these are wealth, income, and other material resources. The distributive definition of justice often includes, however, nonmaterial social goods such as rights, opportunity, power, and self-respect. What marks the distributive paradigm is a tendency to conceive social justice and distribution as coextensive concepts.

A review of how some major theorists define justice makes apparent the prevalence of this conceptual identification of justice with distribution. Rawls defines a "conception of justice as providing in the first instance a standard whereby the distributive aspects of the basic structure of society are to be assessed" (Rawls, 1971, p. 9). W. G. Runciman defines the problem of justice as "the problem of arriving at an ethical criterion by reference to which the distribution of social goods in societies may be assessed"

(Runciman, 1978, p. 37). Bruce Ackerman (1980, p. 25) defines the problem of justice initially as that of determining initial entitlements of a scarce resource, manna, which is convertible into any social good.

William Galston makes more explicit than most theorists the logic of a distributive understanding of justice. Justice, he says, involves an ensemble of possessive relations. In a possessive relation the individual is distinct from the object possessed. Justice, he says, may be defined as rightful possession (Galston, 1980, p. 5). In such a possessive model the nature of the possessing subject is prior to and independent of the goods possessed; the self underlies and is unchanged by alternative distributions (cf. Sandel, 1982). Justice concerns the proper pattern of the allocation of entities among such antecedently existing individuals. Or as Galston puts it, justice is

> the appropriate assignment of entities to individuals; appropriateness encompasses both the relation between some feature of entities and individuals under consideration and the relation between those entities and possible modes of assignment. The domain of entities may include objects, qualities, positions within a system, or even human beings. (Galston, 1980, p. 112)

The distributive paradigm of justice so ensnares philosophical thinking that even critics of the dominant liberal framework continue to formulate the focus of justice in exclusively distributive terms. David Miller, for example, claims that liberal conceptions of justice tend to reflect the prevailing social relations, and argues for a more egalitarian conception of justice than traditional theories propose. Yet he also defines the subject matter of justice as "the manner in which benefits and burdens are distributed among persons, where such qualities and relationships can be investigated" (Miller, 1976, p. 19). Even explicitly socialist or Marxist discussions of justice often fall under the distributive paradigm. In their discussion of justice under socialism, for example, Edward Nell and Onora O'Neill (1980) assume that the primary difference between socialist justice and capitalist liberal justice is in their principles of distribution. Similarly, Kai Nielsen (1979; 1985, chap. 3) elaborates socialist principles of a radical egalitarian justice which have a primarily distributional focus.

Michael Walzer (1983) is interestingly ambiguous in relation to the distributive paradigm. Walzer asserts that philosophers' criticisms of the injustice of a social system usually amount to claims that a dominant good should be more widely distributed, that is, that monopoly is unjust. It is more appropriate, he says, to criticize the structure of dominance itself, rather than merely the distribution of the dominant good. Having one sort of social good—say, money—should not give one automatic access to other social goods. If the dominance of some goods over access to other goods is broken, then the monopoly of some group over a particular good may not be unjust (see Walzer, 1983, pp. 10–13). Walzer's analysis here has resonances with my concern to focus primarily on the social structures and processes that produce distributions rather than on the distributions. At the same time, however, Walzer repeatedly and unambiguously uses the language of distribution to discuss social justice, in sometimes reifying and strange ways. In his chapter on the family, for example, he speaks of the just distribution of love and affection.

Most theorists take it as given, then, that justice is about distributions. The paradigm assumes a single model for all analyses of justice: all situations in which justice is at issue are analogous to the situation of persons dividing a stock of goods and comparing the size of the portions individuals have. Such a model implicitly assumes that individuals or other agents lie as nodes, points in the social field, among whom larger or smaller bundles of social goods are assigned. The individuals are externally related to the goods they possess, and their only relation to one another that matters from the point of view of the paradigm is a comparison of the amount of goods they possess. The distributive paradigm thus implicitly assumes a social atomism, inasmuch as there is no internal relation among persons in society relevant to considerations of justice.

The distributive paradigm is also pattern oriented. It evaluates justice according to the end-state pattern of persons and goods that appear on the social field. Evaluation of social justice involves comparing alternative patterns and determining which is the most just. Such a pattern-oriented conceptualization implicitly assumes a static conception of society.

I find two problems with this distributive paradigm, which I elaborate in the next two sections. First, it tends to ignore, at the same time that it often presupposes, the institutional context that determines material distributions. Second, when extended to nonmaterial goods and resources, the logic of distribution misrepresents them.

THE DISTRIBUTIVE PARADIGM PRESUPPOSES AND OBSCURES
INSTITUTIONAL CONTEXT

Most theorizing about social justice focuses on the distribution of material resources, income, or positions of reward and prestige. Contemporary debates among theorists of justice, as Charles Taylor (1985) points out, are inspired largely by two practical issues. First, is the distribution of wealth and income in advanced capitalist countries just, and if not, does justice permit or even require the provision of welfare services and other redistributive measures? Second, is the pattern of the distribution of positions of high income and prestige just, and if not, are affirmative action policies just means to rectify that injustice? Nearly all of the writers I cited earlier who define justice in distributive terms identify questions of the equality or inequality of wealth and income as the primary questions of social justice (see also Arthur and Shaw, 1978). They usually subsume the second set of questions, about the justice of the distribution of social positions, under the question of economic distribution, since "more desirable" positions usually correspond to those that yield higher income or greater access to resources.

Applied discussions of justice too usually focus on the distribution of material goods and resources. Discussions of justice in medical care, for example, usually focus on the allocation of medical resources such as treatment, sophisticated equipment, expensive procedures, and so on (e.g., Daniels, 1985, esp. chaps. 3 and 4). Similarly, issues of justice enter discussion in environmental ethics largely through consideration of the impact that alternative policies might have on the distribution of natural and social resources among individuals and groups (see, e.g., Simon, 1984).

As we shall see in detail in Chapter 3, the social context of welfare capitalist society helps account for this tendency to focus on the distribution of income and other resources. Public political dispute in welfare corporate society is largely restricted to issues of taxation, and the allocation of public funds among competing social interests. Public discussions of social injustice tend to revolve around inequalities of wealth and income, and the extent to which the state can or should mitigate the suffering of the poor.

There are certainly pressing reasons for philosophers to attend to these issues of the distribution of wealth and resources. In a society and world with vast differences in the amount of material goods to which individuals have access, where millions starve while others can have anything they want, any conception of justice must address the distribution of material goods. The immediate provision of basic material goods for people now suffering severe deprivation must be a first priority for any program that seeks to make the world more just. Such a call obviously entails considerations of distribution and redistribution.

But in contemporary American society, many public appeals to justice do not concern primarily the distribution of material goods. Citizens in a rural Massachusetts town organize against a decision to site a huge hazardous waste treatment plant in their town. Their leaflets convince people that state law has treated the community unjustly by denying them the option of rejecting the plant (Young, 1983). Citizens in an Ohio city are outraged at the announcement that a major employer is closing down its plant. They question the legitimacy of the power of private corporate decisionmakers to throw half the city out of work without warning, and without any negotiation and consultation with the community. Discussion of possible compensation makes them snicker; the point is not simply that we are out of jobs and thus lack money, they claim, but that no private party should have the right to decide to decimate the local economy. Justice may require that former workers and other members of the community have the option of taking over and operating the plant themselves (Schweickart, 1984). These two cases concern not so much the justice of material distributions as the justice of decisionmaking power and procedures.

Black critics claim that the television industry is guilty of gross injustice in its depictions of Blacks. More often than not, Blacks are represented as criminals, hookers, maids, scheming dealers, or jiving connivers. Blacks rarely appear in roles of authority, glamour, or virtue. Arab Americans are outraged at the degree to which television and film present recognizable Arabs only as sinister terrorists or gaudy princes, and conversely that terrorists are almost always Arab. Such outrage at media stereotyping issues in claims about the injustice not of material distribution, but of cultural imagery and symbols.

In an age of burgeoning computer technology, organizations of clerical workers argue that no person should have to spend the entirety of her working day in front of a computer terminal typing in a set of mindless numbers at monitored high speeds. This claim about injustice concerns not the distribution of goods, for the claim would still be made if VDT operators earned $30,000 annually. Here the primary issues of justice concern the structure of the division of labor and a right to meaningful work.

There are many such claims about justice and injustice in our society which are not primarily about the distribution of income, resources, or positions. A focus on the distribution of material goods and resources inappropriately restricts the scope of justice, because it fails to bring social structures and institutional contexts under evaluation. Several writers make this claim about distributive theories specifically with regard to their inability to bring capitalist institutions and class relations under evaluation. In his classic paper, for example, Allen Wood (1972) argues that for Marx justice refers only to superstructural juridical relations of distribution, which are constrained by the underlying mode of production. Because they are confined to distribution, principles of justice cannot be used to evaluate the social relations of production themselves (cf. Wolff, 1977, pp. 199–208).

Other writers criticize distributive theories of justice, especially Rawls's, for presupposing at the same time that they obscure the context of class inequality that the theories are unable to evaluate (Macpherson, 1973; Nielsen, 1978). A distributive conception of justice is unable to bring class relations into view and evaluate them, Evan Simpson suggests, because its individualism prevents an understanding of structural phenomena, the "macroscopic transfer emerging from a complicated set of individual actions" (Simpson, 1980, p. 497) which cannot be understood in terms of any particular individual actions or acquisitions.

Many who make this Marxist criticism of the distributive focus of theories of justice conclude that justice is a concept of bourgeois ideology and thus not useful for a socialist normative analysis. Others disagree, and this dispute has occupied much of the Marxist literature on justice. I will argue later that a criticism of the distributive paradigm does not entail abandoning or transcending the concept of justice. For the moment I wish to focus on the point on which both sides in this dispute agree, namely, that predominant approaches to justice tend to presuppose and uncritically accept the relations of production that define an economic system.

The Marxist analysis of the distributive paradigm provides a fruitful starting point, but it is both too narrow and too general. On the one hand, capitalist class relations are not the only phenomena of social structure or institutional context that the distributive paradigm fails to evaluate. Some feminists point out, for example, that contemporary theories of justice presuppose family structure, without asking how social relations involving sexuality, intimacy, childrearing, and household labor ought best to be organized (see Okin, 1986; Pateman, 1988, pp. 41–43). Like their forebears, contemporary liberal theorists of justice tend to presume that the units among which basic distributions take place are families, and that it is as family members, often heads of families, that individuals enter the public realm where justice operates (Nicholson, 1986, chap. 4). Thus they neglect issues of justice within families—for example, the issue of whether the traditional sexual division of labor still presupposed by much law and employment policy is just.

While the Marxist criticism is too narrow, it is also too vague. The claim that the distributive paradigm fails to bring class relations under evaluation is too general to make clear what specific nondistributive issues are at stake. While property is something distributed, for example, in the form of goods, land, buildings, or shares of stock, the legal relations that define entitlement, possible forms of title, and so on are not goods to be distributed. The legal framework consists of rules defining practices and rights to make decisions about the disposition of goods. Class domination is certainly enacted by agents deciding where to invest their capital—a distributive decision; but the social rules, rights, procedures, and influences that structure capitalist decisionmaking are not distributed goods. In order to understand and evaluate the institutional framework within which distributive issues arise, the ideas of "class" and "mode of production" must be concretized in terms of specific social processes and relations. In Chapter 7 I provide some concretization by addressing issues of the social division of labor.

The general criticism I am making of the predominant focus on the distribution of wealth, income, and positions is that such a focus ignores and tends to obscure the institutional context within which those distributions take place, and which is often at least partly the cause of patterns of distribution of jobs or wealth. Institutional context should be understood in a broader sense than "mode of production." It includes any structures or practices, the rules and norms that guide them, and the language and symbols that mediate social interactions within them, in institutions of state, family, and civil society, as well as the workplace. These are relevant to judgments of justice and injustice insofar as they condition people's ability to participate in determining their actions and their ability to develop and exercise their capacities.

Many discussions of social justice not only ignore the institutional contexts within which distributions occur, but often presuppose specific institutional structures whose justice they fail to bring under evaluation. Some political theories, for example, tend to assume centralized legislative and executive institutions separated from the day-to-day lives of most people in the society, and state officials with the authority to make and enforce policy decisions. They take for granted such institutions of the modern state as bureaucracies and welfare agencies for implementing and enforcing tax schemes and administering services (see, e.g., Rawls, 1971, pp. 274–84). Issues of the just organization of government institutions, and just methods of political decisionmaking, rarely get raised.

To take a different kind of example, to which I will return in Chapter 7, when philosophers ask about the just principles for allocating jobs and offices among persons, they typically assume a stratification of such positions. They assume a hierarchical division of labor in which some jobs and offices carry significant autonomy, decisionmaking power, authority, income, and access to resources, while others lack most of these attributes. Rarely do theorists explicitly ask whether such a definition and organization of social positions is just.

Many other examples of ways in which theorizing about justice frequently presupposes specific structural and institutional background conditions could be cited. In every case a clear understanding of these background conditions can reveal how they affect distribution—what there is to distribute, how it gets distributed, who distributes, and what the distributive outcome is. With Michael Walzer, my intention here is "to shift our attention from distribution itself to conception and creation: the naming of the goods, the giving of meaning, and the collective making" (Walzer, 1983, p. 7). I shall focus most of my discussion on three primary categories of nondistributive issues that distributive theories tend to ignore: decisionmaking structure and procedures, division of labor, and culture.

Decisionmaking issues include not only questions of who by virtue of their positions have the effective freedom or authority to make what sorts of decisions, but also the rules and procedures according to which decisions are made. Discussion of economic justice, for example, often de-emphasizes the decisionmaking structures which are crucial determinants of economic relations. Economic domination in our society occurs not simply or primarily because some persons have more wealth and income than others, as important as this is. Economic domination derives at least as much from the corporate and legal structures and procedures that give some persons the power to make decisions about investment, production, marketing, employment, interest rates, and wages that affect millions of other people. Not all who make these decisions are wealthy or even privileged, but the decisionmaking structure operates to reproduce distributive inequality and the unjust constraints on people's lives that in Chapter 2 I name exploitation and marginalization. As Carol Gould (1988, pp. 133–34) points out, rarely do theories of justice take such structures as an explicit focus. In the chapters that follow I raise several specific issues of decisionmaking structure, and argue for democratic decisionmaking procedures as an element and condition of social justice.

Division of labor can be understood both distributively and nondistributively. As a distributive issue, division of labor refers to how pregiven occupations, jobs, or tasks are allocated among individuals or groups. As a nondistributive issue, on the other hand, division of labor concerns the definition of the occupations themselves. Division of labor as an institutional structure involves the range of tasks performed in a given position, the definition of the nature, meaning, and value of those tasks, and the relations of cooperation, conflict, and authority among positions. Feminist claims about the justice of a sexual division of labor, for example, have been posed both distributively and nondistributively. On the one hand, feminists have questioned the justice of a pattern of distribution of positions that finds a small proportion of women in the most prestigious jobs. On the other hand, they have also questioned the conscious or unconscious association of many occupations or jobs with masculine or feminine characteristics, such as instrumentality or affectivity, and this is not itself a distributive issue. In Chapter 2 I will discuss the justice of the division of labor in the context of exploitation. In Chapter 7 I consider the most important division of labor in advanced industrial societies, that between task definition and task execution.

Culture is the most general of the three categories of nondistributive issues I focus on. It includes the symbols, images, meanings, habitual comportments, stories, and so on through which people express their experience and communicate with one another. Culture is ubiquitous, but nevertheless deserves distinct consideration in discussions of social justice. The symbolic meanings that people attach to other kinds of people and to actions, gestures, or institutions often significantly affect the social standing of persons and their opportunities. In Chapters 2, 4, 5, and 6 I explore the injustice of the cultural imperialism which marks and stereo-types some groups at the same time that it silences their self-expression.

OVEREXTENDING THE CONCEPT OF DISTRIBUTION

The following objection might be made to my argument thus far. It may be true that philosophical discussions of justice tend to emphasize the distribution of goods and to ignore institutional issues of decisionmaking structure and culture. But this is not a necessary consequence of the distributive definition of justice. Theories of distributive justice can and should be applied to issues of social organization beyond the allocation of wealth, income, and resources. Indeed, this objection insists, many theorists explicitly extend the scope of distributive justice to such nonmaterial goods.

Rawls, for example, regards the subject of justice as "the way in which the major social institutions distribute fundamental rights and duties" (Rawls, 1971, p. 7), and for him this clearly includes rights and duties related to decisionmaking, social positions, power, and so on, as well as wealth or income. Similarly, David Miller specifies that "the 'benefits' the distribution of which a conception of justice evaluates should be taken to include intangible benefits such as prestige and self-respect" (Miller, 1976, p. 22). William Galston, finally, insists that "issues of justice involve not only the distribution of property or income, but also such non-material goods as productive tasks, opportunities for development, citizenship, authority, honor, and so on" (Galston, 1980, p. 6; cf. p. 116).

The distributive paradigm of justice may have a bias toward focusing on easily identifiable distributions, such as distributions of things, income, and jobs. Its beauty and simplicity, however, consists in its ability to accommodate any issue of justice, including those concerning culture, decisionmaking structures, and the division of labor. To do so the paradigm simply formulates the issue in terms of the distribution of some material or nonmaterial good among various agents. Any social value can be treated as some thing or aggregate of things that some specific agents possess in certain amounts, and alternative end-state patterns of distribution of that good among those agents can be compared. For example, neo-classical economists have developed sophisticated schemes for reducing all intentional action to a matter of maximizing a utility function in which the utility of all conceivable goods can be quantified and compared.

But this, in my view, is the main problem with the distributive paradigm: it does not recognize the limits to the application of a logic of distribution. Distributive theorists of justice agree that justice is the primary normative concept for evaluating all aspects of social institutions, but at the same time they identify the scope of justice with distribution. This entails applying a logic of distribution to social goods which are not material things or measurable quantities. Applying a logic of distribution to such goods produces a misleading conception of the issues of justice involved. It reifies aspects of social life that are better understood as a function of rules and relations than as things. And it conceptualizes social justice primarily in terms of end-state patterns, rather than focusing on social processes. This distributive paradigm implies a misleading or incomplete social ontology.

But why should issues of social ontology matter for normative theorizing about justice? Any normative claims about society make assumptions about the nature of society, often only implicitly. Normative judgments of justice are about something, and without a social ontology we do not know what they are about. The distributive paradigm implicitly assumes that social judgments are about what individual persons have, how much they have, and how that amount compares with what other persons have. This focus on possession tends to preclude thinking about what people are doing, according to what institutionalized rules, how their doings and havings are structured by institutionalized relations that constitute their positions, and how the combined effect of their doings has recursive effects on their lives. Before developing this argument further, let us look at some examples of the application of the distributive paradigm to three nonmaterial goods frequently discussed by theorists of justice: rights, opportunity, and self-respect.

I quoted Rawls earlier to the effect that justice concerns the distribution of "rights and duties," and talk of distributing rights is by no means limited to him. But what does distributing a right mean? One may talk about having a right to a distributive share of material things, resources, or income. But in such cases it is the good that is distributed, not the right. What can it mean to distribute rights that do not refer to resources or things, like the right of free speech, or the right of trial by jury? We can conceive of a society in which some persons are granted these rights while others are not, but this does not mean that some people have a certain "amount" or "portion" of a good while others have less. Altering the situation so that everyone has these rights, moreover, would not entail that the formerly privileged group gives over some of its right of free speech or trial by jury to the rest of society's members, on analogy with a redistribuion of income.

Rights are not fruitfully conceived as possessions. Rights are relationships, not things; they are institutionally defined rules specifying what people can do in relation to one another. Rights refer to doing more than having, to social relationships that enable or constrain action.

Talk of distributing opportunities involves a similar confusion. If by opportunity we mean "chance," we can meaningfully talk of distributing opportunities, of some people having more opportunities than others, while some have none at all. When I go to the carnival I can buy three chances to knock over the kewpie doll, and my friend can buy six, and she will have more chances than I. Matters are rather different, however, with other opportunities. James Nickel (1988, p. 110) defines opportunities as "states of affairs that combine the absence of insuperable obstacles with the presences of means—internal or external—that give one a chance of overcoming the obstacles that remain." Opportunity in this sense is a condition of enablement, which usually involves a configuration of social rules and social relations, as well as an individual's self-conception and skills.

We may mislead ourselves by the fact that in ordinary language we talk about some people having "fewer" opportunities than others. When we talk that way, the opportunities sound like separable goods that can be increased or decreased by being given out or withheld, even though we know that opportunities are not allocated. Opportunity is a concept of enablement rather than possession; it refers to doing more than having. A person has opportunities if he or she is not constrained from doing things, and lives under the enabling conditions for doing them. Having opportunities in this sense certainly does often entail having material possessions, such as food, clothing, tools, land, or machines. Being enabled or constrained refers more directly, however, to the rules and practices that govern one's action, the way other people treat one in the context of specific social relations, and the broader structural possibilities produced by the confluence of a multitude of actions and practices. It makes no sense to speak of opportunities as themselves things possessed. Evaluating social justice according to whether persons have opportunities, therefore, must involve evaluating not a distributive outcome but the social structures that enable or constrain the individuals in relevant situations (cf. Simpson, 1980; Reiman, 1987).

Consider educational opportunity, for example. Providing educational opportunity certainly entails allocating specific material resources—money, buildings, books, computers, and so on—and there are reasons to think that the more resources, the wider the opportunities offered to children in an educational system. But education is primarily a process taking place in a complex context of social relations. In the cultural context of the United States, male children and female children, working-class children and middle-class children, Black children and white children often do not have equally enabling educational opportunities even when an equivalent amount of resources has been devoted to their education. This does not show that distribution is irrelevant to educational opportunity, only that opportunity has a wider scope than distribution.

Many writers on justice, to take a final example, not only regard self-respect as a primary good that all persons in a society must have if the society is to be just, but also talk of distributing self-respect. But what can it mean to distribute self-respect? Self-respect is not an entity or measurable aggregate, it cannot be parceled out of some stash, and above all it cannot be detached from persons as a separable attribute adhering to an otherwise unchanged substance. Self-respect names not some possession or attribute a person has, but her or his attitude toward her or his entire situation and life prospects. While Rawls does not speak of self-respect as something itself distributed, he does suggest that distributive arrangements provide the background conditions for self-respect (Rawls, 1971, pp. 148–50). It is certainly true that in many circumstances the possession of certain distributable material goods may be a condition of self-respect. Self-respect, however, also involves many nonmaterial conditions that cannot be reduced to distributive arrangements (cf. Howard, 1985).

People have or lack self-respect because of how they define themselves and how others regard them, because of how they spend their time, because of the amount of autonomy and decisionmaking power they have in their activities, and so on. Some of these factors can be conceptualized in distributive terms, but others cannot. Self-respect is at least as much a function of culture as it is of goods, for example, and in later chapters I shall discuss some elements of cultural imperialism that undermine the self-respect of many persons in our society. The point here is that none of the forms and not all of the conditions of self-respect can meaningfully be conceived as goods that individuals possess; they are rather relations and processes in which the actions of individuals are embedded.

These, then, are the general problems with extending the concept of distribution beyond material goods or measurable quantities to non-material values. First, doing so reifies social relations and institutional rules. Something identifiable and assignable must be distributed. In accord with its implicit social ontology that gives primacy to substance over relations, moreover, the distributive paradigm tends to conceive of individuals as social atoms, logically prior to social relations and institutions. As Galston makes clear in the passage I quoted earlier (Galston, 1980, p. 112), conceiving justice as a distribution of goods among individuals involves analytically separating the individuals from those goods. Such an atomistic conception of the individual as a substance to which attributes adhere fails to appreciate that individual identities and capacities are in many respects themselves the products of social processes and relations. Societies do not simply distribute goods to persons who are what they are apart from society, but rather constitute individuals in their identities and capacities (Sandel, 1982; Taylor, 1985). In the distributive logic, however, there is little room for conceiving persons' enablement or constraint as a function of their relations to one another. As we shall see in Chapter 2, such an atomistic social ontology ignores or obscures the importance of social groups for understanding issues of justice.

Second, the distributive paradigm must conceptualize all issues of justice in terms of patterns. It implies a static social ontology that ignores processes. In the distributive paradigm individuals or other agents lie as points in the social field, among whom larger or smaller packets of goods are assigned. One evaluates the justice of the pattern by comparing the size of the packages individuals have and comparing the total pattern to other possible patterns of assignment.

Robert Nozick (1974, chap. 7) argues that such a static or end-state approach to justice is inappropriately ahistorical. End-state approaches to justice, he argues, operate as though social goods magically appear and get distributed. They ignore the processes that create the goods and produce distributive patterns, which they find irrelevant for evaluating justice. For Nozick, only the process is relevant to evaluating distributions. If individuals begin with holdings they are justly entitled to, and undertake free exchanges, then the distributive outcomes are just, no matter what they are. This entitlement theory shares with other theories a possessively individualist social ontology. Society consists only of individuals with "holdings" of social goods which they augment or reduce through individual production and contractual exchange. The theory does not take into account structural effects of the actions of individuals that they cannot foresee or intend, and to which they might not agree if they could. Nevertheless, Nozick's criticism of end-state theories for ignoring social processes is apt.

Important and complex consequences ensue when a theory of justice adopts a narrowly static social ontology. Anthony Giddens claims that social theory in general has lacked a temporal conceptualization of social relations (Giddens, 1976, chap. 2; 1984, chaps. 3 and 4). Action theorists have developed sophisticated accounts of social relations from the point of view of acting subjects with intentions, purposes, and reasons, but they have tended to abstract from the temporal flow of everyday life, and instead talk about isolated acts of isolated individuals. For a theory of justice, this means ignoring the relevance of institutions to justice. Structuralism and functionalist social theories, on the other hand, provide conceptual tools for identifying and explaining social regularities and large-scale institutional patterns. Because they also abstract from the temporal flow of everyday interaction, however, they tend to hypostatize these regularities and patterns and often fail to connect them with accounts of individual action. For a theory of justice, this means separating institutions from choice and normative judgment. Only a social theory that takes process seriously, Giddens suggests, can understand the relation between social structures and action. Individuals are not primarily receivers of goods or carriers of properties, but actors with meanings and purposes, who act with, against, or in relation to one another. We act with knowledge of existing institutions, rules, and the structural consequences of a multiplicity of actions, and those structures are enacted and reproduced through the confluence of our actions. Social theory should conceptualize action as a producer and reproducer of structures, which only exist in action; social action, on the other hand, has those structures and relationships as background, medium, or purpose.

This identification of a weakness in traditional social theory can be applied to the distributive paradigm of justice. I disagree with Nozick that end-state patterns are irrelevant to questions of justice. Because they inhibit the ability of some people to live and be healthy, or grant some people resources that allow them to coerce others, some distributions must come into question no matter how they came about. Evaluating patterns of distribution is often an important starting point for questioning about justice. For many issues of social justice, however, what is important is not the particular pattern of distribution at a particular moment, but rather the reproduction of a regular distributive pattern over time.

For example, unless one begins with the assumption that all positions of high status, income, and decisionmaking power ought to be distributed in comparable numbers to women and men, finding that very few top corporate managers are women might not involve any question of injustice. It is in the context of a social change involving more acceptance of women in corporate management, and a considerable increase in the number of women who obtain degrees in business, that a question of injustice becomes most apparent here. Even though more women earn degrees in business, and in-house policies of some companies aim to encourage women's careers, a pattern of distribution of managerial positions that clusters women at the bottom and men at the top persists. Assuming that justice ultimately means equality for women, this pattern is puzzling, disturbing. We are inclined to ask: what's going on here? why is this general pattern reproduced even in the face of conscious efforts to change it? Answering that question entails evaluation of a matrix of rules, attitudes, interactions, and policies as a social process that produces and reproduces that pattern. An adequate conception of justice must be able to understand and evaluate the processes as well as the patterns.

One might object that this account confuses the empirical issue of what causes a particular distribution with the normative issue of whether the distribution is just. As will be apparent in the chapters that follow, however, in the spirit of critical social theory I do not accept this division between empirical and normative social theory. While there is a distinction between empirical and normative statements and the kinds of reasons required for each, no normative theory meant to evaluate existing societies can avoid empirical inquiry, and no empirical investigation of social structures and relations can avoid normative judgments. Inquiry about social justice must consider the context and causes of actual distributions in order to make normative judgments about institutional rules and relations.

The pattern orientation of the distributive paradigm, then, tends to lead to abstraction from institutional rules and relations and a consequent failure to bring them into evaluation. For many aspects of social structure and institutional context cannot be brought into view without examining social processes and the unintended cumulative consequences of individual actions. Without a more temporal approach to social reality, for example, as we shall see in Chapter 2, a theory of justice cannot conceptualize exploitation, as a social process by which the labor of some unreciprocally supports the privilege of others.

PROBLEMS WITH TALK OF DISTRIBUTING POWER

I have argued that regarding such social values as rights, opportunities, and self-respect as distributable obscures the institutional and social bases of these values. Some theorists of justice might respond to my criticism of the distributive paradigm as follows: What is in question is indeed not goods, but social power; the distributive paradigm, however, can accommodate these issues by giving more attention to the distribution of power. Certainly I agree that many of the issues I have said are confused or obscured by the distributive paradigm concern social power. While talk of the distribution of power is common, however, I think this is a particularly clear case of the misleading and undesirable implications of extending the concept of distribution beyond material goods.

Distributional theorists of justice disagree on how to approach power. Some explicitly exclude power from the scope of their theories. David Miller (1976, p. 22), for example, claims that questions of power are not questions of social justice per se, but concern the causes of justice and injustice. Ronald Dworkin (1983) explicitly brackets issues of power in his discussion of equality, and chooses to consider only issues of welfare, the distribution of goods, services, income, and so on.

Other philosophers and political theorists, however, clearly include questions of power within the scope of the concept of justice. Many would agree that a theory of justice must be concerned not only with end-state patterns, but also with the institutional relations that produce distributions. Their approach to such questions takes the form of assessing the distribution of power in a society or a specific institutional context.

Talk about power in terms of distribution is so common that it does not warrant special notice. The following passage from William Connolly's *Terms of Political Discourse* is typical:

When one speaks of a power structure one conveys, first, the idea that power in at least some domains is distributed unequally; second, that those with more power in one domain are likely to have it in several important domains as well; third, that such a distribution is relatively persistent; and fourth (but not necessarily), that there is more than a random connection between the distribution of power and the distribution of income, status, privilege, and wealth in the system under scrutiny. (Connolly, 1983, p. 117)

Common though it is, bringing power under the logic of distribution, I suggest, misconstrues the meaning of power. Conceptualizing power in distributive terms means implicitly or explicitly conceiving power as a kind of stuff possessed by individual agents in greater or lesser amounts. From this perspective a power structure or power relations will be described as a pattern of the distribution of this stuff. There are a number of problems with such a model of power.

First, regarding power as a possession or attribute of individuals tends to obscure the fact that power is a relation rather than a thing (Bachrach and Baratz, 1969). While the exercise of power may sometimes depend on the possession of certain resources—money, military equipment, and so on—such resources should not be confused with power itself. The power consists in a relationship between the exerciser and others through which he or she communicates intentions and meets with their acquiescence.

Second, the atomistic bias of distributive paradigms of power leads to a focus on particular agents or roles that have power, and on agents over whom these powerful agents or roles have power. Even when they recognize its relational character, theorists often treat power as a dyadic relation, on the model of ruler and subject. This dyadic modeling of power misses the larger structure of agents and actions that mediates between two agents in a power relation (Wartenburg, 1989, chap. 7). One agent can have institutionalized power over another only if the actions of many third agents support and execute the will of the powerful. A judge may be said to have power over a prisoner, but only in the context of a network of practices executed by prison wardens, guards, recordkeepers, administrators, parole officers, lawyers, and so on. Many people must do their jobs for the judge's power to be realized, and many of these people will never directly interact with either the judge or the prisoner. A distributive understanding of power as a possession of particular individuals or groups misses this supporting and mediating function of third parties.

A distributive understanding of power, which treats power as some kind of stuff that can be traded, exchanged, and distributed, misses the structural phenomena of domination (Hartsock, 1983). By domination I mean structural or systemic phenomena which exclude people from participating in determining their actions or the conditions of their actions (cf. Wartenburg, 1989, chap. 6). Domination must be understood as structural precisely because the constraints that people experience are usually the intended or unintended product of the actions of many people, like the actions which enable the judge's power. In saying that power and domination have a structural basis, I do not deny that it is individuals who are powerful and who dominate. Within a system of domination some people can be identified as more powerful and others as relatively powerless. Nevertheless a distributive understanding misses the way in which the powerful enact and reproduce their power.

The structured operation of domination whose resources the powerful draw upon must be understood as a process. A distributive conceptualization of power, however, can construct power relations only as patterns. As Thomas Wartenburg argues (1989, chap. 9), conceptualizing power as relational rather than substantive, as produced and reproduced through many people outside the immediate power dyad, brings out the dynamic nature of power relations as an ongoing process. A distributive understanding of power obscures the fact that, as Foucault puts it, power exists only in action (Foucault, 1980, p. 89; cf. Smart, 1983, chap. 5; Sawicki, 1986):

> What, by contrast, should always be kept in mind is that power, if we do not take too distant a view of it, is not that which makes the difference between those who exclusively possess and retain it, and those who do not have it and submit to it. Power must be analyzed as something that circulates, or rather something which only functions in the form of a chain. It is never localized here or there, never in anybody's hands, never appropriated as a commodity or piece of wealth. Power is employed and exercised through a net-like organization. And not only do individuals circulate between its threads; they are always in the position of simultaneously undergoing and exercising their power. (Foucault, 1980, p. 98)

The logic of distribution, in contrast, makes power a machine or instrument, held in ready and turned on at will, independently of social processes.

Finally, a distributive understanding of power tends to conceive a system of domination as one in which power, like wealth, is concentrated in the hands of a few. Assuming such a condition is unjust, a redistribution of power is called for, which will disperse and decentralize power so that a few individuals or groups no longer have all or most of the power. For some systems of domination such a model may be appropriate. As I will argue in the next two chapters, however, it is not appropriate for understanding the operation of domination and oppression in contemporary welfare corporate societies. For these societies witness the ironic situation in which power is widely dispersed and diffused, yet social relations are tightly defined by domination and oppression. When power is understood as "productive," as a function of dynamic processes of interaction within regulated cultural and decisionmaking situations, then it is possible to say that many widely dispersed persons are agents of power without "having" it, or even being privileged. Without a structural understanding of power and domination as processes rather than patterns of distribution, the existence and nature of domination and oppression in these societies cannot be identified.

DEFINING INJUSTICE AS DOMINATION AND OPPRESSION

Because distributive models of power, rights, opportunity, and self-respect work so badly, justice should not be conceived primarily on the model of the distribution of wealth, income, and other material goods. Theorizing about justice should explicitly limit the concept of distribution to material goods, like things, natural resources, or money. The scope of justice is wider than distributive issues. Though there may be additional nondistributive issues of justice, my concerns in this book focus on issues of decisionmaking, division of labor, and culture.

Political thought of the modern period greatly narrowed the scope of justice as it had been conceived by ancient and medieval thought. Ancient thought regarded justice as the virtue of society as a whole, the well-orderedness of institutions that foster individual virtue and promote happiness and harmony among citizens. Modern political thought abandoned the notion that there is a natural order to society that corresponds to the proper ends of human nature. Seeking to liberate the individual to define "his" own ends, modern political theory also restricted the scope of justice to issues of distribution and the minimal regulation of action among such self-defining individuals (Heller, 1987, chap. 2; cf. MacIntyre, 1981, chap. 17).

While I hardly intend to revert to a full-bodied Platonic conception of justice, I nevertheless think it is important to broaden the understanding of justice beyond its usual limits in contemporary philosophical discourse. Agnes Heller (1987, chap. 5) proposes one such broader conception in what she calls an incomplete ethico-political concept of justice. According to her conception, justice names not principles of distribution, much less some particular distributive pattern. This represents too narrow and substantive a way of reflecting on justice. Instead, justice names the perspectives, principles, and procedures for evaluating institutional norms and rules. Developing Habermas's communicative ethics, Heller suggests that justice is primarily the virtue of citizenship, of persons deliberating about problems and issues that confront them collectively in their institutions and actions, under conditions without domination or oppression, with reciprocity and mutual tolerance of difference. She proposes the following test of the justice of social or political norms:

> Every valid social and political norm and rule (every law) must meet the condition that the foreseeable consequences and side effects the general observance of that law (norm) exacts on the satisfaction of the needs of each and every individual would be accepted by everyone concerned, and that the claim of the norm to actualize the universal values of freedom and/or life could be accepted by each and every individual, regardless of the values to which they are committed. (Heller, 1987, pp. 240–41)

In the course of this book I shall raise some critical questions about the ideas of citizenship, agreement, and universality embedded in the radically democratic ideal which Habermas and Heller, along with others, express. Nevertheless, I endorse and follow this general conception of justice derived from a conception of communicative ethics. The idea of justice here shifts from a focus on distributive patterns to procedural issues of participation in deliberation and decisionmaking. For a norm to be just, everyone who follows it must in principle have an effective voice in its consideration and be able to agree to it without coercion. For a social condition to be just, it must enable all to meet their needs and exercise their freedom; thus justice requires that all be able to express their needs.

As I understand it, the concept of justice coincides with the concept of the political. Politics as I defined it in the Introduction includes all aspects of institutional organization, public action, social practices and habits, and cultural meanings insofar as they are potentially subject to collective evaluation and decisionmaking. Politics in this inclusive sense certainly concerns the policies and actions of government and the state, but in principle can also concern rules, practices, and actions in any other institutional context (cf. Mason, 1982, pp. 11–24).

The scope of justice, I have suggested, is much wider than distribution, and covers everything political in this sense. This coheres with the meaning of justice claims of the sort mentioned at the outset of this chapter. When people claim that a particular rule, practice, or cultural meaning is wrong and should be changed, they are often making a claim about social injustice. Some of these claims involve distributions, but many also refer to other ways in which social institutions inhibit or liberate persons.

Some writers concur that distribution is too narrow a focus for normative evaluation of social institutions, but claim that going beyond this distributive focus entails going beyond the norms of justice per se. Charles Taylor (1985), for example, distinguishes questions of distributive justice from normative questions about the institutional framework of society. Norms of justice help resolve disputes about entitlements and deserts within a particular institutional context. They cannot evaluate that institutional context itself, however, because it embodies a certain conception of human nature and the human good. According to Taylor, confusions arise in theoretical and political discussion when norms of distributive justice are applied across social structures and used to evaluate basic structures. For example, both right and left critics of our society charge it with perpetrating injustices, but according to Taylor the normative perspective from which each side speaks involves a project to construct different institutional forms corresponding to specific conceptions of the human good, a project beyond merely articulating principles of justice.

From a somewhat different perspective, Seyla Benhabib (1986, pp. 330–36) suggests that a normative social theory which evaluates institutions according to whether they are free from domination, meet needs, and provide conditions of emancipation entails going beyond justice as understood by the modern tradition. Because this broader normative social theory entails a critique of culture and socialization in addition to critiques of formal rights and patterns of distribution, it merges questions of justice with questions of the good life.

I am sympathetic with both these discussions, as well as with Michael Sandel's (1982) related argument for recognizing the "limits" of justice and the importance of conceptualizing normative aspects of the self in social contexts that lie beyond those limits. But while I share these writers' general critique of liberal theories of distributive justice, I see no reason to conclude with Taylor and Sandel that this critique reveals the limits of the concept of justice which a normative social philosophy must transcend. I disagree to some extent, moreover, with Taylor's and Benhabib's suggestion that such a wider normative social philosophy merges questions of justice with questions of the good life.

Like many other writers cited earlier in this chapter, Taylor assumes that justice and distribution are coextensive, and therefore that broader issues of institutional context require other normative concepts. Many Marxist theorists who argue that justice is a merely bourgeois concept take a similar position. Whether normative theorists who focus attention on issues of decisionmaking, division of labor, culture, and social organization beyond the distribution of goods call these issues of justice or not is clearly a matter of choice. I can give only pragmatic reasons for my own choice.

Since Plato "justice" has evoked the well-ordered society, and it continues to carry those resonances in contemporary political discussion. Appeals to justice still have the power to awaken a moral imagination and motivate people to look at their society critically, and ask how it can be made more liberating and enabling. Philosophers interested in nurturing this emancipatory imagination and extending it beyond questions of distribution should, I suggest, lay claim to the term justice rather than abandon it.

To a certain extent Heller, Taylor, and Benhabib are right that a postmodern turn to an enlarged conception of justice, reminiscent of the scope of justice in Plato and Aristotle, entails more attention to the definition of ends than the liberal conception of justice allows. Nevertheless, questions of justice do not merge with questions of the good life. The liberal commitment to individual freedom, and the consequent plurality of definitions of the good, must be preserved in any reenlarged conception of justice. The modern restriction of the concept of justice to formal and instrumental principles was meant to promote the value of individual self-definition of ends, or "plans of life," as Rawls calls them. In displacing reflection about justice from a primary focus on distribution to include all institutional and social relations insofar as they are subject to collective decision, I do not mean to suggest that justice should include all moral norms in its scope. Social justice in the sense I intend continues to refer only to institutional conditions, and not to the preferences and ways of life of individuals or groups.

Any normative theorist in the postmodern world is faced with a dilemma. On the one hand, we express and justify norms by appealing to certain values derived from a conception of the good human life. In some sense, then, any normative theory implicitly or explicitly relies on a conception of human nature (cf. Jaggar, 1983, pp. 18–22). On the other hand, it would seem that we should reject the very idea of a human nature as misleading or oppressive.

Any definition of a human nature is dangerous because it threatens to devalue or exclude some acceptable individual desires, cultural characteristics, or ways of life. Normative social theory, however, can rarely avoid making implicit or explicit assumptions about human beings in the formulation of its vision of just institutions. Even though the distributive paradigm carries an individualist conception of society, which considers individual desires and preferences private matters outside the sphere of rational discourse, it assumes a quite specific conception of human nature. It implicitly defines human beings as primarily consumers, desirers, and possessors of goods (Heller, 1987, pp. 180–82). C. B. Macpherson (1962) argues that in presupposing such a possessively individualist view of human nature the original liberal theorists hypostatized the acquisitive values of emergent capitalist social relations. Contemporary capitalism, which depends more upon widespread indulgent consumption than its penny-pinching Protestant ancestor, continues to presuppose an understanding of human beings as primarily utility maximizers (Taylor, 1985).

The idea of human beings that guides normative social theorizing under the distributive paradigm is an image, rather than an explicit theory of human nature. It makes plausible to the imagination both the static picture of social relations entailed by this distributive paradigm and the notion of separate individuals already formed apart from social goods. Displacing the distributive paradigm in favor of a wider, process-oriented understanding of society, which focuses on power, decisionmaking structures, and so on, likewise shifts the imagination to different assumptions about human beings. Such an imaginative shift could be as oppressive as consumerist images if it is made too concrete. As long as the values we appeal to are abstract enough, however, they will not devalue or exclude any particular culture or way of life.

Persons certainly are possessors and consumers, and any conception of justice should presume the value of meeting material needs, living in a comfortable environment, and experiencing pleasures. Adding an image of people as doers and actors (Macpherson, 1973; Bowles and Gintis, 1986) helps to displace the distributive paradigm. As doers and actors, we seek to promote many values of social justice in addition to fairness in the distribution of goods: learning and using satisfying and expansive skills in socially recognized settings; participating in forming and running institutions, and receiving recognition for such participation; playing and communicating with others, and expressing our experience, feelings, and perspective on social life in contexts where others can listen. Certainly many distributive theorists of justice would recognize and affirm these values. The framework of distribution, however, leads to a deemphasizing of these values and a failure to inquire about the institutional conditions that promote them.

This, then, is how I understand the connection between justice and the values that constitute the good life. Justice is not identical with the concrete realization of these values in individual lives; justice, that is, is not identical with the good life as such. Rather, social justice concerns the degree to which a society contains and supports the institutional conditions necessary for the realization of these values. The values comprised in the good life can be reduced to two very general ones: (1) developing and exercising one's capacities and expressing one's experience (cf. Gould, 1988, chap. 2; Galston, pp. 61–69), and (2) participating in determining one's action and the conditions of one's action (cf. Young, 1979). These are universalist values, in the sense that they assume the equal moral worth of all persons, and thus justice requires their promotion for everyone. To these two general values correspond two social conditions that define injustice: oppression, the institutional constraint on self-development, and domination, the institutional constraint on self-determination.

Oppression consists in systematic institutional processes which prevent some people from learning and using satisfying and expansive skills in socially recognized settings, or institutionalized social processes which inhibit people's ability to play and communicate with others or to express their feelings and perspective on social life in contexts where others can listen. While the social conditions of oppression often include material deprivation or maldistribution, they also involve issues beyond distribution, as I shall show in Chapter 2.

Domination consists in institutional conditions which inhibit or prevent people from participating in determining their actions or the conditions of their actions. Persons live within structures of domination if other persons or groups can determine without reciprocation the conditions of their action, either directly or by virtue of the structural consequences of their actions. Thorough social and political democracy is the opposite of domination. In Chapter 3 I discuss some of the issues of decisionmaking that contemporary welfare state politics ignores, and show how insurgent social movements frequently address issues of domination rather than distribution.

As will become clear in the chapters that follow, I think the concepts of oppression and domination overlap, but there is nevertheless reason to distinguish them. Oppression usually includes or entails domination, that is, constraints upon oppressed people to follow rules set by others. But each face of oppression that I shall discuss in Chapter 2 also involves inhibitions not directly produced by relations of domination. As should become clear in that chapter, moreover, not everyone subject to domination is also oppressed. Hierarchical decisionmaking structures subject most people in our society to domination in some important aspect of their lives. Many of those people nevertheless enjoy significant institutionalized support for the development and exercise of their capacities and their ability to express themselves and be heard.

CHAPTER 2

Five Faces of Oppression

> Someone who does not see a pane of glass does not know
> that he does not see it. Someone who, being placed differ-
> ently, does see it, does not know the other does not see it.
> When our will finds expression outside ourselves in ac-
> tions performed by others, we do not waste our time and our
> power of attention in examining whether they have con-
> sented to this. This is true for all of us. Our attention, given
> entirely to the success of the undertaking, is not claimed by
> them as long as they are docile. . . .
> Rape is a terrible caricature of love from which consent is
> absent. After rape, oppression is the second horror of
> human existence. It is a terrible caricature of obedience.
> —Simone Weil

I HAVE proposed an enabling conception of justice. Justice should refer not
only to distribution, but also to the institutional conditions necessary for
the development and exercise of individual capacities and collective communication and cooperation. Under this conception of justice, injustice
refers primarily to two forms of disabling constraints, oppression and
domination. While these constraints include distributive patterns, they
also involve matters which cannot easily be assimilated to the logic of
distribution: decisionmaking procedures, division of labor, and culture.

Many people in the United States would not choose the term "oppression" to name injustice in our society. For contemporary emancipatory
social movements, on the other hand—socialists, radical feminists, American Indian activists, Black activists, gay and lesbian activists—oppression
is a central category of political discourse. Entering the political discourse
in which oppression is a central category involves adopting a general
mode of analyzing and evaluating social structures and practices which is
incommensurate with the language of liberal individualism that dominates
political discourse in the United States.

A major political project for those of us who identify with at least one of
these movements must thus be to persuade people that the discourse of
oppression makes sense of much of our social experience. We are ill prepared for this task, however, because we have no clear account of the

meaning of oppression. While we find the term used often in the diverse philosophical and theoretical literature spawned by radical social movements in the United States, we find little direct discussion of the meaning of the concept as used by these movements.

In this chapter I offer some explication of the concept of oppression as I understand its use by new social movements in the United States since the 1960s. My starting point is reflection on the conditions of the groups said by these movements to be oppressed: among others women, Blacks, Chicanos, Puerto Ricans and other Spanish-speaking Americans, American Indians, Jews, lesbians, gay men, Arabs, Asians, old people, working-class people, and the physically and mentally disabled. I aim to systematize the meaning of the concept of oppression as used by these diverse political movements, and to provide normative argument to clarify the wrongs the term names.

Obviously the above-named groups are not oppressed to the same extent or in the same ways. In the most general sense, all oppressed people suffer some inhibition of their ability to develop and exercise their capacities and express their needs, thoughts, and feelings. In that abstract sense all oppressed people face a common condition. Beyond that, in any more specific sense, it is not possible to define a single set of criteria that describe the condition of oppression of the above groups. Consequently, attempts by theorists and activists to discover a common description or the essential causes of the oppression of all these groups have frequently led to fruitless disputes about whose oppression is more fundamental or more grave. The contexts in which members of these groups use the term oppression to describe the injustices of their situation suggest that oppression names in fact a family of concepts and conditions, which I divide into five categories: exploitation, marginalization, powerlessness, cultural imperialism, and violence.

In this chapter I explicate each of these forms of oppression. Each may entail or cause distributive injustices, but all involve issues of justice beyond distribution. In accordance with ordinary political usage, I suggest that oppression is a condition of groups. Thus before explicating the meaning of oppression, we must examine the concept of a social group.

OPPRESSION AS A STRUCTURAL CONCEPT

One reason that many people would not use the term oppression to describe injustice in our society is that they do not understand the term in the same way as do new social movements. In its traditional usage, oppression means the exercise of tyranny by a ruling group. Thus many Americans would agree with radicals in applying the term oppression to the situation of Black South Africans under apartheid. Oppression also traditionally carries a strong connotation of conquest and colonial domination. The Hebrews were oppressed in Egypt, and many uses of the term oppression in the West invoke this paradigm.

Dominant political discourse may use the term oppression to describe societies other than our own, usually Communist or purportedly Communist societies. Within this anti-Communist rhetoric both tyrannical and colonialist implications of the term appear. For the anti-Communist, Communism denotes precisely the exercise of brutal tyranny over a whole people by a few rulers, and the will to conquer the world, bringing hitherto independent peoples under that tyranny. In dominant political discourse it is not legitimate to use the term oppression to describe our society, because oppression is the evil perpetrated by the Others.

New left social movements of the 1960s and 1970s, however, shifted the meaning of the concept of oppression. In its new usage, oppression designates the disadvantage and injustice some people suffer not because a tyrannical power coerces them, but because of the everyday practices of a well-intentioned liberal society. In this new left usage, the tyranny of a ruling group over another, as in South Africa, must certainly be called oppressive. But oppression also refers to systemic constraints on groups that are not necessarily the result of the intentions of a tyrant. Oppression in this sense is structural, rather than the result of a few people's choices or policies. Its causes are embedded in unquestioned norms, habits, and symbols, in the assumptions underlying institutional rules and the collective consequences of following those rules. It names, as Marilyn Frye puts it, "an enclosing structure of forces and barriers which tends to the immobilization and reduction of a group or category of people" (Frye, 1983a, p. 11). In this extended structural sense oppression refers to the vast and deep injustices some groups suffer as a consequence of often unconscious assumptions and reactions of well-meaning people in ordinary interactions, media and cultural stereotypes, and structural features of bureaucratic hierarchies and market mechanisms—in short, the normal processes of everyday life. We cannot eliminate this structural oppression by getting rid of the rulers or making some new laws, because oppressions are systematically reproduced in major economic, political, and cultural institutions.

The systemic character of oppression implies that an oppressed group need not have a correlate oppressing group. While structural oppression involves relations among groups, these relations do not always fit the paradigm of conscious and intentional oppression of one group by another. Foucault (1977) suggests that to understand the meaning and operation of power in modern society we must look beyond the model of power as "sovereignty," a dyadic relation of ruler and subject, and instead analyze the exercise of power as the effect of often liberal and "humane" practices of education, bureaucratic administration, production and distribution of consumer goods, medicine, and so on. The conscious actions of many individuals daily contribute to maintaining and reproducing oppression, but those people are usually simply doing their jobs or living their lives, and do not understand themselves as agents of oppression.

I do not mean to suggest that within a system of oppression individual persons do not intentionally harm others in oppressed groups. The raped woman, the beaten Black youth, the locked-out worker, the gay man harrassed on the street, are victims of intentional actions by identifiable agents. I also do not mean to deny that specific groups are beneficiaries of the oppression of other groups, and thus have an interest in their continued oppression. Indeed, for every oppressed group there is a group that is *privileged* in relation to that group.

The concept of oppression has been current among radicals since the 1960s partly in reaction to Marxist attempts to reduce the injustices of racism and sexism, for example, to the effects of class domination or bourgeois ideology. Racism, sexism, ageism, homophobia, some social movements asserted, are distinct forms of oppression with their own dynamics apart from the dynamics of class, even though they may interact with class oppression. From often heated discussions among socialists, feminists, and antiracism activists in the last ten years a consensus is emerging that many different groups must be said to be oppressed in our society, and that no single form of oppression can be assigned causal or moral primacy (see Gottlieb, 1987). The same discussion has also led to the recognition that group differences cut across individual lives in a multiplicity of ways that can entail privilege and oppression for the same person in different respects. Only a plural explication of the concept of oppression can adequately capture these insights.

Accordingly, I offer below an explication of five faces of oppression as a useful set of categories and distinctions which I believe is comprehensive, in the sense that it covers all the groups said by new left social movements to be oppressed and all the ways they are oppressed. I derive the five faces of oppression from reflection on the condition of these groups. Because different factors, or combinations of factors, constitute the oppression of different groups, making their oppression irreducible, I believe it is not possible to give one essential definition of oppression. The five categories articulated in this chapter, however, are adequate to describe the oppression of any group, as well as its similarities with and differences from the oppression of other groups. But first we must ask what a group is.

The Concept of a Social Group

Oppression refers to structural phenomena that immobilize or diminish a group. But what is a group? Our ordinary discourse differentiates people according to social groups such as women and men, age groups, racial and ethnic groups, religious groups, and so on. Social groups of this sort are not simply collections of people, for they are more fundamentally intertwined with the identities of the people described as belonging to them. They are a specific kind of collectivity, with specific consequences for how people understand one another and themselves. Yet neither social theory nor philosophy has a clear and developed concept of the social group (see Turner et al., 1987).

A social group is a collective of persons differentiated from at least one other group by cultural forms, practices, or way of life. Members of a group have a specific affinity with one another because of their similar experience or way of life, which prompts them to associate with one another more than with those not identified with the group, or in a different way. Groups are an expression of social relations; a group exists only in relation to at least one other group. Group identification arises, that is, in the encounter and interaction between social collectivities that experience some differences in their way of life and forms of association, even if they also regard themselves as belonging to the same society.

As long as they associated solely among themselves, for example, an American Indian group thought of themselves only as "the people." The encounter with other American Indians created an awareness of difference; the others were named as a group, and the first group came to see themselves as a group. But social groups do not arise only from an encounter between different societies. Social processes also differentiate groups within a single society. The sexual division of labor, for example, has created social groups of women and men in all known societies. Members of each gender have a certain affinity with others in their group because of what they do or experience, and differentiate themselves from the other gender, even when members of each gender consider that they have much in common with members of the other, and consider that they belong to the same society.

Political philosophy typically has no place for a specific concept of the social group. When philosophers and political theorists discuss groups, they tend to conceive them either on the model of aggregates or on the model of associations, both of which are methodologically individualist concepts. To arrive at a specific concept of the social group it is thus useful to contrast social groups with both aggregates and associations.

An aggregate is any classification of persons according to some attribute. Persons can be aggregated according to any number of attributes—eye color, the make of car they drive, the street they live on. Some people interpret the groups that have emotional and social salience in our society as aggregates, as arbitrary classifications of persons according to such attributes as skin color, genitals, or age. George Sher, for example, treats social groups as aggregates, and uses the arbitrariness of aggregate classification as a reason not to give special attention to groups. "There are really as many groups as there are combinations of people and if we are going to ascribe claims to equal treatment to racial, sexual, and other groups with high visibility, it will be mere favoritism not to ascribe similar claims to these other groups as well" (Sher, 1987a, p. 256).

But "highly visible" social groups such as Blacks or women are different from aggregates, or mere "combinations of people" (see French, 1975; Friedman and May, 1985; May, 1987, chap. 1). A social group is defined not primarily by a set of shared attributes, but by a sense of identity. What defines Black Americans as a social group is not primarily their skin color; some persons whose skin color is fairly light, for example, identify themselves as Black. Though sometimes objective attributes are a necessary condition for classifying oneself or others as belonging to a certain social group, it is identification with a certain social status, the common history that social status produces, and self-identification that define the group as a group.

Social groups are not entities that exist apart from individuals, but neither are they merely arbitrary classifications of individuals according to attributes which are external to or accidental to their identities. Admitting the reality of social groups does not commit one to reifying collectivities, as some might argue. Group meanings partially constitute people's identities in terms of the cultural forms, social situation, and history that group members know as theirs, because these meanings have been either forced upon them or forged by them or both (cf. Fiss, 1976). Groups are real not as substances, but as forms of social relations (cf. May, 1987, pp. 22–23).

Moral theorists and political philosophers tend to elide social groups more often with associations than with aggregates (e.g., French, 1975; May, 1987, chap. 1). By an association I mean a formally organized institution, such as a club, corporation, political party, church, college, or union. Unlike the aggregate model of groups, the association model recognizes that groups are defined by specific practices and forms of association. Nevertheless it shares a problem with the aggregate model. The aggregate model conceives the individual as prior to the collective, because it reduces the social group to a mere set of attributes attached to individuals. The association model also implicitly conceives the individual as ontologically prior to the collective, as making up, or constituting, groups.

A contract model of social relations is appropriate for conceiving associations, but not groups. Individuals constitute associations, they come together as already formed persons and set them up, establishing rules, positions, and offices. The relationship of persons to associations is usually voluntary, and even when it is not, the person has nevertheless usually entered the association. The person is prior to the association also in that the person's identity and sense of self are usually regarded as prior to and relatively independent of association membership.

Groups, on the other hand, constitute individuals. A person's particular sense of history, affinity, and separateness, even the person's mode of reasoning, evaluating, and expressing feeling, are constituted partly by her or his group affinities. This does not mean that persons have no individual styles, or are unable to transcend or reject a group identity. Nor does it preclude persons from having many aspects that are independent of these group identities.

The social ontology underlying many contemporary theories of justice, I pointed out in the last chapter, is methodologically individualist or atomist. It presumes that the individual is ontologically prior to the social. This individualist social ontology usually goes together with a normative conception of the self as independent. The authentic self is autonomous, unified, free, and self-made, standing apart from history and affiliations, choosing its life plan entirely for itself.

One of the main contributions of poststructuralist philosophy has been to expose as illusory this metaphysic of a unified self-making subjectivity, which posits the subject as an autonomous origin or an underlying substance to which attributes of gender, nationality, family role, intellectual disposition, and so on might attach. Conceiving the subject in this fashion implies conceiving consciousness as outside of and prior to language and the context of social interaction, which the subject enters. Several currents of recent philosophy challenge this deeply held Cartesian assumption. Lacanian psychoanalysis, for example, and the social and philosophical theory influenced by it, conceive the self as an achievement of linguistic positioning that is always contextualized in concrete relations with other persons, with their mixed identities (Coward and Ellis, 1977). The self is a product of social processes, not their origin.

From a rather different perspective, Habermas indicates that a theory of communicative action also must challenge the "philosophy of consciousness" which locates intentional egos as the ontological origins of social relations. A theory of communicative action conceives individual identity not as an origin but as a product of linguistic and practical interaction (Habermas, 1987, pp. 3–40). As Stephen Epstein describes it, identity is "a socialized sense of individuality, an internal organization of self-perception concerning one's relationship to social categories, that also incorporates views of the self perceived to be held by others. Identity is constituted relationally, through involvement with—and incorporation of—significant others and integration into communities" (Epstein, 1987, p. 29). Group categorization and norms are major constituents of individual identity (see Turner et al., 1987).

A person joins an association, and even if membership in it fundamentally affects one's life, one does not take that membership to define one's very identity, in the way, for example, being Navaho might. Group affinity, on the other hand, has the character of what Martin Heidegger (1962) calls "thrownness": one *finds oneself* as a member of a group, which one experiences as always already having been. For our identities are defined in relation to how others identify us, and they do so in terms of groups which are always already associated with specific attributes, stereotypes, and norms.

From the thrownness of group affinity it does not follow that one cannot leave groups and enter new ones. Many women become lesbian after first identifying as heterosexual. Anyone who lives long enough becomes old. These cases exemplify thrownness precisely because such changes in group affinity are experienced as transformations in one's identity. Nor does it follow fom the thrownness of group affinity that one cannot define the meaning of group identity for oneself; those who identify with a group can redefine the meaning and norms of group identity. Indeed, in Chapter 6 I will show how oppressed groups have sought to confront their oppression by engaging in just such redefinition. The present point is only that one first finds a group identity as given, and then takes it up in a certain way. While groups may come into being, they are never founded.

Groups, I have said, exist only in relation to other groups. A group may be identified by outsiders without those so identified having any specific consciousness of themselves as a group. Sometimes a group comes to exist only because one group excludes and labels a category of persons, and those labeled come to understand themselves as group members only slowly, on the basis of their shared oppression. In Vichy France, for example, Jews who had been so assimilated that they had no specifically Jewish identity were marked as Jews by others and given a specific social status by them. These people "discovered" themselves as Jews, and then formed a group identity and affinity with one another (see Sartre, 1948). A person's group identities may be for the most part only a background or horizon to his or her life, becoming salient only in specific interactive contexts.

Assuming an aggregate model of groups, some people think that social groups are invidious fictions, essentializing arbitrary attributes. From this point of view problems of prejudice, stereotyping, discrimination, and exclusion exist because some people mistakenly believe that group identification makes a difference to the capacities, temperament, or virtues of group members. This individualist conception of persons and their relation to one another tends to identify oppression with group identification. Oppression, on this view, is something that happens to people when they are classified in groups. Because others identify them as a group, they are excluded and despised. Eliminating oppression thus requires eliminating groups. People should be treated as individuals, not as members of groups, and allowed to form their lives freely without stereotypes or group norms.

This book takes issue with that position. While I agree that individuals should be free to pursue life plans in their own way, it is foolish to deny the reality of groups. Despite the modern myth of a decline of parochial attachments and ascribed identities, in modern society group differentiation remains endemic. As both markets and social administration increase the web of social interdependency on a world scale, and as more people encounter one another as strangers in cities and states, people retain and renew ethnic, locale, age, sex, and occupational group identifications, and form new ones in the processes of encounter (cf. Ross, 1980, p. 19; Rothschild, 1981, p. 130). Even when they belong to oppressed groups, people's group identifications are often important to them, and they often feel a special affinity for others in their group. I believe that group differentiation is both an inevitable and a desirable aspect of modern social processes. Social justice, I shall argue in later chapters, requires not the melting away of differences, but institutions that promote reproduction of and respect for group differences without oppression.

Though some groups have come to be formed out of oppression, and relations of privilege and oppression structure the interactions between many groups, group differentiation is not in itself oppressive. Not all groups are oppressed. In the United States Roman Catholics are a specific social group, with distinct practices and affinities with one another, but they are no longer an oppressed group. Whether a group is oppressed depends on whether it is subject to one or more of the five conditions I shall discuss below.

The view that groups are fictions does carry an important antideterminist or antiessentialist intuition. Oppression has often been perpetrated by a conceptualization of group difference in terms of unalterable essential natures that determine what group members deserve or are capable of, and that exclude groups so entirely from one another that they have no similarities or overlapping attributes. To assert that it is possible to have social group difference without oppression, it is necessary to conceptualize groups in a much more relational and fluid fashion.

Although social processes of affinity and differentiation produce groups, they do not give groups a substantive essence. There is no common nature that members of a group share. As aspects of a process, moreover, groups are fluid; they come into being and may fade away. Homosexual practices have existed in many societies and historical periods, for example. Gay men or lesbians have been identified as specific groups and so identified themselves, however, only in the twentieth century (see Ferguson, 1989, chap. 9; Altman, 1981).

Arising from social relations and processes, finally, group differences usually cut across one another. Especially in a large, complex, and highly differentiated society, social groups are not themselves homogeneous, but mirror in their own differentiations many of the other groups in the wider society. In American society today, for example, Blacks are not a simple, unified group with a common life. Like other racial and ethnic groups, they are differentiated by age, gender, class, sexuality, region, and nationality, any of which in a given context may become a salient group identity.

This view of group differentiation as multiple, cross-cutting, fluid, and shifting implies another critique of the model of the autonomous, unified self. In complex, highly differentiated societies like our own, all persons have multiple group identifications. The culture, perspective, and relations of privilege and oppression of these various groups, moreover, may not cohere. Thus individual persons, as constituted partly by their group affinities and relations, cannot be unified, themselves are heterogeneous and not necessarily coherent.

THE FACES OF OPPRESSION

Exploitation

The central function of Marx's theory of exploitation is to explain how class structure can exist in the absence of legally and normatively sanctioned class distinctions. In precapitalist societies domination is overt and accomplished through directly political means. In both slave society and feudal society the right to appropriate the product of the labor of others partly defines class privilege, and these societies legitimate class distinctions with ideologies of natural superiority and inferiority.

Capitalist society, on the other hand, removes traditional juridically enforced class distinctions and promotes a belief in the legal freedom of persons. Workers freely contract with employers and receive a wage; no formal mechanisms of law or custom force them to work for that employer or any employer. Thus the mystery of capitalism arises: when everyone is formally free, how can there be class domination? Why do class distinctions persist between the wealthy, who own the means of production, and the mass of people, who work for them? The theory of exploitation answers this question.

Profit, the basis of capitalist power and wealth, is a mystery if we assume that in the market goods exchange at their values. The labor theory of value dispels this mystery. Every commodity's value is a function of the labor time necessary for its production. Labor power is the one commodity which in the process of being consumed produces new value. Profit comes from the difference between the value of the labor performed and the value of the capacity to labor which the capitalist purchases. Profit is possible only because the owner of capital appropriates any realized surplus value.

In recent years Marxist scholars have engaged in considerable controversy about the viability of the labor theory of value this account of exploitation relies on (see Wolff, 1984, chap. 4). John Roemer (1982), for example, develops a theory of exploitation which claims to preserve the theoretical and practical purposes of Marx's theory, but without assuming a distinction between values and prices and without being restricted to a concept of abstract, homogeneous labor. My purpose here is not to engage in technical economic disputes, but to indicate the place of a concept of exploitation in a conception of oppression.

Marx's theory of exploitation lacks an explicitly normative meaning, even though the judgment that workers are exploited clearly has normative as well as descriptive power in that theory (Buchanan, 1982, chap. 3). C. B. Macpherson (1973, chap. 3) reconstructs this theory of exploitation in a more explicitly normative form. The injustice of capitalist society consists in the fact that some people exercise their capacities under the control, according to the purposes, and for the benefit of other people. Through private ownership of the means of production, and through markets that allocate labor and the ability to buy goods, capitalism systematically transfers the powers of some persons to others, thereby augmenting the power of the latter. In this process of the transfer of powers, according to Macpherson, the capitalist class acquires and maintains an ability to extract benefits from workers. Not only are powers transferred from workers to capitalists, but also the powers of workers diminish by more than the amount of transfer, because workers suffer material deprivation and a loss of control, and hence are deprived of important elements of self-respect. Justice, then, requires eliminating the institutional forms that enable and enforce this process of transference and replacing them with institutional forms that enable all to develop and use their capacities in a way that does not inhibit, but rather can enhance, similar development and use in others.

The central insight expressed in the concept of exploitation, then, is that this oppression occurs through a steady process of the transfer of the results of the labor of one social group to benefit another. The injustice of class division does not consist only in the distributive fact that some people have great wealth while most people have little (cf. Buchanan, 1982, pp. 44–49; Holmstrom, 1977). Exploitation enacts a structural relation between social groups. Social rules about what work is, who does what for whom, how work is compensated, and the social process by which the results of work are appropriated operate to enact relations of power and inequality. These relations are produced and reproduced through a systematic process in which the energies of the have-nots are continuously expended to maintain and augment the power, status, and wealth of the haves.

Many writers have cogently argued that the Marxist concept of exploitation is too narrow to encompass all forms of domination and oppression (Giddens, 1981, p. 242; Brittan and Maynard, 1984, p. 93; Murphy, 1985; Bowles and Gintis, 1986, pp. 20–24). In particular, the Marxist concept of class leaves important phenomena of sexual and racial oppression unexplained. Does this mean that sexual and racial oppression are nonexploitative, and that we should reserve wholly distinct categories for these oppressions? Or can the concept of exploitation be broadened to include other ways in which the labor and energy expenditure of one group benefits another, and reproduces a relation of domination between them?

Feminists have had little difficulty showing that women's oppression consists partly in a systematic and unreciprocated transfer of powers from women to men. Women's oppression consists not merely in an inequality of status, power, and wealth resulting fom men's excluding them from privileged activities. The freedom, power, status, and self-realization of men is possible precisely because women work for them. Gender exploitation has two aspects, transfer of the fruits of material labor to men and transfer of nurturing and sexual energies to men.

Christine Delphy (1984), for example, describes marriage as a class relation in which women's labor benefits men without comparable remuneration. She makes it clear that the exploitation consists not in the sort of work that women do in the home, for this might include various kinds of tasks, but in the fact that they perform tasks for someone on whom they are dependent. Thus, for example, in most systems of agricultural production in the world, men take to market the goods women have produced, and more often than not men receive the status and often the entire income from this labor.

With the concept of sex-affective production, Ann Ferguson (1979; 1984; 1989, chap. 4) identifies another form of the transference of women's energies to men. Women provide men and children with emotional care and provide men with sexual satisfaction, and as a group receive relatively little of either from men (cf. Brittan and Maynard, pp. 142–48). The gender socialization of women makes us tend to be more attentive to interactive dynamics than men, and makes women good at providing empathy and support for people's feelings and at smoothing over interactive tensions. Both men and women look to women as nurturers of their personal lives, and women frequently complain that when they look to men for emotional support they do not receive it (Easton, 1978). The norms of heterosexuality, moreover, are oriented around male pleasure, and consequently many women receive little satisfaction from their sexual interaction with men (Gottlieb, 1984).

Most feminist theories of gender exploitation have concentrated on the institutional structure of the patriarchal family. Recently, however, feminists have begun to explore relations of gender exploitation enacted in the contemporary workplace and through the state. Carol Brown argues that as men have removed themselves from responsibility for children, many women have become dependent on the state for subsistence as they continue to bear nearly total responsibility for childrearing (Brown, 1981; cf. Boris and Bardaglio, 1983; A. Ferguson, 1984). This creates a new system of the exploitation of women's domestic labor mediated by state institutions, which she calls public patriarchy.

In twentieth-century capitalist economies the workplaces that women have been entering in increasing numbers serve as another important site of gender exploitation. David Alexander (1987) argues that typically feminine jobs involve gender-based tasks requiring sexual labor, nurturing, caring for others' bodies, or smoothing over workplace tensions. In these ways women's energies are expended in jobs that enhance the status of, please, or comfort others, usually men; and these gender-based labors of waitresses, clerical workers, nurses, and other caretakers often go unnoticed and undercompensated.

To summarize, women are exploited in the Marxist sense to the degree that they are wage workers. Some have argued that women's domestic labor also represents a form of capitalist class exploitation insofar as it is labor covered by the wages a family receives. As a group, however, women undergo specific forms of gender exploitation in which their energies and power are expended, often unnoticed and unacknowledged, usually to benefit men by releasing them for more important and creative work, enhancing their status or the environment around them, or providing them with sexual or emotional service.

Race is a structure of oppression at least as basic as class or gender. Are there, then, racially specific forms of exploitation? There is no doubt that racialized groups in the United States, especially Blacks and Latinos, are oppressed through capitalist superexploitation resulting from a segmented labor market that tends to reserve skilled, high-paying, unionized jobs for whites. There is wide disagreement about whether such superexploitation benefits whites as a group or only benefits the capitalist class (see Reich, 1981), and I do not intend to enter into that dispute here.

However one answers the question about capitalist superexploitation of racialized groups, is it possible to conceptualize a form of exploitation that is racially specific on analogy with the gender-specific forms just discussed? I suggest that the category of *menial* labor might supply a means for such conceptualization. In its derivation "menial" designates the labor of servants. Wherever there is racism, there is the assumption, more or less enforced, that members of the oppressed racial groups are or ought to be servants of those, or some of those, in the privileged group. In most white racist societies this means that many white people have dark- or yellow-skinned domestic servants, and in the United States today there remains significant racial structuring of private household service. But in the United States today much service labor has gone public: anyone who goes to a good hotel or a good restaurant can have servants. Servants often attend the daily—and nightly—activities of business executives, government officials, and other high-status professionals. In our society there remains strong cultural pressure to fill servant jobs—bellhop, porter, chambermaid, busboy, and so on—with Black and Latino workers. These jobs entail a transfer of energies whereby the servers enhance the status of the served.

Menial labor usually refers not only to service, however, but also to any servile, unskilled, low-paying work lacking in autonomy, in which a person is subject to taking orders from many people. Menial work tends to be auxiliary work, instrumental to the work of others, where those others receive primary recognition for doing the job. Laborers on a construction site, for example, are at the beck and call of welders, electricians, carpenters, and other skilled workers, who receive recognition for the job done. In the United States explicit racial discrimination once reserved menial work for Blacks, Chicanos, American Indians, and Chinese, and menial work still tends to be linked to Black and Latino workers (Symanski, 1985). I offer this category of menial labor as a form of racially specific exploitation, as a provisional category in need of exploration.

The injustice of exploitation is most frequently understood on a distributive model. For example, though he does not offer an explicit definition of the concept, by "exploitation" Bruce Ackerman seems to mean a seriously unequal distribution of wealth, income, and other resources that is group based and structurally persistent (Ackerman, 1980, chap. 8). John Roemer's definition of exploitation is narrower and more rigorous: "An agent is exploited when the amount of labor embodied in *any* bundle of goods he could receive, in a feasible distribution of society's net product, is less than the labor he expended" (Roemer, 1982, p. 122). This definition too turns the conceptual focus from institutional relations and processes to distributive outcomes.

Jeffrey Reiman argues that such a distributive understanding of exploitation reduces the injustice of class processes to a function of the inequality of the productive assets classes own. This misses, according to Reiman, the relationship of force between capitalists and workers, the fact that the unequal exchange in question occurs within coercive structures that give workers few options (Reiman, 1987; cf. Buchanan, 1982, pp. 44–49; Holmstrom, 1977). The injustice of exploitation consists in social processes that bring about a transfer of energies from one group to another to produce unequal distributions, and in the way in which social institutions enable a few to accumulate while they constrain many more. The injustices of exploitation cannot be eliminated by redistribution of goods, for as long as institutionalized practices and structural relations remain unaltered, the process of transfer will re-create an unequal distribution of benefits. Bringing about justice where there is exploitation requires reorganization of institutions and practices of decisionmaking, alteration of the division of labor, and similar measures of institutional, structural, and cultural change.

Marginalization

Increasingly in the United States racial oppression occurs in the form of marginalization rather than exploitation. Marginals are people the system of labor cannot or will not use. Not only in Third World capitalist countries, but also in most Western capitalist societies, there is a growing underclass of people permanently confined to lives of social marginality, most of whom are racially marked—Blacks or Indians in Latin America, and Blacks, East Indians, Eastern Europeans, or North Africans in Europe.

Marginalization is by no means the fate only of racially marked groups, however. In the United States a shamefully large proportion of the population is marginal: old people, and increasingly people who are not very old but get laid off from their jobs and cannot find new work; young people, especially Black or Latino, who cannot find first or second jobs; many single mothers and their children; other people involuntarily unemployed; many mentally and physically disabled people; American Indians, especially those on reservations.

Marginalization is perhaps the most dangerous form of oppression. A whole category of people is expelled from useful participation in social life and thus potentially subjected to severe material deprivation and even extermination. The material deprivation marginalization often causes is certainly unjust, especially in a society where others have plenty. Contemporary advanced capitalist societies have in principle acknowledged the injustice of material deprivation caused by marginalization, and have taken some steps to address it by providing welfare payments and services. The continuance of this welfare state is by no means assured, and in most welfare state societies, especially the United States, welfare redistributions do not eliminate large-scale suffering and deprivation.

Material deprivation, which can be addressed by redistributive social policies, is not, however, the extent of the harm caused by marginalization. Two categories of injustice beyond distribution are associated with marginality in advanced capitalist societies. First, the provision of welfare itself produces new injustice by depriving those dependent on it of rights and freedoms that others have. Second, even when material deprivation is somewhat mitigated by the welfare state, marginalization is unjust because it blocks the opportunity to exercise capacities in socially defined and recognized ways. I shall explicate each of these in turn.

Liberalism has traditionally asserted the right of all rational autonomous agents to equal citizenship. Early bourgeois liberalism explicitly excluded from citizenship all those whose reason was questionable or not fully developed, and all those not independent (Pateman, 1988, chap. 3; cf. Bowles and Gintis, 1986, chap. 2). Thus poor people, women, the mad and the feebleminded, and children were explicitly excluded from citizenship, and many of these were housed in institutions modeled on the modern prison: poorhouses, insane asylums, schools.

Today the exclusion of dependent persons from equal citizenship rights is only barely hidden beneath the surface. Because they depend on bureaucratic institutions for support or services, the old, the poor, and the mentally or physically disabled are subject to patronizing, punitive, demeaning, and arbitrary treatment by the policies and people associated with welfare bureaucracies. Being a dependent in our society implies being legitimately subject to the often arbitrary and invasive authority of social service providers and other public and private administrators, who enforce rules with which the marginal must comply, and otherwise exercise power over the conditions of their lives. In meeting needs of the marginalized, often with the aid of social scientific disciplines, welfare agencies also construct the needs themselves. Medical and social service professionals know what is good for those they serve, and the marginals and dependents themselves do not have the right to claim to know what is good for them (Fraser, 1987a; K. Ferguson, 1984, chap. 4). Dependency in our society thus implies, as it has in all liberal societies, a sufficient warrant to suspend basic rights to privacy, respect, and individual choice.

Although dependency produces conditions of injustice in our society, dependency in itself need not be oppressive. One cannot imagine a society in which some people would not need to be dependent on others at least some of the time: children, sick people, women recovering from childbirth, old people who have become frail, depressed or otherwise emotionally needy persons, have the moral right to depend on others for subsistence and support.

An important contribution of feminist moral theory has been to question the deeply held assumption that moral agency and full citizenship require that a person be autonomous and independent. Feminists have exposed this assumption as inappropriately individualistic and derived from a specifically male experience of social relations, which values competition and solitary achievement (see Gilligan, 1982; Friedman, 1985). Female experience of social relations, arising both from women's typical domestic care responsibilities and from the kinds of paid work that many women do, tends to recognize dependence as a basic human condition (cf. Hartsock, 1983, chap. 10). Whereas on the autonomy model a just society would as much as possible give people the opportunity to be independent, the feminist model envisions justice as according respect and participation in decisionmaking to those who are dependent as well as to those who are independent (Held, 1987b). Dependency should not be a reason to be deprived of choice and respect, and much of the oppression many marginals experience would be lessened if a less individualistic model of rights prevailed.

Marginalization does not cease to be oppressive when one has shelter and food. Many old people, for example, have sufficient means to live comfortably but remain oppressed in their marginal status. Even if marginals were provided a comfortable material life within institutions that respected their freedom and dignity, injustices of marginality would remain in the form of uselessness, boredom, and lack of self-respect. Most of our society's productive and recognized activities take place in contexts of organized social cooperation, and social structures and processes that close persons out of participation in such social cooperation are unjust. Thus while marginalization definitely entails serious issues of distributive justice, it also involves the deprivation of cultural, practical, and institutionalized conditions for exercising capacities in a context of recognition and interaction.

The fact of marginalization raises basic structural issues of justice, in particular concerning the appropriateness of a connection between participation in productive activities of social cooperation, on the one hand, and access to the means of consumption, on the other. As marginalization is increasing, with no sign of abatement, some social policy analysts have introduced the idea of a "social wage" as a guaranteed socially provided income not tied to the wage system. Restructuring of productive activity to address a right of participation, however, implies organizing some socially productive activity outside of the wage system (see Offe, 1985, pp. 95–100), through public works or self-employed collectives.

Powerlessness

As I have indicated, the Marxist idea of class is important because it helps reveal the structure of exploitation: that some people have their power and wealth because they profit from the labor of others. For this reason I reject the claim some make that a traditional class exploitation model fails to capture the structure of contemporary society. It remains the case that the labor of most people in the society augments the power of relatively few. Despite their differences from nonprofessional workers, most professional workers are still not members of the capitalist class. Professional labor either involves exploitative transfers to capitalists or supplies important conditions for such transfers. Professional workers are in an ambiguous class position, it is true, because, as I argue in Chapter 7, they also benefit from the exploitation of nonprofessional workers.

While it is false to claim that a division between capitalist and working classes no longer describes our society, it is also false to say that class relations have remained unaltered since the nineteenth century. An adequate conception of oppression cannot ignore the experience of social division reflected in the colloquial distinction between the "middle class" and the "working class," a division structured by the social division of labor between professionals and nonprofessionals. Professionals are privileged in relation to nonprofessionals, by virtue of their position in the division of labor and the status it carries. Nonprofessionals suffer a form of oppression in addition to exploitation, which I call powerlessness.

In the United States, as in other advanced capitalist countries, most workplaces are not organized democratically, direct participation in public policy decisions is rare, and policy implementation is for the most part hierarchical, imposing rules on bureaucrats and citizens. Thus most people in these societies do not regularly participate in making decisions that affect the conditions of their lives and actions, and in this sense most people lack signficant power. At the same time, as I argued in Chapter 1, domination in modern society is enacted through the widely dispersed powers of many agents mediating the decisions of others. To that extent many people have some power in relation to others, even though they lack the power to decide policies or results. The powerless are those who lack authority or power even in this mediated sense, those over whom power is exercised without their exercising it; the powerless are situated so that they must take orders and rarely have the right to give them. Powerlessness also designates a position in the division of labor and the concomitant social position that allows persons little opportunity to develop and exercise skills. The powerless have little or no work autonomy, exercise little creativity or judgment in their work, have no technical expertise or authority, express themselves awkwardly, especially in public or bureaucratic settings, and do not command respect. Powerlessness names the oppressive situations Sennett and Cobb (1972) describe in their famous study of working-class men.

This powerless status is perhaps best described negatively: the powerless lack the authority, status, and sense of self that professionals tend to have. The status privilege of professionals has three aspects, the lack of which produces oppression for nonprofessionals.

First, acquiring and practicing a profession has an expansive, progressive character. Being professional usually requires a college education and the acquisition of a specialized knowledge that entails working with symbols and concepts. Professionals experience progress first in acquiring the expertise, and then in the course of professional advancement and rise in status. The life of the nonprofessional by comparison is powerless in the sense that it lacks this orientation toward the progressive development of capacities and avenues for recognition.

Second, while many professionals have supervisors and cannot directly influence many decisions or the actions of many people, most nevertheless have considerable day-to-day work autonomy. Professionals usually have some authority over others, moreover—either over workers they supervise, or over auxiliaries, or over clients. Nonprofessionals, on the other hand, lack autonomy, and in both their working and their consumer-client lives often stand under the authority of professionals.

Though based on a division of labor between "mental" and "manual" work, the distinction between "middle class" and "working class" designates a division not only in working life, but also in nearly all aspects of social life. Professionals and nonprofessionals belong to different cultures in the United States. The two groups tend to live in segregated neighborhoods or even different towns, a process itself mediated by planners, zoning officials, and real estate people. The groups tend to have different tastes in food, decor, clothes, music, and vacations, and often different health and educational needs. Members of each group socialize for the most part with others in the same status group. While there is some intergroup mobility between generations, for the most part the children of professionals become professionals and the children of nonprofessionals do not.

Thus, third, the privileges of the professional extend beyond the workplace to a whole way of life. I call this way of life "respectability." To treat people with respect is to be prepared to listen to what they have to say or to do what they request because they have some authority, expertise, or influence. The norms of respectability in our society are associated specifically with professional culture. Professional dress, speech, tastes, demeanor, all connote respectability. Generally professionals expect and receive respect from others. In restaurants, banks, hotels, real estate offices, and many other such public places, as well as in the media, professionals typically receive more respectful treatment than nonprofessionals. For this reason nonprofessionals seeking a loan or a job, or to buy a house or a car, will often try to look "professional" and "respectable" in those settings.

The privilege of this professional respectability appears starkly in the dynamics of racism and sexism. In daily interchange women and men of color must prove their respectability. At first they are often not treated by strangers with respectful distance or deference. Once people discover that this woman or that Puerto Rican man is a college teacher or a business executive, however, they often behave more respectfully toward her or him. Working-class white men, on the other hand, are often treated with respect until their working-class status is revealed. In Chapter 5 I will explore in more detail the cultural underpinnings of the ideal of respectability and its oppressive implications.

I have discussed several injustices associated with powerlessness: inhibition in the development of one's capacities, lack of decisionmaking power in one's working life, and exposure to disrespectful treatment because of the status one occupies. These injustices have distributional consequences, but are more fundamentally matters of the division of labor. The oppression of powerlessness brings into question the division of labor basic to all industrial societies: the social division between those who plan and those who execute. I examine this division in more detail in Chapter 7.

Cultural Imperialism

Exploitation, marginalization, and powerlessness all refer to relations of power and oppression that occur by virtue of the social division of labor—who works for whom, who does not work, and how the content of work defines one institutional position relative to others. These three categories refer to structural and institutional relations that delimit people's material lives, including but not restricted to the resources they have access to and the concrete opportunities they have or do not have to develop and exercise their capacities. These kinds of oppression are a matter of concrete power in relation to others—of who benefits from whom, and who is dispensable.

Recent theorists of movements of group liberation, notably feminist and Black liberation theorists, have also given prominence to a rather different form of oppression, which following Lugones and Spelman (1983) I shall call cultural imperialism. To experience cultural imperialism means to experience how the dominant meanings of a society render the particular perspective of one's own group invisible at the same time as they stereo-type one's group and mark it out as the Other.

Cultural imperialism involves the universalization of a dominant group's experience and culture, and its establishment as the norm. Some groups have exclusive or primary access to what Nancy Fraser (1987b) calls the means of interpretation and communication in a society. As a consequence, the dominant cultural products of the society, that is, those most widely disseminated, express the experience, values, goals, and achievements of these groups. Often without noticing they do so, the dominant groups project their own experience as representative of humanity as such. Cultural products also express the dominant group's perspective on and interpretation of events and elements in the society, including other groups in the society, insofar as they attain cultural status at all.

An encounter with other groups, however, can challenge the dominant group's claim to universality. The dominant group reinforces its position by bringing the other groups under the measure of its dominant norms. Consequently, the difference of women from men, American Indians or Africans from Europeans, Jews from Christians, homosexuals from heterosexuals, workers from professionals, becomes reconstructed largely as deviance and inferiority. Since only the dominant group's cultural expressions receive wide dissemination, their cultural expressions become the normal, or the universal, and thereby the unremarkable. Given the normality of its own cultural expressions and identity, the dominant group constructs the differences which some groups exhibit as lack and negation. These groups become marked as Other.

The culturally dominated undergo a paradoxical oppression, in that they are both marked out by stereotypes and at the same time rendered invisible. As remarkable, deviant beings, the culturally imperialized are stamped with an essence. The stereotypes confine them to a nature which is often attached in some way to their bodies, and which thus cannot easily be denied. These stereotypes so permeate the society that they are not noticed as contestable. Just as everyone knows that the earth goes around the sun, so everyone knows that gay people are promiscuous, that Indians are alcoholics, and that women are good with children. White males, on the other hand, insofar as they escape group marking, can be individuals.

Those living under cultural imperialism find themselves defined from the outside, positioned, placed, by a network of dominant meanings they experience as arising from elsewhere, from those with whom they do not identify and who do not identify with them. Consequently, the dominant culture's stereotyped and inferiorized images of the group must be internalized by group members at least to the extent that they are forced to react to behavior of others influenced by those images. This creates for the culturally oppressed the experience that W.E.B. Du Bois called "double consciousness"—"this sense of always looking at one's self through the eyes of others, of measuring one's soul by the tape of a world that looks on in amused contempt and pity" (Du Bois, 1969 [1903], p. 45). Double consciousness arises when the oppressed subject refuses to coincide with these devalued, objectified, stereotyped visions of herself or himself. While the subject desires recognition as human, capable of activity, full of hope and possibility, she receives from the dominant culture only the judgment that she is different, marked, or inferior.

The group defined by the dominant culture as deviant, as a stereotyped Other, *is* culturally different from the dominant group, because the status of Otherness creates specific experiences not shared by the dominant group, and because culturally oppressed groups also are often socially segregated and occupy specific positions in the social division of labor. Members of such groups express their specific group experiences and interpretations of the world to one another, developing and perpetuating their own culture. Double consciousness, then, occurs because one finds one's being defined by two cultures: a dominant and a subordinate culture. Because they can affirm and recognize one another as sharing similar experiences and perspectives on social life, people in culturally imperialized groups can often maintain a sense of positive subjectivity.

Cultural imperialism involves the paradox of experiencing oneself as invisible at the same time that one is marked out as different. The invisibility comes about when dominant groups fail to recognize the perspective embodied in their cultural expressions as a perspective. These dominant cultural expressions often simply have little place for the experience of other groups, at most only mentioning or referring to them in stereotyped or marginalized ways. This, then, is the injustice of cultural imperialism: that the oppressed group's own experience and interpretation of social life finds little expression that touches the dominant culture, while that same culture imposes on the oppressed group its experience and interpretation of social life.

In several of the following chapters I shall explore more fully the consequences of cultural imperialism for the theory and practice of social justice. Chapter 4 expands on the claim that cultural imperialism is enacted partly through the ability of a dominant group to assert its perspective and experience as universal or neutral. In the sphere of the polity, I argue, claim to universality operates politically to exclude those understood as different. In Chapter 5 I trace the operations of cultural imperialism in nineteenth-century scientific classifications of some bodies as deviant or degenerate. I explore how the devaluation of the bodies of some groups still conditions everyday interactions among groups, despite our relative success at expelling such bodily evaluation from discursive consciousness. In Chapter 6, finally, I discuss recent struggles by the culturally oppressed to take over definition of themselves and assert a positive sense of group difference. There I argue that justice requires us to make a political space for such difference.

Violence

Finally, many groups suffer the oppression of systematic volence. Members of some groups live with the knowledge that they must fear random, unprovoked attacks on their persons or property, which have no motive but to damage, humiliate, or destroy the person. In American society women, Blacks, Asians, Arabs, gay men, and lesbians live under such threats of violence, and in at least some regions Jews, Puerto Ricans, Chicanos, and other Spanish-speaking Americans must fear such violence as well. Physical violence against these groups is shockingly frequent. Rape Crisis Center networks estimate that more than one-third of all American women experience an attempted or successful sexual assault in their lifetimes. Manning Marable (1984, pp. 238–41) catalogues a large number of incidents of racist violence and terror against blacks in the United States between 1980 and 1982. He cites dozens of incidents of the severe beating, killing, or rape of Blacks by police officers on duty, in which the police involved were acquitted of any wrongdoing. In 1981, moreover, there were at least five hundred documented cases of random white teenage violence against Blacks. Violence against gay men and lesbians is not only common, but has been increasing in the last five years. While the frequency of physical attack on members of these and other racially or sexually marked groups is very disturbing, I also include in this category less severe incidents of harrassment, intimidation, or ridicule simply for the purpose of degrading, humiliating, or stigmatizing group members.

Given the frequency of such violence in our society, why are theories of justice usually silent about it? I think the reason is that theorists do not typically take such incidents of violence and harrassment as matters of social injustice. No moral theorist would deny that such acts are very wrong. But unless all immoralities are injustices, they might wonder, why should such acts be interpreted as symptoms of social injustice? Acts of violence or petty harrassment are committed by particular individuals, often extremists, deviants, or the mentally unsound. How then can they be said to involve the sorts of institutional issues I have said are properly the subject of justice?

What makes violence a face of oppression is less the particular acts themselves, though these are often utterly horrible, than the social context surrounding them, which makes them possible and even acceptable.

What makes violence a phenomenon of social injustice, and not merely an individual moral wrong, is its systemic character, its existence as a social practice.

Violence is systemic because it is directed at members of a group simply because they are members of that group. Any woman, for example, has a reason to fear rape. Regardless of what a Black man has done to escape the oppressions of marginality or powerlessness, he lives knowing he is subject to attack or harrassment. The oppression of violence consists not only in direct victimization, but in the daily knowledge shared by all members of oppressed groups that they are *liable* to violation, solely on account of their group identity. Just living under such a threat of attack on oneself or family or friends deprives the oppressed of freedom and dignity, and needlessly expends their energy.

Violence is a social practice. It is a social given that everyone knows happens and will happen again. It is always at the horizon of social imagination, even for those who do not perpetrate it. According to the prevailing social logic, some circumstances make such violence more "called for" than others. The idea of rape will occur to many men who pick up a hitch-hiking woman; the idea of hounding or teasing a gay man on their dorm floor will occur to many straight male college students. Often several persons inflict the violence together, especially in all-male groupings. Sometimes violators set out looking for people to beat up, rape, or taunt. This rule-bound, social, and often premeditated character makes violence against groups a social practice.

Group violence approaches legitimacy, moreover, in the sense that it is tolerated. Often third parties find it unsurprising because it happens frequently and lies as a constant possibility at the horizon of the social imagination. Even when they are caught, those who perpetrate acts of group-directed violence or harrassment often receive light or no punishment. To that extent society renders their acts acceptable.

An important aspect of random, systemic violence is its irrationality. Xenophobic violence differs from the violence of states or ruling-class repression. Repressive violence has a rational, albeit evil, motive: rulers use it as a coercive tool to maintain their power. Many accounts of racist, sexist, or homophobic violence attempt to explain its motivation as a desire to maintain group privilege or domination. I do not doubt that fear of violence often functions to keep oppressed groups subordinate, but I do not think xenophobic violence is rationally motivated in the way that, for example, violence against strikers is.

On the contrary, the violation of rape, beating, killing, and harrassment of women, people of color, gays, and other marked groups is motivated by fear or hatred of those groups. Sometimes the motive may be a simple will to power, to victimize those marked as vulnerable by the very social fact that they are subject to violence. If so, this motive is secondary in the sense that it depends on a social practice of group violence. Violence-causing fear or hatred of the other at least partly involves insecurities on the part of the violators; its irrationality suggests that unconscious processes are at work. In Chapter 5 I shall discuss the logic that makes some groups frightening or hateful by defining them as ugly and loathsome bodies. I offer a psychoanalytic account of the fear and hatred of some groups as bound up with fears of identity loss. I think such unconscious fears account at least partly for the oppression I have here called violence. It may also partly account for cultural imperialism.

Cultural imperialism, moreover, itself intersects with violence. The culturally imperialized may reject the dominant meanings and attempt to assert their own subjectivity, or the fact of their cultural difference may put the lie to the dominant culture's implicit claim to universality. The dissonance generated by such a challenge to the hegemonic cultural meanings can also be a source of irrational violence.

Violence is a form of injustice that a distributive understanding of justice seems ill equipped to capture. This may be why contemporary discussions of justice rarely mention it. I have argued that group-directed violence is institutionalized and systemic. To the degree that institutions and social practices encourage, tolerate, or enable the perpetration of violence against members of specific groups, those institutions and practices are unjust and should be reformed. Such reform may require the redistribution of resources or positions, but in large part can come only through a change in cultural images, stereotypes, and the mundane reproduction of relations of dominance and aversion in the gestures of everyday life. I discuss strategies for such change in Chapter 5.

Applying the Criteria

Social theories that construct oppression as a unified phenomenon usually either leave out groups that even the theorists think are oppressed, or leave out important ways in which groups are oppressed. Black liberation theorists and feminist theorists have argued persuasively, for example, that Marxism's reduction of all oppressions to class oppression leaves out much about the specific oppression of Blacks and women. By pluralizing the category of oppression in the way explained in this chapter, social theory can avoid the exclusive and oversimplifying effects of such reductionism.

I have avoided pluralizing the category in the way some others have done, by constructing an account of separate systems of oppression for each oppressed group: racism, sexism, classism, heterosexism, ageism, and so on. There is a double problem with considering each group's oppression a unified and distinct structure or system. On the one hand, this way of conceiving oppression fails to accommodate the similarities and overlaps in the oppressions of different groups. On the other hand, it falsely represents the situation of all group members as the same.

I have arrived at the five faces of oppression—exploitation, marginalization, powerlessness, cultural imperialism, and violence—as the best way to avoid such exclusions and reductions. They function as criteria for determining whether individuals and groups are oppressed, rather than as a full theory of oppression. I believe that these criteria are objective. They provide a means of refuting some people's belief that their group is oppressed when it is not, as well as a means of persuading others that a group is oppressed when they doubt it. Each criterion can be operationalized; each can be applied through the assessment of observable behavior, status relationships, distributions, texts and other cultural artifacts. I have no illusions that such assessments can be value-neutral. But these criteria can nevertheless serve as means of evaluating claims that a group is oppressed, or adjudicating disputes about whether or how a group is oppressed.

The presence of any of these five conditions is sufficient for calling a group oppressed. But different group oppressions exhibit different combinations of these forms, as do different individuals in the groups. Nearly all, if not all, groups said by contemporary social movements to be oppressed suffer cultural imperialism. The other oppressions they experience vary. Working-class people are exploited and powerless, for example, but if employed and white do not experience marginalization and violence. Gay men, on the other hand, are not qua gay exploited or powerless, but they experience severe cultural imperialism and violence. Similarly, Jews and Arabs as groups are victims of cultural imperialism and violence, though many members of these groups also suffer exploitation or powerlessness. Old people are oppressed by marginalization and cultural imperialism, and this is also true of physically and mentally disabled people. As a group women are subject to gender-based exploitation, powerlessness, cultural imperialism, and violence. Racism in the United States condemns many Blacks and Latinos to marginalization, and puts many more at risk, even though many members of these groups escape that condition; members of these groups often suffer all five forms of oppression.

Applying these five criteria to the situation of groups makes it possible to compare oppressions without reducing them to a common essence or claiming that one is more fundamental than another. One can compare the ways in which a particular form of oppression appears in different groups. For example, while the operations of cultural imperialism are often experienced in similar fashion by different groups, there are also important differences. One can compare the combinations of oppressions groups experience, or the intensity of those oppressions. Thus with these criteria one can plausibly claim that one group is more oppressed than another without reducing all oppressions to a single scale.

Why are particular groups oppressed in the way they are? Are there any causal connections among the five forms of oppression? Causal or explanatory questions such as these are beyond the scope of this discussion. While I think general social theory has a place, causal explanation must always be particular and historical. Thus an explanatory account of why a particular group is oppressed in the ways that it is must trace the history and current structure of particular social relations. Such concrete historical and structural explanations will often show causal connections among the different forms of oppression experienced by a group. The cultural imperialism in which white men make stereotypical assumptions about and refuse to recognize the values of Blacks or women, for example, contributes to the marginalizaion and powerlessness many Blacks and women suffer. But cultural imperialism does not always have these effects.

Succeeding chapters will explore the categories explicated here in different ways. Chapters 4, 5, and 6 explore the effects of cultural imperialism. Those chapters constitute an extended argument that modern political theory and practice wrongly universalize dominant group perspectives, and that attention to and affirmation of social group differences in the polity are the best corrective to such cultural imperialism. Chapters 7 and 8 also make use of the category of cultural imperialism, but focus more attention on social relations of exploitation and powerlessness.

CHAPTER 3

Insurgency and the Welfare Capitalist Society

> Absence of public issues there may well be, but this is not
> due to any absence of problems or contradictions, antagonis-
> tic or otherwise. Impersonal and structural changes have
> not eliminated problems or issues. Their absence from
> many discussions is an ideological condition, regulated in
> the first place by whether or not intellectuals detect and
> state problems as potential *issues* for probable publics, and
> as *troubles* for a variety of individuals.
>
> —C. Wright Mills

FOR CRITICAL THEORY normative reflection arises from a particular social context, to whose social and political conflicts philosophy aims to contribute analysis, clarification, and evaluation. Such normative reflection in a situated social context is not neutral with respect to those conflicts, however, but rather looks for the unrealized possibilities of emancipation latent in institutions and aimed at by social movements in those conflicts.

The welfare capitalist society is the social context within which much theorizing about justice takes place. In this chapter I argue that the distributive paradigm of justice corresponds to the primary formulation of public debate in such societies. Processes of interest-group pluralism restrict public conflict primarily to distribution; issues of the organization of production, public and private decisionmaking structures, and the social meanings that confer status or reinforce disadvantage go unraised. This restriction of public debate has led many writers to claim that welfare capitalist society is depoliticized. Through its welfare orientation it constructs citizens as client-consumers, discouraging their active participation in public life. I argue that the distributive paradigm of justice functions ideologically to reinforce this depoliticization.

The hegemony of welfare capitalist definition of public debate has not gone unchallenged, however. Since the 1960s in most Western capitalist countries insurgent social movements have questioned the welfare state's limitation of public debate to distribution, and sought to politicize the processes of ownership and control, decisionmaking, cultural production, the personal relations of everyday life, and the administered life of work and social service. Although the processes of welfare capitalist society sometimes succeed in containing the insurgent demands of new social movements within the manageable limits of interest-group pluralism, these movements often break out beyond those limits to produce visions of democratized participatory publics. In these movements I locate the social base of a conception of justice that seeks to reduce and eliminate domination and oppression. Democracy is both an element and a condition of social justice.

NORMATIVE PRINCIPLES OF WELFARE CAPITALIST SOCIETY

Welfare capitalist institutions tend to break down the distinction between the public sphere of state activity and the sphere of private-enterprise economic activity. Government assumes overt and widespread responsibility for managing and distributing the benefits of economic processes. At the same time, private institutions such as corporations, unions, and other associations begin to resemble government in organization, power, and scale. Government institutions and agencies, in turn, themselves take on the character of semiautonomous corporations (cf. Unger, 1974, pp. 175–76).

The welfare corporate society embodies at least three important principles largely absent from earlier, more laissez-faire liberal capitalism: (1) the principle that economic activity should be socially or collectively regulated for the purposes of maximizing the collective welfare; (2) the principle that citizens have a right to have some basic needs met by society, and that where private mechanisms fail the state has an obligation to institute policies directed at meeting those needs; and (3) the principle of formal equality and impersonal procedures, in contrast to more arbitrary and personalized forms of authority and more coercive forms of inducing cooperation. While these principles have faced some challenges, nevertheless at least as principles they enjoy wide acceptance.

(1) In an economy as complex and interdependent as modern capitalist economies have become, where the decision of one person or company can affect the activities of so many others, it is sheer irrationality not to bring economic activities under some social control. Most Western European countries engage in some form of government-administered economic planning. While economic coordination and regulation in the United States is less centralized and explicit, there is considerable acceptance of government regulation of the economy. Such government regulation and economic coordination in Western capitalist countries is far from "creeping socialism," as some maintain, since its explicit purpose is the promotion of optimum conditions for private capital accumulation. This regulation of welfare capitalist society nevertheless has a positive value insofar as it affirms the expectation that economic activity should be under

some general public control whenever citizens are so dependent on the economic nexus for their livelihood and well-being.

Despite contemporary rhetoric to the contrary, the primary beneficiary of big government in advanced capitalism is private enterprise, which has become inextricably dependent on government for its continued welfare. Government creates institutions and develops policies explicitly aimed at promoting the long-term interests of capital accumulation. To this end federal and sometimes local government regulates the economic system through tax policy, monetary policy, tariffs and import-export trade policies, debt spending, farm and corporate subsidies, and regulation of its own spending levels. Government increasingly takes on the costs and administration of educating and training the labor forces needed by private enterprise, as well as the costs of research and development. Much of transportation and communications infrastructures, as well as other infrastructure services needed for efficient production and distribution, are now paid for, maintained, and often administered by government agencies. Government takes much responsibility for shouldering the social costs of production, such as pollution control, which can damage the profit-making of other enterprises. And in welfare corporate society government is a primary consumer of the products of private enterprise, in the form of military goods, supplies to its vast agencies and offices, housing, highway, and other public works construction, and so on.

(2) The principle that the state has an obligation to meet needs when private mechanisms fail is perhaps more controversial than the first, but is nevertheless widely accepted in all advanced capitalist societies. Prior to the development of welfare state institutions, the only citizen rights were the formal political rights of liberalism—protection of liberties, rights to due process and equality before the law, voting rights, rights to hold office, and so on. The welfare state promulgates a conception of economic rights, or rights of recipience, as citizen rights. Even when austerity is implemented and the political climate challenges social services that meet needs, a verbal commitment to meeting subsistence needs remains. The Gramm-Rudman budget balancing bill passed by the U.S. Congress in 1985, for example, exempted some of the most basic income support programs, such as AFDC and food stamps, from the automatic cuts it authorized.

Welfare state activity also operates to benefit private citizens, and contributes to their survival and quality of life. Entitlement programs such as social security, unemployment insurance, medicaid, housing support, and direct income support seek to meet some citizen needs. Some aspects of tax policy during the past thirty years in the United States have had the effect of redistributing income from the middle and upper classes to the poor, though recent tax reform has reversed this trend. The middle classes themselves have benefited from loans for college students and home mortgage tax deductions. Support for education and training, as well as enforcement of equal opportunity legislation, creates some employable workers and in a limited way aims to eliminate racial and sexual discrimination. Municipal, state, and federal agencies, moreover, provide a huge sector of jobs, and have been particularly important for expanding professional employment opportunities for Blacks, Latinos, American Indians, and women. Product quality regulation provides some significant level of consumer protection.

These two aspects of government activity in welfare corporate society—the support of capital accumulation and meeting needs of private citizens—reinforce each other. Entitlement programs meeting citizen needs must be paid for through tax revenues, and thus require an expanding economy. Thus under conditions of private enterprise social welfare programs need government regulation of the economy and infrastructure support. Education and training programs benefit the individuals within them as well as the corporations and agencies that hire those individuals.

(3) The welfare capitalist society also aims to embody the values of formal equality and proceduralism as against more arbitrary and personalized forms of authority and more coercive forms of inducing cooperation. Large bureaucratic organizations conduct most collective activity in such societies. Bureaucracies are distinguished from other forms of social organization in operating according to impersonal rules that apply in the same way to all cases. Ideally, people within them have or lack status, privilege, power, or autonomy by virtue of their position in the division of labor, and not by virtue of any personal attributes of birth, family connection, and so on. According to the values of bureaucratic organization, positions should be assigned according to merit. These achievements of bureaucracy are important positive developments in the history of social organization. I say this in spite of the new forms of domination that bureaucratic organization facilitates, which I will discuss below.

The institutions and practices of the welfare state help preserve capitalist institutions in two ways. Structurally, these institutions and practices help create favorable conditions for production and accumulation, help provide a skilled work force, and through direct government consumption and income support to private consumers expand markets for goods. Politically, welfare state policies serve important legitimating functions, by encouraging people's allegiances to the system to the extent that it delivers them something material, or at least the continuing credible promise of something material.

It is not incompatible with this general functionalist view of the welfare state to find its emergence progressive and to recall that most welfare state policies resulted from fierce popular struggles against the rich and powerful. The income support policies that exist in the United States today, for example, would not have come about without mass movements making demands on the state and society, often calling for far more radical change than they achieved. As Piven and Cloward (1982) argue, these popular struggles and the reforms they brought about significantly reduced the insulation of economic issues from political action that had obtained in the nineteenth century. Nor is it inconsistent to insist, on the one hand, that efforts to reduce government-supported welfare measures should be actively and vigorously opposed and, on the other hand, that the form of welfare capitalist institutions should be altered so that they no longer support domination and oppression.

THE DEPOLITICIZATION OF WELFARE CAPITALIST SOCIETY

Welfare capitalist society on the whole is more humane than a capitalist society which gives license to the Invisible Hand, with no social regulation of investment, product quality, or working conditions, and no socially supported provisions for old, poor, and sick people. At the same time that more private economic activity comes under the purview of public policy, however, the public becomes increasingly depoliticized (see Habermas, 1987, pp. 343–56). Social conflict and discussion come to be restricted largely to distributive issues, where background issues of the organization and goals of production, the positions and procedures of decisionmaking, and other such institutional issues do not come into question. Interest-group pluralism functions as the vehicle for resolving conflicts about distribution, a process both unfair and depoliticized (Cohen and Rogers, 1983, chap. 3).

According to many analysts, New Deal reforms began to institutionalize class conflict, and this process was completed by the early 1950s. In this welfare capitalist system capitalists struck a deal with workers. Business and government would accede to demands for collective bargaining rights, more leisure time, more pay, social security and unemployment benefits, and similar measures to improve the material life and security of working people. In return workers would forfeit demands to restructure production, to control the goals and direction of enterprises or the whole economy, or to have community control over administration of services. Social conflict henceforth would be restricted to competition over distributive shares of the total social product. Everyone would agree that economic growth is the primary goal of government and business activity. In order to make the social pie whose distribution they would argue about as large as possible, government and business were to have the authority to do whatever they judged necessary to promote that growth.

This bargain to limit conflict to distribution, leaving production and decisionmaking structures unquestioned, occurred in both private and state sectors. In the private sector, after World War II labor unions implicitly agreed to restrict their demands to distributive issues—pay, hours, benefits, vacation time—and not to bring up issues like working conditions, control over production process, or investment priorities (Bowles and Gintis, 1982; 1986, chap. 2). State regulation of collective bargaining has reinforced this implicit agreement, rarely allowing work process and work organization issues, for example, onto the bargaining agenda.

In federal and state governments, policy issues are restricted largely to the allocation of resources and the provision of social services, within the imperative of fostering corporate economic growth. Conflict takes place over a narrow range of distributive issues: Does reducing the deficit require raising taxes? Should the rich pay a higher proportion of their income in taxes than others? Should funds be appropriated for the MX missile or for public housing and highways? Which appropriations will generate more jobs? The basic ends of government are already given, within the existing structures of power, property, and entitlements, and do not come under discussion. "Policy has always been oriented to the best way to allocate the surplus for individual and collective consumption rather than the more central question of the best way to control the process to realize social needs and the full potentialities of human beings" (Smith and Judd, 1984, p. 184).

The restriction of conflict and policy to distributive issues, within an agreed-upon growth imperative, appears most salient in local politics. An alliance of public officials, businessmen, and bureaucrats effectively operates in most municipalities to channel expressed citizen interests into a system of land-use decisions constrained by the imperative to promote investment (Elkin, 1987; Logan and Molotch, 1987, chap. 3). As I will discuss in Chapter 8, cities themselves become increasingly stripped of state powers, becoming little more than supplicants at the welfare state and corporate table.

Restricting conflict and policy discussion to distributive issues, the welfare capitalist society defines the citizen primarily as a client-consumer. Unlike earlier capitalism, which functioned on low wages and austerity for the working class, welfare state capitalism requires high levels of consumption to keep the growth machine running. Corporate advertising, popular culture media, and government policy collude to encourage people to think of themselves primarily as consumers, to focus their energies on the goods they want, and to evaluate their government's performance according to how well it provides them with goods and services (Habermas, 1987, p. 350; Walzer, 1982). Such a client-consumer orientation toward citizenship privatizes the citizen, rendering goals of popular control or participation difficult or meaningless.

In the welfare capitalist society, processes of interest-group pluralism are the vehicle for the resolution of policy conflict about distributions. Client-consumer citizens and corporate actors organize to promote specific interests in receiving government goods—the oil lobby, the homeless advocates, the trucking interests, the physician lobby, the consumer advocates, and so on. New government programs often create interest groups where they did not exist before. The political game is defined on analogy with the market. Various interests compete with one another for people's loyalties, and those that amass the most members and money have the market advantage in lobbying for legislation, regulations, and the distribution of tax dollars. The different interests must vie with one another for limited resources and the attention of legislators and government officials, so sometimes the interests ally and bargain with one another for their mutual advantage. Government policy and the allocation of resources, according to pluralist theory, are the outcome of this process of competition and bargaining among interest groups.

Critics of the theory and practice of interest-group pluralism argue that the system promotes distributive unfairness. In interest-group competition some groups, especially business, start with greater resources and organization, which enable them better to represent their interests. The outcomes are therefore often biased toward those with these advantages. While I agree with this criticism, I want here to focus on how interest-group pluralism also depoliticizes public life.

In its process of conflict resolution, interest-group pluralism makes no distinction between the assertion of selfish interests and normative claims to justice or right. Public policy dispute is only a competition among claims, and "winning" depends on getting others on your side, making trades and alliances with others, and making effective strategic calculations about how and to whom to make your claims. One does not win by persuading a public that one's claim is just. This strategic conception of policy discussion fosters political cynicism: those who make claims of right or justice are only saying what they want in clever rhetoric. This cynical system often forces movements claiming justice, like the civil rights movement or the movement for the Equal Rights Amendment, to identify themselves as merely another interest group. Those who believe in the justice of equal rights for women must form pressure groups to get what they want, and be prepared to deal and bargain to get it.

This process that collapses normative claims to justice into selfish claims of desire lacks the element of public deliberation that is a hallmark of the political (Arendt, 1958; Michelman, 1986; Sunstein, 1988; Elkin, 1987, chap. 7). A politicized public resolves disagreement and makes decisions by listening to one another's claims and reasons, offering questions and objections, and putting forth new formulations and proposals, until a decision can be reached.

When each agent or organization acts to promote its own specific interests through government agency channels that rarely receive publicity, much less public discussion, a fragmented public life results. There is no forum within the public sphere of discussion and conflict where people can examine the overall patterns of justice or fairness produced by these processes (Howe, 1982; Barber, 1984, chap. 3). Nor is it possible to bring the basic structures, assumptions, constraints, and decisionmaking procedures producing the distributive patterns into public discussion, because for the most part these are not effectively public. Moreover, bringing them into view requires a more comprehensive perspective than the fragmentation of interest-group pluralism allows, because one needs to know the relationship between the desires of different interests and the collective consequences of their simultaneous enactment.

Interest-group politics effectively locks individual citizens out of direct participation in public decisionmaking, and often also keeps them ignorant of the proposals deliberated and the decisions made. Citizens cannot voice their demands or participate in policy discussions except as constituencies organized around some specific government program or interest. Since policies are directed not at persons as such, but at persons constituted piecemeal as taxpayers, health service consumers, parents, workers, residents of cities, and so on, calculations of what might ultimately be in a particular individual's self-interest become incoherent (Janowitz, 1976, chap. 4). Under these circumstances it is little wonder that citizens are often politically apathetic.

Finally, and perhaps most importantly, the interest-group structure of decisionmaking in welfare capitalist society depoliticizes because the decisions are often made in privacy. Increased public regulation of private economic and social activity produces interest-oriented government agencies that often work in daily partnership with the representatives of those private interests. The result is what Alan Wolfe (1977) calls the "franchise state," the carving out of government authority for institutionalized interest groups.

In this system of interest-group pluralism most public policy decisionmaking takes place as part of the day-to-day operations of these government agencies, which receive with their legislative or executive creation wide powers to formulate and enforce regulations. Most of these policies are hammered out in complex and informal negotiating processes within the agencies and between those agencies and the business or other private organizations that have specific interests at stake in the policies and enough power and influence to gain access to the agencies (see Lowi, 1969, esp. chaps. 3 and 4). Usually these policy decisions are made in semisecret, and thus the substantive decisions of the welfare corporate society are depoliticized. In the words of Claus Offe:

> If politics has to do with the working out of visions about the just order of social life, and the conflict among divergent visions of such order, then it is, given this condition of blocked mediation, only a slight exaggeration to say that we experience a condition in which politics and the state have become divorced from each other. (Offe, 1984, p. 173)

Two decades ago Theodore Lowi (1969) argued that this uncoupling meant that effectively much government activity is no longer subject to the rule of law. Legislative bodies are one of the few forums for the public discussion of policy. Most active policies enacted by government in the welfare capitalist society are not laws, however, but regulations established by agency department heads, often without any public discussion. Of course, legislative action is necessary to create many agencies, and their continued existence as well as the extent of their activity is decided by budgetary action in legislatures. Proposals for new agencies and programs, as well as funding proposals, however, are worked out in negotiations between agencies and their private constituencies.

THE IDEOLOGICAL FUNCTION OF THE DISTRIBUTIVE PARADIGM

Ideas function ideologically, as I understand that term, when they represent the institutional context in which they arise as natural or necessary. They thereby forestall criticism of relations of domination and oppression, and obscure possible more emancipatory social arrangements. In the context of welfare capitalist society, the distributive paradigm of justice functions ideologically in this sense.

The predominance of a distributive paradigm in contemporary philosophical theories of justice can be accounted for, I suggest, at least partly by the fact that distributive issues dominate policy discussion in welfare capitalist society (cf. Heller, 1987, p. 155). This theoretical orientation fits comfortably with our intuitions because to the extent that justice is discussed at all in our society, issues of income distribution, resource allocation, and the awarding of positions predominate. The distributive paradigm reflects and sometimes justifies welfare capitalist society's tentative and tenuous commitment to meeting basic needs and regulating economic activity for the collective good. The possessive individualist conception of human nature which in Chapter 1 I argued underlies the distributive paradigm fits the social context of welfare capitalist society, which constructs citizens primarily as client-consumers (cf. Taylor, 1985).

In asserting this I do not mean that distributive theories of justice necessarily mirror or endorse existing distributions and the interests that support them. On the contrary, the distributive paradigm dominates contemporary philosophical discourse partly because many theorists believe that there is considerable distributive injustice in existing welfare capitalist societies. Within the limits of the distributive paradigm, many theories of justice argue for principles whose application implies criticisms of these social conditions.

Operating within the confines of distributive issues, interest-group pluralism, as we have seen, perpetuates a depoliticized public life that fragments social life and privatizes citizens' relationship to the state. It discourages public deliberation about collective decisions, especially about the goals of government, or the organization of institutions and relations of power. The depoliticized process of policy formation in welfare capitalist society thus makes it difficult to see the institutional rules, practices, and social relations that support domination and oppression, much less to challenge them.

A similar blindness afflicts the distributive paradigm of justice, as I argued in Chapter 1. By focusing on distribution, theories of justice usually fail to bring issues of decisionmaking power, division of labor, and culture under evaluation. These are often more basic than distributions, to the extent that they causally condition distributions. The distributive paradigm implicitly assumes an atomistic and static social ontology, when an ontology that includes relations and processes would better capture many aspects of domination and oppression.

The distributive paradigm of justice does not produce the depoliticized client-consumer citizen characteristic of welfare capitalist society. The hegemony of this paradigm, however, reinforces the one-dimensionality of contemporary policy discourse and the containment function it serves. Because it reflects the processes of interest-group pluralism, and hypostatizes these as the subject matter of justice in general, the distributive paradigm functions to legitimate those processes and the depoliticization of public life they encourage. Insofar as predominant approaches to theorizing about justice fail to evaluate the institutional structures that provide the context and conditions of distributions, they help forestall criticism of relations of power and culture in welfare capitalist society. To that extent they reinforce domination and oppression, and block the political imagination from envisioning more emancipatory institutions and practices.

A critical theoretical approach to justice begins with the insight that any normative or social theory is and should be conditioned by the particular historical and social context in which it speaks. Thus my claim that the distributive paradigm functions ideologically does not assume that theorizing about justice could be neutral about or independent of particular social conditions. Necessarily surrounded by already existing institutions and social relations, normative theorizing can be either supportive or critical of them, or in some cases, perhaps, a mixture of both. While welfare capitalist society is less oppressive in some respects than some other societies, it nevertheless contains many structures of domination and oppression which political philosophy should locate and criticize. Some of these have a source in welfare and corporate bureaucracies.

THE ADMINISTERED SOCIETY AND NEW FORMS OF DOMINATION

Domination, as I defined it in Chapter 1, consists in institutional conditions which inhibit or prevent people from participating in determining their actions or the conditions of their actions. Welfare capitalist society creates specifically new forms of domination. Increasingly the activities of everyday work and life come under rationalized bureaucratic control, subjecting people to the discipline of authorities and experts in many areas of life.

By bureaucracy I mean a system that defines and organizes social projects as the object of technical control. Bureaucracy extends the object of technical or instrumental reason beyond the natural world to coordinated human action and interaction. Taking the ends of action—whether producing a bomb, taking the census, or bringing food to a famine-stricken area—as given, bureaucratic reason determines the most efficient means to the realization of those ends. Because the definition of ends always lies outside the particular bureaucratic system, and the system of means is developed by a technical science that claims to be value-free, bureaucratic organization is largely depoliticized—its activity is not understood as the product of value-laden decisions (Keane, 1984, chap. 2).

In the progressive vision of many nineteenth- and early twenieth-century social revolutionaries and reformers, both in Eastern and Western Europe and in the United States, bureaucratization was conceived as the way to eliminate domination, especially class domination. The formalization embedded in bureaucracy often has been designed to transform traditional systems of power in which one agent is arbitrarily able to force another to submit to the dictates of his or her will. Thus collectivized agricultural production replaced the rule of the kosaks, corporate managerial systems replaced the rule of the owner-bosses, city-manager government replaced the rule of party machine patriarchs, and family law and social service agencies replaced some of the rule of the husband-father.

In traditional forms of rule, rulers exercise power in accordance with their particular desires, values, or ends. The ruler has a right to expect obedience because he is sovereign, and need give no other reason. Bureaucratic administration replaces such personal sovereignty with the rule of laws and procedures. For each area of its activity bureaucracy develops formal, explicit rules, impersonal in the sense that they must be followed by whoever occupies the positions or engages in the activities they describe. Thus bureaucracy introduces a universalization and standardization of social or cooperative activity.

Defining a cooperative project as the object of technical control, bureaucracy discovers the objectively best way to realize that project, not with a view to someone's personal ends, but with a view to the ends of the organization or project itself. In so doing bureaucracy develops a detailed division of labor. It defines positions in a hierarchy of authority, where each position is bound by rules, and movement between positions is governed by a formal meritocratic system.

Formalizing collective action through explicitly articulated rules and procedures, however, separates it from normative inquiry and commitment. Decisions and actions will be evaluated less according to whether they are right or just than according to their legal validity, that is, whether they are consistent with the rules and follow the appropriate procedures. This uncoupling of legal rationality from normative reasoning constitutes the meaning of bureaucratic depoliticization (see Habermas, 1987, pp. 307–10).

Along with bureaucratic administration of cooperative projects, a new understanding of the meaning and responsibilities of work develops for those involved in such administration, namely, the ethic of professionalism. Professionalization depoliticizes work activity insofar as it removes the ends of the activity from determination by the individual worker. As work becomes professionalized workers understand themselves as following the procedures of an ethical and scientific discipline, whether medicine, library cataloging, or child care, in which they receive formal training. Strong explicit or implicit rules prohibit professionals from bringing their personal desires and commitments to the job, or allowing personal feelings about others to influence their performance. Professional workers subordinate their individual whims or desires to the team effort, taking as the highest value the smooth operation of the organization and the realization of its goals. The professional ethic incorporates a strong notion of loyalty, both to the practioners of one's profession and to one's organization.

There are many advantages to regularized practices of social cooperation guided by formalized rules and procedures, and to the development of professional disciplines. While changing the rules is often more difficult in bureaucratic organizations than changing rulers was in traditional societies, it is still better to subject persons to formalized regulations which at least in principle they can know and anticipate than to subject them to the often arbitrary and selfish whims of individual rulers. As many students of the welfare corporate society have argued, however, the expansion of bureaucratic administration over increasing areas of work and life brings with it new experiences of domination.

Welfare corporate society presents us with the irony of a huge system of production, distribution, and service provision depending on the detailed cooperation of millions of people most of whom have no part in determining their actions or the conditions of their actions. Most people in such societies are not powerless, in the sense that I described in Chapter 2; many have some autonomy in their work, some institutionalized authority over others, some position that commands a modicum of respect. Even relatively enabled people, however, are subject to structures of domination. They experience themselves as subject to the unreciprocated authority of others. They find their actions constrained by structural or bureaucratic imperatives that often seem both to result from no one's decisions and to serve the interests of a specific set of agents. People experience bureaucratic domination not only as workers, but also as clients and consumers subject to rules they have had no part in making, which are designed largely to convenience the provider or agency rather than the consumer.

Corporate administrative workplaces are hierarchically structured, in that most workers in them are subordinate to the authority of others. If people have decisionmaking power, it is generally over others' actions rather than their own. This structure of hierarchical authority reestablishes the personal domination that bureaucratic organization was alleged to have eliminated. For however explicitly a bureaucracy formalizes rules and procedures, it still cannot eliminate individual and subjective choices (Unger, 1974, pp. 169–71). Heads of divisions and departments, for example, normally have a great deal of discretion in making, interpreting, applying, and enforcing rules according to their particular understanding of the goals of the organization and their choice of priorities.

The very universalism and formal characteristics of bureaucratic rules produce within the bureaucracy an experience of personal dependency and necessary submission to arbitrary will. The formalism, universality, and impersonality of the rules are supposed to protect persons from the arbitrariness of whim and personal likes and dislikes—everyone is to be treated in the same way, impersonally and impartially, and no particular values should enter. But people applying the impersonal rules must make judgments about how they apply to each particular case. By their very nature, formal and universal rules have no automatic mechanism for their application to particular cases, and in their application the decision-maker's feelings, values, and particular perceptions inevitably enter.

As I shall develop in more detail in Chapter 7, the point is not that substantive personal values enter bureaucratic decisionmaking when they ought not to; on the contrary, the entrance of particular substantive values into decisions is inevitably and properly part of what decisionmaking is about. The scientistic ideology of bureaucratic administration, however, purports to remove all particular values from decisions. How is this bureaucratic ideology validated? Generally the justice of hierarchical decisionmaking is justified by the claim that any professional with the proper knowledge acting impartially would come to the same decision. Since in fact personal judgment inevitably enters many important decisions, however, subordinates experience themselves as subject to the arbitrary will of a superior on whom they are personally dependent. Life inside the bureaucracy thus becomes a scary funhouse of "impression management" and "psyching out" games. To remove the wide latitude of subjective judgment superiors are able to exercise with respect to subordinates, bureaucracies often institute detailed, formalized, "objective" methods of supervision and surveillance. These only increase the sense of domination, however, since they apply more detailed rules more frequently to the behavior and performance of subordinates, and subjective judgment inevitably enters in the application of these rules as well (cf. Lefort, 1986).

Domination in welfare corporate society extends beyond the workplace to many other areas of everyday life. In the phenomenon that Habermas refers to as the "colonization of the life world," both government and private agencies subject clients and consumers to meshes of microauthority. Clients and consumers submit to the authority of hospitals, schools, universities, social service agencies, government offices, banks, fast-food restaurants, and countless other institutions. Officials in these institutions not only prescribe much of the behavior of clients or consumers within the institutions, but perhaps more importantly, through social scientific, managerial, or marketing disciplines, they define for the client or consumer the very form and meaning of the needs the institutions aim to meet (Habermas, 1987, pp. 362–63; cf. Fraser, 1987a; Laclau and Mouffe, 1984, pp. 161–63). The colonization of the life world means that life activities formerly subject to traditional norms, spontaneous action, or collective decision become commodified or are brought under the control of state institutions, and thus become normalized, universalized, and standardized (cf. K. Ferguson, 1984).

Persons within welfare corporate society often do not challenge these forms of domination and depoliticization, partly because they seem to be the price of the material comfort the majority of people have. Those without material comfort are even less likely to challenge the authority of institutions that define their behavior and needs, because they are more dependent on them than others. Two other phenomena legitimate the structure of welfare corporate society and make it difficult to challenge its forms of domination: the ideology of expertism, and the hope of social and career mobility.

In welfare corporate society knowledge is power. Depoliticization of public life succeeds apparently because most people are convinced that issues of legislation, production, and planning are too complex to be understood except by fiscal, legal, and managerial experts. In the ideology of expertism, the knowledgeable and only the knowledgeable have a right to rule, because they are masters of the objective and value-neutral discipline applying to the area of social life in question, and thus their decisions are necessary and correct (Bay, 1981, pp. 65–67; cf. Habermas, 1987, p. 326). Rule by experts claims to transcend politics, claims not to entail submission by some to the will of others. With the rule of experts we seem to witness an end to ideology and achieve scientific organization in social life. It is therefore difficult for people to challenge the doctors, social workers, engineers, statisticians, economists, job analysts, city planners, and the myriad of other experts whose judgments determine their actions or the conditions of their actions.

Within bureaucratic organizations the ideology of merit operates in the same way. A professional acquires the right to rule more persons as he or she develops greater expertise in his or her profession, as judged by those already designated experts. Careerism is therefore another legitimating mechanism in welfare corporate society (Habermas, 1975, pp. 74–78). When there is a commitment to a principle of equal opportunity, when channels of promotion are clear, and when merit criteria are applied impartially, then persons rise in the hierarchy of authority in a manner commensurate with their expertise. Subordinates accept the hierarchical structure and the authority of their superiors because they themselves have legitimate hopes of rising to positions of greater authority. Careerism contributes to the privatization of social life. Rather than collectively challenging the legitimacy of the authority of the experts, people on the career track have their own advancement primarily in view. A necessary condition for such advancement, in fact, is not politicizing the decisions of either the organization or the larger public. In Chapter 7 I shall focus on showing the ideological character of the merit principles that both expertism and careerism presuppose.

I argued in Chapter 1 that talk of distributing and redistributing power makes little sense because power is not a possession to be distributed. This cursory glance at typical experiences of domination in welfare corporate society should make clear that the problem cannot be described as a monopoly of power, which could be solved by redistributing power. The shift from bosses to bureaucracies entails a diffusion as well as a proliferation of power. To be sure, in contemporary bureaucratic hierarchies some people have more power than others, in the sense of authority to give orders or make decisions. Many others, I have noted, are powerless. But all power and domination within these large-scale organizations depends on the cooperation of a multitude of different people. Most people in the society outside of these organizations also feel the dominating effects of the administered life world. Only a democratization of welfare corporate institutions that introduces procedures of collective discussion and decisionmaking about ends and means can bring people some control over their action. Democratization is less fruitfully conceived as a redistribution of power than as a reorganization of decisionmaking rules. Later in this chapter I shall argue that democracy is an element and condition of social justice, not just in government institutions, but in principle in all institutions.

INSURGENCY AND THE REPOLITICIZATION OF PUBLIC LIFE

The depoliticization of welfare capitalist society succeeds only if certain structural contradictions can be contained. First, there is a fiscal contradiction. The welfare capitalist system relies on government programs to foster private accumulation and maintain high levels of consumption. These state functions require massive state spending, however, and the money must come from somewhere. Commitment to maximum levels of private accumulation clashes with the needs of the welfare state (Offe, 1984, chap. 6; cf. Gough, 1979). As the fiscal crisis generated by this contradiction magnifies, the goals of state activity can come more explicitly into question.

Second, there is a contradiction involved in bringing increasing areas of everyday life under rationalized and directed human control, and at the same time keeping such control depoliticized. Since the polity retains formal ideals of democracy, the more social spheres come under the purview of state policy, the more likely it is that people will demand meaningful public discussion of such policy (Habermas, 1975; 1987, pp. 354–68; Offe, 1984, chap. 7).

In the context of these contradictions of welfare capitalist society, since the 1960s diverse insurgent campaigns and movements have responded to the domination and colonization of administered life. I take the term insurgency from Michael Walzer:

> Insurgency is the demand that bureaucratic services make possible, instead of replacing, local decisionmaking. Or rather it is the acting out of a new dialectic, which denies conventional definitions of good behavior and seeks to make the "helpfulness" of the welfare bureaucracy into the starting point of a new politics of resistance and self-determination. (Walzer, 1982, p. 152)

Insurgent campaigns and movements arise within welfare capitalist society, on the fringes of bureaucratic institutions or carving out new social spaces not dreamt of in their rules. They are often local and spontaneous, though not unorganized, with a sense of limitation—the limits of an act, or a particular goal, or a particular constituency. Insurgency often carries with it the dramatic spirit of the quick strike in the belly of the beast—witches throwing dried blood on pornographic magazines, priests smashing up the nose of a Trident missile. But insurgency also describes the ongoing pulse and mass organization that many writers have referred to as the "new social movements."

What is new about these insurgent social movements, according to Jean Cohen and Andrew Arato (1984), is their self-limiting character. Unlike Marxist or social democratic oppositional movements earlier in this century, the new social movements are particularistic and oriented to specific issues, rather than global. Unlike radical political movements of an earlier time, their aim is usually not to seize and transform state power; rather, they seek to limit state and corporate power, to push back the bounds of their commodifying and bureaucratizing influence. They seek to loosen social life from the colonizing influence of welfare state and corporate bureaucracy, to create alternative institutional forms and independent discussion.

Insurgent movements exploit and expand the sphere of civil society (Habermas, 1981; Cohen, 1985), the space between individuals and families, on the one hand, and state and large corporate institutions, on the other. Civil society involves, in the words of Maria Markus, "the whole network of the voluntary and particular (that is, not all-encompassing) associations and organizations, together with the autonomous instruments of opinion formation, articulation, and oppression which are distinct both from the state and from the proper institutions of economy" (Markus, 1986, p. 441). In the United States this is a vast field of social life that includes religious organizations, schools and universities, many small businesses, many nonprofit agencies and organizations, and a huge diversity of voluntary organizations, as well as publishing and other media associated with or expressing the perspectives of those organizations.

In response to the domination exercised over everyday life by welfare and corporate bureaucracies, the principle of insurgent organizing is not unification, but proliferation. Contemporary insurgencies are local and heterogeneous, with loosely networked groups, sharing newsletters or meeting at conferences. Different groups may spin off around an issue or campaign, and coexist as a movement without the unity of a common program or central organization. The most recent upsurge of the peace movement in the United States, for example, consists of a wild array of organizations and affinity groups with varying identities—feminist, Christian, socialist, ecological, and so on—sponsoring a mixed bag of tactics—guerrilla theater, legislative lobbying, nonviolent civil disobedience, marches, and chain letters. Such heterogeneity sometimes produces conflict in the goals and political positions of these movements.

While these new social movements often press for specific allocations of state resources, their main focus, at least at the time of their upsurge and growing strength, is not distributive. They focus on broad issues of decisionmaking power and political participation. Often they seek less to expand the scope of the state's welfare services than to respond to the invasion of nearly every area of social life by both public and private bureaucracies (Habermas, 1981; 1987, pp. 392–96). Most focus on issues of oppression and domination; they usually seek democratization of institutions and practices, to bring them under more direct popular control. These insurgent campaigns and movements may be divided into three major categories: (1) those that challenge decisionmaking structures and the right of the powerful to exert their will; (2) those organizing autonomous services; and (3) movements of cultural identity.

(1) Some contemporary insurgencies effectively question the prerogatives of government and corporate officials to make decisions affecting a broad public according to private bureaucratic priorities of profit or efficiency (cf. Luke, 1987). Since the early 1970s the environmental movement has challenged the prerogative of private companies to produce whatever they wish however they wish. The movement has successfully raised the consciousness of a broad mass of people about environmental dangers, and has even succeeded to some degree in winning legislation to regulate corporate activity and altering corporate practices. In the wake of numerous plant closings in the last ten years, a movement has grown that seeks to limit the power of private corporations to sneak out of town without warning. Though there was a lull in protests of foreign policy after the Vietnam War, since the early 1980s steady citizen insurgency has questioned the aims of the U.S. government and its right to make decisions that affect the rest of the world, especially Central America and South Africa.

The anti–nuclear power movement represents, I think, the most strikingly successful insurgency movement questioning what until then had been taken for granted as a *fait accompli*. Since the Eisenhower "atoms for peace" initiative in the late 1950s, an enormous amount of public and private resources and planning has been devoted to building nuclear power plants. The anti–nuclear power movement called into question the entire framework of energy understanding that most establishment officials had been assuming, insisting that the very idea of nuclear power is a bad social choice, and staging well-organized occupations of existing and planned nuclear sites, sometimes including tens of thousands of people. These protest actions perfected the theory and practice of the "affinity group," which has become a model of disciplined democratic decisionmaking for many subsequent protest movements. The affinity group model of organization aptly illustrates the principle of proliferation as distinct from unification. Affinity groups are relatively autonomous and distinguished by the various principles of their affinity, such as political standpoint, gender, age, religion, or neighborhood, and on many occasions dozens of distinct affinity groups have successfully planned and staged joint protest actions.

Since the late 1960s urban social movements have sprouted all over the United States that challenge the decisionmaking structure of local government. Urban social movements have demanded citizen participation in development planning, and in many cities generated neighborhood organizations aiming at more participatory structures (Clavel, 1986). Some urban movements have directly challenged the atomizing forces of interest-group pluralism, which emphasizes individual consumption, and instead called for construction of institutions to provide for more collective consumption (Castells, 1983, chap. 32).

As the protest heat picked up one spring when a vote on aid to the Nicaraguan contras was approaching, Jean Kirkpatrick noted in a speech that foreign policy cannot be made by the citizenry, but must be decided by the experts. Most of the insurgencies that have challenged the decisionmaking prerogatives of official power have also sought to demystify the ideology of expertism. Community groups challenging the decision to construct a hazardous waste treatment plant or a nuclear plant or a nuclear waste disposal site must acquire considerable technical knowledge of waste management, local geology, and law in order to conduct their campaign; in the process they discover that these matters can be understood by ordinary citizens, and that experts are rarely neutral. Peace movement activists have sat on panels with nuclear strategy specialists, appearing at least as knowledgeable and exposing deterrence policies as choices, not necessities. Other peace activists have mastered the supposedly arcane complexities of the economic system to challenge the claim that military production is economically beneficial.

In the peace and Central America solidarity movements other kinds of democratically run and participatory alternative institutions have arisen that both bypass and challenge official channels of international diplomacy. The movement to give illegal sanctuary to refugees from Central America in this country has been prosecuted so vigorously by the U.S. government not because it represents an anti-American extremist revolutionary movement, but precisely because it has the broad participation of ordinary respectable churchgoing citizens who have taken it upon themselves to do something directly about policies whose rightness and legitimacy they question. Many U.S. and Soviet citizens have likewise rejected the legitimacy of their governments in seeking a dissolution of U.S.-Soviet antagonism, developing people-to-people forms of exchange.

(2) Much contemporary insurgency includes efforts to decolonize service provision and the meeting of needs through the establishment of autonomous organizations of politicized self-help (Zola, 1987). Rather than demand that the state provide more services or support policies, these movements instead have determined to develop more participatory institutions to provide services or promote political goals marginal to or outside the authority of the state (Withorn, 1984). These autonomous politicized self-help agencies should not be identified, however, with efforts on the part of the federal government to withdraw from service provision, returning caring functions to family and private charity. At the same time that these insurgent agencies try to maintain democratic local control, many of them also demand access to public resources to support their activity.

The women's movement has been a vanguard in such activity, establishing health services, rape crisis services and shelters for battered women. Typically these began as collectives making decisions democratically, with persons rotating among the different kinds of jobs. They seek not merely to meet the client's needs, but to empower her to define and meet her own needs, as well as to bring her to some political awareness of the sources of her suffering. As both the need for these services and the success of these autonomous women's institutions in providing them became apparent by the mid 1970s, these institutions began to join the orbit of the welfare state. To receive state or federal funding many were required to designate official boards of directors and to have certified, professionalized staffs. While some women's services have become part of the bureaucratic establishment as a result, most fought to maintain significant autonomy, most still rely heavily on volunteer workers with significant participation in decisionmaking, and most still identify with a feminist movement that politicizes the needs women bring to these institutions.

Similar kinds of alternative institutions for politicized self-help service provision have mushroomed in many Black, Latino, American Indian, and white working-class communities. They often combine service provision with political agitation and direct action protest, involving the participation of those served (see Boyte, 1984; Boyte and Reissman, 1986). While hoping to channel the distribution of goods and services more toward the oppressed, these institutions aim to go beyond distribution to empower persons, develop their capacities, and sponsor new institutional forms in which people can collectively take some contol over their environment.

The recent unsuccessful campaign to charter a new city of Mandela out of the predominantly Black sections of Boston exhibits how projects for democratic self-determination can extend far beyond small collectives.

Tenant organizations are self-organized to apprise tenants of their rights against landlords and in the face of condominium and cooperative conversions, and to represent tenants in their relations with property owners. In the face of rising housing costs, a scarcity of housing, and consequent homelessness, however, insurgencies have arisen that seek democratic control over housing. The most dramatic of these have been various forms of squatters' movements, where people simply take over abandoned buildings and renovate them to make them livable. More often groups acquire buildings legally and, often with the participation of the people who will live there, renovate them into low-cost housing units; in doing so these groups have faced the issue of speculative resale and have found innovative ways to form cooperatives and land trusts to ensure that these new units of housing will not be out of the reach of the people most in need (Dreier, 1987). Most of these cooperative housing organizations have sought to institutionalize procedures of democratic decisionmaking in sometimes complex organizational forms (White, 1982).

(3) Many social movements, finally, have focused on politicizing culture. Culture is a broad category, and I do not intend to give it a precise definition here. Culture refers to all aspects of social life from the point of view of their linguistic, symbolic, affective, and embodied norms and practices. Culture includes the background and medium of action, the unconscious habits, desires, meanings, gestures, and so on that people grow into and bring to their interactions. Usually culture is just there, a set of traditions and meanings that change, but seldom as the result of conscious reflection and decision.

Politicizing culture, then, means bringing language, gestures, forms of embodiment and comportment, images, interactive conventions, and so on into explicit reflection. Cultural politics questions certain everyday symbols, practices, and ways of speaking, making them the subject of public discussion, and explicitly matters of choice and decision. The politicization of culture should be distinguished from a libertarian insistence on the right of individuals to "do their own thing," however unconventional. Cultural politics does often celebrate suppressed practices and novel expressions, especially when these arise from and speak for oppressed groups. But cultural politics has primarily a critical function: to ask what practices, habits, attitudes, comportments, images, symbols, and so on contribute to social domination and group oppression, and to call for collective transformation of such practices.

Historically the welfare state has taken some steps toward conscious public decisionmaking about whether and how to meet people's needs. It has thus helped create the possibility of a more politicized approach to meeting needs, which welfare capitalist society suppresses. In a similar fashion, the colonization of much of everyday life by government and corporate bureaucracies, who deliberately manipulate meanings and symbols and consciously condition consumption choices, has helped create the conditions for a politicized culture. For once some aspects of culture come under the conscious deliberation of some people, it is not difficult to call for everyone to participate in cultural choices.

In the late 1960s and early 1970s the counterculture movement made the body and its adornment the site of struggle: hippies challenged "straight" society's norms of respectability, which required short, clipped hair for men and little or no facial hair, as well as tailored angular clothes. The punk movement continued in a different form this challenge to the aesthetic of professional culture. Beginning in the late 1960s food also became politicized; the "natural foods" movement, which changed enormously the eating practices of millions of people, asked political questions about food—questions about nutrient quality, about how food is produced and whether its production involves potentially harmful pesticides, about the acceptability of killing animals for food and whether this "small planet" can afford to feed so much grain to animals instead of directly to people, about where food comes from and who is exploited in its production. Besides making demands on government for environmental regulations and on corporations to employ production processes that do not damage the environment, the environmental movement has questioned the appropriateness of a plastic-dependent, throwaway consumer culture.

Though it is much more than a cultural movement, contemporary feminism represents probably the most far-reaching movement of cultural politics. Its slogan "the personal is political" signaled that no aspect of everyday life would be exempt from reflection and potential criticism—language, jokes, styles of advertising, dating practices, dress, norms of childrearing, and countless other supposedly mundane and trivial elements of behavior and comportment. Many resist such thorough politicization of everyday habits, because it seems onerous to reflect upon and deliberate about what pronouns to use or whether one is interrupting other people too much. Feminists have nevertheless succeeded in encouraging such reflection and discussion and in significantly changing many people's behavior and practices.

Sexual and erotic experience has been a major focus of feminist cultural politics, of course. Feminist discussion, sometimes acrimonious, has raised fundamental issues about what sexual practices and sexual imagery can both promote free expression for women and not contribute to their oppression. The gay and lesbian liberation movements have further politicized sexual and erotic experience by resisting notions of "normal" sexuality and raising issues of decisionmaking rights in matters of love, intimacy, and erotic imagery.

Finally, there have emerged movements of oppressed racial and ethnic minorities, as well as of old people, disabled people, and others culturally oppressed by being defined as the Other, the different and the deviant. These movements have politicized culture by confronting the stereotypes and norms that make such definition acceptable. Many groups experiencing cultural imperialism have organized and asserted the positivity of their specific experience and culture, rejecting melting-pot ideals of assimilation and unity. Post–World War II ethnopolitics in Western capitalist societies can be understood at least partly as a reaction to the colonization of the everyday life world by welfare state and corporate bureaucracies. The state has become too large, impersonal, and ubiquitous to foster a sense of unity, and at the same time oppressed groups often experience state policies as biased against them (Rothschild, 1982, p. 19). As I shall discuss in more detail in the chapters that follow, politicization of culture by groups experiencing cultural imperialism involves examining how media images, speech, modes of comportment, and interactive dynamics contribute to the oppression that defines some people as different and deviant.

Because in welfare capitalist society the state is largely depoliticized, insurgent movements can best create and nurture autonomous publics in the space of civil society (Keane, 1984, pp. 225–56; 1988, chap. 4). These movements repoliticize social life, treating many given and unquestioned institutions and practices as alterable, subject to choice. They generate discussions about how those institutions might be best organized and those practices best conducted.

As we shall see in Chapter 4, modern republican theorizing which defines the political in terms of a public tends to assume a unitary public sphere structured by simultaneous face-to-face relations (Arendt, 1958; Barber, 1984). It is important to observe that public life in our society, to the degree that it exists at all, fails to meet these conditions. Public discussion led by insurgent movements most often occurs not in some single assembly but in a heterogeneous proliferation of groups, associations, and forums, with diverse perspectives and orientations. A single public discussion, moreover, facilitated by print and electronic media, may take place over months or even years, and involve persons separated by vast spaces who never meet one another. What makes a discussion public is neither unity nor proximity, but the openness with which it takes place.

THE DIALECTIC OF RECONTAINMENT VERSUS DEMOCRACY

The welfare corporate society, I have argued, depoliticizes public life by restricting discussion to distributive issues in a context of interest-group pluralism where each group competes for its share of public resources. During the 1950s and through most of the 1960s this interest-group structure successfully depoliticized much policymaking. Protest and criticism was fairly easily churned into the cogs of the welfare capitalist mechanism, where the protesting agents either got a piece of the pie or got lost in the works. The society that Herbert Marcuse described as one-dimensional mostly succeeded in absorbing any negations into the consumer-oriented passive relation between the state and individuals.

By the late 1960s, however, urban social movements of Blacks, Chicanos, and Puerto Ricans, the student and youth movements, and the emerging radical feminist movement burst through the bounds of business as usual, questioning the Establishment itself. Based outside or on the margins of institutionalized interest-group pluralism, such insurgent social movements seek to repoliticize social life. They treat many given and unquestioned institutions and practices as subject to choice. The radical movements of the late 1960s went far beyond distributive issues to challenge fundamental givens about the organization of power in every institution. The threatened Establishment sometimes responded viciously (Lader, 1979), but more frequently sought to reintegrate the radical demands, as well as the agents voicing them, back into the pluralist system.

Ira Katznelson (1981, chap. 7) finds that this is just what welfare capitalist politics succeeded in doing with the urban Black liberation movement. That movement had begun to connect a diversity of issues to a system of institutionalized racism—from education, to housing, to jobs, to police treatment. Black identity united the movement across different neighborhoods and regions. These and other factors combined to make it possible for that movement to reflect on and challenge some of the basic structures of welfare capitalist urban society in a more forceful and fundamental way than had occurred in the United States since the 1930s. Federal and city policymakers responded with programs that brought Black leaders into the business of distributing welfare, housing, health, and educational services within their own neighborhoods, once again fragmenting political consciousness and the ability of Blacks to act collectively across neighborhood and regional lines (cf. Elkin, 1987, p. 58).

Challenges to institutional structure and demands for change in decisionmaking structures have often been rechanneled into distributive solutions by the politics of welfare capitalist society. The demands of women and nonwhites for an end to institutional racism and sexism filter into a feeble effort to distribute a few more professional jobs and places in professional schools to members of these groups. The call for structural alterations in decisions that affect housing construction and rent is whittled down to a question of government-subsidized housing. Demands that corporations be accountable to communities regarding environmental issues are met with offers of monetary compensation.

Manuel Castells tells a story similar to Katznelson's about the neighborhood movement in the Mission district of San Francisco in the late 1970s. The movement began as a well-organized and widely supported challenge to the assumptions of government and business about the proper direction of development, and the right of business and government institutions to determine that direction. But in the end it failed to achieve institutional changes or to change the parameters of power, because it was successfully reabsorbed into the interest-group process (Castells, 1983, chap. 13). In a similar fashion much of the movement dubbed the New Populism, while asserting principles of people's power, local control, and institutional change, has been reabsorbed into the distributive orientation of interest-group politics (Boggs, 1987, chap. 4; Gottdiener, 1985, pp. 180–90).

The last two decades in the United States and Western Europe have witnessed cycles of insurgency and recontainment, in which insurgent movements break out of the interest-group distributive framework, and are then partially or totally reabsorbed into the interest-group system. The 1970s and 1980s saw a time of economic decline and retrenchment in which the contradictions of the welfare state became more apparent, prompting the state to cut back on welfare provision. When the benefits of welfare state policies must be defended from attack, it is especially difficult for insurgent movements to avoid being reabsorbed in and reinforcing the game of interests competing for shares in the consumption pie. As the state itself experiences increasing fiscal and economic crisis, policymakers are less able or willing to promote distributive fairness. This not only causes serious declines in the standard of living for many, but also prompts questions about the conditions of fair distribution, the basic structure of control and decision, and the self-determination of needs and services.

Much contemporary politics, I have suggested, consists in a dialectic between movements of insurgency that seek democratization, collective decisionmaking, and grass-roots empowerment, on the one hand, and established institutions and structures that seek to reabsorb such demands into a distributive framework, on the other. This process of insurgency and recontainment exhibits a political struggle between the two visions of justice I articulated in Chapter 1: justice as distribution, presuming a consumer-oriented, possessively individualist conception of persons, and justice as enablement and empowerment, presuming a more active conception of persons.

These are not the only normative and political positions with significant following in advanced capitalist societies, but they are two of the most important. Philosophers and theorists of justice, I suggest, cannot be indifferent or neutral with respect to the differing normative orientations reflected in the discourses of conflicting political actors. Many insurgent social movements name injustice as social domination and oppression. They implicitly, and sometimes explicitly, reject as incomplete a conception of justice that limits normative political judgment to the distribution of social benefits, and raise fundamental issues of decisionmaking structure and procedure and of the normative implications of cultural meanings. If they are not to be irrelevant or simply to reinforce existing discourses, theorists of justice must take part in the struggle between these two conceptions of justice.

DEMOCRACY AS A CONDITION OF SOCIAL JUSTICE

I have defined justice as the institutionalized conditions that make it possible for all to learn and use satisfying skills in socially recognized settings, to participate in decisionmaking, and to express their feelings, experience, and perspective on social life in contexts where others can listen. This understanding of justice specifies a certain range of distributive outcomes. In particular, justice in modern industrial societies requires a societal commitment to meeting the basic needs of all persons whether or not they contribute to the social product (see Sterba, 1980, chap. 2; Gutmann, 1980, chap. 5; Walzer, 1983, chap. 3). If persons suffer material deprivation of basic needs for food, shelter, health care, and so on, then they cannot pursue lives of satisfying work, social participation, and expression.

Justice equally requires, however, participation in public discussion and processes of democratic decisionmaking. All persons should have the right and opportunity to participate in the deliberation and decisionmaking of the institutions to which their actions contribute or which directly affect their actions. Such democratic structures should regulate decisionmaking not only in government institutions, but in all institutions of collective life, including, for example, production and service enterprises, universities, and voluntary organizations. Democracy is both an element and a condition of social justice.

If justice is defined negatively as the elimination of structures of domination, then justice implies democratic decisionmaking. Democracy is a condition of freedom in the sense of self-determination (Young, 1979; cf. Cunningham, 1987, chap. 4). The social contract tradition of political theory provides the major argument for democracy on grounds of self-determination. If all persons are of equal moral worth, and no one by nature has greater capacity for reason or moral sense, then people ought to decide collectively for themselves the goals and rules that will guide their action. While this argument for democracy has never been entirely submerged, and periodically reemerges in populist, socialist, or syndicalist waves, in the mainstream tradition of modern political theory the idea of a social contract has also been used to justify authoritarian political forms (Pateman, 1979). In authoritarian contract theory, while the people have a moral right to self-rule, they delegate their authority to government officials, who, because they are limited by impartial laws, make decisions in the public interest. In Chapter 4 I shall argue that the ideal of impartiality used to legitimate political authority is impossible, and consequently that only democratic processes are consistent with justice.

As an element of justice that minimizes domination, democracy has both instrumental and intrinsic value. Instrumentally, participatory processes are the best way for citizens to ensure that their own needs and interests will be voiced and will not be dominated by other interests. The problem with interest-group pluralism is not, as some critics charge, that people promote their own interests. Rather, the normative defects of interest-group politics are, first, that the privatized form of representation and decisionmaking it encourages does not require these expressions of interests to appeal to justice, and, second, that inequality of resources, organization, and power allows some interests to dominate while others have little or no voice.

As many democratic theorists have argued, democratic participation has an intrinsic value over and above the protection of interests, in providing important means for the development and exercise of capacities. This argument for the intrinsic value of participatory democratic institutions was put forward in the classical tradition by Rousseau and J. S. Mill (cf. Pateman, 1970, chap. 3). Having and exercising the opportunity to participate in making collective decisions that affect one's actions or the conditions of one's actions fosters the development of capacities for thinking about one's own needs in relation to the needs of others, taking an interest in the relation of others to social institutions, reasoning and being articulate and persuasive, and so on. Only such participation, moreover, can give persons a sense of active relation to social institutions and processes, a sense that social relations are not natural but subject to invention and change. The virtues of citizenship are best cultivated through the exercise of citizenship (Cunningham, 1987, chap. 4; Elkin, 1987, pp. 150–70; Gutmann, 1980, chap. 7; Barber, 1984).

Democracy is also a condition for a public's arriving at decisions whose substance and implications best promote substantively just outcomes, including distributive justice. The argument for this claim relies on Habermas's conception of communicative ethics. In the absence of a philosopher-king with access to transcendent normative verities, the only ground for a claim that a policy or decision is just is that it has been arrived at by a public which has truly promoted the free expression of all needs and points of view. Tyrannized publics, publics manipulated by officials, and media publics with little access to information and communication do not satisfy this requirement. Deliberation is most likely to arrive at a fair distribution of resources, just rules of cooperation, the best and most just division of labor and definition of social positions, if it involves the open participation of all those affected by the decisions. With such participation, people will persuade, ideally, only if they phrase their proposals as appeals to justice, because others will call them to account if they believe their own interests endangered. With such participation, people will most likely introduce relevant information. Democratic decisionmaking tends to promote just outcomes, then, because it is most likely to introduce standards of justice into decisionmaking processes and because it maximizes the social knowledge and perspectives that contribute to reasoning about policy.

Some theorists express skepticism about the justice of participatory democracy because they doubt that democratic procedures in fact usually lead to just outcomes. Allowing all affected people to participate in social decisions can result in serious injustices when groups have conflicting interests and differ in numbers and privilege. Amy Gutmann (1980, pp. 191–97) offers the example of community control of schools, where increased democracy led to increased segregation in many cities because the materially more privileged and more articulate whites were able to promote their perceived interests against the just demand of Blacks for equal treatment in an integrated system. Because of this "paradox of democracy" Gutmann argues that distributive fairness is a necessary condition for institutions of democratic participation, and that democratic processes must be limited by principles of equal liberty and rough distributive equality.

Many similar examples can be cited of ways that grass-roots participation in decisionmaking can lead to unjust and oppressive outcomes. Tax revolt in the United States has often been accomplished through referendum, and the reduced government revenues that result have contributed to increased exploitation and marginalization. In many cities and regions of the United States today, to take another example, if one put a gay rights proposal to a direct vote it would be defeated. Moreover, much evidence could be offered that in the United States in the last fifty years policies to undermine domination and oppression have been enacted more frequently by executive order and the courts than by legislation, and more frequently at the federal than at the state or local level. Social justice to some degree has been imposed on resistant people.

This objection to the claim that democratic decisionmaking processes promote justice must be taken seriously. The first important response is that democracy must indeed always be constitutional: the rules of the game must not change with each majority's whim, but rather must be laid down as constraints on deliberation and outcomes, and must be relatively immune to change. Such rules should spell out basic rights that democratically arrived at decisions cannot violate, including economic as well as civil and political rights (cf. Green, 1985, chap. 10).

Second, the objection tends to equate democracy and participation with local control. But this equation is unnecessary, and in many cases may be undesirable for precisely the reasons the objectors raise. Permitting autonomous local control over the use of resources, for example, when resources are unequally distributed among locales, is likely to produce exploitation rather than justice. In Chapter 8 I argue against the common but too simple equation of democratization with decentralization and local autonomy.

Third, the objection assumes that democratic processes occur only in institutions that make laws and state policies, while other institutions, such as private corporations or the bureaucracies that administer state policies, remain undemocratic. The leverage of inequality that allows participatory processes to favor the will of the stronger, as in Gutmann's example, is often traceable to the authority and power that some derive from these other institutions. If constitutional democracy restructures all institutional forms, and not merely institutions now falling under public policy decisions, then people are less likely to be powerless to express their voice in any one forum. Democracy in one institution reinforces democracy in others.

An extensive redistribution of wealth and a restructuring of control over capital and resources is a necessary aspect of the link between democracy and justice. To suggest that the institutionalization of participatory processes should wait upon the achievement of distributive justice, however, as Gutmann does, is not only to postpone such democratization into an indefinite utopian future, but to make the achievement of distributive justice equally unlikely. On the other hand, weakening relations of domination so that persons have greater institutionalized opportunity to participate in discussion about and the making of decisions that affect them itself is a condition for achieving greater distributive fairness. In contemporary welfare capitalist society the parameters of distributive possibilities are fairly fixed; thus only challenging the given structure and procedures for making distributive decisions can further the material equality necessary for fair participation. Economic equalization and democratization, that is, foster one another and should occur together to promote social justice.

Finally, the objection Gutmann raises presumes a unified public in which all citizens are the same qua citizens. In Gutmann's example, the formally equal procedures allow the group with greater numbers and resources to dominate the rest. Even the achievement of economic equality would not necessarily eliminate this "paradox of democracy," however, as long as differences continued to exist in other respects by virtue of which one group is stereotyped, silenced, or marginalized, or differences of experience and activities between groups produced perceived conflicts of interest. Only if oppressed groups are able to express their interests and experience in the public on an equal basis with other groups can group domination through formally equal processes of participation be avoided. The next three chapters develop an extended argument for such a group-differentiated participatory public.

CHAPTER 4

The Ideal of Impartiality and the Civic Public

> A table, and behind this table, which distances them from
> the two litigants, the "third party," that is, the judges. Their
> position indicates firstly that they are neutral with respect to
> each litigant, and secondly this implies that their decision is
> not already arrived at in advance, that it will be made after
> an aural investigation of the two parties, on the basis of a
> certain conception of truth and a certain number of ideas
> concerning what is just and unjust, and thirdly that they
> have the authority to enforce their decision. . . . Now this
> idea that there can be people who are neutral in relation to
> the two parties, that they can make judgments about them
> on the basis of ideas of justice which have absolute validity,
> and that their decisions must be acted upon, I believe that
> all this is far removed from and quite foreign to the very idea
> of popular justice.
>
> —Michel Foucault

A GROWING BODY of feminist-inspired moral theory has challenged the
paradigm of moral reasoning as defined by the discourse of justice and
rights. In this paradigm moral reasoning consists in adopting an impartial
and impersonal point of view on a situation, detached from any particular
interests at stake, weighing all interests equally, and arriving at a conclusion which conforms to general principles of justice and rights, impartially
applied to the case at hand. Critics argue that this paradigm describes not
moral reasoning as such, but the specific moral reasoning called for in the
impersonal public contexts of law, bureaucracy, and the regulation of economic competition. This "ethic of rights" corresponds poorly to the social
relations typical of family and personal life, whose moral orientation requires not detachment from but engagement in and sympathy with the
particular parties in a situation; it requires not principles that apply to all
people in the same way, but a nuanced understanding of the particularities of the social context, and the needs particular people have and express
within it. Philosophers should recognize that the paradigm of moral reasoning as the impartial application of general principles describes only a

restricted field of moral life, and develop moral theories adequate to the private, personal, and informal contexts it ignores (Gilligan, 1982; Blum, 1980; 1988; Friedman, 1986; Noddings, 1984).

More recently some feminist theorists have begun to question this opposition between justice and care (Friedman, 1987; Okin, 1989). In this chapter I extend this line of argument. The feminist critiques of traditional moral theory retain a distinction between public, impersonal institutional roles in which the ideal of impartiality and formal reason applies, on the one hand, and private, personal relations which have a different moral structure. Instead of retaining this public/private dichotomy, these criticisms of an ethic of rights should lead us to question the ideal of impartiality itself, as an appropriate ideal for any concrete moral context.

I argue that the ideal of impartiality in moral theory expresses a logic of identity that seeks to reduce differences to unity. The stances of detachment and dispassion that supposedly produce impartiality are attained only by abstracting from the particularities of situation, feeling, affiliation, and point of view. These particularities still operate, however, in the actual context of action. Thus the ideal of impartiality generates a dichotomy between universal and particular, public and private, reason and passion. It is, moreover, an impossible ideal, because the particularities of context and affiliation cannot and should not be removed from moral reasoning. Finally, the ideal of impartiality serves ideological functions. It masks the ways in which the particular perspectives of dominant groups claim universality, and helps justify hierarchical decisionmaking structures.

The ideal of impartial moral reason corresponds to the Enlightenment ideal of the public realm of politics as attaining the universality of a general will that leaves difference, particularity, and the body behind in the private realms of family and civil society. Recent attempts to revive republican thinking appeal to the ideal of a civic public which transcends particularities of interest and affiliation to seek a common good. In Chapter 3 I followed this new republican initiative in criticizing the depoliticized public life of interest-group pluralism, and agreed with its proponents that politics should involve public forums of deliberation and collective decisionmaking. In this chapter, however, I argue that the modern ideal of the civic public is inadequate. The traditional public realm of universal citizenship has operated to exclude persons associated with the body and feeling—especially women, Blacks, American Indians, and Jews. Many contemporary theorists of participatory democracy retain the ideal of a civic public in which citizens leave behind their particularity and differences. Because such a universalist ideal continues to threaten the exclusion of some, the meaning of "public" should be transformed to exhibit the positivity of group differences, passion, and play.

POSTMODERNIST CRITIQUE OF THE LOGIC OF IDENTITY

Several writers seek to expose and deconstruct a logic they find in Western philosophical and theoretical discourse that denies and represses difference. Often referred to as postmodern, these thinkers include Theodor Adorno (1973), Jacques Derrida (1977), and Luce Irigaray (1985). I shall follow Adorno in calling this logic the logic of identity. For the purposes of this exposition I take the critique of the logic of identity to resonate with Derrida's critique of a metaphysics of presence.

The logic of identity expresses one construction of the meaning and operations of reason: an urge to think things together, to reduce them to unity. To give a rational account is to find the universal, the one principle, the law, covering the phenomena to be accounted for. Reason seeks essence, a single formula that classifies concrete particulars as inside or outside a category, something common to all things that belong in the category. The logic of identity tends to conceptualize entities in terms of substance rather than process or relation; substance is the self-same entity that underlies change, that can be identified, counted, measured.

Any conceptualization brings the impressions and flux of experience into an order that unifies and compares. But the logic of identity goes beyond the attempt to order and compare the particulars of experience. It constructs totalizing systems in which the unifying categories are themselves unified under principles, where the ideal is to reduce everything to one first principle.

The logic of identity denies or represses difference. Difference, as I understand it, names both the play of concrete events and the shifting differentiation on which signification depends. Reason, discourse, is always already inserted in a plural, heterogeneous world that outruns totalizing comprehension. Any identifiable something presupposes a something else against which it stands as background, from which it is differentiated. No utterance can have meaning unless it stands out differentiated from another. Understood as different, entities, events, meanings, are neither identical nor opposed. They can be likened in certain respects, but similarity is never sameness, and the similar can be noticed only through difference. Difference, however, is not absolute otherness, a complete absence of relationship or shared attributes.

The logic of identity flees from the sensuous particularity of experience, with its ambiguities, and seeks to generate stable categories. Through the logic of identity thought aims to master that sensuous heterogeneous embodiment by bringing the object fully under a concept. It thereby denies the difference between the object and the subject; it seeks a unity of the thinking subject with the object thought, that thought might grasp, comprehend the real. Through the logic of identity thought seeks to bring everything under control, to eliminate uncertainty and unpredictability, to spiritualize the bodily fact of sensuous immersion in a world that outruns the subject, to eliminate otherness.

This project of reducing the heterogeneity of sensuous particulars to the unity of thought itself submits to a relentless logic of identity, as thought itself, the thinking subject, must be reduced to unity. Such a subject is conceived as a pure transcendental origin: it has no foundation outside itself, it is self-generating and autonomous. Its pure identity of origin ensures that its representation of reality will be unambiguous and true. The logic of identity also seeks to reduce the plurality of particular subjects, their bodily, perspectival experience, to a unity, by measuring them against the unvarying standard of universal reason.

The irony of the logic of identity is that by seeking to reduce the differently similar to the same, it turns the merely different into the absolutely other. It inevitably generates dichotomy instead of unity, because the move to bring particulars under a universal category creates a distinction between inside and outside. Since each particular entity or situation has both similarities and differences with other particular entities or situations, and they are neither completely identical nor absolutely other, the urge to bring them into unity under a category or principle necessarily entails expelling some of the properties of the entities or situations. Because the totalizing movement always leaves a remainder, the project of reducing particulars to a unity must fail. Not satisfied then to admit defeat in the face of difference, the logic of identity shoves difference into dichotomous hierarchical oppositions: essence/accident, good/bad, normal/deviant.

Difference, as the relatedness of things with more or less similarity in a multiplicity of possible respects, here congeals as the binary opposition a/not-a. In every case the unity of the positive category is achieved only at the expense of an expelled, unaccounted for chaotic realm of the accidental. In the history of Western thought this logic of identity has created a vast number of such mutually exclusive oppositions that structure whole philosophies: subject/object, mind/body, nature/culture. These dichotomies in Western discourse are structured by the dichotomy good/bad, pure/impure. The first side of the dichotomy is elevated over the second because it designates the unified, the self-identical, whereas the second side lies outside the unified as the chaotic, unformed, transforming, that always threatens to cross the border and break up the unity of the good.

THE IDEAL OF IMPARTIALITY AS DENYING DIFFERENCE

Modern ethics establishes impartiality as the hallmark of moral reason. This conception of moral reason assumes that in order for the agent to escape egoism, and attain objectivity, he or she must adopt a universal point of view that is the same for all rational agents (see Darwall, 1983, chap. 1). The ideal of impartiality is the result of this search for a universal, objective "moral point of view." Its conception of reason expresses the logic of identity.

How does the moral theorist or rational agent arrive at the moral point of view? By abstracting from all the particularities of the circumstances on which moral reason reflects. The impartial reasoner is detached: reason abstracts from the particular experiences and histories that constitute a situation. The impartial reasoner must also be dispassionate, abstracting from feelings, desires, interests, and commitments that he or she may have regarding the situation, or that others may have. The impartial reasoner is, finally, a universal reasoner. The moral point of view abstracts from the partiality of affiliation, of social or group perspective, that constitutes concrete subjects (cf. Darwall, 1983, pp. 133–43).

Impartial reason aims to adopt a point of view outside concrete situations of action, a transcendental "view from nowhere" that carries the perspective, attributes, character, and interests of no particular subject or set of subjects. This ideal of the impartial transcendental subject denies or represses difference in three ways. First, it denies the particularity of situations. The reasoning subject, emptied of all its particularity, treats all situations according to the same moral rules, and the more the rules can be reduced to a single rule or principle, the more this impartiality and universality will be guaranteed. Whatever her or his particular situation, any subject can reason from this universal point of view according to universal principles that apply to all moral situations in the same way.

Second, in its requirement of dispassion, impartiality seeks to master or eliminate heterogeneity in the form of feeling. Only by expelling desire or affectivity from reason can impartiality achieve its unity. The construct of an impartial point of view is arrived at by abstracting from the concrete particularity of the person in situation. This requires abstracting from the particularity of bodily being, its needs and inclinations, and from the feelings that attach to the experienced particularity of things and events. Normative reason is defined as impartial, and reason defines the unity of the moral subject, both in the sense that it knows the universal principles of morality and in the sense that it is what all moral subjects have in common in the same way. This reason thus stands opposed to desire and affectivity as what differentiate and particularize persons.

Third, the most important way that the ideal of impartiality reduces particularity to unity is in reducing the plurality of moral subjects to one subjectivity. In its requirement of universality, the ideal of impartial reason is supposed to represent a point of view that any and all rational subjects can adopt, precisely by abstracting from the situational particularities that individualize them. The impartial moral judge, moreover, ideally should treat all persons alike, according to the same principles, impartially applied.

In its will to reduce plurality to unity, impartiality seeks one transcendental moral subjectivity. Impartial reason judges from a point of view outside of the particular perspectives of persons involved in interaction, able to totalize these perspectives into a whole, or a general will. From this point of view of a solitary transcendent god, the moral reasoner silently deduces its judgment from weighing the evidence and conflicting claims, and applying to them universal principles. Because it already takes all perspectives into account, the impartial subject need acknowledge no subjects other than itself to whose interests, opinions, and desires it should attend.

This monological character of philosophical presentations of moral reasoning holds even among those who make an effort not to ignore the plurality of moral subjects. Rawls, for example, criticizes utilitarianism on the grounds that it does not recognize the plurality of moral subjects. Through its conception of the impartial spectator, utilitarianism seeks to organize the desires of all persons into one coherent system of desire, and thereby to make the principle of choice for a society the same as that for individuals (Rawls, 1971, pp. 26–27). Rawls asserts that his "original position" provides a better representation of impartiality, because it defines 'impartiality from the standpoint of the litigants themselves. It is they who must choose their conception of justice once and for all in an original position of equality" (Rawls, 1971, p. 190).

While Rawls insists on the plurality of selves as a necessary starting point for a conception of justice, the reasoning of the original position is nevertheless monological. He interprets the process of choosing principles as a bargaining game in which individuals all reason privately in terms of their own interests. This bargaining game model does presume a plurality of selves; each subject reasons in terms of its own interests alone with full knowledge that there is a plurality of others doing the same with whom it must come to agreement. The constraints on reasoning that Rawls builds into this original position in order to make it a representation of impartiality, however, rule out not only any difference among participants in the original position, but also any discussion among them. The veil of ignorance removes any differentiating characteristics among individuals, and thus ensures that all will reason from identical assumptions and the same universal point of view. The requirement that participants in the original position be mutually disinterested precludes any of the participants from listening to others' expression of their desires and interests and being influenced by them. The bargaining game model rules out genuine discussion and interaction among participants in the original position. To ensure that they have as little opportunity for interaction as possible, Rawls even suggests that we imagine a courier mediating between them collecting proposals, announcing them, and informing them when they have come to agreement (Rawls, 1971, p. 139; cf. Young, 1981).

Stephen Darwall is explicit that the conditions of impartiality reduce the plurality of selves and points of view that obtains in actual social life to the unity of one rational agent. He presumes a thicker veil of ignorance than Rawls's, one that forbids not only knowledge of one's preferences but also motivation by them: "Suppose that those behind our thicker veil are both ignorant of any preferences they may have that are not common to any rational agent as such and hence immune to their motive force. This means there is in effect only one chooser behind the veil: an arbitrary rational agent" (Darwall, 1983, p. 231).

THE IMPOSSIBILITY OF IMPARTIALITY

Moral reason that seeks impartiality tries to reduce the plurality of moral subjects and situations to a unity by demanding that moral judgment be detached, dispassionate, and universal. But as I have already suggested, such an urge to totalization necessarily fails. Reducing differences to unity means bringing them under a universal category, which requires expelling those aspects of the different things that do not fit into the category. Difference thus becomes a hierarchical opposition between what lies inside and what lies outside the category, valuing more what lies inside than what lies outside.

The strategy of philosophical discourse which Derrida calls deconstruction, and Adorno calls negative dialectic, exposes the failure of reason's claim to reduce difference to unity. Thomas Nagel in effect deconstructs impartial reason's claim to totality. The attempt to adopt an impartial and universal perspective on reality leaves behind the particular perspectives from which it begins, and reconstructs them as mere appearances as opposed to the reality that objective reason apprehends. The experience of these appearances, however, is itself part of reality. If reason seeks to know the whole of reality, then, it must apprehend all the particular perspectives from their particular points of view. The impartiality and therefore objectivity of reason, however, depends on its detaching itself from particulars and excluding them from its account of the truth. So reason cannot know the whole and cannot be unified (Nagel, 1986, pp. 26–27).

Like other instances of the logic of identity, the desire to construct an impartial moral reason results not in unity, but in dichotomy. In everyday moral life, prior to the totalizing moves of universal reason, there are only situated contexts of action, with all their particularities of history, affiliation, and preconceived value. The ideal of impartiality reconstructs this moral context into an opposition between its formally impartial aspects and those of its aspects that are *merely* partial and particular.

Impartial reason, as we have seen, also generates a dichotomy between reason and feeling. Because of their particularity, feeling, inclination, needs, and desire are expelled fom the universality of moral reason. Dispassion requires that one abstract from the personal pull of desire, commitment, care, in relation to a moral situation and regard it impersonally. Feeling and commitment are thereby expelled from moral reason; all feelings and desires are devalued, become equally irrational, equally irrelevant to moral judgment (Spraegens, 1981, pp. 250–56). This drive to unity fails, however. Feelings, desires, and commitments do not cease to exist and motivate just because they have been excluded from the definition of moral reason. They lurk as inarticulate shadows, belying the claim to comprehensiveness of universalist reason.

In its project of reducing the plurality of subjects to one universal point of view, the ideal of impartiality generates another dichotomy, between a general will and particular interests. The plurality of subjects is not in fact eliminated, but only expelled from the moral realm; the concrete interests, needs, and desires of persons and the feelings that differentiate them from one another become merely private, subjective. In modern political theory this dichotomy appears as that between a public authority that represents the general interest, on the one hand, and private individuals with their own private desires, unshareable and incommunicable. We shall explore this dichotomy further in the next section.

The ideal of impartiality expresses in fact an impossibility, a fiction. No one can adopt a point of view that is completely impersonal and dispassionate, completely separated from any particular context and commitments. In seeking such a notion of moral reason philosophy is *utopian*; as Nagel expresses it, the impartial view is a view from nowhere. Philosophers typically depict this utopia through stories, myths, or thought experiments. Here's Nagel's:

> Suppose all the news feeding sensory data to my brain were cut but I were somehow kept breathing and nourished and conscious. And suppose auditory and visual experiences could be produced in me not by sound and light but by direct stimulation of the nerves, so that I could be fed information in words and images about what was going on in the world, what other people saw and heard, and so forth. There I would have a conception of the world without having any perspective on it. (Nagel, 1986, p. 63)

Bruce Ackerman's imagination also has a rather science-fiction cast. To think ourselves into an impartial point of view from which we can formulate an ideal of justice, he has us imagine that we are on a spaceship that has just landed on a planet on which a substance, mana, can be converted into anything anybody might want. Presumably we bring with ourselves no histories and particular hopes, no group affiliations or religions, and although Ackerman refers to his characters with gendered pronouns, gender difference appears to have no effect on their experience or point of view. The job of these newly arrived earthlings is to discuss how to distribute mana, how to construct a just society for themselves. Ackerman ensures the impartiality of the reasoning this dialogue produces by building in a Commander who serves as dialogic umpire; she decides—from an impartial point of view, of course—when speakers are breaking the only rule that guides their discussion, namely, that no one can give as a reason that his or her person or ideas are better than anyone else's. To get impartiality out of the dialogue, Ackerman has to build it into its ground rules.

Rawls presents us with not so flashy a fiction, but the original position which he constructs as the point of view of impartiality is just as utopian, especially in its provision of the veil of ignorance. The veil separates each from any knowledge of or connection with a particular history, set of group affiliations, or set of commitments, and the requirement of mutual disinterestedness ensures that none will develop among them as they talk. Darwall's "thicker" veil, which I referred to earlier, is even more counterfactual.

The ideal of impartiality is an idealist fiction. It is impossible to adopt an unsituated moral point of view, and if a point of view is situated, then it cannot be universal, it cannot stand apart from and understand all points of view. It is impossible to reason about substantive moral issues without understanding their substance, which always presupposes some particular social and historical context; and one has no motive for making moral judgments and resolving moral dilemmas unless the outcome matters, unless one has a particular and passionate interest in the outcome. As Bernard Williams points out, the difference between factual or scientific reflection and practical or moral reflection is precisely that the former is impersonal while the latter is not:

> Practical deliberation is in every case first-personal, and the first person is not derivative or naturally replaced by *anyone*. The action I decide on will be mine, and its being mine means not just that it will be arrived at by this deliberation, but that it will involve changes in the world of which I shall be empirically the cause, and of which these desires and this deliberation itself will be, in some part, the cause. (Williams, 1985, p. 68)

Some writers who agree with this critique of the dichotomy between reason and feeling, general and particular, generated by the traditional ideal of impartiality in moral theory suggest that rather than think of impartiality as a view from nowhere, one can arrive at the same results by thinking of the view from everywhere. Susan Okin, for example, reconstructs Rawls's idea of the original position as a reasoning process that takes account of all the particular positions and perspectives in the society in order to arrive at the just outcome. Unlike a more universalist Kantian approach, she suggests, this idea of taking the point of view of everyone does not oppose reason to feeling or exclude particularity. Indeed, it depends on the ability of the moral reasoner to be sympathetic with every particular position and point of view (Okin, 1989; cf. Sunstein, 1988).

This move to particularize impartiality retains a totalizing urge, however, and is no more possible than its more universalistic counterpart. The idea remains that *one* subject, the impartial reasoner, can adopt the point of view of everyone. This construction of a particularist notion of impartiality assumes that from my particular perspective, with my particular history and experience, I can nevertheless empathize with the feelings and perspectives of others differently situated. This assumption denies the difference among subjects. To be sure, subjects are not opaque to one another, their difference is not absolute. But especially when class, race, ethnicity, gender, sexuality, and age define different social locations, one subject cannot fully empathize with another in a different social location, adopt her point of view; if that were possible then the social locations would not be different (cf. Friedman, 1989, pp. 649–53).

Some might object that by rejecting the universality of the ideal of impartiality I am rejecting the very possibility of moral reflection itself. Such an objection rests on an identification of reflection with impartiality, and this is the very identification I deny. Moral reason certainly does require reflection, an ability to take some distance from one's immediate impulses, intuitions, desires, and interests in order to consider their relation to the demands of others, their consequences if acted upon, and so on. This process of reflection, however, does not require that one adopt a point of view emptied of particularity, a point of view that is the same for everyone; indeed, it is hard to see how such a universal point of view could aid reflection that leads to action at all (Williams, 1985, pp. 63–69, 110–11; cf. Walzer, 1987, pp. 48–56).

One might also object that by rejecting the universality of the ideal of impartiality I thereby deny the universality of moral commitment, expressed in the assumption that all persons are of equal moral worth. Here it is necessary to distinguish between meanings of universality. Universality in the sense of the participation and inclusion of everyone in moral and social life does not imply universality in the sense of the adoption of a general point of view that leaves behind particular affiliations, feelings, commitments, and desires. Indeed, as I shall argue in the next section, universality as generality has often operated precisely to inhibit universal inclusion and participation (cf. Young, 1989).

The moral theory that promotes the ideal of impartiality begins with an inappropriate dichotomy: either egoism or impartiality (see Darwall, 1983, chap. 1). Either an agent reasons only selfishly, considering only what will best promote his or her own selfish desires and goals, or he or she reasons from an impartial, general point of view that has no particular desires or interests in view. The theory of impartial reason wrongly identifies partiality with selfishness, and constructs its counterfactual universalist abstraction in order to move the subject beyond egoism. But there is another way the subject moves beyond egoism: the encounter with other people. A "moral point of view" arises not from a lonely self-legislating reason, but from the concrete encounter with others, who demand that their needs, desires, and perspectives be recognized (cf. Levinas, 1969; Derrida, 1978). As I have argued, the theory of impartiality assumes a monologic moral reason, a single subject attempting to get out of its myopic point of view. If one assumes instead that moral reason is dialogic, the product of discussion among differently situated subjects all of whom desire recognition and acknowledgment from the others, then there is no need for a universal point of view to pull people out of egoism. A selfish person who refuses to listen to the expression of the needs of others will not himself be listened to.

The alternative to a moral theory founded on the assumption of impartial reason, then, is a communicative ethics. Habermas has gone further than any other contemporary thinker in elaborating the project of a moral reason that recognizes the plurality of subjects. He insists that subjectivity is a product of communicative interaction. Moral rationality should be understood as dialogic, the product of the interaction of a plurality of subjects under conditions of equal power that do not suppress the interests of any.

Yet even Habermas seems unwilling to abandon a standpoint of universal normative reason that transcends particularist perspectives. As Seyla Benhabib (1986, pp. 327–51) argues, he vacillates between privileging the neutral and impartial standpoint of the "generalized other" and what she calls the standpoint of the "concrete other." Like the theories of Rawls and Ackerman, one strain of Habermas's theory relies on an a priori conception of moral reason. Normative reason must be rationally reconstructed as constituted by subjects who begin with a commitment to discursive understanding and to being persuaded by the force of the stronger argument. This initial shared motive to reach consensus, coupled with the assumption of a discussion situation free from domination, accounts for how moral norms can be general and binding. Like the theories of Rawls and Ackerman, this strain in Habermas's theory relies on counterfactuals which build in an impartial starting point in order to get universality out of the moral dialogue.

Habermas's conception of dialogic reason finds valid only the expression of generalizable interests, a term whose meaning is equivocal. Sometimes it seems to mean only those interests that are universal, which everyone shares and everyone agrees to respect for everyone else. This interpretation of generalizable interests yields a dichotomy between universal and particular, public and private, as needs and interests which may not be shareable, because they derive from a person's particular history and affiliations, drop out.

Another interpretation of generalizable interests, as Benhabib argues, derives from the insight that an emancipatory politics involves the expression and interpretation of needs. In a democratic discussion where participants express their needs, no one speaks from an impartial point of view, nor does anyone appeal to a general interest. Since having their needs met depends on the actions of others in the polity, people are forced, in Hannah Pitkin's words,

> to acknowledge the power of others and appeal to their standards, even as we try to get them to acknowledge our power and standards. We are forced to find or create a common language of purposes and aspirations, not merely to clothe our private outlook in public disguise, but to become aware ourselves of its public meaning. We are forced . . . to transform "I want" into "I am entitled to," a claim that becomes negotiable by public standards. (Pitkin, 1981, p. 347)

In this move from an expression of desire to a claim of justice, dialogue participants do not bracket their particular situations and adopt a universal and shared standpoint. They only move from self-regarding need to recognition of the claims of others. On this interpretation, those claims are normatively valid which are generalizable in the sense that they can be recognized without violating the rights of others or subjecting them to domination. Interests generalizable in this sense may nevertheless be particular, tied to the situation and needs of a particular group and thus not shared by everyone.

THE LOGIC OF IDENTITY IN THE IDEAL OF THE CIVIC PUBLIC

The dichotomy between reason and desire also appears in modern political theory in the distinction between the universal, public realm of sovereignty and the state, on the one hand, and the particular, private realm of needs and desires, on the other. Modern normative political theory and political practice aim to embody impartiality in the public realm of the state. Like impartial moral reason, this public realm attains its generality only by the exclusion of particularity, desire, feeling, and those aspects of life associated with the body. In modern political theory and practice the civic public associated with this realm achieves a unity in particular by the exclusion of women and others associated with nature and the body.

Richard Sennett (1974) and others have described the developing urban centers of the eighteenth century as engendering a unique public life. As commerce increased and more people came into the city, the space of the city itself was changed to make for more openness, vast boulevards where people fom different classes mingled in the same spaces (Berman, 1982). According to Habermas, one of the functions of this public life of the mid-eighteenth century was to provide a critical space where people discussed and criticized the affairs of the state in newspapers, coffeehouses, and other forums (Habermas, 1974). While dominated by bourgeois men, public discussion in the coffeehouses admitted men of any class on equal terms. Through the institution of the salons, moreover, as well as the theater and reading societies, aristocratic and bourgeois women participated and sometimes took the lead in such public discussion (Landes, 1988, pt. 2).

Public life in this period appears to have been wild, playful, and sexy. The theater was a social center, a forum where wit and satire challenged the state and predominant mores. This unbridled public mixed sexes and classes to some degree, mixed serious discourse with play, and mixed the aesthetic with the political. It did not survive republican philosophy. The idea of the universalist state that expresses an impartial point of view transcending any particular interests was in part a reaction to this differentiated public. The republicans grounded their universalist state in the idea of the civic public which political theory and practice institutionalized by the end of the eighteenth century in Europe and the United States to suppress the popular and linguistic heterogeneity of the urban public. Civic institutionalization reordered social life on a strict division of public and private.

Rousseau's political philosophy is the paradigm of this ideal of the civic public. Rousseau develops his conception of politics in reaction to his experience of the urban public of the eighteenth century (Ellison, 1985), as well as in reaction to the premises and conclusions of the atomistic and individualist theory of the state expressed by Hobbes. The civic public expresses the universal and impartial point of view of reason, standing opposed to and expelling desire, sentiment, and the particularity of needs and interests. From the narrow premises of individual desire and want we cannot arrive at a strong enough normative conception of social relations. The difference between atomistic egoism and civil society does not consist simply in the fact that the infinity of individual appetite has been curbed by laws enforced by threat of punishment. Rather, reason brings people together to recognize common interests and a general will.

For Rousseau the sovereign people embodies the universal point of view of the collective interest and equal citizenship. In their pursuit of individual interests people have a particularist orientation. Normative reason reveals an impartial point of view, however, that all rational persons can adopt, which expresses a general will not reducible to an aggregate of particular interests. To participate in the general will as a citizen is to express human nobility and genuine freedom. Such rational commitment to collectivity is not compatible with personal satisfaction, however, and for Rousseau this is the tragedy of the human condition (Shklar, 1969, chap. 5).

Rousseau conceived this public realm as unified and homogeneous, and indeed suggested methods of fostering commitment to such unity through civic celebrations. While the purity, unity, and generality of this public realm require transcending and repressing the partiality and differentiation of need, desire, and affectivity, Rousseau hardly believed that human life can or should be without emotion and the satisfaction of need and desire. Man's particular nature as a feeling, needful being finds expression in the private realm of domestic life, over which women are the proper moral guardians.

Recent feminist analyses of the dichotomy between public and private in modern political theory imply that the ideal of the civic public as impartial and universal is itself suspect. Modern political theorists and politicians proclaimed the impartiality and generality of the public and at the same time quite consciously found it fitting that some persons, namely, women, nonwhites, and sometimes those without property, should be excluded from participation in that public. If this was not just a mistake, it suggests that the ideal of the civic public as expressing the general interest, the impartial point of view of reason, itself results in exclusion. By assuming that reason stands opposed to desire, affectivity, and the body, this conception of the civic public excludes bodily and affective aspects of human existence. In practice this assumption forces homogeneity upon the civic public, excluding from the public those individuals and groups that do not fit the model of the rational citizen capable of transcending body and sentiment. This exclusion has a twofold basis: the tendency to oppose reason and desire, and the association of these traits with kinds of persons.

In the social scheme expounded by Rousseau, and Hegel after him, women must be excluded from the public realm of citizenship because they are the caretakers of affectivity, desire, and the body. Allowing appeals to desires and bodily needs to move public debates would undermine public deliberation by fragmenting its unity. Even within the domestic realm, moreover, women must be dominated. Their dangerous, heterogeneous sexuality must be kept chaste and confined to marriage. Enforcing chastity on women will keep each family a separated unity, preventing the chaos and blood mingling that would be produced by illegitimate children. Only then can women be the proper caretakers of men's desire, by tempering its potentially disruptive impulses through moral education. Men's desire for women itself threatens to shatter and disperse the universal rational realm of the public, as well as to disrupt the neat distinction between the public and the private. As guardians of the private realm of need, desire, and affectivity, women must ensure that men's impulses do not remove them from the universality of reason. The moral neatness of the female-tended hearth, moreover, will temper the possessively individualistic impulses of the particularistic realm of business and commerce, which like sexuality constantly threatens to explode the unity of society (see Okin, 1978, pt. 3; Lange, 1979; Elshtain, 1981, chap. 4; Pateman, 1988, chap. 4).

The bourgeois world instituted a moral division of labor between reason and sentiment, identifying masculinity with reason and femininity with sentiment and desire (Glennon, 1979; Lloyd, 1984). The sphere of family and personal life is as much a modern creation as the modern realm of state and law, and comes about as part of the same process (Nicholson, 1986, chap. 4; cf. Okin, 1981). The impartiality and rationality of the state depend on containing need and desire in the private realm of the family. The public realm of citizens achieves unity and universality only by defining the civil individual in opposition to the disorder of womanly nature, which embraces feeling, sexuality, birth and death, the attributes that concretely distinguish persons from one another. The universal citizen is disembodied, dispassionate (male) reason (Pateman, 1986; 1988, chaps. 1–4).

The universal citizen is also white and bourgeois. Women have not been the only persons excluded from participation in the modern civic public. In Europe until recently in many nations both Jews and working-class people were excluded from citizenship. In the United States the designers of the Constitution specifically restricted the access of the laboring class to the rational public, and of course excluded slaves and Indians from participation in the civic public as well. George Mosse (1985) and Ronald Takaki (1979) expose the structure of such exclusion in bourgeois republican life in Europe and the United States respectively. The white male bourgeoisie conceived republican virtue as "respectability." The "respectable" man was rational, restrained, and chaste, unyielding to passion, sentimental attachments, or the desire for luxury. The respectable man should be straight, dispassionate, rule-bound. The bodily, sexual, uncertain, disorderly aspects of existence in these cultural images were and are identified with women, homosexuals, Blacks, Indians, Jews, and Orientals.

The idea of the unified nation which developed in Europe in the nineteenth century, Mosse argues, depended precisely on opposing manly virtue to the heterogeneity and uncertainty of the body, and associating despised groups with the body, setting them outside the homogeneity of the nation (cf. Anderson, 1983). Takaki shows that early American republicans were quite explicit about the need for the homogeneity of citizens, a need which from the earliest days of the republic involved the relationship of the white republicans to the Black and Indian peoples (cf. Herzog, 1985). These republican fathers, such as Jefferson, identified the Red and Black people in their territories with wild nature and passions, just as they feared that women outside the domestic realm were wanton and avaricious. They defined moral, civilized republican life in opposition to this backward-looking, uncultivated desire they identified with women and nonwhites. Most important, they explicitly justified the restriction of citizenship to white men on the grounds that the unity of the nation depended on homogeneity and dispassionate reason.

To summarize, the ideal of normative reason, moral sense, stands opposed to desire and affectivity. Impartial civilized reason characterizes the virtue of the republican man who rises above passion and desire. Instead of cutting bourgeois man entirely off from the body and affectivity, however, the culture of the rational public confines them to the domestic sphere, which also confines women's passions and provides emotional solace to men and children. Indeed, within this domestic realm sentiments can flower, and each individual can recognize and affirm his particularity. Precisely because the virtues of impartiality and universality define the civic public, that public must exclude human particularity. Modern normative reason and its political expression in the idea of the civic public, then, attain unity and coherence through the expulsion and confinement of everything that would threaten to invade the polity with differentiation: the specificity of women's bodies and desire, differences of race and culture, the variability and heterogeneity of needs, the goals and desires of individuals, the ambiguity and changeability of feeling.

IDEOLOGICAL FUNCTIONS OF THE IDEAL OF IMPARTIALITY

One might object that I have asked too much of impartiality. Impartiality in its strongest sense is impossible, this objection admits; real moral agents are particular and cannot simply bracket their particular histories and affiliations, nor the substantial practical interests at stake in a decision. Impartiality should be understood as a regulative ideal of rea-

.tion claims—unrealizable, but nevertheless important as

/ is impartiality impossible, however, but commitment to the
adverse ideological consequences. To reiterate the definition of
.y given in Chapter 3, an idea functions ideologically when belief in
ps reproduce relations of domination or oppression by justifying
m or by obscuring possible more emancipatory social relations. Widespread commitment to the ideal of impartiality serves at least three ideological functions. It supports the idea of the neutral state, which in turn
provides some ground for the distributive paradigm of justice. It legitimates bureaucratic authority and hierarchical decisionmaking processes,
defusing calls for democratic decisionmaking. And finally, it reinforces
oppression by hypostatizing the point of view of privileged groups into a
universal position. Instead of impartiality, I argue, we should seek public
fairness, in a context of heterogeneity and partial discourse.

Impartiality designates a point of view that any rational person can
adopt, a detached and universal point of view that takes all particular
points of view equally into account. If one is impartial in the making of
a moral or political decision, then that decision will be the right one,
the best, the one which does in fact represent the interests of everyone affected as much as possible. The decision arrived at by the impartial
decisionmaker is one all those affected would have arrived at if they had
discussed it under circumstances of mutual respect and equal power.
So provided we find impartial decisionmakers, there is no need for discussion.

The idea of the impartial decisionmaker functions in our society to legitimate an undemocratic, authoritarian structure of decisionmaking. In
modern liberal society the rule of some people over others, their power to
make decisions that affect the actions and conditions of action of others,
cannot be justified on the grounds that some people are simply better than
others. If all people are equal in their capacity for reason, empathy, and
creativity, and if all people are of equal worth, it seems to follow that
decisions about the rules and policies guiding their cooperative life should
be made by them collectively: sovereignty should rest with the people. In
the myth of the social contract, the people delegate their authority to
government officials, who are charged with making decisions impartially,
looking only to the general interest, and not favoring any particular interests. Autonomy is consistent with hierarchical authority provided the authorities act from impartial rationality.

Thus a different aspect of the dichotomy between the public realm of
the state and the private realm of partial interests emerges. The state
stands above society, apart and detached, overseeing and refereeing the
competition and conflict that arises in individuals' private pursuit of their

private gain. Thus Locke, for example, explicitly uses the metaphor of an umpire to describe the function of government. The state impartially officiates over the activities of the competitive accumulative economy, and citizens owe allegiance and obedience to this state precisely because it supposedly stands impartially apart from any particular interests (Pateman, 1979, pp. 70–71).

Hegel's political philosophy provides the most thorough and explicit account of the state as expressing impartiality and universality as against the particularity of desire and interest. For Hegel the liberal account of social relations as based on the liberty of self-defining individuals to pursue their own ends properly describes only one aspect of social life, the sphere of civil society. As a member of civil society, the individual pursues private ends for himself and his family, in association with others who have similar particular interests. These particular interests within civil society may conflict, but transactions of exchange produce much harmony and satisfaction. Conceived as a member of the state, on the other hand, the individual is not a locus of particular desire, but the bearer of universally articulated rights and responsibilities. The point of view of the state and law transcends all particular interests, to express the universal and rational spirit of humanity. State laws and action express the general will, the interests of the whole society (see Pelczynski, 1971, pp. 1–29; Walton, 1983).

But the pursuit of the general interest is not compatible with the pursuit of particular interests in the same person. Thus there must be a distinct class of citizens who are not involved in the pursuit of private interest in market society, whose job it is to maintain the public good and the universal point of view of the state. These bureaucrats will be chosen by objective examination that identifies those best qualified to perceive and institute the general interest, and they will be supported from state funds to ensure their impartiality. Being entirely independent of civil society, the bureaucracy represents for Hegel the social instantiation of moral rules. Without participating in their formation, all citizens can be confident that the laws and policies set down by the bureaucracy express their objective freedom, the fulfillment of their universality as citizens, and thus they have an absolute duty to obey them (see Pateman, 1979, pp. 109–10; Buchanan, 1982, pp. 6–10).

The rule of government officials in our society is legitimated by an ideology of impartiality. We give no mandate to the legislators we elect precisely so that they can make laws impartially, the laws that will reflect the general interest. These laws are themselves impartial; they should apply to all in the same way. With wise laws arrived at by legislators looking to the general interest, executors and judges need only apply them impartially to particular cases for justice to be ensured.

According to this image of the state, government administrators, judges, and bureaucrats are supposed to be the experts in impartial decisionmaking. Unlike those of other people, their jobs do not involve immersion in particular activities with particular ends; rather their jobs are to stand apart, regard the whole of the diversity of interests and aims, and make decisions. People affected by decisions must sometimes provide information to the judges and bureaucrats at hearings and trials. But it is up to the authority to decide the outcome, because only the authority is impartial and represents the general interest. Turning over decisions to a popular assembly of people discussing their various needs and interests is positively a bad idea, because it would create irresolvable conflict. For people in civil society are partial, committed to promoting their own self-interest or the particular aims of the organizations and groups with which they are affiliated, and these are in inevitable conflict. Because democratic decisionmaking cannot work, the state must serve as a neutral arbitrator.

The idea of the neutral state that stands above the particular interests and conflicts of civil society is, however, a myth. Marxist critiques of the liberal state also apply to this image of the state as the umpire in interest-group competition. If there are significant differences of power, resources, access to publicity, and so on among different classes, groups, or interests, decisionmaking procedures that are impartial in the sense of allowing equal formal opportunity to all to press their interests will usually yield outcomes in the interests of the more powerful.

Impartiality is just as impossible for bureaucratic decisionmakers, moreover, as it is for other moral agents. It is simply not possible for flesh-and-blood decisionmakers, whether in government or not, to adopt the standpoint of transcendental reason when they make decisions, divorcing themselves from the group affiliations and commitments that constitute their identities and give them a perspective on social life. But it does not follow from the particularity of their histories and interests that people are only self-regarding, unable and unwilling to consider other interests and points of view. The pluralist ideology that defines economic and social interests as purely self-regarding and the state as impartial, however, encourages thinking in only self-regarding terms. Each is supposed to press his or her own interests, and the impartial state will see to it that fairness is done. I have already argued that being fair does not require stepping out of one's skin. The history and commitments of a person or group are nevertheless *partial*, precisely because they never do comprehend all relevant points of view from the outside. Legislators, government administrators, and other government officials, moreover, usually develop a partial view of social life and a set of particular interests that derive from their government context; government does not in fact transcend civil society and view it as a whole (Noedlinger, 1981).

The myth of the neutral state serves an ideological function insofar as it helps account for the distributive paradigm of justice. Most discussions of justice assume, implicitly or explicitly, that justice is "dispensed" by an authority, and that this authority is impartial. Most discussions of social justice also assume that issues of justice concern solely or primarily the principles by which government policy should be guided. If reflection on justice assumes the state as a realm of impartial decisionmaking that transcends and comprehends all partial interests, perspectives, and commitments, then the only significant issues of justice are distributive. If we assume the distributors are impartial and thus take all interests in the society into account, then there is no reason to make an explicit issue of the just organization of decisionmaking power.

The ideal of impartiality, I have argued, legitimates bureaucratic authority. This is true of authority in the private corporation or organization as much as in government. There too authority is justified not on aristocratic grounds, but on the grounds of a necessity of separating managerial tasks from others, making managers oversee the different and partial perspectives on the organization. Having risen in the hierarchy of an organization because his, and once in a while her, intelligence, creativity, and hard work demonstrated his or her merit, the manager's task is to supervise subordinates in a "professional" manner, which means taking a point of view of objective and impartial reason in making decisions. Rules of a corporation or agency should themselves be impartial and formal, and the administrator should apply them impartially. The administrator's decisions should reflect the interests of the organization as a whole. Bureaucratic hierarchy is just because positions are assigned impartially according to merit. As long as decisionmakers strive for impartiality, democracy is unnecessary; their decisions will best serve the interests of all. The ideal of impartiality thus helps legitimate the hierarchical organization of most workplaces, and the idea of merit allocation of its positions. In Chapter 7 I shall challenge this myth of merit, which assumes the possibility of normatively and culturally impartial standards of evaluation.

Insistence on the ideal of impartiality in the face of its impossibility functions to mask the inevitable partiality of perspective from which moral deliberation actually takes place. The situated assumptions and commitments that derive from particular histories, experiences, and affiliations rush to fill the vacuum created by counterfactual abstraction; but now they are asserted as "objective" assumptions about human nature or moral psychology. The ideal of impartiality generates a propensity to universalize the particular.

Where social group differences exist, and some groups are privileged while others are oppressed, this propensity to universalize the particular reinforces that oppression. The standpoint of the privileged, their particular experience and standards, is constructed as normal and neutral. If some groups' experience differs from this neutral experience, or they do not measure up to those standards, their difference is constructed as deviance and inferiority. Not only are the experience and values of the oppressed thereby ignored and silenced, but they become disadvantaged by their situated identities. It is not necessary for the privileged to be selfishly pursuing their own interests at the expense of others to make this situation unjust. Their partial manner of constructing the needs and interests of others, or of unintentionally ignoring them, suffices. If oppressed groups challenge the alleged neutrality of prevailing assumptions and policies and express their own experience and perspectives, their claims are heard as those of biased, selfish special interests that deviate from the impartial general interest. Commitment to an ideal of impartiality thus makes it difficult to expose the partiality of the supposedly general standpoint, and to claim a voice for the oppressed.

The ideal of impartiality legitimates hierarchical decisionmaking and allows the standpoint of the privileged to appear as universal. The combination of these functions often leads to concrete decisions that perpetuate the oppression and disadvantage of some groups and the privilege of others. Positions of decisionmaking authority are usually occupied by members of privileged groups—white Anglo nominally heterosexual men—for access to such positions is part of their privilege. Based on assumptions and standards they claim as neutral and impartial, their authoritative decisions often silence, ignore, and render deviant the abilities, needs, and norms of others. The remedy for the domination and oppression that ensues is to dismantle the hierarchy. If normative reason is dialogic, just norms are most likely to arise from the real interaction of people with different points of view who are drawn out of themselves by being forced to confront and listen to others. Just decisionmaking structures must thus be democratic, ensuring a voice and vote to all the particular groups involved in and affected by the decisions.

Participatory Democracy and the Idea of a Heterogeneous Public

If we give up the ideal of impartiality, there remains no moral justification for undemocratic processes of decisionmaking concerning collective action. Instead of a fictional contract, we require real participatory structures in which actual people, with their geographical, ethnic, gender, and occupational differences, assert their perspectives on social issues within institutions that encourage the representation of their distinct voices.

Theoretical discussion of justice, then, requires theoretical discussion of participatory democracy. As Carole Pateman (1986) points out, however, many contemporary theorists of participatory democracy are no less committed to the ideal of the civic public than their classical forebears.

This ideal of the civic public, I have argued, excludes women and other groups defined as different, because its rational and universal status derives only from its opposition to affectivity, particularity, and the body. Republican theorists insisted on the unity of the civic public: insofar as he is a citizen every man leaves behind his particularity and difference, to adopt a universal standpoint identical for all citizens, the standpoint of the common good or general will. In practice republican politicians enforced homogeneity by excluding from citizenship all those defined as different, and associated with the body, desire, or need influences that might veer citizens away from the standpoint of pure reason. Two contemporary theorists of participatory democracy, Benjamin Barber and Jürgen Habermas, retain important features of the universalist ideal of the civic public, though both ambiguously.

Barber (1984) argues fiercely against contemporary political theorists who construct a model of political discourse purified of affective dimensions. Ritual, myth, passion, emotional expression, and poetic discourse have political meaning, he argues, as much as rational argumentation. Thus Barber does not fear the disruption of the unity and the rationality of the public by desire and the body, as a number of republican theorists appear to do. In his concept of strong democracy he retains, however, a conception of the civic public as defined by unity and universality, as opposed to group affinity and particular need and interest. He distinguishes clearly between the public realm of citizenship and civic activity, on the one hand, and a private realm of particular identities, roles, affiliations, and interests. Strong democracy, he claims, regrets any division in the public, which ideally expresses a common will and common judgment of all the citizenry. Citizenship by no means exhausts people's social identities, but it takes moral priority over all other social activities in strong democracy. The pursuit of particular interests, the pressing of the claims of particular groups, all must take place within a framework of community and common vision established by the public realm. Thus Barber's vision of participatory democracy continues to rely on a strong opposition between the public sphere of citizenship and the private sphere of particular interest and affiliation. The process of participatory democracy for him requires the submerging of social differences, which I have argued tends to lead to privilege for some groups whose voice and perspective dominate the allegedly common public.

Habermas's theory of communicative action is more ambiguous than Barber's as regards the degree to which it retains the republican legacy of unity and universalism in its definition of the public as a realm of reason opposed to a private realm of desire and feeling. As I argued earlier, the main tendencies of a theory of communicative action aim at a genuinely intersubjective and contextual participatory democracy. Without the transcendental point of view of impartiality, the rationality of norms can be grounded only by understanding them as the outcome of discussion including all those who will be bound by them. As I discussed earlier, one possible interpretation of communicative ethics is that normative claims are the outcome of the expression of needs, feelings, and desires which individuals claim to have met and recognized by others under conditions where all have an equal voice in the expression of their needs and desires. This interpretation thus tends to collapse the distinction between public reason and a private realm of desire, need, and feeling.

A strong strain of Kantian universalism remains in Habermas, however, which undermines this move to a radically pluralist participatory politics of need interpretation. Habermas retains vestiges of a dichotomy between reason and affectivity. He rather firmly separates discourse about feelings from discourse about norms. His model of language itself, moreover, relies heavily on a paradigm of discursive argumentation, deemphasizing the metaphorical, rhetorical, playful, embodied aspects of speech that are an important aspect of its communicative effect (see Young, 1987; cf. Keane, 1984, pp. 169–72). Despite the possibilities of a communicative ethics, Habermas himself retains a commitment to the "moral point of view" as that of a "generalized other," in which the reasoning subject abstracts from her or his own concrete contexts of need, desire, and commitment and regards others also from this general standpoint. In that form he retains a distinction between a public realm of rights and principles and a private realm of contextualized need (Benhabib, 1986, pp. 348–51). Finally, the claim that participants in dialogue implicitly aim at consensus is reminiscent of the ideal unity of the civic public.

As we saw in Chapter 3, many writers assert that welfare corporate society is depoliticized through the institutionalization of interest-group pluralism. Just as Barber calls for a strong democratic public, many of these writers also call for a reinstitution of a civic public in which citizens transcend their particular contexts, needs, and interests to address the common good. I have been arguing, however, that such a desire for political unity will suppress difference, and tend to exclude some voices and perspectives from the public, because their greater privilege and dominant position allows some groups to articulate the "common good" in terms influenced by their particular perspective and interests.

Contrary to Barber's account, for example, the problem with interest-group pluralism is not that it is plural and particular, but that it is privatized. It institutionalizes and encourages an egoist, self-regarding view of the political process; each party enters the political competition for scarce goods and privileges only in order to maximize its own gain, and need not listen to or respond to the claims of others for their own sake. Thus interest-group pluralism allows little space for claims that some parties have a responsibility to attend to the claims of others because they are needy or oppressed. The processes and often the outcomes of interest-group bargaining, moreover, take place largely in private; they are neither revealed nor discussed in a forum that genuinely includes all those potentially affected by the decisions.

The repoliticization of public life does not require the creation of a unified public realm in which citizens leave behind their particular group affiliations, histories, and needs to discuss a mythical "common good." In a society differentiated by social groups, occupations, political positions, differences of privilege and oppression, regions, and so on, the perception of anything like a common good can only be an outcome of public interaction that expresses rather than submerges particularities. Those seeking the democratization of politics in our society, in my view, should reconceptualize the meaning of public and private and their relation, to break decisively with the tradition of Enlightenment republicanism. While there are good theoretical and practical reasons to maintain a distinction between public and private, this distinction should not be constructed as a hierarchical opposition corresponding to oppositions between reason and feeling, masculine and feminine, universal and particular.

The primary meaning of public is what is open and accessible. The public is in principle not exclusionary. While general in that sense, this conception of a public does not imply homogeneity or the adoption of some general or universal standpoint. Indeed, in open and accessible public spaces and forums, one should expect to encounter and hear from those who are different, whose social perspectives, experience, and affiliations are different. To promote a politics of inclusion, then, participatory democrats must promote the ideal of a heterogeneous public, in which persons stand forth with their differences acknowledged and respected, though perhaps not completely understood, by others.

The private, as Hannah Arendt (1958, pp. 58–67) points out, is etymologically related to deprivation. The private, as traditionally conceived, is what should be hidden from view, or what cannot be brought to view. It is connected wih shame and incompleteness. As Arendt points out, this notion of the private implies the exclusion of bodily and affective aspects of human life from the public.

Instead of defining the private as what the public excludes, I suggest, the private should be defined, as in one strain of liberal theory, as that aspect of his or her life and activity that any person has a right to exclude others from. The private in this sense is not what public institutions exclude, but what the individual chooses to withdraw from public view. With the growth of both state and nonstate bureaucracies, the protection of privacy has become a burning public issue. In welfare capitalist society, the defense of personal privacy has become not merely a matter of keeping the state out of certain affairs, but of calling for positive state regulation to ensure that both its own agencies and nonstate organizations, such as corporations, respect the claims of individuals to privacy.

This manner of formulating the concepts of public and private, which is inspired by feminist confrontations with traditional political theory, does not deny their distinction. It does deny, however, a social division between public and private spheres, each with different kinds of institutions, activities, and human attributes. The concept of a heterogeneous public implies two political principles: (a) no persons, actions, or aspects of a person's life should be forced into privacy; and (b) no social institutions or practices should be excluded a priori from being a proper subject for public discussion and expression.

The modern conception of the public, I have argued, creates a conception of citizenship which excludes from public attention most particular aspects of persons. Public life is supposed to be "blind' to sex, race, age, and so on, and all persons are supposed to enter the public and its discussion on identical terms. This conception of the public has resulted in the exclusion of persons and aspects of persons from public life.

Ours is still a society that forces persons or aspects of persons into privacy. Repression of homosexuality is perhaps the most striking example. In the United States today most people seem to hold the liberal view that persons have a right to be gay as long as they keep their activities private. Calling attention in public to the fact that one is gay, making public displays of gay affection, or even publicly asserting gay needs and rights, provokes ridicule and fear in many people. Our society is only beginning to change the practice of keeping the physically and mentally disabled out of public view. For almost a century "respectable" women have had access to public spaces and public expression, but prevailing norms still pressure us to privatize the most obvious manifestations of our femaleness—menstruation, pregnancy, lactation—to keep these out of public speech, public view, and public consideration. By extension, children should be kept out of public view, and of course their voices should not receive public expression.

The feminist slogan "the personal is political" expresses the principle that no social practices or activities should be excluded as improper subjects for public discussion, expression, or collective choice. The contemporary women's movement has made public issues out of many practices claimed to be too trivial or private for public discussion: the meaning of pronouns, domestic violence against women, the practice of men's opening doors for women, the sexual assault of women and children, the sexual division of housework, and so on.

Socialist and populist politics call for making public issues out of many actions and activities deemed properly private, such as how individuals and enterprises invest their money, what they produce, and how they produce it. Welfare corporate society allows many large institutions whose actions have an enormous impact on many people to define their activity as private, and thus gives them the right to exclude others. Participatory democrats interested in undermining economically caused oppressions such as exploitation and marginalization usually call for bringing some or all of the activities of such institutions under the purview of public democratic decisions.

These examples show that public and private do not easily correspond to institutional spheres, such as work versus family, or state versus economy. In democratic politics, where the line of privacy should be drawn itself becomes a public issue (Cunningham, 1987, p. 120). The purpose of protecting privacy is to preserve liberties of *individual* action, opportunity, and participation. The claim of any institution or collective to privacy, to the right to exclude others, can be justified only on grounds of enabling a justified range of individual privacy.

As I suggested at the beginning of this chapter, challenging the traditional opposition between public and private that aligns it with oppositions between universality and particularity, reason and affectivity, implies challenging a conception of justice that opposes it to care. A theory that limits justice to formal and universal principles that define a context in which each person can pursue her or his personal ends without hindering the ability of others to pursue theirs entails not merely too limited a conception of social life, as Michael Sandel (1982) suggests, but too limited a conception of justice. As a virtue, justice cannot stand opposed to personal need, feeling, and desire, but names the institutional conditions that enable people to meet their needs and express their desires. Needs can be expressed in their particularity in a heterogeneous public. In Chapter 6 I shall develop in more detail principles of public life that attend to and affirm difference. But first, in Chapter 5, I shall explore further the dynamics of identity that contribute to a fear of difference and its construction as absolute otherness.

CHAPTER 5

The Scaling of Bodies and the Politics of Identity

> Racism and homophobia are real conditions of all our lives in
> this place and time. I urge each one of us here to reach down
> into that deep place of knowledge inside herself and touch
> that terror and loathing of any difference that lives there.
> See whose face it wears. Then the personal as the political
> can begin to illuminate all our choices.
>
> —Audre Lorde

My body was given back to me sprawled out, distorted, recolored, clad in
mourning in that white winter day. The Negro is ugly, the Negro is animal, the
Negro is bad, the Negro is mean, the Negro is ugly; look, a nigger, it's cold, the
nigger is shivering, because he is cold, the little boy is trembling because he is
afraid of the nigger, the nigger is shivering with cold, that cold goes through
your bones, the handsome little boy is trembling because he thinks that the
nigger is quivering with rage, the little white boy throws himself into his
mother's arms; Momma, the nigger's going to eat me up.

All round me the white man, above the sky tears at its navel, the earth rasps
under my feet, and there is a white song, a white song. All this whiteness that
burns me. . . .

I sit down at the fire and I become aware of my uniform. I had not seen it. It
is indeed ugly. I stop there, for who can tell me what beauty is? (Fanon, 1967,
p. 114)

RACISM, as well as other group oppressions, should be thought of not as a
single structure, but in terms of several forms of oppression that in the
United States condition the lives of most or all Blacks, Latinos, Asians,
American Indians, and Semitic peoples. The oppressions experienced by
many members of these groups are certainly conditioned by the specific
structures and imperatives of American capitalism—structures of exploitation, segregated division of labor, and marginalization. Racism, like
sexism, is a convenient means of dividing workers from one another and
legitimating the superexploitation and marginalization of some. Clearly
experiences like that evoked by Fanon above, however, cannot be reduced to capitalist processes or encompassed within the structures of oppression just mentioned. They belong instead to the general forms of

oppression I have called cultural imperialism and violence. Cultural imperialism consists in a group's being invisible at the same time that it is marked out and stereotyped. Culturally imperialist groups project their own values, experience, and perspective as normative and universal. Victims of cultural imperialism are thereby rendered invisible as subjects, as persons with their own perspective and group-specific experience and interests. At the same time they are marked out, frozen into a being marked as Other, deviant in relation to the dominant norm. The dominant groups need not notice their own group being at all; they occupy an unmarked, neutral, apparently universal position. But victims of cultural imperialism cannot forget their group identity because the behavior and reactions of others call them back to it.

The Fanon passage evokes a particular and crucially important aspect of the oppression of cultural imperialism: the group-connected experience of being regarded by others with aversion. In principle, cultural imperialism need not be structured by the interactive dynamics of aversion, but at least in supposedly liberal and tolerant contemporary societies, such reactions of aversion deeply structure the oppression of all culturally imperialized groups. Much of the oppressive experience of cultural imperialism occurs in mundane contexts of interaction—in the gestures, speech, tone of voice, movement, and reactions of others (cf. Brittan and Maynard, 1984, pp. 6–13). Pulses of attraction and aversion modulate all interactions, with specific consequences for experience of the body. When the dominant culture defines some groups as different, as the Other, the members of those groups are imprisoned in their bodies. Dominant discourse defines them in terms of bodily characteristics, and constructs those bodies as ugly, dirty, defiled, impure, contaminated, or sick. Those who experience such an epidermalizing of their world (Slaughter, 1982), moreover, discover their status by means of the embodied behavior of others: in their gestures, a certain nervousness that they exhibit, their avoidance of eye contact, the distance they keep.

The experience of racial oppression entails in part existing as a group defined as having ugly bodies, and being feared, avoided, or hated on that account. Racialized groups, moreover, are by no means the only ones defined as ugly or fearful bodies. Women's oppression, like the oppression of Blacks, exhibits all the five forms described in Chapter 2. The sexual division of labor at home and in the workplace produces gender-specific forms of exploitation and powerlessness. Women's oppression, however, is also clearly structured by the interactive dynamics of desire, the pulses of attraction and aversion, and people's experience of bodies and embodiment. While a certain cultural space is reserved for revering feminine beauty and desirability, in part that very cameo ideal renders most women drab, ugly, loathsome, or fearful bodies. Old people, gay men and lesbians, disabled people and fat people also occupy as groups the position of ugly, fearful, or loathsome bodies. The interactive dynamics and cultural stereotypes that define groups as the ugly other have much to do with the oppressive harrassment and physical violence that endangers the peace and bodies of most members of most of these groups.

This chapter explores the construction of ugly bodies and the implications of unconscious fears and aversions for the oppression of despised groups. I expand the suggestion made in the last chapter that racist and sexist exclusions from the public have a source in the structure of modern reason and its self-made opposition to desire, body, and affectivity. Modern philosophy and science established unifying, controlling reason in opposition to and mastery over the body, and then identified some groups with reason and others with the body.

The objectification and overt domination of despised bodies that obtained in the nineteenth century, however, has receded in our own time, and a discursive commitment to equality for all has emerged. Racism, sexism, homophobia, ageism, and ableism, I argue, have not disappeared with that commitment, but have gone underground, dwelling in everyday habits and cultural meanings of which people are for the most part unaware. Through Kristeva's category of the abject, I explore how the habitual and unconscious fears and aversions that continue to define some groups as despised and ugly bodies modulate with anxieties over loss of identity. Our society enacts the oppression of cultural imperialism to a large degree through feelings and reactions, and in that respect oppression is beyond the reach of law and policy to remedy.

The analysis in this chapter raises questions for moral theory, about whether and how moral judgments can be made about unintended behavior. If unconscious behavior and practices reproduce oppression, they must be morally condemnable. I argue that moral theory must in such cases distinguish between blaming and holding responsible the perpetrators.

The dissolution of cultural imperialism thus requires a cultural revolution which also entails a revolution in subjectivity. Rather than seeking a wholeness of the self, we who are the subjects of this plural and complex society should affirm the otherness within ourselves, acknowledging that as subjects we are heterogeneous and multiple in our affiliations and desires. Social movement practices of consciousness raising, I note, offer beginning models of methods of revolutionizing the subject.

THE SCALING OF BODIES IN MODERN DISCOURSE

In Chapter 4 I suggested that the claim of modern reason to universality and neutrality, and its opposition to affectivity and the body, leads to the devaluation and exclusion of some groups. Here I will explore the meaning of this process at greater length. Modern racism, sexism, homophobia, ageism, and ableism are not superstitious carry-overs from the Dark Ages that clash with Enlightenment reason. On the contrary, modern scientific and philosophical discourse explicitly propound and legitimate formal theories of race, sex, age, and national superiority. Nineteenth- and early twentieth-century scientific, aesthetic, and moral culture explicitly constructed some groups as ugly or degenerate bodies, in contrast to the purity and respectability of neutral, rational subjects.

Critical theoretical accounts of instrumental reason, postmodernist critiques of humanism and of the Cartesian subject, and feminist critiques of the disembodied coldness of modern reason all converge on a similar project of puncturing the authority of modern scientific reason. Modern science and philosophy construct a specific account of the subject as knower, as a self-present origin standing outside of and opposed to objects of knowledge—autonomous, neutral, abstract, and purified of particularity. They construct this modern subjectivity by fleeing from material reality, from the body's sensuous continuity with flowing, living things, to create a purified abstract idea of formal reason, disembodied and transcendent. With all its animation removed and placed in that abstract transcendent subject, nature is frozen into discrete, inert, solid objects, each identifiable as one and the same thing, which can be counted, measured, possessed, accumulated, and traded (Merchant, 1978; Kovel, 1970, chap. 5; Irigaray, 1985, pp. 26–28, 41).

An important element of the discourse of modern reason is the revival of visual metaphors to describe knowledge. In the logic of identity I discussed in Chapter 4, rational thought is defined as infallible vision; only what is seen clearly is real, and to see it clearly makes it real. One sees not with the fallible senses, but with the mind's eye, a vision standing outside all, surveying like a proud and watchful lord. This subject seeks to know a Truth as pure signifier that completely and accurately mirrors reality. The knowing subject is a gazer, an observer who stands above, outside of, the object of knowledge. In the visual metaphor the subject stands in the immediate presence of reality without any involvement with it. The sense of touch, by comparison, involves the perceiver with the perceived; one cannot touch something without being touched. Sight, however, is distanced, and conceived as unidirectional; the gazer is pure originating focusing agency and the object is a passive being-seen (Irigaray, 1985, pp. 133–51).

The gaze of modern scientific reason, moreover, is a normalizing gaze (Foucault, 1977; West, 1982). It is a gaze that assesses its object according to some hierarchical standard. The rational subject does not merely observe, passing from one sight to another like a tourist. In accordance with the logic of identity the scientific subject measures objects according to scales that reduce the plurality of attributes to unity. Forced to line up on calibrations that measure degrees of some general attribute, some of the particulars are devalued, defined as deviant in relation to the norm.

Foucault summarizes five operations that this normalizing gaze brings into play: comparison, differentiation, hierarchization, homogenization, and exclusion. Normalizing reason

> refers individual actions to a whole that is at once a field of comparison, a space of differentiation and the principle of a rule to be followed. It differentiates individuals from one another, in terms of the following overall rule: that the rule be made to function as a minimal threshold, as an average to be respected or an optimum towards which one must move. It measures in quantitative terms and hierarchizes in terms of value the abilities, the level, the "nature" of individuals. It introduces, through this "value-giving" measure, the constraint of conformity that must be achieved. Lastly, it traces the limit that will define difference in relation to all other differences, the external frontier of the abnormal. (Foucault, 1977, pp. 182–83)

Much recent scholarship has revealed the white, bourgeois, male, European biases that have attached to the expression of the idea of the rational subject in modern discourse. In thinly veiled metaphors of rape, the founders of modern science construct nature as the female mastered and controlled by the (masculine) investigator. The virtues of the scientist become also the virtues of masculinity—disembodied detachment, careful measurement and the manipulation of instruments, comprehensive generalizing and reasoning, authoritative speech backed by evidence (Keller, 1985; Merchant, 1978).

The attributes of the knowing subject and normative gazer become attached just as closely to class and race. Class position arises not from tradition or family, but from superior intelligence, knowledge, and rationality. Reason itself shifts in meaning. Its mission is no longer, as it was with the ancients, to contemplate the eternity of the heavens and the subtlety of the soul, but rather to figure out the workings of nature in order to direct its processes to productive ends. "Intelligence" and "rationality" now mean primarily the activity of strategic and calculative thinking, abstraction from particulars to formulate general laws of operation, logical organization of systems, the development and mastery of formalized and technical language, and the designing of systems of surveillance and supervision. Nature and the body are objects of such manipulation and observation. As I shall discuss further in Chapter 7, moreover, this reason/body dichotomy also structures the modern division between "mental" and "material" labor. From the dawn of modern instrumental reason the idea of whiteness has been associated with reason purified of any material body, while body has been identified with blackness (Kovel, 1970, chaps. 5–7). This identification enables people who claim whiteness for themselves to put themselves in the position of the subject, and to identify people of color with the object of knowledge (cf. Said, 1978, pp. 31–49).

It is important not to construe accounts such as these as claiming either that class, race, gender, and other oppressions are grounded in or caused by scientific reason or that scientific reason simply reflects the social relations of domination. Scientific and philosophic reason express a view of subjectivity and objectivity that has come to have enormous influence and repercussions in modern Western culture. The association of this reason with a white, male bourgeoisie arises and persists in the context of a society structured by hierarchical relations of class, race, gender, and nationality which have an independent dynamic.

Without doubt an association of abstract reason with masculinity and whiteness did emerge, but quite possibly it came about through a set of fateful historical accidents. Those articulating and following the codes of modern reason were white bourgeois men. In articulating their visual metaphors of reason they spoke for themselves, unmindful that there might be other positions to articulate. As this modern detached and objectifying reason assumed the meaning of humanity and subjectivity, and acquired the authoritative position of truth-seeing, privileged groups assumed the privilege of that authoritative subject of knowledge. Groups they defined as different thereby slid into the position of objects correlated with the subject's distancing and mastering gaze.

The imposition of scientific reason's dichotomy between subject and object on hierarchical relations of race, gender, class, and nationality, however, has deep and abiding consequences for the structuring of privilege and oppression. The privileged groups lose their particularity; in assuming the position of the scientific subject they become disembodied, transcending particularity and materiality, agents of a universal view from nowhere. The oppressed groups, on the other hand, are locked in their objectified bodies, blind, dumb, and passive. The normalizing gaze of science focused on the objectified bodies of women, Blacks, Jews, homosexuals, old people, the mad and feeble-minded. From its observations emerged theories of sexual, racial, age, and mental or moral superiority. These are by no means the first discourses to legitimate the rule of the rich, or men, or Europeans. As Foucault argues, however, late eighteenth- and early nineteenth-century discourse instituted an epistemological break that found a theoretical expression in the "sciences of man" (Foucault, 1970). In this *episteme* bodies are both naturalized, that is, conceived as subject to deterministic scientific laws, and normalized, that is, subject to evaluation in relation to a teleological hierarchy of the good. The naturalizing theories were biological or physiological, and explicitly associated with aesthetic standards of beautiful bodies and moral standards of upstanding character.

In the developing sciences of natural history, phrenology, physiognomy, ethnography, and medicine, the gaze of the scientific observer was applied to bodies, weighing, measuring, and classifying them according to a normative hierarchy. Nineteenth-century theorists of race explicitly assumed white European body types and facial features as the norm, the perfection of human form, in relation to which other body types were either degenerate or less developed. Bringing these norms into the discourse of science, however, *naturalized* them, gave the assertions of superiority an additional authority as truths of nature. In nineteenth-century biological and medical schemes white male bourgeois European bodies are the "best" body types by nature, and their natural superiority determines directly the intellectual, aesthetic, and moral superiority of persons in this group over all other types (West, 1982, chap. 2).

In the nineteenth century in Europe and the United States the normalizing gaze of science endowed the aesthetic scaling of bodies with the authoritativeness of objective truth. All bodies can be located on a single scale whose apex is the strong and beautiful youth and whose nadir is the degenerate. The scale measured at least three crucial attributes: physical health, moral soundness, and mental balance. The degenerate is physically weak, frail, diseased. Or the degenerate is mentally imbalanced: raving, irrational or childlike in mental simplicity. But most important, moral impropriety is a sign of degeneracy, and a cause of physical or mental disease. Moral degeneracy usually means sexual indulgence or deviant sexual behavior, though it also refers to indulgence in other physical pleasures. Thus the homosexual and the prostitute are primary degenerates, whose sexual behavior produces physical and mental disease.

In scientific discourse about the normal and the deviant, the healthy and the degenerate, it was crucial that any form of degeneracy, whether physical, mental, or moral, make itself manifest in physical signs identifiable by the scientific gaze. Degeneracy was thought to appear on the surface of the body, whose beauty or ugliness was objectively measurable according to detailed characteristics of facial features, degree and kind of hair, skin color and complexion, shape of head, location of eyes, and structure of the genitals, buttocks, hips, chest, and breasts (Gilman, 1985, pp. 64–70, 156–58, 191–94). The prostitute, the homosexual, the criminal, are all easy to identify because of the physical symptoms of ugliness and degeneracy they exhibit.

The nineteenth-century ideal of beauty was primarily an ideal of manly virtue (Mosse, 1985, pp. 31, 76–80), of the strong, self-controlled rational man distanced from sexuality, emotion, and all else disorderly and disturbing. Even white bourgeois men are capable of disease and deviance, especially if they give themselves over to sexual impulse. Manly men must therefore vigilantly defend their health and beauty through discipline and chastity (cf. Takaki, 1979, chap. 2). In much nineteenth-century scientific discourse, however, whole groups of people are essentially and irrevocably degenerate: Blacks, Jews, homosexuals, poor and working people, and women.

As a group women are physically delicate and weak due to the specific constitution of their bodies, the operation of their reproductive and sexual parts. Because of their ovaries and uterus women are subject to madness, irrationality, and childlike stupidity, and they have greater tendencies toward sexual licentiousness than men. Beauty in women, like beauty in men, is a disembodied, desexualized, unfleshy aesthetic: light-colored hair and skin, and slenderness. Women of a certain class who are maintained under the disciplined rule of respectable and rational men can be saved from the insanity, degeneracy, and vice to which all women are prone.

Women are essentially identified with sexuality, as are the other groups scientifically classified as essentially degenerate: Blacks, Jews, homosexuals, in some places and times working people, and "criminal elements." A striking aspect of nineteenth-century discourse and iconography is the interchangeability of these categories: Jews and homosexuals are called black and often depicted as black, and all degenerate males are said to be effeminate. Medical science occupies itself with classifying the bodily features of members of all these groups, dissecting their corpses, often with particular attention to their sexual parts. The sexualization of racism in particular associates both men and women of degenerate races with unbridled sexuality. But scientists show particular fascination with Black, Jewish, and Arab women (Gilman, 1985, chap. 3).

The medicalization of difference brings about a strange and fearful logic. On the one hand, the normal/abnormal distinction is a pure good/bad exclusive opposition. On the other hand, since these opposites are located on one and the same scale, it is easy to slide from one to the other, the border is permeable. The normal and the abnormal are distinct natures, men and women, white and black, but it is possible to get sick, to lose moral vigilance, and to degenerate. Nineteenth-century moral and medical texts are full of male fears of becoming effeminate (Mosse, 1985, chap. 2).

In this context a new discourse about aging develops. Only in the nineteenth century does there emerge a general cultural and medical association between old age and disease, degeneracy, and death. Traditional patriarchal society more often revered the old man, and sometimes even the old woman, as an emblem of strength, endurance, and wisdom. Now old age comes increasingly to be associated with frailty, incontinence, senility, and madness (Cole, 1986). While such associations do not originate in the nineteenth century (witness King Lear), once again the normalizing discourse of science and medicine endows such associations with the authority of objective truth. The degeneracy of age, like that of race, is supposedly apparent in the objective ugliness of old people, especially old women.

Modern scientific reason thus generated theories of human physical, moral, and aesthetic superiority, which presumed the young white bourgeois man as the norm. The unifying structure of that reason, which presumed a knowing subject purified of sensuous immersion in things, made possible the objectification of other groups, and their placement under a normalizing gaze.

Conscious Acceptance, Unconscious Aversion

So far I have addressed the question of how some groups become ugly and fearful bodies by reviewing the construction of theories of racial, sexual, and mental superiority generated by nineteenth-century scientific reason. Many of the writers I have cited suggest that these nineteenth-century structures condition the ideology and psychology of group-based fears and prejudices in contemporary Western capitalist societies. Cornel West asserts, for example, that the racist consequences of Enlightenment conceptions of reason and science 'continue to haunt the modern West: on the non-discursive level, in ghetto streets, and on the discursive level, in methodological assumptions in the disciplines of the humanities" (West, 1982, p. 48).

But can we assume such an easy continuity between the racist, sexist, homophobic, and ageist ideologies of the past and the contemporary social situation of Europe and North America? Many would argue that conditions have so changed as to render these nineteenth- and early twentieth-century theories and ideologies mere historical curiosities, with no relationship to contemporary thoughts, feelings, and behavior. Rational discussion and social movements discredited these tracts of nineteenth-century scientific reason. After much bitter struggle and not a few setbacks, legal and social rules now express commitment to equality among groups, to the principle that all persons deserve equal respect and consideration, whatever their race, gender, religion, age, or ethnic identification.

Those of us who argue that racism, sexism, homophobia, ageism, and ableism are deep structures in contemporary social relations cannot dismiss as illusory the common conviction that ideologies of natural inferiority and group domination no longer exercise significant influence in our society. Nor can we plausibly regard the aversions and stereotypes we claim perpetuate oppression today as simple, though perhaps weakened, extensions of the grosser xenophobia of the past. Many people deny claims that ours is a racist, sexist, ageist, ableist, heterosexist society, precisely because they identify these "isms" with scientifically legitimated theories of group inferiority and socially sanctioned exclusion, domination, and denigration. To be clear and persuasive in our claims about contemporary group oppression and its reproduction, we must affirm that explicit and discursively focused racism and sexism have lost considerable legitimacy. We must identify a different social manifestation of these forms of group oppression corresponding to specific contemporary circumstances, new forms which have both continuities and discontinuities with past structures.

To formulate such an account of contemporary manifestations of group opppression I adopt the three-leveled theory of subjectivity that Anthony Giddens (1984) proposes for understanding social relations and their reproduction in action and social structures. Action and interaction, says Giddens, involve discursive consciousness, practical consciousness, and a basic security system. Discursive consciousness refers to those aspects of action and situation which are either verbalized, founded on explicit verbal formula, or easily verbalizable. Practical consciousness, on the other hand, refers to those aspects of action and situation which involve often complex reflexive monitoring of the relation of the subject's body to those of other subjects and the surrounding environment, but which are on the fringe of consciousness, rather than the focus of discursive attention (cf. Bourdieu, 1977). Practical consciousness is the habitual, routinized background awareness that enables persons to accomplish focused, immediately purposive action. For example, the action of driving to the grocery store and buying goods on my shopping list involves a highly complex set of actions at the level of practical consciousness, such as driving the car itself and maneuvering the cart in the grocery store, where I have acquired a habitual sense of the space in relation to the items I seek.

"Basic security system" for Giddens designates the basic level of identity security and sense of autonomy required for any coherent action in social contexts; one might call it the subject's ontological integrity. Psychotics are those for whom a basic security system has broken down or never been formed. Giddens's theory of structuration assumes that social structures exist only in their enactment through reflexively monitored action, the aggregate effects of that action, and the unintended consequences of action. Action, in its turn, involves the socially situated *body* in a dynamic of trust and anxiety in relation to its environment, and especially in relation to other actors:

> The prevalence of tact, trust or ontological security is achieved and sustained by a bewildering range of skills which agents deploy in the production and reproduction of interaction. Such skills are founded first and foremost in the normatively regulated control of what might seem . . . to be the tiniest, most insignificant details of bodily movement and expression. (Giddens, 1984, p. 79)

What psychoanalysis refers to as unconscious experience and motivation occurs at the level of this basic security system. In the personality development of each individual, some experiences are repressed in the process of contructing a basic sense of competence and autonomy. An independent unconscious "language" results from the splitting of this experiential material off from the self's identity: it emerges in bodily behavior and reactions, including gestures, tone of voice, and even, as Freud found, certain forms of speech or symbolization themselves. In everyday action and interaction, the subject reacts, introjects, and reorients itself in order to maintain or reinstate its basic security system.

Racism, sexism, homophobia, ageism, and ableism, I suggest, have receded from the level that Giddens refers to as discursive consciousness. Most people in our society do not consciously believe that some groups are better than others and for this reason deserve different social benefits (see Hochschild, 1988, pp. 75–76). Public law in Western capitalist societies, as well as the explicit policies of corporations and other large institutions, has become committed to formal equality and equal opportunity for all groups. Explicit discrimination and exclusion are forbidden by the formal rules of our society for most groups in most situations.

Commitment to formal equality for all persons tends also to support a public etiquette that disapproves of speech and behavior calling attention in public settings to a person's sex, race, sexual orientation, class status, religion, and the like. In a fine restaurant waiters are supposed to be deferential to all patrons—whether Black or white, trucker or surgeon—as though they were aristocrats; on the supermarket line, on the other hand, nobody gets special privileges. Public etiquette demands that we relate to people as individuals only, according everyone the same respect and courtesies. Calling attention to a person's being Black, or Jewish, or Arab, or old, or handicapped, or rich, or poor, in public settings is in distinctly poor taste, as is behaving toward some people with obvious condescension, while deferring to others. Contemporary social etiquette remains more ambiguous about calling attention to a woman's femininity, but the women's movement has helped create social trends that make it poor taste to behave in deferential or patronizing ways to women as well. The ideal promoted by current social etiquette is that these group differences should not matter in our everyday encounters with one another, that especially in formal and impersonal dealings, but more generally in all non-familiar settings and situations, we should ignore facts of sex, race, ethnicity, class, physical ability, and age. These personal facts are supposed to make no difference to how we treat one another.

I should not exaggerate the degree to which beliefs about the inferiority, degeneracy, or malignancy of some groups have receded from consciousness. There continue to be individuals and groups who are committed sexists and racists, though in the dominant liberal context they must often be careful about how they make their claims if they wish to be heard. Theories of racial and sexual inferiority, moreover, continue to surface in our intellectual culture, as in Jensen's theory of IQ differential. They too, however, are on the defensive and generally fail to achieve wide acceptance. But although public etiquette may forbid discursively conscious racism and sexism, in the privacy of the living room or locker room people are often more frank about their prejudices and preferences. Self-conscious racism, sexism, homophobia, ageism, and ableism are fueled by unconscious meanings and reactions that take place at the levels Giddens calls practical consciousness and the basic security system. In a society committed to formal equality for all groups, these unconscious reactions are more widespread than discursive prejudice and devaluation, and do not need the latter to reproduce relations of privilege and oppression. Judgments of beauty or ugliness, attraction or aversion, cleverness or stupidity, competence or ineptness, and so on are made unconsciously in interactive contexts and in generalized media culture, and these judgments often mark, stereotype, devalue, or degrade some groups.

Group differences, I argued in Chapter 2, are not "natural' facts. They are made and constantly remade in social interactions in which people identify themselves and one another. As long as group differences matter for the identification of self and others—as they certainly do in our society—it is impossible to ignore those differences in everyday encounters. In my interactions a person's sex, race, and age affect my behavior toward that person, and when a person's class status, occupation, sexual orientation, or other forms of social status are known or suspected, these also affect behavior. White people tend to be nervous around Black people, men nervous around women, especially in public settings. In social interaction the socially superior group often avoids being close to the lower-status group, avoids eye contact, does not keep the body open.

A Black man walks into a large room at a business convention and finds that the noise level reduces, not to a hush, but definitely reduces. A woman at a real estate office with her husband finds the dealer persistently failing to address her or to look at her, even when she speaks to him directly. A woman executive is annoyed that her male boss usually touches her when they talk, putting his hand on her elbow, his arm around her shoulder, in gestures of power and fatherliness. An eighty-year-old man whose hearing is as good as a twenty-year-old's finds that many people shout at him when they speak, using babylike short sentences they might also use to speak to a preschooler (Vesperi, 1985, pp. 50–59).

Members of oppressed groups frequently experience such avoidance, aversion, expressions of nervousness, condescension, and stereotyping.

For them such behavior, indeed the whole encounter, often painfully fills their discursive consciousness. Such behavior throws them back onto their group identity, making them feel noticed, marked, or conversely invisible, not taken seriously, or worse, demeaned.

Those exhibiting such behavior, however, are rarely conscious of their actions or how they make the others feel. Many people are quite consciously committed to equality and respect for women, people of color, gays and lesbians, and disabled people, and nevertheless in their bodies and feeling have reactions of aversion or avoidance toward members of those groups. People suppress such reactions from their discursive consciousness for several reasons. First, as I will discuss in a later section, these encounters and the reactions they provoke threaten to some degree the structure of their basic security system. Second, our culture continues to separate reason from the body and affectivity, and therefore to ignore and devalue the significance of bodily reactions and feelings. Finally, the liberal imperative that differences should make no difference puts a sanction of silence on those things which at the level of practical consciousness people "know" about the significance of group differences.

Groups oppressed by structures of cultural imperialism that mark them as the Others, as different, thus not only suffer the humiliation of aversive, avoiding, or condescending behavior, but must usually experience that behavior in silence, unable to check their perceptions against those of others. The dominant social etiquette often finds it indecorous and tactless to point out racial, sexual, age, or ableist difference in public and impersonal settings and encounters. The discomfort and anger of the oppressed at this behavior of others toward them must therefore remain unspoken if they expect to be included in those public contexts, and not disturb the routines by calling attention to forms of interaction. When the more bold of us do complain of these mundane signs of systematic oppression, we are accused of being picky, overreacting, making something out of nothing, or of completely misperceiving the situation. The courage to bring to discursive consciousness behavior and reactions occurring at the level of practical consciousness is met with denial and powerful gestures of silencing, which can make oppressed people feel slightly crazy.

Unconscious racism, sexism, homophobia, ageism, and ableism occur not only in bodily reactions and feelings and their expression in behavior, but also in judgments about people or policies. When public morality is committed to principles of equal treatment and the equal worth of all persons, public morality requires that judgments about the superiority or inferiority of persons be made on an individual basis according to individual competences. As I will discuss further in Chapter 7, however, fears, aversions, and devaluations of groups marked as different often unconsciously enter these judgments of competence. Through a phenomenon

that Adrian Piper (1988) calls higher-order discrimination, people frequently disparage attributes that in another person would be considered
praiseworthy, because they are attached to members of certain groups.
Assertiveness and independent thinking may be regarded as signs of good
character, of someone you would want on your team, but when found in
a woman they can become stridency or inability to cooperate. A woman
may value gentleness and softspokenness in a man, but find these attributes in a gay man signs of secretiveness and a lack of integrity. Aversion
to or devaluation of certain groups is displaced onto a judgment of character or competence supposedly unconnected with group attributes. Because the judger recognizes and sincerely believes that people should not
be devalued or avoided simply because of group membership, the judger
denies that these judgments of competence have a racist, sexist, or homophobic basis.

Similar processes of displacement often occur in public policy judgments and the reasons given for them. Since law and policy are formally
committed to equality, assertions of race or gender privilege come coded
and under rubrics other than the assertion of racial or sexual superiority
(Omi and Winant, 1983). Affirmative action discussion is an important
locus of covert or unconscious racism and sexism. Charles Lawrence
(1987) argues that unconscious racism underlies many public policy decisions where race is not explicitly at stake and the policymakers have no
racist intentions. In the late 1970s, for example, the city of Memphis
erected a wall between the white and Black sections of the city; city
officials' motives were to preserve order and protect property. In many
cities there are struggles over the location and character of public housing, in which the white participants do not discuss race and may not think
in terms of race. Lawrence argues that in cases such as these unconscious
racism has a powerful effect, and that one tests the presence of racism by
looking at the cultural meaning of issues and decisions: walls mean separation, public housing means poor Black ghettos, in the cultural vocabulary
of the society. The cultural meaning of AIDS in contemporary America associates it with gay men and gay life style, despite vigorous efforts on the
part of many people to break this association; consequently much discussion about AIDS policy may involve homophobia, even when the discussants do not mention gay men.

Unconscious racism, sexism, homophobia, ageism, and ableism are
often at work, I have suggested, in social interactions and policymaking.
A final area where these aversions, fears, and devaluations are at work is
the mass entertainment media—movies, television, magazines and their
advertisements, and so forth. How is it possible, for example, for a society
to proclaim in its formal rules and public institutions that women are as
competent as men and should be considered on their merits for profes-

sional jobs, when that same society mass-produces and distributes slick magazines and movies depicting the abuse and degradation of women in images intended to be sexually arousing? There is no contradiction here if reality and reason are boarded off from fantasy and desire. The function of mass entertainment media in our society appears to be to express unbridled fantasy; so feelings, desires, fears, aversions, and attractions are expressed in the products of mass culture when they appear nowhere else. Racist, sexist, homophobic, ageist, and ableist stereotypes proliferate in these media, often in stark categories of the glamourously beautiful and the grotesquely ugly, the comforting good guy and the threatening evil one. If politicizing agents call attention to such stereotypes and devaluations as evidence of deep and harmful oppression of the groups stereotyped and degraded, they are often met with the response that they should not take these images seriously, because their viewers do not; these are only harmless fantasies, and everyone knows they have no relationship to reality. Once more reason is separated from the body and desire, and rational selves deny attachment to their bodies and desires.

BEHAVIORAL NORMS OF RESPECTABILITY

I have considered how the discourse of modern reason created the naturalized categories of deviant, deficient, and diseased women, Blacks, Jews, homosexuals, and old people. The constitution of modern scientific reason itself sanctioned the objectification of groups expelled from the privileged subject position occupied by the white male bourgeois, bringing them under the scrutiny of a gaze that measured, weighed, and classified their bodily attributes according to a standard of white male youthfulness. Modern racism, misogyny, and homophobia, however, are not only grounded in the discourse of science and philosophy. Normalizing reason, the reason of a subject purified of body and change, a reason that masters and controls the objects fixed by its measuring gaze, enters everyday life in what George Mosse calls the ideal of respectability that dominated nineteenth-century bourgeois morality. I am not concerned here with the causes of these norms of respectability—with how, for example, the ideal of respectability was connected with the development industrial capitalism. I shall describe only some of the content and significance of those norms, to show how they structure racism, sexism, homophobia, and ageism.

Respectability consists in conforming to norms that repress sexuality, bodily functions, and emotional expression. It is linked to an idea of order: the respectable person is chaste, modest, does not express lustful desires, passion, spontaneity, or exuberance, is frugal, clean, gently spoken, and well mannered. The orderliness of respectability means things are under control, everything in its place, not crossing the borders.

Respectable behavior is preoccupied with cleanliness and propriety, meticulous rules of decency. Rules govern minute aspects of everyday behavior concerning bodily function and the arrangement of the environment. The body should be clean in all respects, and cleaned of its aspects that betoken its fleshiness—fluids, dirt, smells. The environment in which respectable people dwell must also be clean, purified: no dirt, no dust, no garbage, and all signs of bodily function—eating, excreting, sex, birthing—should be hidden behind closed doors. Bourgeois morality created a sphere of individual privacy, where the respectable individual would be alone with his or her body, taking care, bringing it under control and making it ready for public view. Respectable behavior involves keeping the body covered and not exhibiting its functions: so strict norms govern how to eat, silently, with no belching, burping, or farting. Speech is also governed by rules of decency: some words are clean and respectable, others dirty, and many, especially those relating to the body or sexuality, should not be mentioned in respectable company. Many bourgeois rules of decorum—such as these governing modes of address, gestures of respect, where to sit, or how to sip brandy—do not apply directly to bodily functions. But all manners come to be associated with bodily decency, restraint, and cleanliness.

As I discussed in Chapter 4, gender polarization was a crucial aspect of the orderliness of bourgeois respectability. Modern bourgeois society created a complementary opposition of genders much stronger than had existed before: women are identified with the body and sexuality, especially as emotion, while men stand on the side of disembodied reason. The bourgeois ideology of gender in the nineteenth century allocated each gender its proper physical and social sphere, the sphere of politics and commerce for men, the sphere of home and family for women. As morally inferior, tied to maternal instinct and the particularity of love, women could not attain the heights of discipline, virtue, and self-control required of respectable men. But women too were to observe strict codes of propriety many of which attached to the body and sexuality.

The codes of bourgeois respectability made masculinity and femininity mutually exclusive and yet complementary opposites. As such, gender dichotomy is ruled by a logic of identity that denies or represses difference, in the sense of plurality, heterogeneity, the incommensurability of experiences that cannot be brought under a common measure. The strict dimorphism and complementarity of masculinity and femininity bring respectable women under control, in the paternal care of respectable men. These men are the subjects, and their women reflect and reinforce them in love, service, and nurturance. With woman serving as man's helpmeet and complement, working as guardian over his bodily, sexual, and emotional needs and at the same time exempting him from association with her, the society is orderly.

Bourgeois gender polarization represents a denial of difference because in the respectable couple there was only one subjectivity. Mosse shows how the virtues of respectability were primarily virtues of manliness. The primary virtue of manliness is self-mastery—the ability to restrain the expression of passion, desire, sexuality, bodily need, impulse. Self-mastery requires discipline and vigilance, and only he who achieves them is truly rational, competent, and deserving of positions of authority; only the man who properly disciplines himself should be in the position to discipline others. This man is truly independent and autonomous: there is nothing about his behavior that overflows, gets away from him; he is completely the author and origin of his action.

Mosse argues that in the nineteenth-century ideal of respectable manly virtue lay a homoeroticism that legitimated bonds of attachment among men by repressing sexual definition of those bonds. As I already noted, the white male youth expressed the ideal of a passionate, but desexualized, beauty. The white male bourgeois unity and universality which implicitly defined the idea of the public in the nineteenth century reached its most arrogant development in nationalism. In nationalism sexuality was sublimated into love of nation and empire. Nationalist sentiments and loyalty were pursued in a homoerotic brotherhood that excluded women, the refined clubs and fields of the soldier, statesman, and Empire bureaucrat. This nationalism contributed both materially and ideologically to the racialization of nonwhite peoples, to their confinement outside the border of respectability (cf. Anderson, 1983). To be respectable means to belong to a "civilized" people, whose manners and morals are more "advanced" than those of "savage" or backward peoples. In this schema people of color are naturally embodied, amoral, expressive, undisciplined, unclean, lacking in self-control.

I have suggested that it is a mistake to construe the racism, sexism, classism, homophobia, ageism, and ableism of contemporary Western industrial societies as simply continuous with their nineteenth-century predecessors. An account of these contemporary privileges and oppressions must proceed as much from the historical differences as from the continuities. One major difference is that racism, sexism, homophobia, ageism, and ableism are no longer for the most part discursively conscious, but exist in behavior, images, and attitudes primarily at the level of practical consciousness and the basic security system. Similarly, one can ask to what degree contemporary society retains the cult of manly virtue and respectability, which inherently excludes women, nonwhites, and homosexuals from the rational public because these groups are associated with sexuality and the body.

A discontinuity seems obvious: whereas Victorian morality repressed and devalued sexual expression, at least for respectable people, contemporary Western advanced industrial societies allow, if not indeed glorify, sexual expression, for just about everyone. We can agree with Marcuse (1964, chap. 3) that in many ways this modern sexuality is *repressively* desublimated, a performance-oriented, accumulation-promoting superficial sexuality, but there seems no doubt that in gentrified consumer society sex is raw, not sublimated. The sexualization of society has entailed a blurring of the border between types of persons who are respectable and those who are not. As the bodies of white men are increasingly and openly sexualized the stigma of embodied sexuality no longer attaches so completely to women, Blacks, and homosexuals. Simultaneously it becomes possible to admit for these formerly despised groups a level of rationality denied them before. The dichotomies between reason and the body, self-discipline and sexual expression, cool detachment and affectivity, no longer so clearly map onto a distinction between groups, but enter into the composition of everyone's life.

The oppression of powerlessness derives in part from an ideal of respectability which contemporary society retains in the virtues and behavior of the "professional." It is paradigmatically in the office, or at business meetings, that persons in contemporary society follow the rules of decorum typical of bourgeois respectability, and in these settings people evaluate one another according to those rules. Whereas in the nineteenth century respectability attached to a single group or class, whose duty it was to exhibit its virtues in all aspects of their lives, today the code of respectability has been narrowed to public institutions and practices of business. In principle, moreover, anyone can be respectable, though we shall see below how group difference undermines this principle.

The norms of "professional" comportment entail repression of the body's physicality and expressiveness. It goes without saying that respectable, professional norms require eliminating or covering all bodily odors, being clean and "clean-cut." In dress, professional men follow the basic form of nineteenth-century respectable male dress. The "business suit" is straight and angular, with no frills or decoration, in fabric of fine weave and durable weight, in drab colors revealingly referred to as "neutral." Since women's clothes have in modern Western society been so different from men's, with more color, fabric, and decoration, the age of the businesswoman has created ambiguities and variations in professional dress. The code for the truly professional woman's dress, however, seems to have settled on a female version of the business suit, with a simple knee-length skirt instead of pants, and permitting more colorful blouses than the shirts appropriate with the male business suit.

Professional behavior, which in this society signifies rationality and authoritativeness, requires specific ways of sitting, standing, walking, and speaking—namely, without undue expression. Professional comportment entails an affable cheer, but without excitement or demonstrativeness. In speaking one should keep one's voice steady, certainly not giggling or expressing sadness, anger, disappointment, or uncertainty. One should speak firmly, without hesitation or ambiguity, and slang, dialect, and accent should be absent from one's speech. It is inappropriate to speak excitedly or to embellish one's speech with broad gestures.

In the nineteenth century norms of respectability most guided the behavior of a particular group, white bourgeois men, with a complementary set of norms for the women under their rule. Blacks, Jews, women, homosexuals, and working-class people all tended to be associated with the unruly heterogeneity of the body and affectivity, and therefore were regarded as outside the culture of respectability. In contemporary society, I have suggested, the dichotomy between reason and the body is no longer so firmly tied to groups. In principle all groups are said to be both rational and bodily. I have argued, however, that racist, sexist, and heterosexist reactions of aversion of nervousness still mark out the bodily being of some groups, but that such marking sometimes does not appear at the level of discursive consciousness. While certain groups are no longer excluded from formal opportunity to participate in respected professions, nevertheless the situation of groups victimized by cultural imperialism impedes their successful attainment of professional equality.

Despite the claim that professional comportment is neutral, it is in fact the product of socialization into a particular culture. White Anglo heterosexual middle-class men are most socialized into this culture, whereas women, Blacks, Latinos, poor and working-class people, gay men and lesbians, tend to exhibit cultural habits that deviate from or conflict with professional culture. The reasons for these differences are multiple. These groups promote a positive culture among themselves that has more "colorful" or expressive styles than are deemed appropriate in straight professional culture. The socializing agents of professional culture, moreover, particularly teachers, often give more reinforcement to white middle-class men in developing a disciplined, articulate, rational comportment than to members of other groups, because dominant cultural imagery continues to identify them as the paradigm professionals.

"Assimilation" into the dominant culture, acceptance into the rosters of relative privilege, requires that members of formerly excluded groups adopt professional postures and suppress the expressiveness of their bodies. Thus emerges for all who have not lost the impulses of life and expression a new kind of distinction between public and private, in bodily behavior. My public self is my behavior in bureaucratic institutions, sitting, standing, walking 'correctly," managing my impression. My "private" behavior is relaxed, more expressive in the body, at home with my family or socializing with members of the group with which I identify.

The lived distinction between public, respectable comportments and private, more casual comportments intersects with the interactive dynamics of racism, sexism, homophobia, ageism, and ableism. In "private" settings, where people are more relaxed, they may express devaluing judgments about members of other groups that they repress in "public" settings of formal rules and bureaucratic impersonality.

For women, disabled people, Blacks, Latinos, gay men, lesbians, and others that continue to be marked out as the Other, however, there remains another obstacle to respectability. Even if they successfully exhibit the norms of respectability, their physical presence continues to be marked, something others take note of, and, I have argued, often evokes unconscious reactions of nervousness or aversion in others. In being thus chained to their bodily being they cannot be fully and un-self-consciously respectable and professional, and they are not so considered. Upon first meeting someone they must "prove" through their professional comportment that they are respectable, and their lives are constantly dogged by such trials, which, though surely not absent from the lives of white men, are less regular.

XENOPHOBIA AND ABJECTION

In his study of white racism, Joel Kovel (1970) distinguishes three ideal types: dominative racism, aversive racism, and metaracism. Dominative racism involves direct mastery that has its most obvious manifestations in enslavement and other forms of forced labor, race status rules that privilege whites, and genocide. Whereas such domination usually entails frequent, often daily and intimate association between members of racial groups, aversive racism is a racism of avoidance and separation. From what Kovel calls metaracism, finally, almost all traces of a commitment to race superiority have been removed, and only the grinding processes of a white-dominated economy and technology account for the continued misery of many people of color.

While according to Kovel all three types of racism exist in contemporary American society, he thinks they nevertheless correspond roughly to stages in the history of white racism, especially in the United States. The nineteenth century, especially in the South, saw dominative racism as the primary form, with strong strains of aversive racism among the liberal Northern bourgeoisie who claimed to be free of racism. In the contemporary United States, racism takes primarily the form of aversive racism, with the increasing significance of metaracism.

The distinction between dominative and aversive racism can be mapped onto the shift I have outlined from discursive consciousness to practical consciousness and basic security system. In nineteenth-century racist culture, along with sexism and heterosexism, explicit theories of superior bodies and character were expressed, and Blacks, Jews, women, homosexuals, and working people were constructed as having degenerate or inferior natures that justified their domination by white bourgeois men. In contemporary society these oppressions exist less in the form of overt domination than as avoidances, aversions, and separations enacted by the privileged in relation to the oppressed.

Kovel's project is to give a psychodynamic account of racism. He suggests that dominative racism and aversive racism involve different issues and processes in the unconscious of white Western culture. Dominative racism, he suggests, involves primarily oedipal issues of sexual object and conquest, and the issues of competition and aggression played out (for men) in the oedipal drama. The explicit preoccupation with genitals and sexuality in nineteenth-century racist discourse is a symptom of this oedipal psyche. Aversive racism, on the other hand, digs more deeply into a preoedipal, anal moment of fundamental fantasies of dirt and pollution. Kovel finds this racism more consonant with the spirit of modern capitalist and instrumental rationality. Modern scientific consciousness seeks to reduce the self to pure mind abstracted from sensuality and material immersion in nature. Such an urge for purity in the context of power creates some groups as scapegoats, representative of the expelled body standing over against the purified and abstracted subject.

Oppression in contemporary society as structured by reactions of aversion, I have suggested, is not limited to racism, but also describes an aspect of sexism, homophobia, ageism, and ableism. Blacks, Latinos, Asians, gays and lesbians, old people, disabled people and often poor people, experience nervousness or avoidance from others, even from those whose discursive consciousness aims to treat them with respect as equals. This does not mean that all these group oppressions are the same. Each oppressed group has a specific identity and history that cannot be reduced to any other. In Chapter 2 I explicated five aspects of oppression, various combinations and instances of which a particular oppressed group may experience, but none of which is a necessary condition of oppression. One function of such a plural model of oppression is to avoid reductionism in discussing group oppression. I believe that all the groups named above occupy a similar status as despised, ugly, or fearful bodies, as a crucial element of their oppression. Below I offer an account of that status, which I think applies in similar ways to all these groups. This account represents only one slice, if you will, of the oppressions of racism, sexism, homophobia, ageism, and ableism.

With the concept of the abject, Julia Kristeva offers a means of understanding behavior and interactions that express group-based fear or loathing which is similar to Kovel's account of aversive racism, though not so thoroughly Freudian. In *Powers of Horror* (1982), as in much of her other work, Kristeva quarrels with the emphasis of Freudian psychoanalysis on ego development, the development of the capacity for symbolization and representation that signals the emergence of an identical self over against which stand objects, representable, definable, desired, and manipulable. In Kristeva's view psychoanalytic theory has paid too little attention to preoedipal processes of drive organization in which the figure of the mother structures affect, as opposed to the oedipal episode structured by the law-giving father.

In other writings Kristeva introduces a distinction between the symbolic and the semiotic as two irreducible, heterogeneous aspects of language (Kristeva, 1977). The symbolic is the capacity to signify, to make one element stand for an absent other, the possibility of representation, sense, logic. Symbolic capacity depends on certain repressions, on the opposition between conscious and unconscious association. The semiotic, on the other hand, is the heterogeneous, bodily, material, nonsensical aspect of speech always present with, but not integrated into, its signification: gesture, tone of voice, the musicality of speech, arrangement of words, the material aspects of all language that are expressive, affective without having definable significance. The speaking self always carries along this shadow, its spilled-over body expressed in comportment and excitation.

In the idea of the abject Kristeva locates one mode of such self-baggage. Abjection does not produce a subject in relation to objects—the ego—but rather the moment of separation, the border between the "I" and the other, before an "I" is formed, that makes possible the relation between the ego and its objects. Before desire—the movement out from a self to the objects on which it is directed—there is bare want, lack, loss and breach that is unrepresentable, that exists only as affect.

Abjection is the feeling of loathing and disgust the subject has in encountering certain matter, images, and fantasies—the horrible, to which it can only respond with aversion, with nausea and distraction. The abject is at the same time fascinating; it draws the subject in order to repel it. The abject is meaningless, repulsive in an irrational, unrepresentable way. Kristeva claims that abjection arises from the primal repression in which the infant struggles to separate from the mother's body that nourishes and comforts, from the reluctant struggle to establish a separate corporeal schema, in tension and continuity with the mother's body which it seeks to incorporate.

For the subject to enter language, to become a self, it must separate from its joyful continuity with the mother's body and acquire a sense of a border between itself and the other. In the primal fluidity of maternal *jouissance* the infant introjects the Other. Thus the border of separation can be established only by expelling, rejecting, the mother, which is only then distinguished from the infant itself; the expulsion that creates the border between inside and outside is an expulsion of itself. The infant struggles with its own drives in relation to the Other, to attain a sense of body control, but the struggle is reluctant, and the separation experienced as a loss, a wound, a want. The moment of separation can only be "a violent, clumsy breaking away, with the constant risk of falling back under the sway of a power as secure as it is shifting" (Kristeva, 1982, p. 13).

The expelled self turns into a loathsome menace because it threatens to reenter, to obliterate the border established between it and the separated self. The separation is tenuous, the subject feels it as a loss and yearns for, while rejecting, a reenclosure by the Other. The defense of the separated self, the means of keeping the border firm, is aversion from the Other, repulsion, for fear of disintegration.

Abjection is expressed in reactions of disgust to body excretions—matter expelled from the body's insides: blood, pus, sweat, excrement, urine, vomit, menstrual fluid, and the smells associated with each of these. The process of life itself consists in the expulsion outward of what is in me, in order to sustain and protect my life. I react to the expelled with disgust because the border of myself must be kept in place. The abject must not touch me, for I fear that it will ooze through, obliterating the border between inside and outside necessary for my life, which arises in the process of expulsion. If by accident or force I come to touch the abject matter, I react again with the reflex of expelling what is inside me: nausea.

Abjection, then, Kristeva says, is prior to the emergence of a subject in opposition to an object, and makes possible that distinction. The movement of abjection makes signification possible by creating a being capable of dividing, repeating, separating. The abject, as distinct from the object, does not stand opposed to the subject, at a distance, definable. The abject is other than the subject, but is only just the other side of the border. So the abject is not opposed to and facing the subject, but next to it, too close for comfort:

> The "unconscious" contents remain here *excluded* but in a strange fashion; not radically enough to allow for a secure differentiation between subject and object, and yet clearly enough for a defensive *position* to be established—one that implies a refusal but also a sublimating elaboration. (Kristeva, 1982, p. 7)

The abject provokes fear and loathing because it exposes the border between self and other as constituted and fragile, and threatens to dissolve the subject by dissolving the border. Phobia is the name of this fear, an irrational dread that latches onto a material to which it is drawn in horrified fascination. Unlike fear of an object, to which one reacts with attempts at control, defense, and counteraction, phobic fear of the abject is a paralyzing and vertiginous dread of the unnameable. At the same time the abject is fascinating, bringing out an obsessed attraction.

Abjection, Kristeva says, is a peculiar experience of ambiguity. 'Because, while releasing a hold, it does not radically cut off the subject from what threatens it—on the contrary, abjection acknowledges it to be in perpetual danger" (Kristeva, 1982, p. 9). The abject arises potentially in "whatever disturbs identity, system, order. What does not respect borders, positions, rules" (Kristeva, 1982, p. 4). Any border ambiguity may become for the subject a threat to its own borders. Separation between self and Other is the product of a violent break from a prior continuity. As constructed, the border is fragile, because the self experiences this separation as a loss and lack without name or reference. The subject reacts to this abject with loathing as the means of restoring the border separating self and other.

This account of the meaning of the abject enhances, I suggest, an understanding of a body aesthetic that defines some groups as ugly or fearsome and produces aversive reactions in relation to members of those groups. Racism, sexism, homophobia, ageism, and ableism, are partly structured by abjection, an involuntary, unconscious judgment of ugliness and loathing. This account does not explain how some groups become culturally defined as ugly and despised bodies. The symbolic association of some people and groups with death and degeneracy must in every case be explained socially and historically, and is historically variable. Even if abjection is a result of any subject's construction, nothing in the subject's formation makes group loathing necessary. The association between groups and abject matter is socially constructed; once the link is made, however, the theory of abjection describes how these associations lock into the subject's identities and anxieties. As they represent what lies just beyond the borders of the self, the subject reacts with fear, nervousness, and aversion to members of these groups because they represent a threat to identity itself, a threat to what Giddens calls the "basic security system."

Xenophobia as abjection is present throughout the history of modern consciousness, structured by a medicalized reason that defines some bodies as degenerate. The role of abjection may increase, however, with the shift from a discursive consciousness of group superiority to such group superiority lived primarily at the levels of practical consciousness and the basic security system.

When racism, sexism, heterosexism, ageism, and ableism, exist at the level of discursive consciousness, the despised groups are objectified. Scientific, medical, moral, and legal discourse construct these groups as objects, having their own specific nature and attributes, different from and over against the naming subject, who controls, manipulates, and dominates them. When these group-based claims of superiority and inferiority recede from discursive consciousness, however, these groups no longer face a dominant subject as clearly identifiable objects different from and opposed to itself. Women, Blacks, homosexuals, the mad, and the feebleminded become more difficult to name as the Others, identifiable creatures with degenerate and inferior natures. In xenophobic subjectivity they recede to a murky affect without representation.

The repression of sexism, racism, heterosexism, ageism, and ableism from discursive consciousness enhances an ambiguity characteristic of the movement of abjection. In many societies there exists a broad-based commitment to principles of equal respect and equal treatment for all persons, whatever their group identification. At the same time, the routines of practical consciousness, forms of identification, interactive behavior, rules of deference, and so on clearly differentiate groups, privileging some over others. There exists a dissonance between the group-blind egalitarian truisms of discursive consciousness and the group-focused routines of practical consciousness. This dissonance creates the sort of border crisis ripe for the appearance of the abject.

Today the Other is not so different from me as to be an object; discursive consciousness asserts that Blacks, women, homosexuals, and disabled people are like me. But at the level of practical consciousness they are affectively marked as different. In this situation, those in the despised groups threaten to cross over the border of the subject's identity because discursive consciousness will not name them as completely different (cf. Frye, 1983b, pp. 114–15). The face-to-face presence of these others, who do not act as though they have their own "place," a status to which they are confined, thus threatens aspects of my basic security system, my basic sense of identity, and I must turn away with disgust and revulsion.

Homophobia is the paradigm of such border anxiety. The construction of the idea of race, its connection with physical attributes and lineage, still makes it possible for a white person to know that she is not Black or Asian. But as homosexuality has become increasingly deobjectified, no specific characteristics, no physical, genetic, mental, or moral "character," marks off homosexuals from heterosexuals. It thus becomes increasingly difficult to assert any difference between homosexuals and heterosexuals except their choice of sexual partners. Homophobia is one of the deepest fears of difference precisely because the border between gay and straight is constructed as the most permeable; anyone at all can become gay, especially me, so the only way to defend my identity is to turn away with irrational disgust. Thus we can understand why people who have fairly successfully eliminated the symptoms of racism and sexism nevertheless often exhibit deep homophobia.

Ageism and ableism also exhibit the border anxiety of the abject. For in confronting old or disabled people I confront my own death. Kristeva believes that the abject is connected with death, the disintegration of the subject. The aversion and nervousness that old and disabled people evoke, the sense of their being ugly, arises from the cultural connection of these groups with death. Thomas Cole (1986) shows that prior to the nineteenth century old age was not linked to death; indeed, just the opposite was the case. In a time when death might come to persons at any age, and often took children and young adults, old age represented a triumph over death, a sign of virtue. During this time of patriarchal family domination, old people were highly regarded and venerated. Now, when it has become increasingly likely that people will live to be old, old age has become associated with degeneracy and death. At a time when most people can expect to be old, old people produce a border anxiety like that structuring homophobia. I cannot deny that the old person will be myself, but that means my death, so I avert my gaze from the old person, or treat her as a child, and want to leave her presence as soon as possible. My relation to disabled people has a similar structure. The only difference between myself and the wheelchair-bound person is my good luck. Encounter with the disabled person again produces the ambiguity of recognizing that the person whom I project as so different, so other, is nevertheless like me.

The story I have told is related from the point of view of privileged groups who experience abjection in encountering Blacks, Latinos, Asians, Jews, gays, lesbians, old people, disabled people, women. But what about the subjectivity of members of these groups themselves? It would be a mistake to think that this account of abjection presumes that, for example, Blacks construct white people as an abjected Other, and so on. For cultural imperialism consists precisely in the fact that the subject point of view for any subject, whatever his or her specific group membership, is identified with that of privileged groups. The form of cultural imperialism in the modern West provides and insists on only one subject position, that of the unified, disembodied reason identified with white bourgeois men. Within the unifying logic of modern reason and respectability, the subjectivity of members of culturally imperialized groups tends to stand in the same position as that of the privileged groups. From that supposedly neutral subject position all these despised and deviant groups are experienced as the abjected Other.

Members of culturally imperialized groups, that is, themselves often exhibit symptoms of fear, aversion, or devaluation toward members of their own groups and other oppressed groups. Blacks, for example, not infrequently have racist reactions to other Blacks, as the differentiation between "light-skinned" and "dark-skinned" Blacks exhibits. Gay men and lesbians themselves exhibit homophobia, old people denigrate the aged, and women are sometimes sexist. Insofar as members of these groups assume the position of subjects within the dominant culture, that is, they experience members of their own group abjectly. Even more commonly, members of culturally imperialized groups fear and despise members of other oppressed groups: Latinos are sometimes racist toward Blacks and vice versa, both are often deeply homophobic, and so on.

Even when they do not strictly assume the dominant subject position as their own point of view, members of these groups nevertheless internalize the cultural knowledge that dominant groups fear and loathe them, and to that extent assume the position of the dominant subjectivity toward themselves and other members of the groups with which they identify. But members of culturally imperialized groups also live a subjectivity different from the dominant subject position, one derived from their positive identification and social networks with others in their group. The dialectic between these two subjectivities—the point of view of the dominant culture which defines them as ugly and fearsome, and the point of view of the oppressed who experience themselves as ordinary, companionate, and humorous—represents what I referred to in Chapter 2 as double consciousness. In this respect culturally imperialized groups live a subjectivity different from that lived by privileged groups, an experience of themselves as split, divided, of their subjectivity as fragile and plural. A way out of culturally defined racism, sexism, homophobia, ageism, and ableism, I suggest in the final section of this chapter, is to push all subjects to an understanding of themselves as plural, shifting, heterogeneous. But first I shall examine the issue of responsibility for oppression that this analysis raises.

MORAL RESPONSIBILITY AND UNINTENDED ACTION

I have argued that oppression persists in our society partly through interactive habits, unconscious assumptions and stereotypes, and group-related feelings of nervousness or aversion. Group oppressions are enacted in this society not primarily in official laws and policies but in informal, often unnoticed and unreflective speech, bodily reactions to others, conventional practices of everyday interaction and evaluation, aesthetic judgments, and the jokes, images, and stereotypes pervading the mass media.

The oppression of cultural imperialism in our society partly involves defining some groups as Other, specially marked, locked in their bodies. Even when discursive reason no longer defines women or people of color as having a specific nature different from men or white people, affective and symbolic associations still tie these groups to a certain kind of body.

The presumption of unconscious fears and aversions also helps to account for the violence that victimizes these groups, as well as the degree to which it is accepted by others. I argued in Chapter 2 that this form of violence differs from other forms of group-related violence—for example, warfare or repressive violence—though these forms may be intertwined. Warfare and repression have rational objectives: to defeat a formally defined enemy, or to prevent a subjugated group from challenging, weakening, or overturning authority structures. The violence of rape, random beating, the harrassment of threats, taunts, display of pictures and symbols, and so on, is irrational in the sense that it is not explicitly instrumental to an end. It is performed for its own sake, for sport or out of random frustration, and has as its object only the humiliation and degradation of its victims. An account of racism, sexism, and homophobia that includes an understanding of the deep threats to identity that difference poses for many people helps account not only for such acts themselves, but for a social climate that makes them institutional possibilities.

Normative social philosophy and political theory rarely focus on such phenomena. The dichotomy between reason and affectivity which structures modern normative philosophy here appears in what normative philosophy and political theory take as the proper subjects of inquiry. Typically, political theory is about laws, policies, the large-scale distribution of social goods, countable quantities like votes and taxes; it is not about bodily reactions, comportments, and feelings. To the extent that normative philosophy ignores these aspects of oppression enacted in practical consciousness and the unconscious, however, it contributes not only little to ending oppression, but also something to the silencing of the oppressed. If contemporary oppression is enacted through a body aesthetic, through nervousness and avoidance motivated by threats to the basic security system, and through images and stereotypes that simultaneously feed such behavior, legitimate it, and allay the fears it expresses, then normative reflection on justice should include attention to such phenomena.

Many moral philosophers would find it odd to include gestures, informal remarks, judgments of ugliness, and feelings of discomfort under the rubric of issues of justice. They might have difficulty regarding them as *moral* phenomena at all, that is, as phenomena appropriately subject to moral judgment. For the dominant paradigm of moral theory tends to restrict the scope of moral judgment to deliberate action. Implicitly or explicitly, many moral theorists direct their attention to intended or voluntary action, where the actor knows what he or she is doing and could have done otherwise. One of the main aims of moral theory is to discover principles and maxims that justify action or form obligations. Such an aim implicitly conceives moral life as conscious, deliberate, a rational weighing of alternatives. Much moral theorizing is devoted to discussion of dilemmas and hard cases, where alternatives are explicit, and the question is which one to choose. Within this paradigm it is often regarded as inappropriate to submit habits, feelings, or unconscious reactions to normative judgment, because the subjects having them are not aware of their behavior, and thus have not intended or chosen it.

The implicit assumption that only intentional actions should be subject to moral or political judgment perhaps underlies a response members of oppressed groups often encounter when they express anger or indignation at another person's ordinary unthinking behavior. A woman complains of a male colleague's guiding her by the elbow out of the board room, or a wheelchair-bound person expresses indignation about not being addressed directly, while matters relevant to him are referred to his able-bodied companion. The response frequently heard to such complaints is, "Oh, he didn't mean anything by it." Such a response implies that the anger and moral judgment of the woman or the wheelchair-bound person are misplaced, that they do not have the right to complain of or condemn another person's behavior if that person intends to be courteous and respectful.

A conception of justice that starts from the concept of oppression must break with such a limitation of moral and political judgment to discursively conscious and intended action. If unconscious reactions, habits, and stereotypes reproduce the oppression of some groups, then they should be judged unjust, and therefore should be changed. Robert Adams (1985) argues that everyday moral intuitions include moral judgments about people's unintended or involuntary behavior. We judge people morally wrong who are unjustly angry at others, or who are self-righteous or ungrateful. Larry May (1990) argues that it makes sense to condemn people morally for being insensitive, for being unable or unwilling to understand and sympathize with the way actions, social practices, and so on appear from a different social position.

If social philosophy assumes that intended and deliberate action is the primary focus of moral judgment, it risks ignoring or even excusing some of the most important sources of oppression. Only moral judgment that extends to habitual interaction, bodily reactions, unthinking speech, feelings, and symbolic associations can capture much about such oppression.

In the essay I referred to earlier, Charles Lawrence (1987) makes a similar argument for legal theory. The dominant model of responsibility in legal judgment requires that behavior and action which litigants claim is wrong and for which they seek legal remedy be intended—that people know what they are doing and why. Lawrence cites several cases in which litigants argued that a certain action or policy was racist, but courts found against them, on the grounds that the perpetrators did not have race in mind in their actions. Such an intentional model of fault or responsibility, Lawrence argues, is much too narrow, and should be broadened to include actions and policies whose social meanings associate them with race, even when race is not what the agents or policymakers had in mind.

My claim that unintended actions and unconscious reactions should be subject to moral judgment nevertheless poses a puzzle for moral theory. Should unintended actions be judged in the same way as intended actions? Everyday intuitions tend to excuse people for unintended actions; even though someone has done something harmful, we often claim the person should not be condemned, because she didn't mean it. Conversely, everyday moral judgment is often inclined to give people moral credit for good intentions. Imagine a white person committed to social equality for people of color who enters political struggle to advance such equality, and who nevertheless sometimes has aversive reactions to people of color, makes thoughtless, insensitive remarks about and to them, and so on. Isn't such a person less to be condemned morally than one who insists that there is nothing left for policy to do, or that all proposed policies are inappropriate?

To take account of such intuitions we can distinguish between blaming people and holding them responsible (cf. Blum, 1980, p. 189; Calhoun, 1989; Card, 1989). It is inappropriate to blame people for actions they are unaware of and do not intend. People and institutions nevertheless can and should be held responsible for unconscious and unintended behavior, actions, or attitudes that contribute to oppression. To blame an agent means to make that agent liable to punishment. I mean punishment in a broad sense, including not only imprisonment and fines, but also being made to do something in restitution, exclusion from associations, removal of privileges, public censure, and social ostracism. Blame is a backward-looking concept. Calling on agents to take responsibility for their actions, habits, feelings, attitudes, images, and associations, on the other hand, is forward-looking; it asks the person "from here on out" to submit such unconscious behavior to reflection, to work to change habits and attitudes.

A distinction between blame and responsibility is important for legal and institutional contexts as well (cf. Lawrence, 1987, pp. 325–26). In conformity with its propensity to tie fault to intention, legal judgment too often identifies liability with blame for a damage which must be "made whole." Social change to break the cycle of exclusion and disadvantage that women, people of color, disabled people, gay men and lesbians, old people, and others suffer will not be aided by the law unless courts are willing to require forward-looking remedies of institutions whose unconscious and unintended actions contribute to that disadvantage.

JUSTICE AND CULTURAL REVOLUTION

Saying that certain habitual and unconscious actions, manners, forms of response, ways of speaking, and so on should be judged unjust means that the people who perform these actions should be asked to take responsibility, to bring to their discursive awareness the meaning and implications of these habitual actions. But why consider this an issue of social justice rather than simply of individual moral action? In Chapter 1 I argued that injustice should be defined primarily in terms of oppression and domination. The scope of justice, I argued, is not limited to distribution, but includes all social processes that support or undermine oppression, including culture. The behavior, comportments, images, and stereotypes that contribute to the oppression of bodily marked groups are pervasive, systemic, mutually generating, and mutually reinforcing. They are elements of dominant cultural practices that lie as the normal background of our liberal democratic society. Only changing the cultural habits themselves will change the oppressions they produce and reinforce, but change in cultural habits can occur only if individuals become aware of and change their individual habits. This is cultural revolution.

Culture is to a significant degree a matter of social choice; we can choose to change the elements of culture and to create new ones. Sometimes such change can be facilitated by passing laws or establishing policies. Nicaragua has a law against the use of women's bodies for advertising commodities. A glossy magazine can establish a policy of having more articles, photographs, and advertisements that depict Blacks in ordinary life activities. Most cultural change cannot occur, however, by edict. One cannot pass a law regulating the appropriate distance people ought to stand from one another, or whether and how they should touch. Similarly, in most situations one does not wish formally to regulate the expression of fantasy, jokes, and so on, because the dangers to liberty are too great. While aesthetic judgment always carries implicit rules, and the project of revaluing some people's bodies involves changing those rules, aesthetic judgment cannot be formally regulated. The injunction to "be just" in such matters amounts to no more and no less than a call to bring these phenomena of practical consciousness and unconsciousness under discussion, that is, to *politicize* them. The requirements of justice, then, concern less the making of cultural rules than providing institutional means for fostering politicized cultural discussion, and making forums and media available for alternative cultural experiment and play.

Cultural revolution that confronts and undermines the fears and aversions that structure unconscious behavior entails a revolution in the subject itself. Kristeva's notion of the subject in process suggests that the subject is always split, heterogeneous (Kristeva, 1977; cf. Smith, 1988, pp. 117–23). The monologic culture of respectable rationality, however, encourages the subject to desire a unified self, solid, coherent, integrated. Much popular psychology in our society promotes this image of the authentic, healthy subject as unified. We enjoin ourselves to get ourselves "together'; contradiction or plurality in our sense of self we find reproachable, a state to be overcome. But if, as I have suggested, oppressive fears and aversions toward others have a source in fears of identity loss, then such an urge to unity may be part of the problem. For people to become comfortable around others whom they perceive as different, it may be necessary for them to become more comfortable with the heterogeneity within themselves. The varying and contradictory social contexts in which we live and interact, along with the multiplicity of our own group memberships and the multiple identities of others with whom we interact, make the heterogeneity of the subject inevitable. The question is whether to repress or to affirm it.

Cultural revolution that challenges the association of some groups with abject bodies also involves the politicization of these group definitions. Despised and oppressed groups challenge cultural imperialism when they question the dominant norms of virtue, beauty, and rationality, putting forward their own positive definition of themselves as a group and thereby pluralizing norms. In Chapter 6 I will discuss more extensively the meaning and implications of this politics of asserting positive group difference.

The process of politicizing habits, feelings, and expressions of fantasy and desire that can foster cultural revolution entails a kind of social therapy. Engaging in such therapy through strictly psychoanalytic methods on a mass scale would indeed be a massive undertaking hard to imagine. I think some cultural change toward these ends can be realistically undertaken, however, in the processes of politicized personal discussion that social movements have come to call "consciousness raising."

The phrase "consciousness raising" was used by the women's movement in the late 1960s to describe a process in which women share their experiences of frustration, unhappiness, and anxiety, and find common patterns of oppression structuring these very personal stories. They found that "the personal is political," that what was originally experienced as a private, personal problem in fact has political dimensions, as exhibiting an aspect of power relations between men and women. The Black liberation movement of the late 1960s similarly strove through personal discussion to displace oppressed people's depression and self-deprecation onto social sources. Aspects of social life that appear as given and natural come into question and appear as social constructions and therefore as changeable. The process by which an oppressed group comes to define and articulate the social conditions of its oppression, and to politicize culture by confronting the cultural imperialism that has denigrated or silenced its specific group experience, is a necessary and crucial step in confronting and reducing oppression.

Another form of consciousness raising involves making the privileged aware of how their habitual actions, reactions, images, and stereotypes contribute to oppression. Again, my own experience with this group process of politicizing culture derives from the women's movement. By the late 1970s, the soul-searching generated by angry accusations that the women's movement was racist had engendered forms of discussion concretely addressing women's experiences of group differences and seeking to change relations of group privilege and oppression among women. Women's groups provided the structure for intensive, often emotion-laden discussions designed to bring to the discursive consciousness of the participants the feelings, reactions, stereotypes, and assumptions they had about women of other groups, as well as the ways their behavior toward these women might participate in and reproduce relations of privilege and oppression between them. Such group processes can be generalized to any social setting. Institutionalized consciousness-raising policies can take many forms, of which I will give just two examples.

In recent years some enlightened corporations, motivated in part also by a desire to stave off conflict and lawsuits, have instituted consciousness-raising workshops for male managers and other male employees on issues of sexual harrassment. The very concept of sexual harrassment resulted from feminist consciousness raising among women no longer willing to accept as inevitable and individual behavior they found annoying, humiliating, or coercive. Bringing men to be able to identify behavior that women collectively judge annoying, humiliating, or coercive, however, and explaining why women find it so, has been no easy task.

Differential privilege of members of different racial groups is perpetuated in part by the process of schooling. If my account of unconscious aversion as a typical dynamic of racism is at all accurate, many if not most teachers unconsciously behave differently toward Blacks or Latinos than they behave toward whites. A school system committed to racial justice can distribute literature describing processes of unconscious differential treatment, and conduct workshops in which teachers reflect on and discuss their own behavior and attitudes toward students of different races.

Consciousness raising about homophobia may be the most important and productive strategy for such a revolution of the subject. As I have said, homophobia may be one of the strongest experiences of abjection because sexual identity is more ambiguous than other group identities. The border between attraction to persons of the other sex and attraction to those of the same sex is fluid. At the same time, homophobia is deeply wrapped up with issues of gender identity, for in this society gender identity continues to be heterosexist: the genders are considered mutually exclusive opposites that complement and complete one another. Order thus depends on the unambiguous settling of the genders: men must be men and women must be women. Homosexuality produces a special anxiety, then, because it seems to unsettle this gender order. Because gender identity is a core of everyone's identity, homophobia seems to go to the core of identity.

Thus confronting homophobia involves confronting the very desire to have a unified, orderly identity, and the dependence of such a unified identity on the construction of a border that excludes aspects of subjectivity one refuses to face. If through consciousness raising one accepts the possibility that one might become different, be different, in sexual orientation, I suggest, this loosens the exclusion of others defined as different from one's self-conception in other ways. Efforts to undermine the oppressions of racism, sexism, heterosexism, ageism, and ableism mutually reinforce one another not only because these groups have some common interests and certain persons or institutions tend to reproduce the oppression of them all. There are more direct connections among these oppressions in the structure of identity and self-protection. Just as nineteenth-century stereotyping of these groups tended to assimilate them to one another, especially through the mediation of sexual images, so contemporary discourse can help subvert one group-based fear by breaking down another.

A strategy of consciousness raising presumes that those participating already understand something about how interactive dynamics and cultural imagery perpetuate oppression, and are committed to social justice enough to want to change them. Such activity cannot take place in the abstract. People will be motivated to reflect on themselves and their relations with others only in concrete social circumstances of cooperation where they recognize problems—the political group in which gays and lesbians voice dissatisfaction, the company that never seems to promote women and therefore loses them, the school or neighborhood with racial conflict.

There is a step in politicizing culture prior to the therapeutic, namely, the affirmation of a positive identity by those experiencing cultural imperialism. Assumptions of the universality of the perspective and experience of the privileged are dislodged when the oppressed themselves expose those assumptions by expressing the positive difference of their experience. By creating their own cultural images they shake up received stereotypes about them. Having formed a positive self-identity through organization and public cultural expression, those oppressed by cultural imperialism can then confront the dominant culture with demands for recognition of their specificity. I shall discuss some of the implications of this process in the next chapter.

CHAPTER 6

Social Movements and the Politics of Difference

> The idea that I think we need today in order to make deci-
> sions in political matters cannot be the idea of a totality, or
> of the unity, of a body. It can only be the idea of a multiplic-
> ity or a diversity. . . . To state that one must draw a critique
> of political judgment means today to do a politics of opinions
> that at the same time is a politics of Ideas . . . in which jus-
> tice is not placed under a rule of convergence but rather a
> rule of divergence. I believe that this is the theme that one
> finds constantly in present day writing under the name
> "minority."
>
> —Jean-François Lyotard

THERE WAS once a time of caste and class, when tradition decreed that
each group had its place, and that some are born to rule and others to
serve. In this time of darkness, law and social norms defined rights, privileges, and obligations differently for different groups, distinguished by
characteristics of sex, race, religion, class, or occupation. Social inequality
was justified by church and state on the grounds that people have different
natures, and some natures are better than others.

Then one day Enlightenment dawned, heralding a revolutionary conception of humanity and society. All people are equal, the revolutionaries
declared, inasmuch as all have a capacity for reason and moral sense. Law
and politics should therefore grant to everyone equal political and civil
rights. With these bold ideas the battle lines of modern political struggle
were drawn.

For over two hundred years since those voices of Reason first rang out,
the forces of light have struggled for liberty and political equality against
the dark forces of irrational prejudice, arbitrary metaphysics, and the
crumbling towers of patriarchal church, state, and family. In the New
World we had a head start in this fight, since the American War of Independence was fought on these Enlightenment principles, and our Constitution stood for liberty and equality. So we did not have to throw off the
yokes of class and religious privilege, as did our Old World comrades. Yet
the United States had its own oligarchic horrors in the form of slavery and
the exclusion of women from public life. In protracted and bitter struggles

these bastions of privilege based on group difference began to give way, finally to topple in the 1960s.

Today in our society a few vestiges of prejudice and discrimination remain, but we are working on them, and have nearly realized the dream those Enlightenment fathers dared to propound. The state and law should express rights only in universal terms applied equally to all, and differences among persons and groups should be a purely accidental and private matter. We seek a society in which differences of race, sex, religion, and ethnicity no longer make a difference to people's rights and opportunities. People should be treated as individuals, not as members of groups; their life options and rewards should be based solely on their individual achievement. All persons should have the liberty to be and do anything they want, to choose their own lives and not be hampered by traditional expectations and stereotypes.

We tell each other this story and make our children perform it for our sacred holidays—Thanksgiving Day, the Fourth of July, Memorial Day, Lincoln's Birthday. We have constructed Martin Luther King Day to fit the narrative so well that we have already forgotten that it took a fight to get it included in the canon year. There is much truth to this story. Enlightenment ideals of liberty and political equality did and do inspire movements against oppression and domination, whose success has created social values and institutions we would not want to lose. A people could do worse than tell this story after big meals and occasionally call upon one another to live up to it.

The very worthiness of the narrative, however, and the achievement of political equality that it recounts, now inspires new heretics. In recent years the ideal of liberation as the elimination of group difference has been challenged by movements of the oppressed. The very success of political movements against differential privilege and for political equality has generated movements of group specificity and cultural pride.

In this chapter I criticize an ideal of justice that defines liberation as the transcendence of group difference, which I refer to as an ideal of assimilation. This ideal usually promotes equal treatment as a primary principle of justice. Recent social movements of oppressed groups challenge this ideal. Many in these movements argue that a positive self-definition of group difference is in fact more liberatory.

I endorse this politics of difference, and argue that at stake is the meaning of social difference itself. Traditional politics that excludes or devalues some persons on account of their group attributes assumes an essentialist meaning of difference; it defines groups as having different natures. An egalitarian politics of difference, on the other hand, defines difference more fluidly and relationally as the product of social processes.

An emancipatory politics that affirms group difference involves a reconception of the meaning of equality. The assimilationist ideal assumes that equal social status for all persons requires treating everyone according to the same principles, rules, and standards. A politics of difference argues, on the other hand, that equality as the participation and inclusion of all groups sometimes requires different treatment for oppressed or disadvantaged groups. To promote social justice, I argue, social policy should sometimes accord special treatment to groups. I explore pregnancy and birthing rights for workers, bilingual-bicultural rights, and American Indian rights as three cases of such special treatment. Finally, I expand the idea of a heterogeneous public here by arguing for a principle of representation for oppressed groups in democratic decisionmaking bodies.

COMPETING PARADIGMS OF LIBERATION

In "On Racism and Sexism," Richard Wasserstrom (1980a) develops a classic statement of the ideal of liberation from group-based oppression as involving the elimination of group-based difference itself. A truly nonracist, nonsexist society, he suggests, would be one in which the race or sex of an individual would be the functional equivalent of eye color in our society today. While physiological differences in skin color or genitals would remain, they would have no significance for a person's sense of identity or how others regard him or her. No political rights or obligations would be connected to race or sex, and no important institutional benefits would be associated with either. People would see no reason to consider race or gender in policy or everyday interactions. In such a society, social group differences would have ceased to exist.

Wasserstrom contrasts this ideal of assimilation with an ideal of diversity much like the one I will argue for, which he agrees is compelling. He offers three primary reasons, however, for choosing the assimilationist ideal of liberation over the ideal of diversity. First, the assimilationist ideal exposes the arbitrariness of group-based social distinctions which are thought natural and necessary. By imagining a society in which race and sex have no social significance, one sees more clearly how pervasively these group categories unnecessarily limit possibilities for some in existing society. Second, the assimilationist ideal presents a clear and unambiguous standard of equality and justice. According to such a standard, any group-related differentiation or discrimination is suspect. Whenever laws or rules, the division of labor, or other social practices allocate benefits differently according to group membership, this is a sign of injustice. The principle of justice is simple: treat everyone according to the same principles, rules, and standards. Third, the assimilationist ideal maximizes choice. In a society where differences make no social difference people can develop themselves as individuals, unconstrained by group norms and expectations.

There is no question that the ideal of liberation as the elimination of group difference has been enormously important in the history of emancipatory politics. The ideal of universal humanity that denies natural differences has been a crucial historical development in the struggle against exclusion and status differentiation. It has made possible the assertion of the equal moral worth of all persons, and thus the right of all to participate and be included in all institutions and positions of power and privilege. The assimilationist ideal retains significant rhetorical power in the face of continued beliefs in the essentially different and inferior natures of women, Blacks, and other groups.

The power of this assimilationist ideal has inspired the struggle of oppressed groups and the supporters against the exclusion and denigration of these groups, and continues to inspire many. Periodically in American history, however, movements of the oppressed have questioned and rejected this "path to belonging" (Karst, 1986). Instead they have seen self-organization and the assertion of a positive group cultural identity as a better strategy for achieving power and participation in dominant institutions. Recent decades have witnessed a resurgence of this "politics of difference" not only among racial and ethnic groups, but also among women, gay men and lesbians, old people, and the disabled.

Not long after the passage of the Civil Rights Act and the Voting Rights Act, many white and Black supporters of the Black civil rights movement were surprised, confused, and angered by the emergence of the Black Power movement. Black Power advocates criticized the integrationist goal and reliance on the support of white liberals that characterized the civil rights movement. They encouraged Blacks to break their alliance with whites and assert the specificity of their own culture, political organization, and goals. Instead of integration, they encouraged Blacks to seek economic and political empowerment in their separate neighborhoods (Carmichael and Hamilton, 1967; Bayes, 1982, chap. 3; Lader, 1979, chap. 5; Omi and Winant, 1986, chap. 6). Since the late 1960s many Blacks have claimed that the integration successes of the civil rights movement have had the effect of dismantling the bases of Black-organized social and economic institutions at least as much as they have lessened Black-white animosity and opened doors of opportunity (Cruse, 1987). While some individual Blacks may be better off than they would have been if these changes had not occurred, as a group, Blacks are no better off and may be worse off, because the Blacks who have succeeded in assimilating into the American middle class no longer associate as closely with lower-class Blacks (cf. Wilson, 1978).

While much Black politics has questioned the ideal of assimilation in economic and political terms, the past twenty years have also seen the assertion and celebration by Blacks of a distinct Afro-American culture, both as a recovery and revaluation of an Afro-American history and in the creation of new cultural forms. The slogan "Black is beautiful" pierced American consciousness, deeply unsettling the received body aesthetic which I argued in Chapter 5 continues to be a powerful reproducer of racism. Afro-American hairstyles pronounced themselves differently stylish, not less stylish. Linguistic theorists asserted that Black English is English differently constructed, not bad English, and Black poets and novelists exploited and explored its particular nuances.

In the late 1960s Red Power came fast on the heels of Black Power. The American Indian Movement and other radical organizations of American Indians rejected perhaps even more vehemently than Blacks the goal of assimilation which has dominated white-Indian relations for most of the twentieth century. They asserted a right to self-government on Indian lands and fought to gain and maintain a dominant Indian voice in the Bureau of Indian Affairs. American Indians have sought to recover and preserve their language, rituals, and crafts, and this renewal of pride in traditional culture has also fostered a separatist political movement. The desire to pursue land rights claims and to fight for control over resources on reservations arises from what has become a fierce commitment to tribal self-determination, the desire to develop and maintain Indian political and economic bases in but not of white society (Deloria and Lytle, 1983; Ortiz, 1984, pt. 3; Cornell, 1988, pt. 2).

These are but two examples of a widespread tendency in the politics of the 1970s and 1980s for oppressed, disadvantaged, or specially marked groups to organize autonomously and assert a positive sense of their cultural and experiential specificity. Many Spanish-speaking Americans have rejected the traditional assumption that full participation in American society requires linguistic and cultural assimilation. In the last twenty years many have developed a renewed interest and pride in their Puerto Rican, Chicano, Mexican, or other Latin American heritage. They have asserted the right to maintain their specific culture and speak their language and still receive the benefits of citizenship, such as voting rights, decent education, and job opportunities. Many Jewish Americans have similarly rejected the ideal of assimilation, instead asserting the specificity and positive meaning of Jewish identity, often insisting publicly that Christian culture cease to be taken as the norm.

Since the late 1960s the blossoming of gay cultural expression, gay organization, and the public presence of gays in marches and other forums have radically altered the environment in which young people come to sexual identity, and changed many people's perceptions of homosexuality. Early gay rights advocacy had a distinctly assimilationist and universalist orientation. The goal was to remove the stigma of being homosexual, to prevent institutional discrimination, and to achieve societal recognition that gay people are "no different" from anyone else. The very process of political organization against discrimination and police harassment and for the achievement of civil rights, however, fostered the development of gay and lesbian communities and cultural expression, which by the mid 1970s flowered in meeting places, organizations, literature, music, and massive street celebrations (Altman, 1982; D'Emilio, 1983; Epstein, 1987).

Today most gay and lesbian liberation advocates seek not merely civil rights, but the affirmation of gay men and lesbians as social groups with specific experiences and perspectives. Refusing to accept the dominant culture's definition of healthy sexuality and respectable family life and social practices, gay and lesbian liberation movements have proudly created and displayed a distinctive self-definition and culture. For gay men and lesbians the analogue to racial integration is the typical liberal approach to sexuality, which tolerates any behavior as long as it is kept private. Gay pride asserts that sexual identity is a matter of culture and politics, and not merely "behavior" to be tolerated or forbidden.

The women's movement has also generated its own versions of a politics of difference. Humanist feminism, which predominated in the nineteenth century and in the contemporary women's movement until the late 1970s, finds in any assertion of difference between women and men only a legacy of female oppression and an ideology to legitimate continued exclusion of women from socially valued human activity. Humanist feminism is thus analogous to an ideal of assimilation in identifying sexual equality with gender blindness, with measuring women and men according to the same standards and treating them in the same way. Indeed, for many feminists, androgyny names the ideal of sexual liberation—a society in which gender difference itself would be eliminated. Given the strength and plausibility of this vision of sexual equality, it was confusing when feminists too began taking the turn to difference, asserting the positivity and specificity of female experience and values (see Young, 1985; Miles, 1985).

Feminist separatism was the earliest expression of such gynocentric feminism. Feminist separatism rejected wholly or partly the goal of entering the male-dominated world, because it requires playing according to rules that men have made and that have been used against women, and because trying to measure up to male-defined standards inevitably involves accommodating or pleasing the men who continue to dominate socially valued institutions and activities. Separatism promoted the empowerment of women through self-organization, the creation of separate and safe spaces where women could share and analyze their experiences, voice their anger, play with and create bonds with one another, and develop new and better institutions and practices.

Most elements of the contemporary women's movement have been separatist to some degree. Separatists seeking to live as much of their lives as possible in women-only institutions were largely responsible for the creation of the women's culture that burst forth all over the United States by the mid 1970s, and continues to claim the loyalty of millions of women—in the form of music, poetry, spirituality, literature, celebrations, festivals, and dances (see Jaggar, 1983, pp. 275–86). Whether drawing on images of Amazonian grandeur, recovering and revaluing traditional women's arts, like quilting and weaving, or inventing new rituals based on medieval witchcraft, the development of such expressions of women's culture gave many feminists images of a female-centered beauty and strength entirely outside capitalist patriarchal definitions of feminine pulchritude. The separatist impulse also fostered the development of the many autonomous women's institutions and services that have concretely improved the lives of many women, whether feminists or not—such as health clinics, battered women's shelters, rape crisis centers, and women's coffeehouses and bookstores.

Beginning in the late 1970s much feminist theory and political analysis also took a turn away from humanist feminism, to question the assumption that traditional female activity expresses primarily the victimization of women and the distortion of their human potential and that the goal of women's liberation is the participation of women as equals in public institutions now dominated by men. Instead of understanding the activities and values associated with traditional femininity as largely distortions and inhibitions of women's truly human potentialities, this gynocentric analysis sought to revalue the caring, nurturing, and cooperative approach to social relations they found associated with feminine socialization, and sought in women's specific experiences the bases for an attitude toward the body and nature healthier than that predominant in male-dominated Western capitalist cuture.

None of the social movements asserting positive group specificity is in fact a unity. All have group differences within them. The Black movement, for example, includes middle-class Blacks and working-class Blacks, gays and straight people, men and women, and so it is with any other group. The implications of group differences within a social group have been most systematically discussed in the women's movement. Feminist conferences and publications have generated particularly fruitful, though often emotionally wrenching, discussions of the oppression of racial and ethnic blindness and the importance of attending to group differences among women (Bulkin, Pratt, and Smith, 1984). From such discussions emerged principled efforts to provide autonomously organized forums for Black women, Latinas, Jewish women, lesbians, differently abled women, old women, and any other women who see reason for claiming that they have as a group a distinctive voice that might be silenced in a general feminist discourse. Those discussions, along with the practices feminists instituted to structure discussion and interaction among differently identifying groups of women, offer some beginning models for the development of a heterogeneous public. Each of the other social movements has also generated discussion of group differences that cut across their identities, leading to other possibilities of coalition and alliance.

EMANCIPATION THROUGH THE POLITICS OF DIFFERENCE

Implicit in emancipatory movements asserting a positive sense of group difference is a different ideal of liberation, which might be called democratic cultural pluralism (cf. Laclau and Mouffe, 1985, pp. 166–71; Cunningham, 1987, pp. 186–99; Nickel, 1987). In this vision the good society does not eliminate or transcend group difference. Rather, there is equality among socially and culturally differentiated groups, who mutually respect one another and affirm one another in their differences. What are the reasons for rejecting the assimilationist ideal and promoting a politics of difference?

As I discussed in Chapter 2, some deny the reality of social groups. For them, group difference is an invidious fiction produced and perpetuated in order to preserve the privilege of the few. Others, such as Wasserstrom, may agree that social groups do now exist and have real social consequences for the way people identify themselves and one another, but assert that such social group differences are undesirable. The assimilationist ideal involves denying either the reality or the desirability of social groups.

Those promoting a politics of difference doubt that a society without group differences is either possible or desirable. Contrary to the assumption of modernization theory, increased urbanization and the extension of equal formal rights to all groups has not led to a decline in particularist affiliations. If anything, the urban concentration and interactions among groups that modernizing social processes introduce tend to reinforce group solidarity and differentiation (Rothschild, 1981; Ross, 1980; Fischer, 1982). Attachment to specific traditions, practices, language, and other culturally specific forms is a crucial aspect of social existence. People do not usually give up their social group identifications, even when they are oppressed.

Whether eliminating social group difference is possible or desirable in the long run, however, is an academic issue. Today and for the foreseeable future societies are certainly structured by groups, and some are privileged while others are oppressed. New social movements of group specificity do not deny the official story's claim that the ideal of liberation as eliminating difference and treating everyone the same has brought significant improvement in the status of excluded groups. Its main quarrel is with the story's conclusion, namely, that since we have achieved formal equality, only vestiges and holdovers of differential privilege remain, which will die out with the continued persistent assertion of an ideal of social relations that make differences irrelevant to a person's life prospects. The achievement of formal equality does not eliminate social differences, and rhetorical commitment to the sameness of persons makes it impossible even to name how those differences presently structure privilege and oppression.

Though in many respects the law is now blind to group differences, some groups continue to be marked as deviant, as the Other. In everyday interactions, images, and decisions, assumptions about women, Blacks, Hispanics, gay men and lesbians, old people, and other marked groups continue to justify exclusion, avoidance, paternalism, and authoritarian treatment. Continued racist, sexist, homophobic, ageist, and ableist institutions and behavior create particular circumstances for these groups, usually disadvantaging them in their opportunity to develop their capacities. Finally, in part because they have been segregated from one another, and in part because they have particular histories and traditions, there are cultural differences among social groups—differences in language, style of living, body comportment and gestures, values, and perspectives on society.

Today in American society, as in many other societies, there is widespread agreement that no person should be excluded from political and economic activities because of ascribed characteristics. Group differences nevertheless continue to exist, and certain groups continue to be privileged. Under these circumstances, insisting that equality and liberation entail ignoring difference has oppressive consequences in three respects.

First, blindness to difference disadvantages groups whose experience, culture, and socialized capacities differ from those of privileged groups. The strategy of assimilation aims to bring formerly excluded groups into the mainstream. So assimilation always implies coming into the game after it is already begun, after the rules and standards have already been set, and having to prove oneself according to those rules and standards. In the assimilationist strategy, the privileged groups implicitly define the standards according to which all will be measured. Because their privilege involves not recognizing these standards as culturally and experientially specific, the ideal of a common humanity in which all can participate without regard to race, gender, religion, or sexuality poses as neutral and universal. The real differences between oppressed groups and the dominant norm, however, tend to put them at a disadvantage in measuring up to these standards, and for that reason assimilationist policies perpetuate their disadvantage. Later in this chapter and in Chapter 7 I shall give examples of facially neutral standards that operate to disadvantage or exclude those already disadvantaged.

Second, the ideal of a universal humanity without social group differences allows privileged groups to ignore their own group specificity. Blindness to difference perpetuates cultural imperialism by allowing norms expressing the point of view and experience of privileged groups to appear neutral and universal. The assimilationist ideal presumes that there is a humanity in general, an unsituated group-neutral human capacity for self-making that left to itself would make individuality flower, thus guaranteeing that each individual will be different. As I argued in Chapter 4, because there is no such unsituated group-neutral point of view, the situation and experience of dominant groups tend to define the norms of such a humanity in general. Against such a supposedly neutral humanist ideal, only the oppressed groups come to be marked with particularity; they, and not the privileged groups, are marked, objectified as the Others.

Thus, third, this denigration of groups that deviate from an allegedly neutral standard often produces an internalized devaluation by members of those groups themselves. When there is an ideal of general human standards according to which everyone should be evaluated equally, then Puerto Ricans or Chinese Americans are ashamed of their accents or their parents, Black children despise the female-dominated kith and kin networks of their neighborhoods, and feminists seek to root out their tendency to cry, or to feel compassion for a frustrated stranger. The aspiration to assimilate helps produce the self-loathing and double consciousness characteristic of oppression. The goal of assimilation holds up to people a demand that they "fit," be like the mainstream, in behavior, values, and goals. At the same time, as long as group differences exist, group members will be marked as different—as Black, Jewish, gay—and thus as unable simply to fit. When participation is taken to imply assimilation the oppressed person is caught in an irresolvable dilemma: to participate means to accept and adopt an identity one is not, and to try to participate means to be reminded by oneself and others of the identity one is.

A more subtle analysis of the assimilationist ideal might distinguish between a conformist and a transformational ideal of assimilation. In the conformist ideal, status quo institutions and norms are assumed as given, and disadvantaged groups who differ from those norms are expected to conform to them. A transformational ideal of assimilation, on the other hand, recognizes that institutions as given express the interests and perspective of the dominant groups. Achieving assimilation therefore requires altering many institutions and practices in accordance with neutral rules that truly do not disadvantage or stigmatize any person, so that group membership really is irrelevant to how persons are treated. Wasserstrom's ideal fits a transformational assimilation, as does the group-neutral ideal advocated by some feminists (Taub and Williams, 1987). Unlike the conformist assimilationist, the transformational assimilationist may allow that group-specific policies, such as affirmative action, are necessary and appropriate means for transforming institutions to fit the assimilationist ideal. Whether conformist or transformational, however, the assimilationist ideal still denies that group difference can be positive and desirable; thus any form of the ideal of assimilation constructs group difference as a liability or disadvantage.

Under these circumstances, a politics that asserts the positivity of group difference is liberating and empowering. In the act of reclaiming the identity the dominant culture has taught them to despise (Cliff, 1980), and affirming it as an identity to celebrate, the oppressed remove double consciousness. I am just what they say I am—a Jewboy, a colored girl, a fag, a dyke, or a hag—and proud of it. No longer does one have the impossible project of trying to become something one is not under circumstances where the very trying reminds one of who one is. This politics asserts that oppressed groups have distinct cultures, experiences, and perspectives on social life with humanly positive meaning, some of which may even be superior to the culture and perspectives of mainstream society. The rejection and devaluation of one's culture and perspective should not be a condition of full participation in social life.

Asserting the value and specificity of the culture and attributes of oppressed groups, moreover, results in a relativizing of the dominant culture. When feminists assert the validity of feminine sensitivity and the positive value of nurturing behavior, when gays describe the prejudice of heterosexuals as homophobic and their own sexuality as positive and self-developing, when Blacks affirm a distinct Afro-American tradition, then the dominant culture is forced to discover itself for the first time as specific: as Anglo, European, Christian, masculine, straight. In a political struggle where oppressed groups insist on the positive value of their specific culture and experience, it becomes increasingly difficult for dominant groups to parade their norms as neutral and universal, and to construct the values and behavior of the oppressed as deviant, perverted, or inferior. By puncturing the universalist claim to unity that expels some groups and turns them into the Other, the assertion of positive group specificity introduces the possibility of understanding the relation between groups as merely difference, instead of exclusion, opposition, or dominance.

The politics of difference also promotes a notion of group solidarity against the individualism of liberal humanism. Liberal humanism treats each person as an individual, ignoring differences of race, sex, religion, and ethnicity. Each person should be evaluated only according to her or his individual efforts and achievements. With the institutionalization of formal equlity some members of formerly excluded groups have indeed succeeded, by mainstream standards. Structural patterns of group privilege and oppression nevertheless remain. When political leaders of oppressed groups reject assimilation they are often affirming group solidarity. Where the dominant culture refuses to see anything but the achievement of autonomous individuals, the oppressed assert that we shall not separate from the people with whom we identify in order to "make it" in a white Anglo male world. The politics of difference insists on liberation of the whole group of Blacks, women, American Indians, and that this can be accomplished only through basic institutional changes. These changes must include group representation in policymaking and an elimination of the hierarchy of rewards that forces everyone to compete for scarce positions at the top.

Thus the assertion of a positive sense of group difference provides a standpoint from which to criticize prevailing institutions and norms. Black Americans find in their traditional communities, which refer to their members as "brother" and "sister," a sense of solidarity absent from the calculating individualism of white professional capitalist society. Feminists find in the traditional female values of nurturing a challenge to a militarist world-view, and lesbians find in their relationships a confrontation with the assumption of complementary gender roles in sexual relationships. From their experience of a culture tied to the land American Indians formulate a critique of the instrumental rationality of European culture that results in pollution and ecological destruction. Having revealed the specificity of the dominant norms which claim universality and neutrality, social movements of the oppressed are in a position to inquire how the dominant institutions must be changed so that they will no longer reproduce the patterns of privilege and oppression.

From the assertion of positive difference the self-organization of oppressed groups follows. Both liberal humanist and leftist political organizations and movements have found it difficult to accept this principle of group autonomy. In a humanist emancipatory politics, if a group is subject to injustice, then all those interested in a just society should unite to combat the powers that perpetuate that injustice. If many groups are subject to injustice, moreover, then they should unite to work for a just society. The politics of difference is certainly not against coalition, nor does it hold that, for example, whites should not work against racial injustice or men against sexist injustice. This politics of group assertion, however, takes as a basic principle that members of oppressed groups need separate organizations that exclude others, especially those from more privileged groups. Separate organization is probably necessary in order for these groups to discover and reinforce the positivity of their specific experience, to collapse and eliminate double consciousness. In discussions within autonomous organizations, group members can determine their specific needs and interests. Separation and self-organization risk creating pressures toward homogenization of the groups themselves, creating new privileges and exclusions, a problem I shall discuss in Chapter 8. But contemporary emancipatory social movements have found group autonomy an important vehicle for empowerment and the development of a group-specific voice and perspective.

Integration into the full life of the society should not have to imply assimilation to dominant norms and abandonment of group affiliation and culture (Edley, 1986; cf. McGary, 1983). If the only alternative to the oppressive exclusion of some groups defined as Other by dominant ideologies is the assertion that they are the same as everybody else, then they will continue to be excluded because they are not the same.

Some might object to the way I have drawn the distinction between an assimilationist ideal of liberation and a radical democratic pluralism. They might claim that I have not painted the ideal of a society that transcends group differences fairly, representing it as homogeneous and conformist. The free society envisaged by liberalism, they might say, is certainly pluralistic. In it persons can affiliate with whomever they choose; liberty encourages a proliferation of life styles, activities, and associations. While I have no quarrel with social diversity in this sense, this vision of liberal pluralism does not touch on the primary issues that give rise to the politics of difference. The vision of liberation as the transcendence of group difference seeks to abolish the public and political significance of group difference, while retaining and promoting both individual and group diversity in private, or nonpolitical, social contexts. In Chapter 4 I argued that this way of distinguishing public and private spheres, where the public represents universal citizenship and the private individual differences, tends to result in group exclusion from the public. Radical democratic pluralism acknowledges and affirms the public and political significance of social group differences as a means of ensuring the participation and inclusion of everyone in social and political institutions.

RECLAIMING THE MEANING OF DIFFERENCE

Many people inside and outside the movements I have discussed find the rejection of the liberal humanist ideal and the assertion of a positive sense of group difference both confusing and controversial. They fear that any admission by oppressed groups that they are different from the dominant groups risks justifying anew the subordination, special marking, and exclusion of those groups. Since calls for a return of women to the kitchen, Blacks to servant roles and separate schools, and disabled people to nursing homes are not absent from contemporary politics, the danger is real. It may be true that the assimilationist ideal that treats everyone the same and applies the same standards to all perpetuates disadvantage because real group differences remain that make it unfair to compare the unequals. But this is far preferable to a reestablishment of separate and unequal spheres for different groups justified on the basis of group difference.

Since those asserting group specificity certainly wish to affirm the liberal humanist principle that all persons are of equal moral worth, they appear to be faced with a dilemma. Analyzing W.E.B. Du Bois's arguments for cultural pluralism, Bernard Boxill poses the dilemma this way: "On the one hand, we must overcome segregation because it denies the idea of human brotherhood; on the other hand, to overcome segregation we must self-segregate and therefore also deny the idea of human brotherhood" (Boxill, 1984, p. 174). Martha Minow finds a dilemma of difference facing any who seek to promote justice for currently oppressed or disadvantaged groups. Formally neutral rules and policies that ignore group differences often perpetuate the disadvantage of those whose difference is defined as deviant; but focusing on difference risks recreating the stigma that difference has carried in the past (Minow, 1987, pp. 12–13; cf. Minow, 1985; 1990).

These dilemmas are genuine, and exhibit the risks of collective life, where the consequences of one's claims, actions, and policies may not turn out as one intended because others have understood them differently or turned them to different ends. Since ignoring group differences in public policy does not mean that people ignore them in everyday life and interaction, however, oppression continues even when law and policy declare that all are equal. Thus I think for many groups and in many circumstances it is more empowering to affirm and acknowledge in political life the group differences that already exist in social life. One is more likely to avoid the dilemma of difference in doing this if the meaning of difference itself becomes a terrain of political struggle. Social movements asserting the positivity of group difference have established this terrain, offering an emancipatory meaning of difference to replace the old exclusionary meaning.

The oppressive meaning of group difference defines it as absolute otherness, mutual exclusion, categorical opposition. This essentialist meaning of difference submits to the logic of identity. One group occupies the position of a norm, against which all others are measured. The attempt to reduce all persons to the unity of a common measure constructs as deviant those whose attributes differ from the group-specific attributes implicitly presumed in the norm. The drive to unify the particularity and multiplicity of practices, cultural symbols, and ways of relating in clear and distinct categories turns difference into exclusion.

Thus I explored in the previous two chapters how the appropriation of a universal subject position by socially privileged groups forces those they define as different outside the definition of full humanity and citizenship.

The attempt to measure all against some universal standard generates a logic of difference as hierarchical dichotomy—masculine/feminine, civilized/savage, and so on. The second term is defined negatively as a lack of the truly human qualities; at the same time it is defined as the complement to the valued term, the object correlating with its subject, that which brings it to completion, wholeness, and identity. By loving and affirming him, a woman serves as a mirror to a man, holding up his virtues for him to see (Irigaray, 1985). By carrying the white man's burden to tame and educate the savage peoples, the civilized will realize universal humanity. The exotic orientals are there to know and master, to be the completion of reason's progress in history, which seeks the unity of the world (Said, 1978). In every case the valued term achieves its value by its determinately negative relation to the Other.

In the objectifying ideologies of racism, sexism, anti-Semitism, and homophobia, only the oppressed and excluded groups are defined as different. Whereas the privileged groups are neutral and exhibit free and malleable subjectivity, the excluded groups are marked with an essence, imprisoned in a given set of possibilities. By virtue of the characteristics the group is alleged to have by nature, the ideologies allege that group members have specific dispositions that suit them for some activities and not others. Difference in these ideologies always means exclusionary opposition to a norm. There are rational men, and then there are women; there are civilized men, and then there are wild and savage peoples. The marking of difference always implies a good/bad opposition; it is always a devaluation, the naming of an inferiority in relation to a superior standard of humanity.

Difference here always means absolute otherness; the group marked as different has no common nature with the normal or neutral ones. The categorical opposition of groups essentializes them, repressing the differences within groups. In this way the definition of difference as exclusion and opposition actually denies difference. This essentializing categorization also denies difference in that its universalizing norms preclude recognizing and affirming a group's specificity in its own terms.

Essentializing difference expresses a fear of specificity, and a fear of making permeable the categorical border between oneself and the others. This fear, I argued in the previous chapter, is not merely intellectual, and does not derive only from the instrumental desire to defend privilege, though that may be a large element. It wells from the depths of the Western subject's sense of identity, especially, but not only, in the subjectivity of privileged groups. The fear may increase, moreover, as a clear essentialism of difference wanes, as belief in a specifically female, Black, or homosexual nature becomes less tenable.

The politics of difference confronts this fear, and aims for an understanding of group difference as indeed ambiguous, relational, shifting, without clear borders that keep people straight—as entailing neither amorphous unity nor pure individuality. By asserting a positive meaning for their own identity, oppressed groups seek to seize the power of naming difference itself, and explode the implicit definition of difference as deviance in relation to a norm, which freezes some groups into a self-enclosed nature. Difference now comes to mean not otherness, exclusive opposition, but specificity, variation, heterogeneity. Difference names relations of similarity and dissimilarity that can be reduced to neither coextensive identity nor nonoverlapping otherness.

The alternative to an essentializing, stigmatizing meaning of difference as opposition is an understanding of difference as specificity, variation. In this logic, as Martha Minow (1985; 1987; 1990) suggests, group differences should be conceived as relational rather than defined by substantive categories and attributes. A relational understanding of difference relativizes the previously universal position of privileged groups, which allows only the oppressed to be marked as different. When group difference appears as a function of comparison between groups, whites are just as specific as Blacks or Latinos, men just as specific as women, able-bodied people just as specific as disabled people. Difference thus emerges not as a description of the attributes of a group, but as a function of the relations between groups and the interaction of groups with institutions (cf. Littleton, 1987).

In this relational understanding, the meaning of difference also becomes contextualized (cf. Scott, 1988). Group differences will be more or less salient depending on the groups compared, the purposes of the comparison, and the point of view of the comparers. Such contextualized understandings of difference undermine essentialist assumptions. For example, in the context of athletics, health care, social service support, and so on, wheelchair-bound people are different from others, but they are not different in many other respects. Traditional treatment of the disabled entailed exclusion and segregation because the differences between the disabled and the able-bodied were conceptualized as extending to all or most capacities.

In general, then, a relational understanding of group difference rejects exclusion. Difference no longer implies that groups lie outside one another. To say that there are differences among groups does not imply that there are not overlapping experiences, or that two groups have nothing in common. The assumption that real differences in affinity, culture, or privilege imply oppositional categorization must be challenged. Different groups are always similar in some respects, and always potentially share some attributes, experiences, and goals.

Such a relational understanding of difference entails revising the meaning of group identity as well. In asserting the positive difference of their experience, culture, and social perspective, social movements of groups that have experienced cultural imperialism deny that they have a common identity, a set of fixed attributes that clearly mark who belongs and who doesn't. Rather, what makes a group a group is a social process of interaction and differentiation in which some people come to have a particular *affinity* (Haraway, 1985) for others. My "affinity group" in a given social situation comprises those people with whom I feel the most comfortable, who are more familiar. Affinity names the manner of sharing assumptions, affective bonding, and networking that recognizably differentiates groups from one another, but not according to some common nature. The salience of a particular person's group affinities may shift according to the social situation or according to changes in her or his life. Membership in a social group is a function not of satisfying some objective criteria, but of a subjective affirmation of affinity with that group, the affirmation of that affinity by other members of the group, and the attribution of membership in that group by persons identifying with other groups. Group identity is constructed from a flowing process in which individuals identify themselves and others in terms of groups, and thus group identity itself flows and shifts with changes in social process.

Groups experiencing cultural imperialism have found themselves objectified and marked with a devalued essence from the outside, by a dominant culture they are excluded from making. The assertion of a positive sense of group difference by these groups is emancipatory because it reclaims the definition of the group by the group, as a creation and construction, rather than a given essence. To be sure, it is difficult to articulate positive elements of group affinity without essentializing them, and these movements do not always succeed in doing so (cf. Sartre, 1948, p. 85; Epstein, 1987). But they are developing a language to describe their similar social situation and relations to one another, and their similar perceptions and perspectives on social life. These movements engage in the project of cultural revolution I recommended in the last chapter, insofar as they take culture as in part a matter of collective choice. While their ideas of women's culture, Afro-American culture, and American Indian culture rely on past cultural expressions, to a significant degree these movements have self-consciously constructed the culture that they claim defines the distinctiveness of their groups.

Contextualizing both the meaning of difference and identity thus allows the acknowledgment of difference within affinity groups. In our complex, plural society, every social group has group differences cutting across it, which are potential sources of wisdom, excitement, conflict, and oppression. Gay men, for example, may be Black, rich, homeless, or old, and these differences produce different identifications and potential conflicts among gay men, as well as affinities with some straight men.

RESPECTING DIFFERENCE IN POLICY

A goal of social justice, I will assume, is social equality. Equality refers not primarily to the distribution of social goods, though distributions are certainly entailed by social equality. It refers primarily to the full participation and inclusion of everyone in a society's major institutions, and the socially supported substantive opportunity for all to develop and exercise their capacities and realize their choices. American society has enacted formal legal equality for members of all groups, with the important and shameful exception of gay men and lesbians. But for many groups social equality is barely on the horizon. Those seeking social equality disagree about whether group-neutral or group-conscious policies best suit that goal, and their disagreement often turns on whether they hold an assimilationist or culturally pluralist ideal. In this section I argue for the justice of group-conscious social policies, and discuss three contexts in which such policies are at issue in the United States today: women's equality in the workplace, language rights of non-English speakers, and American Indian rights. Another category of group-conscious policies, namely, affirmative action, I will discuss in Chapter 7.

The issue of formally equal versus group-conscious policies arises primarily in the context of workplace relations and access to political power. I have already discussed one of the primary reasons for preferring group-conscious to neutral policies: policies that are universally formulated and thus blind to differences of race, culture, gender, age, or disability often perpetuate rather than undermine oppression. Universally formulated standards or norms, for example, according to which all competitors for social positions are evaluated, often presume as the norm capacities, values, and cognitive and behavioral styles typical of dominant groups, thus disadvantaging others. Racist, sexist, homophobic, ageist, and ableist aversions and stereotypes, moreover, continue to devalue or render invisible some people, often disadvantaging them in economic and political interactions. Policies that take notice of the specific situation of oppressed groups can offset these disadvantages.

It might be objected that when facially neutral standards or policies disadvantage a group, the standards or policies should simply be restructured so as to be genuinely neutral, rather than replaced by group-conscious policies. For some situations this may be appropriate, but in many the group-related differences allow no neutral formulation. Language policy might be cited as paradigmatic here, but as I will discuss shortly, some gender issues may be as well.

More important, however, some of the disadvantages that oppressed groups suffer can be remedied in policy only by an affirmative acknowledgment of the group's specificity. The oppressions of cultural imperialism that stereotype a group and simultaneously render its own experience invisible can be remedied only by explicit attention to and expression of that group's specificity. For example, removing oppressive stereotypes of Blacks, Latinos, Indians, Arabs, and Asians and portraying them in the same roles as whites will not eliminate racism from television programming. Positive and interesting portrayals of people of color in situations and ways of life that derive from their own self-perceptions are also necessary, as well as a great deal more positive presence of all these groups than currently exists.

These considerations produce a second reason for the justice of group-conscious policies, in addition to their function in counteracting oppression and disadvantage. Group-conscious policies are sometimes necessary in order to affirm the solidarity of groups, to allow them to affirm their group affinities without suffering disadvantage in the wider society.

Some group-conscious policies are consistent with an assimilationist ideal in which group difference has no social significance, as long as such policies are understood as means to that end, and thus as temporary divergences from group-neutral norms. Many people look upon affirmative action policies in this way, and as I shall discuss shortly, people typically understand bilingual education in this way. A culturally pluralist democratic ideal, however, supports group-conscious policies not only as means to the end of equality, but also as intrinsic to the ideal of social equality itself. Groups cannot be socially equal unless their specific experience, culture, and social contributions are publicly affirmed and recognized.

The dilemma of difference exposes the risks involved both in attending to and in ignoring differences. The danger in affirming difference is that the implementation of group-conscious policies will reinstate stigma and exclusion. In the past, group-conscious policies were used to separate those defined as different and exclude them from access to the rights and privileges enjoyed by dominant groups. A crucial principle of democratic cultural pluralism, then, is that group-specific rights and policies should stand together with general civic and political rights of participation and inclusion. Group-conscious policies cannot be used to justify exclusion of or discrimination against members of a group in the exercise of general political and civil rights. A democratic cultural pluralism thus requires a dual system of rights: a general system of rights which are the same for all, and a more specific system of group-conscious policies and rights (cf. Wolgast, 1980, chap. 2) In the words of Kenneth Karst:

When the promise of equal citizenship is fulfilled, the paths to belonging are opened in two directions for members of cultural minorities. As full members of the larger society, they have the option to participate to whatever degree they choose. They also may look inward, seeking solidarity within their cultural group, without being penalized for that choice. (Karst, 1986, p. 337)

If "cultural minority" is interpreted to mean any group subject to cultural imperialism, then this statement applies to women, old people, disabled people, gay men and lesbians, and working-class people as much as it applies to ethnic or national groups. I will now briefly consider three cases in which group-specific policies are necessary to support social equality: women, Latinos, and American Indians.

(1) Are women's interests best promoted through gender-neutral or group-conscious rules and policies? This question has been fiercely debated by feminists in recent years. The resulting literature raises crucial questions about dominant models of law and policy that take equality to mean sameness, and offers some subtle analyses of the meaning of equality that do not assume identity (see Vogel, 1990). Most of this discussion has focused on the question of pregnancy and childbirth rights in the workplace.

Advocates of an equal treatment approach to pregnancy argue that women's interests are best served by vigorously pressing for the inclusion of pregnancy leaves and benefits within gender-neutral leave and benefit policies relevant to any physical condition that renders men or women unable to work. The history of protective legislation shows that women cannot trust employers and courts not to use special classification as an excuse for excluding and disadvantaging women, and we are best protected from such exclusion by neutral policies (Williams, 1983). Even such proponents of equal treatment, however, agree that gender-neutral policies that take male lives as the norm will disadvantage women. The answer, according to Nadine Taub and Wendy Williams, is a model of equality in the workplace that recognizes and accommodates the specific needs of all workers; such a model requires significant restructuring of most workplace policy (Taub and Williams, 1986).

In my view an equal treatment approach to pregnancy and childbirth is inadequate because it either implies that women do not have any right to leave and job security when having babies, or assimilates such guarantees under the supposedly gender-neutral category of "disability." Such assimilation is unacceptable because pregnancy and childbirth are usually normal conditions of normal women, because pregnancy and childbirth themselves count as socially necessary work, and because they have unique and variable characteristics and needs (Scales, 1981; Littleton, 1987). Assimilating pregnancy and childbirth to disability tends to stigmatize these processes as "unhealthy." It suggests, moreover, that the primary or only reason that a woman has a right to leave and job security is that she is physically unable to work at her job, or that doing so would be more difficult than when she is not pregnant and recovering from childbirth. While these are important considerations, another reason is that she ought to have the time to establish breast-feeding and develop a relationship and routine with her child, if she chooses. At issue is more than eliminating the disadvantage women suffer because of male models of uninterrupted work. It is also a question of establishing and confirming positive public recognition of the social contribution of childbearing. Such recognition can and should be given without either reducing women to childbearers or suggesting that all women ought to bear children and are lacking if they do not.

Feminists who depart from a gender-neutral model of women's rights generally restrict this departure to the biological situation of childbirth. Most demand that parental leave from a job, for example, should be gender-neutral, in order not to perpetuate the connection of women with the care of children, and in order not to penalize those men who choose more than average childrearing responsibilities. I myself agree with gender-neutral policy on this issue.

Restricting the issue of group-conscious policies for women to childbirth, however, avoids some of the hardest questions involved in promoting women's equality in the workplace. Women suffer workplace disadvantage not only or even primarily because of their birthing capacity, but because their gender socialization and identity orients the desires, temperaments, and capacities of many women toward certain activities and away from others, because many men regard women in inappropriately sexual terms, and because women's clothes, comportment, voices, and so on sometimes disrupt the disembodied ideal of masculinist bureaucracy. Differences between women and men are not only biological, but also socially gendered. Such gender differences are multiple, variable, and do not reduce men and women to segregating essences. Perhaps such differences should not exist, but without doubt they do now. Ignoring these differences sometimes disadvantages women in public settings where masculine norms and styles predominate.

In a model she calls "equality as acceptance," Christine Littleton argues for a gender-conscious approach to policy directed at rendering femininely gendered cultural attributes costless for women. This model begins with the assumption of structured social gender differences—for example, gender-dominated occupational categories, woman-dominated childrearing and other family member caretaking, and gender differences in the sports people wish to pursue. None of these are essences; it is not as though all men or all women follow the gendered patterns, but the patterns are identifiable and apply broadly to many people's lives. Littleton's model of equality as acceptance supports policies which not only will not disadvantage women who engage in traditionally feminine activity or behavior, but which value the feminine as much as the masculine:

The focus of equality as acceptance, therefore, is not on the question of whether *women* are different, but rather on the question of how the social fact of gender asymmetry can be dealt with so as to create some symmetry in the lived-out experience of all members of the community. I do not think it matters so much whether differences are "natural" or not; they are built into our structures and selves in either event. As social facts, differences are created by the interaction of person with person or person with institution; they inhere in the relationship, not in the person. On this view, the function of equality is to make gender differences, perceived or actual, costless relative to each other, so that anyone may follow a male, female, or androgynous lifestyle according to their natural inclination or choice without being punished for following a female lifestyle or rewarded for following a male one. (Littleton, 1987, p. 1297)

The acceptance model of equality, then, publicly acknowledges culturally based gender differences, and takes steps to ensure that these differences do not disadvantage. Though Littleton does not emphasize it, this model implies, first, that gender differences must not be used implicitly or explicitly as a basis for excluding persons from institutions, positions, or opportunities. That is, general rights to equal opportunity, as well as other civil and political rights, must obtain. Over and above this, equality as acceptance explicitly revalues femininely coded activity and behavior as the equal of masculine-coded activity.

Comparable worth policies are a widely discussed strategy for revaluing the culturally feminine. Schemes of equal pay for work of comparable worth require that predominantly male and predominantly female jobs have similar wage structures if they involve similar degrees of skill, difficulty, stress, and so on. The problem in implementing these policies, of course, lies in designing methods of comparing different jobs. Most schemes of comparison still choose to minimize sex differences by using supposedly gender-neutral criteria, such as educational attainment, speed of work, whether the work involves manipulation of symbols, pleasantness of work conditions, decisionmaking ability, and so on. Some writers have suggested, however, that standard classifications of job traits may be systematically biased to keep specific kinds of tasks involved in many female-dominated occupations hidden (Beatty and Beatty, 1981; Treiman and Hartman, 1981, p. 81). Many female-dominated occupations involve gender-specific kinds of labor—such as nurturing, smoothing over social relations, or the exhibition of sexuality—which most task observation ignores (Alexander, 1987). A fair assessment of the skills and complexity of many female-dominated jobs may therefore involve paying explicit attention to gender differences rather than applying gender-blind categories of comparison (cf. Littleton, 1987, p. 1312).

Littleton offers sports as another area of revaluation. An "equality as acceptance" approach, she suggests, would support an equal division of resources between male and female programs rather than divide up the available sports budget per capita (Littleton, 1987, p. 1313). If the disparities in numbers of people involved were too great, I do not think this proposal would be fair, but I agree with the general principle Littleton is aiming at. Women who wish to participate in athletic activities should not be disadvantaged because there are not more women who currently wish to; they should have as many well-paid coaches, for example, as do men, their locker room facilities should be as good, and they should have access to all the equipment they need to excel. More importantly, femininely stereotyped sports, such as synchronized swimming or field hockey, should receive a level of support comparable to more masculine sports like football or baseball.

(2) In November 1986 the majority of voters in California supported a referendum declaring English the official language of that state. The ramifications of this policy are not clear, but it means at least that state institutions have no obligation to print ballots and other government literature or provide services in any language other than English. The California success has spurred a national movement to declare English the official language of the United States, as well as many additional local movements, especially in regions with fast-growing populations of people whose first language is not English. In winter 1989, for example, an English-only proposal went before the legislature of Suffolk County, Long Island, that even some English-first advocates thought was too strong. Not only would it have made English the official language of Suffolk County, but it would have forbidden public service providers from speaking to clients in any language other than English (Schmitt, 1989).

Many English-only advocates justify their position as another of many measures that should be taken to cut the costs of government. But the movement's primary appeal is to a normative ideal of the unity of the polity. As a nation, the United States was founded by English speakers; non-English speakers are not "real" Americans, no matter how many generations they can trace on American soil. A polity cannot sustain itself without significant commonality and mutual identification among its citizens, this argument goes, and a common language is one of the most important of such unifying forces. Linguistic and cultural pluralism leads to conflict, divisiveness, factionalism, and ultimately disintegration. Giving public preference to English supports this unity and encourages non-English speakers to assimilate more quickly.

There are at least three arguments against this appeal to the unity of a single harmonious polity. First, it is simply unrealistic. From its beginnings the United States has always harbored sizeable linguistic and cultural minorities. Its history of imperialism and annexation and its immigration policy have resulted in more. In the past twenty-five years U.S. military and foreign policy has led to a huge influx of Latin Americans and Asians. Some estimate, moreover, that by the year 2000 Hispanic and Asian populations in the United States will have increased by 84 and 103 percent respectively (Sears and Huddy, 1987). Many individuals belonging to cultural minorities choose to assimilate, as do some whole groups. But many do not. Even without official support for their doing so and with considerable pressures against it, many groups have retained distinct linguistic and cultural identities, even some whose members have lived in the United States for several generations. Spanish speakers may be the most salient here because their relative numbers are large, and because their connections with Puerto Rico, Mexico, or other parts of Latin America remain strong. Given the determination of many linguistic and cultural minorities to maintain a specific identity even as they claim rights to the full benefits of American citizenship, a determination which seems to be increasing, the desire of the English-only movement to create unity through enforced language policy is simply silly.

Second, as I have already argued at several points, this norm of the homogeneous public is oppressive. Not only does it put unassimilated persons and groups at a severe disadvantage in the competition for scarce positions and resources, but it requires that persons transform their sense of identity in order to assimilate. Self-annihilation is an unreasonable and unjust requirement of citizenship. The fiction, poetry, and songs of American cultural minorities brim over with the pain and loss such demands inflict, documenting how thoroughly assimilationist values violate basic respect for persons.

Thus, third, the normative ideal of the homogeneous public does not succeed in its stated aim of creating a harmonious nation. In group-differentiated societies conflict, factionalism, divisiveness, civil warfare, do often occur between groups. The primary cause of such conflict, however, is not group difference per se, but rather the relations of domination and oppression between groups that produce resentment, hostility, and resistance among the oppressed. Placing a normative value on homogeneity only exacerbates division and conflict, because it gives members of the dominant groups reason to adopt a stance of self-righteous intractability.

I argued in Chapter 4 that a just polity must embrace the ideal of a heterogeneous public. Group differences of gender, age, and sexuality should not be ignored, but publicly acknowledged and accepted. Even more so should group differences of nation or ethnicity be accepted. In the twentieth century the ideal state is composed of a plurality of nations or cultural groups, with a degree of self-determination and autonomy compatible with federated equal rights and obligations of citizenship. Many states of the world embrace this ideal, though they often realize it only very imperfectly (see Ortiz, 1984, pt. 2). English-only advocates often look with fear at the large and rapidly growing cultural minorities in the United States, especially the Spanish-speaking minority, and argue that only enforcing the primacy of English can prevent us from becoming a culturally plural society like Canada. Such arguments stubbornly refuse to see that we already are.

The difference between an assimilationist and a culturally pluralist ideal becomes particularly salient in educational policy. Bilingual education is highly controversial in the United States today, partly because of the different cultural meanings given to it. In 1974 the Supreme Court ruled that the state has an obligation to remedy the English-language deficiency of its students so they will have equal opportunity to learn all subjects; but the Court did not specify how this should be done. The Bilingual Education Act, passed in 1978 and amended several times, sets aside federal funds for use by school systems to develop bilingual education programs (see Minow, 1985; Kleven, 1989). Even so, in 1980, 77 percent of Hispanic children in the United States received no form of special programming corresponding to their linguistic needs (Bastian, 1986, p. 46). In 1986 in Texas, 80 percent of school districts were found out of compliance with a state-mandated bilingual education program (Canter, 1987).

There are several different models of language support programs. Some, like English as a Second Language, provide no instruction in the student's native language, and are often not taught by persons who can speak the student's language. Others, called immersion programs, involve English-language instruction primarily, but are taught by bilingual instructors whom the student can question in his or her native language. Transitional bilingual education programs involve genuinely bilingual instruction, with the proportions of English and native language changing as the student progresses. Transitional programs instruct students in such subjects as math, science and history in their native language at the same time that they develop English-language skills; they aim to increase the amount of time of instruction in English.

All these programs are assimilationist in intent. They seek to increase English proficiency to the point where native-language instruction is unnecessary; none has the goal of maintaining and developing proficiency in the native language. The vast majority of programs for students with limited English proficiency in the United States take one of these forms. The use of transitional bilingual programs instead of ESL or immersion programs is hotly debated. The majority of Americans support special language programs for students with limited English, in order to help them learn English; but the more programs instruct in a native language, especially when they instruct in subjects like math or science, the more they are considered by English speakers to be unfair coddling and a waste of taxpayer dollars (Sears and Huddy, 1987). Transitional bilingual educational programs, on the other hand, are usually preferred by linguistic minorities.

Another model of bilingual education is rarely practiced in the United States, and is hardly on the public agenda: bilingual-bicultural maintenance programs. These aim to reinforce knowledge of the students' native language and culture, at the same time that they train them to be proficient in the dominant language, English. Few advocates of cultural pluralism and group autonomy in the United States would deny that proficiency in English is a necessary condition for full participation in American society. The issue is only whether linguistic minorities are recognized as full participants in their specificity, with social support for the maintenance of their language and culture. Only bilingual-bicultural maintenance programs can both ensure the possibility of the full inclusion and participation of members of linguistic minorities in all society's institutions and at the same time preserve and affirm their group-specific identity (cf. Nickel, 1987, p. 119).

(3) American Indians are the most invisible oppressed group in the United States. Numbering just over one million, they are too small a proportion of most regional populations to organize influential pressure groups or threaten major disruptions of the lives of white society. Federal and state policy often can safely ignore Indian interests and desires. Many Indians live on reservations, where non-Indians have little contact with them. Even in cities Indians often form their own support systems and networks, mingling little with non-Indians (Cornell, 1988, pp. 132–37). Whether on or off the reservation, Indians suffer the most serious marginalization and deprivation of any social group; by every measure—income, unemployment rates, infant mortality, and so on—Indians are the poorest Americans.

At the same time, Indians are the most legally differentiated people in the United States, the only group granted formally special status and rights by the federal government. Indians represent the *arche*-difference that from the beginning subverts the claim to origin, to a New World, that founds the myth of America as the home of English-speaking farmers, traders, and inventors. Agents of the U.S. government have poisoned, burned, looted, tricked, relocated, and confined Indians many times over, in persistently genocidal policies, attempting to purge this difference within. Legal history and the string of federal treaties, however, also testify to a begrudging acknowledgment of the Indian peoples as independent political entities with which the government must negotiate. Until the twentieth century the special legal status of Indians was conceptualized almost entirely as a relation of wardship and dependence between an inferior savage people and a superior civilized sovereign, and the shadow of this conceptualization darkens even recent legal decisions (Williams, 1987). As with women, Blacks, and the feebleminded, Indian difference was codified in normalizing law as an inferior infantile nature that justified less than full citizenship.

At the turn of the century policymakers assumed that an end to this position of tutelage and wardship implied assimilation to the dominant culture. Thus the land reallocation policies of the late 1800s were intended to encourage Indians to value private property and the virtues of yeoman husbandry. In the 1920s, when Congress voted to grant Indians full U.S. citizenship, federal policy forced assimilation by forbidding Indian children to speak their native language in the boarding schools to which they were transported, sometimes thousands of miles from home. During the same period Indians were prohibited from practicing many of their traditional religious rites.

In the 1930s the Indian Reorganization Act eliminated and reversed many of these policies, creating the contemporary system of federally recognized tribal governments. But in the 1950s the pendulum swung back with the effort by Congress to terminate the federal relationship with tribes, withdrawing all recognition of Indians as distinct peoples, and once again attempting to force Indians to assimilate into white society. This brutal seesaw history of U.S.-Indian relations caused Indians to change and adapt their values, practices, and institutions and even their identities. Many distinct Indian identities have disappeared, as Indian groups merged or reorganized their relations with one another under the oppression of white policies. Throughout this history, however, assimilation was not a live option for the Indians. While many individuals may have left their groups and successfully integrated into the dominant white culture, Indians as groups persistently preserved their differences from white society against the fiercest opposition. Many Indians today find much fault wih the present organization of the tribes, the definition of their role, and their legal relationship with the U.S. government, but few would propose the elimination of the tribal system that formally recognizes specific independently defined Indian groups and guarantees them specific rights in defining and running tribal affairs.

The case of American Indians especially exemplifies the arguments of this chapter because it is perhaps clearest here that justice toward groups requires special rights, and that an assimilationist ideal amounts to genocide. Such special rights, however, should not justify exclusion from full participation in the American dream of liberty, equal opportunity, and the like. The justice of recognizing both specific needs of a group and rights of full participation and inclusion in the polity has clear precedence in U.S.-Indian law. Indians are the only group to have what almost amounts to a dual citizenship: as members of a tribe they have specific political, legal, and collective rights, and as U.S. citizens they have all the civil and political rights of other citizens (Deloria and Lytle, 1984, pp. 3–4). Recognized Indian tribes have specific rights to jurisdictional and territorial sovereignty, and many specific religious, cultural, and gaming rights (see Pevar, 1983).

Many Indians believe this system of particular rights remains too much at the discretion of the federal government, and some have taken their claims for greater self-determination to international judicial bodies (Ortiz, 1984, pp. 32–46). Justice in the form of unambiguous recognition of American Indian groups as full and equal members of American society requires, in my view, that the U.S. government relinquish the absolute power to alter or eliminate Indian rights.

Even in the absence of full justice the case of Indians provides an important example of the combination of general rights and particular rights which, I have argued, is necessary for the equality of many oppressed or disadvantaged groups. The system of tribal rights, and their relation to general rights, is certainly complex, and there is often disagreement about the meaning and implications of these rights. Many Indians believe, moreover, that their rights, especially territorial rights to make decisions about land, water, and resources, are not sufficiently recognized and enforced because economic interests profit from ignoring them. I do not wish to argue that this system of particular rights, or the bureaucratic form it takes, should extend to other oppressed or disadvantaged social groups. The specificity of each group requires a specific set of rights for each, and for some a more comprehensive system than for others. The case of American Indians, however, illustrates the fact that there is a precedent for a system of particular rights that a group wants for reasons of justice, namely, because they enforce the group's autonomy and protect its interests as an oppressed minority.

THE HETEROGENEOUS PUBLIC AND GROUP REPRESENTATION

I have argued that participatory democracy is an element and condition of social justice. Contemporary participatory democratic theory, however, inherits from republicanism a commitment to a unified public that in practice tends to exclude or silence some groups. Where some groups are materially privileged and exercise cultural imperialism, formally democratic processes often elevate the particular experiences and perspectives of the privileged groups, silencing or denigrating those of oppressed groups.

In her study of the functioning of a New England town meeting government, for example, Jane Mansbridge demonstrates that women, Blacks, working-class people, and poor people tend to participate less and have their interests represented less than whites, middle-class professionals, and men. White middle-class men assume authority more than others, and they are more practiced at speaking persuasively; mothers and old people find it more difficult than others to get to meetings (Mansbridge, 1980, chap. 9). In Chapter 3 I cited Amy Gutmann's example of how increasing democracy in some school systems led to increased segregation because the more numerous, materially privileged, and articulate whites were able to promote their perceived interests against Blacks' just demand for equal treatment in an integrated system (Gutmann, 1980, pp. 191–202).

In these and similar cases, the group differences of privilege and oppression that exist in society have an effect on the public, even though the public claims to be blind to difference. Traditionally political theory and practice have responded to evidence of such bias by attempting yet once again to institute a genuinely universal public. Such a pure perspective that transcends the particularity of social position and consequent partial vision, I argued in Chapter 4, is impossible. If the unified public does not transcend group differences and often allows the perspective and interests of privileged groups to dominate, then a democratic public can counteract this bias only by acknowledging and giving voice to the group differences within it.

I assert, then, the following principle: a democratic public should provide mechanisms for the effective recognition and representation of the distinct voices and perspectives of those of its constituent groups that are oppressed or disadvantaged. Such group representation implies institutional mechanisms and public resources supporting (1) self-organization of group members so that they achieve collective empowerment and a reflective understanding of their collective experience and interests in the context of the society; (2) group analysis and group generation of policy proposals in institutionalized contexts where decisionmakers are obliged to show that their deliberations have taken group perspectives into consideration; and (3) group veto power regarding specific policies that affect a group directly, such as reproductive rights policy for women, or land use policy for Indian reservations.

Specific representation for oppressed groups in the decisionmaking procedures of a democratic public promotes justice better than a homogeneous public in several ways, both procedural and substantial (cf. Beitz,

1988, pp. 168–69). First, it better assures procedural fairness in setting the public agenda and hearing opinions about its items. Social and economic privilege means, among other things, that the groups which have it behave as though they have a right to speak and be heard, that others treat them as though they have that right, and that they have the material, personal, and organizational resources that enable them to speak and be heard. As a result, policy issues are often defined by the assumptions and priorities of the privileged. Specific representation for oppressed groups interrupts this process, because it gives voice to the assumptions and priorities of other groups.

Second, because it assures a voice for the oppressed as well as the privileged, group representation better assures that all needs and interests in the public will be recognized in democratic deliberations. The privileged usually are not inclined to protect or advance the interests of the oppressed, partly because their social position prevents them from understanding those interests, and partly because to some degree their privilege depends on the continued oppression of others. While different groups may share many needs, moreover, their difference usually entails some special needs which the individual groups themselves can best express. If we consider just democratic decisionmaking as a politics of need interpretation, as I have already suggested, then democratic institutions should facilitate the public expression of the needs of those who tend to be socially marginalized or silenced by cultural imperialism. Group representation in the public facilitates such expression.

In the previous section I argued for the assertion of a positive sense of difference by oppressed groups, and for a principle of special rights for those groups. I discussed there the legitimate fears of many in emancipatory social movements that abandoning group-blind policies and adopting group-specific ones will restigmatize the groups and justify new exclusions. Group representation can help protect against such a consequence. If oppressed and disadvantaged groups can self-organize in the public and have a specific voice to present their interpretation of the meaning of and reasons for group-differentiated policies, then such policies are more likely to work for than against them.

Group representation, third, encourages the expression of individual and group needs and interests in terms that appeal to justice, that transform an "I want" into an "I am entitled to," in Hannah Pitkin's words. In Chapter 4 I argued that publicity itself encourages this transformation because a condition of the public is that people call one another to account. Group representation adds to such accountability because it serves as an antidote to self-deceiving self-interest masked as an impartial or general interest. Unless confronted with different perspectives on social relations and events, different values and language, most people tend to assert their perspective as universal. When social privilege allows some group perspectives to dominate a public while others are silent, such universalizing of the particular will be reaffirmed by many others. Thus the test of whether a claim upon the public is just or merely an expression of self-interest is best made when those making it must confront the opinion of others who have explicitly different, though not necessarily conflicting, experiences, priorities, and needs (cf. Sunstein, 1988, p. 1588). As a person of social privilege, I am more likely to go outside myself and have regard for social justice when I must listen to the voice of those my privilege otherwise tends to silence.

Finally, group representation promotes just outcomes because it maximizes the social knowledge expressed in discussion, and thus furthers practical wisdom. Group differences are manifest not only in different needs, interests, and goals, but also in different social locations and experiences. People in different groups often know about somewhat different institutions, events, practices, and social relations, and often have differing perceptions of the same institutions, relations, or events. For this reason members of some groups are sometimes in a better position than members of others to understand and anticipate the probable consequences of implementing particular social policies. A public that makes use of all such social knowledge in its differentiated plurality is most likely to make just and wise decisions.

I should allay several possible misunderstandings of what this principle of group representation means and implies. First, the principle calls for specific representation of social groups, not interest groups or ideological groups. By an interest group I mean any aggregate or association of persons who seek a particular goal, or desire the same policy, or are similarly situated with respect to some social effect—for example, they are all recipients of acid rain caused by Ohio smokestacks. Social groups usually share some interests, but shared interests are not sufficient to constitute a social group. A social group is a collective of people who have affinity with one another because of a set of practices or way of life; they differentiate themselves from or are differentiated by at least one other group according to these cultural forms.

By an ideological group I mean a collective of persons with shared political beliefs. Nazis, socialists, feminists, Christian Democrats, and antiabortionists are ideological groups. The situation of social groups may foster the formation of ideological groups, and under some circumstances an ideological group may become a social group. Shared political or moral beliefs, even when they are deeply and passionately held, however, do not themselves constitute a social group.

A democratic polity should permit the expression of all interests and opinions, but this does not imply specific representation for any of them.

A democratic public may wish to provide representation for certain kinds of interests or political orientations; most parliamentary systems, for example, give proportional representation to political parties according to the number of votes they poll. The principle of group representation that I am arguing for here, however, refers only to social groups.

Second, it is important to remember that the principle calls for specific representation only of oppressed or disadvantaged groups. Privileged groups are already represented, in the sense that their voice, experience, values, and priorities are already heard and acted upon. The faces of oppression explicated in Chapter 2 provide at least beginning criteria for determining whether a group is oppressed and therefore deserves representation. Once we are clear that the principle of group representation refers only to oppressed social groups, then the fear of an unworkable proliferation of group representation should dissipate.

Third, while I certainly intend this principle to apply to representative bodies in government institutions, its application is by no means restricted to that sphere. In earlier chapters I have argued that social justice requires a far wider institutionalization of democracy than currently obtains in American society. Persons should have the right to participate in making the rules and policies of any institution with authority over their actions. The principle of group representation applies to all such democratized publics. It should apply, for example, to decisionmaking bodies formed by oppressed groups that aim to develop policy proposals for a heterogeneous public. Oppressed groups within these groups should have specific representation in such autonomous forums. The Black caucus should give specific representation to women, for example, and the women's caucus to Blacks.

This principle of group representation, finally, does not necessarily imply proportional representation, in the manner of some recent discussions of group representation (see Bell, 1987, chap. 3; Beitz, 1988, p. 163). Insofar as it relies on the principle of "one person one vote," proportional representation retains the assumption that it is primarily individuals who must be represented in decisionmaking bodies. Certainly they must, and various forms of proportional representation, including proportional representation of groups or parties, may sometimes be an important vehicle for representing individuals equally. With the principle I argue for here, however, I am concerned with the representation of group experience, perspectives, and interests. Proportional representation of group members may sometimes be too little or too much to accomplish that aim. A system of proportional group representation in state and federal government in the United States might result in no seats for American Indians, for example. Given the specific circumstances and deep oppression of Indians as a group, however, the principle would certainly require that they have a specific voice. Allocating strictly half of all places to women, on the other hand, might be more than is necessary to give women's perspectives an empowered voice, and might make it more difficult for other groups to be represented.

A principle of group representation has been implicitly and sometimes explicitly asserted in several contemporary social movements struggling against oppression and domination. In response to the anger and criticism that women, Blacks, gays and lesbians, American Indians, and others have leveled against traditionally unitary radical groups and labor unions, many of them have implemented some form of group representation in their decisionmaking bodies. Some political organizations, unions, and feminist groups have formal caucuses for Blacks, Latinos, women, gay men and lesbians, disabled people, and old people, whose perspectives might be silenced without explicit representation. Frequently these organizations have procedures for giving the caucuses a voice in organization-wide discussion and caucus representation in decisionmaking. Some organizations also require representation of members of disadvantaged groups in leadership bodies.

At the height of efforts to occupy nuclear power construction sites, for example, many anti–nuclear power actions and organizations responded to criticisms by feminists or people of color that the movement was dominated by straight white men. Social group affinity groups formed and were generally encouraged, providing solidarity and representation to formerly invisible groups. The National Women's Studies Association, to take another example, has a complex and effective system of representation for group caucuses in its decisionmaking bodies.

The idea of a Rainbow Coalition expressed a heterogeneous public with forms of group representation. The traditional coalition corresponded to the idea of a unified public that transcends particular differences of experience and concerns. In traditional coalitions diverse groups work together for specific ends which they agree interest or affect them all in a similar way, and they generally agree that the differences of perspective, interests, or opinion among them will not surface in the public statements and actions of the coalition. This form ideally suits welfare state interest-group politics. In a Rainbow Coalition, by contrast, each of the constituent groups affirms the presence of the others as well as the specificity of their experience and perspective on social issues (Collins, 1986). In the Rainbow public Blacks do not simply tolerate the participation of gays, labor activists do not grudgingly work alongside peace movement veterans, and none of these paternalistically concede to feminist participation. Ideally, a Rainbow Coalition affirms the presence and supports the claims of each of the oppressed groups or political movements constituting it, and arrives at a political program not by voicing some "principles of unity" that hide difference, but rather by allowing each constituency to analyze economic and social issues from the perspective of its experience. This implies that each group maintains significant autonomy, and requires provision for group representation. Unfortunately, the promise of the Jesse Jackson campaign to launch a viable grassroots organization expressing these Rainbow Coalition ideals has not been fulfilled.

A principle of representation for oppressed or disadvantaged groups has been implemented most frequently in organizations and movements that challenge politics as usual in welfare capitalist society. Some more mainstream organizations, however, also have implemented this principle in some form. The National Democratic Party has had rules requiring representation of women and people of color as delegates, and many state Democratic parties have had similar rules. Many nonprofit agencies call for representation of specific groups, such as women, Blacks, Latinos, and disabled people, on their boards of directors. In a program that some of them call "valuing difference," some corporations have instituted limited representation of oppressed social groups in corporate discussions. One can imagine such a principle of group representation extended to other political contexts. Social justice would be enhanced in many American cities, for example, if a citywide school committee formally and explicitly represented Blacks, Hispanics, women, gay men and lesbians, poor and working-class people, disabled people, and students.

Some might object that implementing a principle of group representation in governing bodies would exacerbate conflict and divisiveness in public life, rendering decisions even more difficult to reach. Especially if groups have veto power over policies that fundamentally and uniquely affect members of their group, it seems likely, it might be claimed, that decisionmaking would be stalled. This objection presupposes that group differences imply essential conflicts of interest. But this is not so; groups may have differing perspectives on issues, but these are often compatible and enrich everyone's understanding when they are expressed. To the extent that group differences produce or reflect conflict, moreover, group representation would not necessarily increase such conflict and might decrease it. If their differences bring groups into conflict, a just society should bring such differences into the open for discussion. Insofar as structured relations of privilege and oppression are the source of the conflict, moreover, group representation can change those relations by equalizing the ability of groups to speak and be heard. Thus group representation should mitigate, though not eliminate, certain kinds of conflict. If, finally, the alternative to stalled decisionmaking is a unified public that makes decisions ostensibly embodying the general interest which systematically ignore, suppress, or conflict with the interests of particular groups, then stalled decisionmaking may sometimes be just.

A second objection might be that the implementation of this principle can never get started. For to implement it a public must be constituted to decide which groups, if any, deserve specific representation in decision-making procedures. What principles will guide the composition of such a "constitutional convention'? Who shall decide what groups should receive representation, and by what procedures shall this decision be made? If oppressed groups are not represented at this founding convention, then how will their representation be ensured at all? And if they are represented, then why is implementation of the principle necessary?

These questions pose a paradox of political origins which is not specific to this proposal, and which no philosophical argument can resolve. No program or set of principles can found a politics, because politics does not have a beginning, an original position. It is always a process in which we are already engaged. Normative principles such as those I have proposed in this chapter can serve as proposals in this ongoing political discussion, and means of envisioning alternative institutional forms, but they cannot found a polity. In actual political situations application of any normative principle will be rough and ready, and always subject to challenge and revision. If democratic publics in American society accept this principle of group representation, as I have suggested a few have, they also are likely to name candidates for groups within them that deserve specific representation. Such an opening might sensitize the public to the need for other groups to be represented. But if it does not, these groups will have to petition with arguments that may or may not be persuasive. I see no practical way out of this problem of origin, but that does not stand as a reason to reject this or any other normative principle.

One might ask how the idea of a heterogeneous public which encourages self-organization of groups and group representation in decisionmaking differs from the interest-group pluralism I criticized in Chapter 3. Interest-group pluralism, I suggest, operates precisely to forestall the emergence of public discussion and decisionmaking. Each interest group promotes its own specific interest as thoroughly and forcefully as it can, and need not consider the other interests competing in the political marketplace except strategically, as potential allies or adversaries in its own pursuit. The rules of interest-group pluralism do not require justifying one's interest as right, or compatible with social justice. A heterogeneous public, however, is a *public*, where participants discuss together the issues before them and come to a decision according to principles of justice. Group representation, I have argued, nurtures such publicity by calling for claimants to justify their demands before others who explicitly stand in different social locations.

Implementing principles of group representation in national and local politics in the United States, or in restructured democratic publics within particular institutions such as factories, offices, universities, churches, and social service agencies, would obviously require creative thinking and flexibility. There are no models to follow. European models of consociational democratic institutions, for example, cannot be removed from the contexts in which they have evolved, and even within them it is not clear that they constitute models of participatory democracy. Reports of experiments with institutionalized self-organization among women, indigenous peoples, workers, peasants, and students in contemporary Nicaragua offer an example closer to the conception I am advocating (Ruchwarger, 1987).

Social justice entails democracy. Persons should be involved in collective discussion and decisionmaking in all the settings that depend on their commitment, action, and obedience to rules—workplaces, schools, neighborhoods, and so on. When such institutions privilege some groups over others, actual democracy requires group representation for the disadvantaged. Not only do just procedures require group representation in order to ensure that oppressed or disadvantaged groups have a voice, but such representation is also the best means to promote just outcomes of the deliberative process.

I have argued that the ideal of the just society as eliminating group differences is both unrealistic and undesirable. Instead justice in a group-differentiated society demands social equality of groups, and mutual recognition and affirmation of group differences. Attending to group-specific needs and providing for group representation both promotes that social equality and provides the recognition that undermines cultural imperialism.

CHAPTER 7

Affirmative Action and the Myth of Merit

> We have no words to speak about our oppression, our dis-
> tress, our bitterness, and our revolt against the exhaustion,
> the stupidity, the monotony, the lack of meaning of our
> work and of our life, against the contempt in which our work
> is held; against the despotic hierarchy of the factory; against
> a society in which we remain the underdogs and in which
> goods and enjoyments that are considered normal by other
> classes are denied to us and are parceled out to us only re-
> luctantly, as though we were asking for a privilege. We have
> no words to say what it is and how it feels to be workers, to
> be held in suspicion, to be ordered around by people who
> have more and who pretend to know more and who compel
> us to work according to rules *they* set and for purposes that
> are *theirs*, not ours. And we have no words to say all this
> because the ruling class has monopolized not only the power
> of decision-making and of material wealth; they have also
> monopolized culture and language.
>
> —André Gorz

INJUSTICE, I have argued, should be defined primarily in terms of the
concepts of oppression and domination, rather than distribution. Racism
and sexism are major forms of oppression in our society. Philosophical
discussion of racial and gender injustice tends to be largely restricted to
issues of equal opportunity, with a major focus on the question of whether
affirmative action programs that give preference to women or people of
color in order to equalize their opportunities are just.

In this chapter I suggest that affirmative action programs challenge
principles of liberal equality more directly than many proponents are willing to admit, and that making this challenge explicit strengthens the case
for these programs. In particular, affirmative action challenges the primacy of a principle of nondiscrimination and the conviction that persons
should be treated only as individuals and not as members of groups. The
equal opportunity discussion of which the affirmative action debate is a
part, however, represents a very narrow mode of thinking about racial and
gender justice. I argue that affirmative action debate is an instance of the

application of the distributive paradigm of justice. It defines racial and gender justice in terms of the distribution of privileged positions among groups, and fails to bring into question issues of institutional organization and decisionmaking power.

The bulk of this chapter focuses on and criticizes two assumptions about institutional organization that often underlie discussions of equal opportunity, assumptions whose justice is not questioned. Philosophers and policymakers usually assume as given, and thus as not unjust, a hierarchical division of labor with scarce positions of high income, power, and prestige at the top, and less privileged positions at the bottom. They also assume that these positions should be distributed according to merit, by measuring the individual technical competence of persons and awarding the most competitive positions to those judged most qualified according to impartial measures of such competence. I question both these assumptions.

For the merit principle to apply it must be possible to identify, measure, compare, and rank individual performance of job-related tasks using criteria that are normatively and culturally neutral. For most jobs, however, this is not possible, and most criteria of evaluation used in our society, including educational credentials and standardized testing, have normative and cultural content. Since impartial, value-neutral, scientific measures of merit do not exist, I argue that a major issue of justice must be who decides what are the appropriate qualifications for a given position, how they will be assessed, and whether particular individuals have them.

If objective, value-neutral merit evaluation is difficult or impossible, the legitimacy of a hierarchical division of labor is called seriously into question. I do not argue that any division among tasks and functions is wrong, but only the division between task design and task execution, which appears in the social class division between professional and nonprofessional jobs. This division allows only relatively few to develop and exercise their capacities. It subjects most people to structures of domination and many to the oppressions of exploitation, powerlessness, and cultural imperialism. Development of workplace democracy can do much to remedy this injustice, but a workplace democracy that retains the given division of labor is not enough. Relations of knowledge, autonomy, and cooperation must themelves be restructured in the definition of tasks in order to reduce or undermine oppression.

AFFIRMATIVE ACTION AND THE PRINCIPLE OF NONDISCRIMINATION

My purpose in this section is not to engage in a thorough justification of educational and employment policies that specially attend to excluded or disadvantaged groups and prefer members of those groups some of the time. Rather, I wish to put this much-discussed issue of justice and group difference in the context of the arguments I have made in previous chapters. Thus my discussion will be restricted largely to considering how affirmative action policies violate a principle of equal treatment, and to illustrating how much affirmative action discussion presumes a distributive paradigm of social justice.

Most affirmative action policies mandated or upheld by the courts have been justified as compensation for past discriminatory practices. In traditional legal terms, such a justification is least controversial when redress benefits the actual persons who have suffered discrimination, as when a court orders preferential promotion procedures for those who were wrongfully segregated into race- or gender-specific job categories. But where they have found evidence of intentional past discrimination courts have often ordered or upheld an affirmative action remedy even though the individuals benefiting are not the same as those discriminated against.

Justifying affirmative action policies as redress or compensation for past discrimination is fairly uncontroversial, but such a justification also tends to restrict permissible programs to a very narrow range. Some writers and litigants attempt to justify affirmative action policies as compensation or redress for a history of general societal discrimination against women or Blacks (see Boxill, 1984, pp. 148–67). Such arguments are weak because, as I will argue shortly, they render the concept of discrimination unacceptably vague. Arguments that affirmative action policies counteract the current biases and prejudices of decisionmakers are more compelling. Although explicitly discriminatory policies are no longer legal, and many institutions have in good faith eliminated explicitly discriminatory practices, women and people of color continue to be subject to often unconscious stereotypes, reactions, and expectations of decisionmakers, who continue to be white or male, and usually both. Affirmative action procedures are a necessary and just means of combating such assumptions and perceptions, which persist in excluding and disadvantaging women and people of color (Davidson, 1976; cited in Fullinwider, 1980, pp. 151–52).

Robert Fullinwider suggests that this reasoning creates a dilemma. On this argument, he says, "if we do not use preferential hiring, we permit discrimination to exist. But preferential hiring is also discrimination. Thus, if we use preferential hiring, we also permit discrimination to exist. The dilemma is that whatever we do, we permit discrimination" (Fullinwider, 1980, p. 156). Proponents of broad affirmative action policies often find themselves in this dilemma because they share with their opponents the conviction that the primary principle of justice at stake is a principle of nondiscrimination. Fullinwider's formulation of the dilemma also relies on an equivocation on the term discrimination; in the first use it means unconscious biases, prejudices, and assumptions that disadvantage women or people of color, and in the second it means conscious preferential practices that favor group members on grounds of their group membership. The dilemma disappears, I suggest, if proponents of affirmative action abandon the assumption that nondiscrimination is a paramount principle of justice, and stop assuming that racial and sexual injustice must come under the concept of discrimination.

Those who oppose affirmative action policies usually do so on the grounds that they discriminate. For them a principle of equal treatment, a principle of nondiscrimination, has absolute moral primacy. On this conception of social justice, policies that are group blind and apply the same formal rules to everyone are both necessary and sufficient for social justice. Since affirmative action policies violate this principle of equal treatment, they are wrong (see, e.g., Reynolds, 1986). Supporters of affirmative action policies would be less on the defensive, I suggest, if they positively acknowledged that these policies discriminate, instead of trying to argue that they are an extension of or compatible with a principle of nondiscrimination. We should, moreover, deny the assumption, widely held by both proponents and opponents of affirmative action, that discrimination is the only or primary wrong that groups suffer. Oppression, not discrimination, is the primary concept for naming group-related injustice. While discriminatory policies sometimes cause or reinforce oppression, oppression involves many actions, practices, and structures that have little to do with preferring or excluding members of groups in the awarding of benefits.

In Chapter 6 I argued against an assimilationist ideal that equates social equality with the elimination or transcendence of group differences. Taking a principle of equal treatment, or nondiscrimination, as an absolute or primary principle of justice assumes such an ideal of equality as sameness. I have argued that equal treatment should not receive such primacy. Equality, defined as the participation and inclusion of all groups in institutions and positions, is sometimes better served by differential treatment. This argument shifts the context for discussing the justice of affirmative action policies that favor members of oppressed or disadvantaged groups. No longer need affirmative action be seen as an exception to the otherwise operative principle of nondiscrimination. Instead, it becomes one of many group-conscious policies instrumental in undermining oppression.

Considering discrimination the only or primary injustice that women or people of color suffer in American society focuses attention on the wrong issues. Discrimination is primarily an agent-oriented, fault-oriented concept. Thus it tends to focus attention on the perpetrator and a particular action or policy, rather than on victims and their situation (see Freeman,

1982). Identifying group-based injustice with discrimination tends to put the onus on the victims to prove a harm is done, case by case.

As a concept of fault, moreover, discrimination tends to present the injustice groups suffer as aberrant, the exception rather than the rule. Now that law and public sentiment agree that specific discrimination which excludes or disadvantages women or people of color is wrong, people have come to think of the normal condition as the absence of discrimination (Fitzpatrick, 1987). Since explicit discrimination against women and people of color has decreased, the equation of group-based injustice with discrimination leads people to assume that injustices against these groups have also been eliminated.

The concept of discrimination, I suggest, should be restricted to the explicit exclusion or preference of some people in the distribution of benefits, the treatment they receive, or the positions they occupy, on account of their social group membership. Ironically, when discrimination in this sense becomes illegal and socially unacceptable, it becomes very difficult to prove that it takes place. People easily retreat into appeals to qualifications, or into asserting preferences for kinds of character and comportment, instead of for groups. Many legal theorists have argued for a results test rather than an intent test of discrimination; that is, a policy or practice should be found discriminatory if it results in a disproportionate exclusion of women or people of color, whatever the intent of its makers. The "disparate impact" doctrine articulated by the Supreme Court in 1971 in the Griggs case suggests such a broadened meaning of discrimination. In recent years, however, neither courts nor the general public have appeared willing to accept such an expanded concept of discrimination.

I agree that the moral focus should be on victims and results, rather than perpetrators and intents. But it confuses issues to bring such a focus on results under the concept of discrimination. A much better strategy for addressing the injustice suffered by disadvantaged groups is to restrict the concept of discrimination to intentional and explicitly formulated policies of exclusion or preference, and to argue that discrimination is not the only or necessarily the primary wrong that women and people of color suffer. As groups, the primary wrong we suffer is oppression.

In Chapter 2 I argued that oppression should not necessarily be understood as perpetrated by particular oppressing agents. While many individuals contribute to oppression, and particular groups of people are privileged because of the oppression of other groups, one misses the mundane and systematic character of oppression if one assumes that particular oppressors can and should always be identified and blamed. In its focus on individual agents, the concept of discrimination obscures and even tends to deny the structural and institutional framework of oppression. If one focuses on discrimination as the primary wrong groups suffer, then the more profound wrongs of exploitation, marginalization, powerlessness, cultural imperialism, and violence that we still suffer go undiscussed and unaddressed. One misses how the weight of society's institutions and people's assumptions, habits, and behavior toward others are directed at reproducing the material and ideological conditions that make life easier for, provide greater real opportunities to, and establish the priority of the point of view of white heterosexual men.

A focus on oppression rather than discrimination as the primary wrong that women, people of color, and other groups suffer allows us to admit that affirmative action policies are indeed discriminatory (see Sumner, 1987). They call for consciously and explicitly preferring members of particular groups on account of their group membership. Discrimination in this sense may or may not be wrong, depending on its purpose. An all-male club of city officials and business people is wrong, for example, because it reinforces and augments networks of privilege among men that exist even in its absence. It is not wrong to found an all-women's professional association, on the other hand, to counteract the isolation and strains that many professional women experience as a result of being less than welcome minorities in their fields.

If differentiation of groups reinforces undesirable stereotypes about their members, excludes them, segregates them, or puts them in subordinate positions, then it is wrong (Rhode, 1989, chap. 10; cf. Colker, 1986). Most historical discriminations have been wrong not because they distinguished people according to group attributes, but because they aimed at or resulted in formally and explicitly restricting the actions and opportunities of group members. They have been wrong, that is, because they have contributed to and helped enforce oppression. If discrimination serves the purpose of undermining the oppression of a group, it may be not only permitted, but morally required.

Institutions and policies too often have differential adverse impact on formerly excluded or segregated groups, even though this may not be intended. Bias against women, people of color, disabled people, and gays and lesbians is embedded in institutions, either because they are designed with the lives and perspectives of the privileged in mind, or because their structure still reflects the subordination that formal rules have outlawed. Explicit policies of exclusion, segregation, and subordination, finally, have left a deep legacy of group-differentiated capacities, culture, and socialization that continue to privilege white men in the competition for the most rewarded social positions. Much of this difference in capacity or preference should be conceived simply as difference rather than inferiority, but as I will discuss shortly, merit standards often translate difference into hierarchy. Oppression thus remains an ongoing process reproduced by many rules, practices, actions, and images.

Thus the primary argument for policies that consciously aim to increase the participation and inclusion of women, Blacks, Latinos, or disabled people in schools and offices and in positions of high reward and authority is that these policies intervene in the processes of oppression (Hawkesworth, 1984, pp. 343–44; Livingston, 1979, chaps. 1–3; Fullinwider, 1980, pp. 151–52; 1986, pp. 183–84; Boxill, 1984, chap. 7; Wasserstrom, 1980b; 1986; Rhode, 1989, chap. 10; Sumner, 1987). This positive intervention has several dimensions. Through strong affirmative action policies an institution announces its acceptance of formerly excluded groups. Affirmative action policies also counter the particular group-related biases of institutions and decisionmakers which put women and people of color at a disadvantage. Finally, inclusion and participation of women, people of color, disabled people, and so on in institutions and positions carries the advantages of group representation in decisionmaking bodies. Because of their differing experiences, cultures, values, and interactive styles, people from different groups often bring unique perspectives to a collective endeavor, supplementing those of others. The primary purpose of affirmative action policies, then, is neither to compensate for past discrimination nor to make up for supposed deficiencies of formerly excluded groups. Instead, the primary purpose of affirmative action is to mitigate the influence of current biases and blindnesses of institutions and decisionmakers.

AFFIRMATIVE ACTION DISCUSSION AND THE DISTRIBUTIVE PARADIGM

In Chapter 1 I argued that a distributive paradigm dominates philosophical and policy discussions of social justice. While distributive issues are important concerns of social justice, an approach that focuses solely on distribution tends to obscure questions of the justice of social institutions at least as important as distributions. Theories of justice that focus on distribution tend to assume the institutional structures which produce distributions as given background conditions whose justice is not brought into question. Insofar as this paradigm of justice limits evaluation to distribution, ignoring and obscuring questions of the justice of institutional organization, it serves an ideological function; it implicitly supports the institutional relations it assumes as given.

Both philosophical and policy discussions of affirmative action exhibit the distributive paradigm of social justice. Richard Wasserstrom is representative of those who conceptualize affirmative action as an issue of distributive justice:

> There is, at present, a maldistribution of power and authority along racial and sexual lines that is part of the social structure. Within the major political and

social institutions, such as the university, the bench, and the bar, the state and federal executive branches, and the corporate world, the great majority of positions are held by those who are white and male. One thing to be said for programs of preferential treatment is that by their operation they directly alter the composition of these institutions by increasing the number of nonwhites and women who in fact fill these positions of power and authority. This is desirable in itself because it is a redistribution of positions in a way that creates a new social reality—one which more nearly resembles the one captured by the conception of the good society. . . . To the degree that the present distribution of services and goods is unfair to members of these groups, the distributional change is justifiable simply because it is now a more just distribution. (Wasserstrom, 1980b, p. 56)

Where affirmative action programs are in place they do indeed have some success in redistributing desirable positions among women and people of color who otherwise probably would not get them. While some would argue that procedures of formally equal treatment should not be violated in order to produce more just patterns in the distribution of positions, I agree with Wasserstrom that the goal of achieving greater justice legitimates preferential treatment. Even if strong affirmative action programs existed in most institutions, however, they would have only a minor effect in altering the basic structure of group privilege and oppression in the United States. Since these programs require that racially or sexually preferred candidates be qualified, and indeed often highly qualified, they do nothing directly to increase opportunities for Blacks, Latinos, or women whose social environment and lack of resources make getting qualified nearly impossible for them. Change in the overall social patterns of racial and gender stratification in our society would require major changes in the structure of the economy, the process of job allocation, the character of the social division of labor, and access to schooling and training (cf. Wilson, 1978; 1986; Livingston, 1979, chap. 11; Hochschild, 1988). Intersecting the oppressions of race and gender are the oppressions of class.

In the past twenty years debate about affirmative action policies has occupied a great deal of the attention of policymakers, policy analysts, courts, unions, and professional associations. This debate is important because it raises fundamental issues of principle. So much energy invested in the issue of affirmative action, however, means energy deflected from other aspects of racial or gender justice, and from imagining other policy proposals that might undermine racial and sexual oppression. Affirmative action is one of the few policy proposals on the social agenda in the United States that address issues of sexual and racial oppression. I suggest that one reason it is so much discussed, even though more rarely supported, is that it is a "safer" proposal for addressing group inequality than others that might be voiced.

The terms of the affirmative action debate define a set of assumptions that accept the basic structure of the division of labor and the basic process of allocating positions. In their debate, both proponents and opponents of affirmative action assume as a prima facie principle that social positions should be distributed to the "most qualified," disagreeing only on whether it is just to override that principle. Both sides assume as given a hierarchical division of labor in which some few people are winners in the competition for scarce desirable positions, and most people must settle for positions of little reward, or no positions at all. Without this division of labor, the stakes that make the affirmative action debate so bitter would not be so high. Some participants in the affirmative action debate may in other contexts not accept these assumptions; but the terms of the debate itself presume them. Because the affirmative action issue is restricted to the distribution and redistribution of positions, broader structural questions about justice in the definition of positions and how admission to them is determined rarely get raised in public. To the degree that the affirmative action debate limits public attention to the relatively narrow and superficial issue of the redistribution of positions within an already given framework, that debate serves the function of supporting the structural status quo.

The remainder of this chapter examines in detail two assumptions about institutional structure that usually underlie affirmative action debate: the assumption that positions should be distributed to the most qualified, and the assumption that a hierarchical division of labor is just.

The Myth of Merit

A widely held principle of justice in our society is that positions and rewards should be distributed according to individual merit. The merit principle holds that positions should be awarded to the most qualified individuals, that is, to those who have the greatest aptitude and skill for performing the tasks those positions require. This principle is central to legitimating a hierarchical division of labor in a liberal democratic society which assumes the equal moral and political worth of all persons. Assuming as given a structural division between scarce highly rewarded positions and more plentiful less rewarded positions, the merit principle asserts that this division of labor is just when no group receives privileged positions by birth or right, or by virtue of arbitrary characteristics such as race, ethnicity, or sex. The unjust hierarchy of caste is to be replaced by a "natural" hierarchy of intellect and skill.

Just how this principle of merit should be interpreted, and whether it should function as the principle of the distribution of positions and rewards, is the subject of some controversy. Rawls, for example, argues that using natural talents as a criterion for awarding positions can be considered just as arbitrary as awarding them according to race or sex, because a person is just as little responsible for his or her talents as for his or her race (Rawls, 1971, pp. 101–4; cf. Sandel, 1982, pp. 72–82). Thus many argue that effort and achievement should be a large part of merit criteria (e.g., Nielsen, 1985, pp. 104–12). Many argue, further, that a principle of merit distribution should apply only after basic needs are met for everyone (Sterba, 1980, pp. 47–62; Nielsen, 1985, chap. 6; Galston, 1980, pp. 162–70, 197–200). Others question whether a principle of merit has any moral force, arguing that claims about efficiency or productivity cannot support claims of right or desert (see Daniels, 1978).

In his thorough and thoughtful study of the conflict of values he perceives in the goals of equal opportunity, James Fishkin defines the merit principle as entailing "widespread procedural fairness in the evaluation of qualifications for positions" (Fishkin, 1983, p. 22). Procedural fairness requires that the processes of evaluation "approach the model of an impartial competition." Qualifications are "criteria that are job related in that they fairly can be interpreted as indicators of competence or motivation for an individual's performance in a given position." Education, job history, fairly administered test results, or other tokens of ability or effort, says Fishkin, can all be used to assess qualifications. A fair assessment of an individual's qualifications must rest on that person's own past or present actual performance of relevant tasks; determination of qualifications cannot rest on statistical inferences (Fishkin, 1983, pp. 23–24).

Use of a principle of merit to allocate scarce and desirable positions in a job hierarchy, and in the educational institutions that train people for those jobs, is just only if several conditions are met. First, qualifications must be defined in terms of technical skills and competence, independently of and neutral with respect to values and culture. By technical competence I mean competence at producing specified results. If merit criteria do not distinguish between technical skills and normative or cultural attributes, there is no way to separate being a "good" worker of a certain sort from being the sort kind of person—with the right background, way of life, and so on. Second, to justify differential job privilege the purely technical skills and competences must be "job related," in that they operate as predictors for excellent performance in the position. Third, for merit criteria to be applied justly, performance and competence must be judged individually. In order to say that one individual is more qualified than another, finally, the performances and predicted performances of individuals must be compared and ranked according to measures which are independent of and neutral with respect to values and culture.

Proponents of a merit principle rarely doubt that these conditions can be met. Fishkin, for example, finds it obvious that the technical competence of individuals can be measured and predicted apart from values, purposes, and cultural norms. "It is hard to believe," he says, "in a modern industrial society, with a complex differentiation of tasks that qualifications that are performance related could not be defined so as to predict better performances" (Fishkin, 1983, p. 56). It may be hard to believe, but in fact such normatively and culturally neutral measures of individual performance do not exist for most jobs. The idea of merit criteria that are objective and unbiased with respect to personal attributes is a version of the ideal of impartiality, and is just as impossible.

First, most jobs are too complex and multifaceted to allow for a precise identification of their tasks and thus measurement of levels of performance of those tasks. Precise, value-neutral, task-specific measures of job performance are possible only for jobs with a limited number of definable functions each of which is a fairly straightforward identifiable task, requiring little verbal skill, imagination, or judgment (Fallon, 1980). Data entry work or quality control sorting may satisfy these requirements, but a great many jobs do not. A travel agent, for example, must keep records, communicate effectively on the telephone and through ever-changing computer networks of information, and study and keep at hand options in tour packages for many places. Service sector work, a vastly expanding portion of jobs, in general can rarely be evaluated in terms of the criteria of productivity and efficiency applied to industrial production, because it makes much less sense to count services rendered than items that come off the assembly line.

Second, in complex industrial and office organizations, it is often not possible to identify the contribution that each individual makes, precisely because the workers cooperate in producing an outcome or product. The performance of a team, department, or firm may be measurable, but this is of little use in justifying the position or level of reward of any particular team members (cf. Offe, 1976, pp. 54–57; Collins, 1979, p. 31).

Third, a great many jobs require wide discretion in what the worker does and how best to do it. In many jobs the worker's role is more negative than positive; he or she oversees a process and intervenes to prevent something from going wrong. In automated processes, from individual machines to entire factories, for example, workers routinely contribute little to the actual making of things, but they must be vigilant in tending the machines to make sure the process goes as it should. The negative role increases worker discretion about whether, when, and how often to intervene. Perhaps there is one easily identifiable and measurable way to perform many positive actions. But there are many ways of preventing a process from going wrong, and it is not usually possible to measure a worker's productivity level in terms of the costs that would have been incurred if she or he had not intervened, or the costs that would have been saved if she or he had intervened differently (Offe, 1976, p. 56).

Finally, the division of labor in most large organizations means that those evaluating a worker's performance often are not familiar with the actual work process. Modern organizational hierarchies are what Claus Offe calls task discontinuous hierarchies (Offe, 1976, pp. 25–28). In a task continuous hierarchy, like that exemplified by medieval guild production, superiors do the same kind of work as their subordinates, but with a greater degree of skill and competence. In the task discontinuous hierarchies of contemporary organizations, job ladders are highly segregated. Superiors do not do the same kind of work as subordinates, and may never have done that sort of work. Thus the superior is often not competent to evaluate the technical work performance itself, and must rely on evaluating workers' attitudes, their compliance with the rules, their self-presentation, their cooperativeness—that is, their social comportment.

While these four impediments to a normatively and culturally neutral definition and assessment of job performance occur in many types of work, they are most apparent in professional and managerial work. These types of work usually involve a wide diversity of skills and tasks. Most or all of these tasks rely on the use of judgment, discretion, imagination, and verbal acuity, and none of these qualities is precisely measurable according to some objective, value-neutral scale. The achievement of professional and managerial objectives usually involves a complex series of social relationships and dependencies, to the extent that it is often unreasonable to hold professionals responsible for not meeting objectives (Rausch, 1985, pp. 97–103). Professional and managerial jobs, finally, often are evaluated not only by superiors in a task discontinuous hierarchy, but by clients who are even less aware of the nature of the jobs and the skills required, and who are thus not in a position to apply criteria of technical performance that are normatively and culturally neutral.

If professional and managerial positions are even less liable to value-neutral assessment than other jobs, then this creates a particular problem for the legitimation of a hierarchical division of labor. Since these are the most scarce and most rewarded positions, and thus the positions for which there is the greatest competition, it is these for which value-neutral merit criteria are most needed. For these positions it is not enough that decisionmakers be able to justify the claim that the person chosen can do the job; they must also justify the claim that out of all candidates this one can do the job best. For such comparative claims under circumstances of stiff competition to be legitimate, it must be possible precisely to define and measure the technical competence of individuals. But this requirement is least present in those jobs for which it is most needed (cf. Fallon, 1980, p. 849; Wasserstrom, 1980b, p. 68).

Even though the merit principle requires impartial technical definition of qualifications, the criteria actually used to determine qualifications tend to embody or include particular values, norms, and cultural attributes— such as whether those being evaluated behave according to certain social norms, whether they promote specifically defined organizational goals, and whether they demonstrate generally valued social competences and characteristics. Factory workers are often evaluated for their punctuality, obedience, loyalty, and positive attitude; professional workers may be evaluated for their articulateness, authoritativeness, and ability to work effectively in groups.

Let me emphasize that using criteria such as these is not necessarily inappropriate; the point is that they are normative and cultural rather than neutrally scientific. That is, they concern whether the person evaluated supports and internalizes specific values, follows implicit or explicit social rules of behavior, supports social purposes, or exhibits specific traits of character, behavior, or temperament that the evaluators find desirable. Use of normative and cultural criteria in addition to and intertwined with evaluation of technical competence is for the most part unavoidable.

Experts in managerial performance evaluation make no secret of the fact that systems of merit evaluation do not impartially measure technical productivity. One writer about job performance defines an evaluation criterion as "a behavior, or set of behaviors, that management values enough to want to be able to describe it, predict it (select for it), and/or control it." The choice of criteria, this writer admits, is entirely a "subjective" judgment management makes, the result of consensus among managers or between managers and employees (Blumfield, 1976, pp. 6–7; cf. Sher, 1987b, p. 199).

One study of performance evaluation practices finds that evaluators of professional or managerial performance commonly rely on assessment of broadly defined traits such as leadership, initiative, cooperation, judgment, creativity, and dependability, rather than on more specific behavior and performance outcomes (Devrie, et al., 1980, p. 20). The authors of this study regard assessment by personality or character traits as an inferior form of evaluation, because such traits can only be vaguely defined and the judgment that someone exhibits them seems tied to the evaluators' purposes and preferences. They recommend management by objectives as the most objective or value-neutral system of evaluation. Here managers' performance is evaluated according to whether and to what extent they meet objectives previously defined by supervisors or by employees and supervisors together. While surely more objective than assessment of character traits, management by objectives is hardly value-neutral, since values are usually built into the definition of objectives. Rausch (1985, chap. 6) claims, moreover, that management by objectives has lost favor because managers are often unable to meet objectives for reasons beyond their control. He claims that performance evaluation is inevitably subjective and value-laden, and for that reason recommends use of peer ratings and ratings by several supervisors instead of only one.

If merit evaluation is inevitably subjective and depends on the judgment of evaluators, then merit evaluation will justify hierarchy only if the evaluators are impartial in the strong sense of not being influenced by the social perspective of a particular group or culture. I have argued in Chapter 4 that such an impartial standpoint in the public is a fiction. It is equally so in individual institutions. The conviction that evaluators can and should be neutral with respect to groups, ways of life, and cultural norms in the assessment of performance and competence masks their actual situatedness and partiality. As I shall discuss further in the next section, moreover, such impartial, objective methods of evaluation are impossible even with quantified measures and standardized tests.

Within the hierarchical division of labor, evaluators of merit are usually superordinate to those they evaluate, occupying positions of relative privilege. Their criteria of evaluation often emphasize norms of conformity which contribute to the smooth maintenance and reproduction of the existing relations of privilege, hierarchy, and subordination, rather than neutrally evaluating only technical competence and performance. The hierarchies of privilege in our society are clearly structured by race, gender, and other group differences, moreover, so evaluators are most often white heterosexual able-bodied men, and those they evaluate from other groups.

At least two sources of group-related disadvantage affect members of subordinated groups, even when their evaluators believe they are being impartial. As I argued in Chapter 4, the ideal of impartiality encourages the universalization of the particular. Criteria of evaluation necessarily carry normative and cultural implications and so often will not be group-neutral. These criteria often carry assumptions about ways of life, styles of behavior, and values that derive from and reflect the experience of the privileged groups who design and implement them. Since the ideology of impartiality leads evaluators to deny the particularity of these standards, groups with different experiences, values, and ways of life are evaluated as falling short. For example, in Chapter 6 I discussed feminist arguments that many supposedly neutral and unquestioned norms of the corporate workplace implicitly assume male socialization and a male life style. To take another example, an employee who does not look a white male employer in the eye may be perceived as shifty or dishonest; but the employee may have been raised in a culture where averting the eyes is a sign of deference.

Second, as I argued in Chapter 5, everyday judgment of and interaction with women, people of color, gay men and lesbians, disabled people, and old people is often influenced by unconscious aversions and devaluations. Thus evaluators, especially those belonging to groups defined as neutral, often carry unconscious biases and prejudices against specially marked groups. A number of studies have shown, for example, that many whites rate black job candidates more negatively than whites with identical credentials (McConohay, 1986). Similar studies have shown that the same résumé receives a significantly lower rating when it has a woman's name than when it has a man's (Rhode, 1988, p. 1220).

EDUCATION AND TESTING AS PERFORMANCE PROXIES

I have argued that the merit principle's requirement of normatively and culturally neutral measures of individual job performance usually cannot be met. The maintenance of a hierarchical division of labor with scarce privileged positions at the top will be just, however, only if those positions are filled according to normatively and culturally neutral criteria of technical competence. The pressure is on, then, to find performance proxies— measures of individual competence and achievement that can substitute for performance measures, and that are independent of and neutral with respect to values and culture. Educational credentials and standardized test results function in our society as the primary proxies for direct assessment and prediction of job performance. Despite beliefs to the contrary, however, educational attainment and test results are no more neutral than more direct evaluations of performance.

In a liberal democratic society, education is understood as the means of providing equal opportunity for all groups. But there is no evidence that education equalizes. Despite educators' bemoaning the fact for several decades, the system of education stubbornly reproduces class, race, and gender hierarchies (Gintis and Bowles, 1986, chap. 4). Educators mistakenly believe they have produced equal educational opportunity when no one is barred from following a course of study because of race or gender, and when in principle all students follow the same curriculum and are measured according to the same standards. Schools do not attend enough to differential learning needs, and place responsibility on parents and students when students do not achieve (Bastian et al., 1986, pp. 26–31). Schools continue to be racially segregated in many regions of the United States. Even when they do not actively reinforce gender and racial stereotyping, schools generally do very little to confront cultural images of appropriate pursuits for girls and boys, or to make visible the achievements of women and people of color. Serious racial and gender differentiation persists in math and science study and achievement in junior high and high school, the subjects most needed for the pursuit of privileged and lucrative careers in a high-tech society. Eleanor Orr (1987) argues that a coherent separate dialect of Black English leads some children systematically to mistranslate instruction in science and mathematics, accounting at least partly for the poorer performance and lesser interest of Black children in these subjects. Similar arguments have been made about gender bias in the culture of math and science.

Money continues to be a major discriminator. Middle- and upper-class children have better schools than poor and working-class children. Thus they are better prepared to compete for college admission. If by chance poor and working-class children qualify for college, they often cannot pay for it, or for the postgraduate training that can lead them to positions of privilege.

According to Randall Collins (1979, pp. 19–21), studies show little correlation between educational attainment and job performance or occupational success. Much of what schools teach is not technical skills, but cultural values and social norms such as obedience, attentiveness, and deference to authority. Students are often graded according to how well they have internalized these values and norms rather than how well they are able to perform certain tasks.

Educational achievement has nevertheless become a major criterion of job qualifications. As one might predict, this has led directly to a credential inflation. Once a high school diploma became genuinely attainable for the majority of people, a college degree became a *sine qua non* for many jobs. As state support begins to make community college and state four-year college degrees widely available, these too become relatively devalued. One must come from a "better school" or have an advanced degree to "get ahead." The promise of education as a ticket to the top of the division of labor is not fulfilled because the hierarchical system permits only relatively few positions of privilege, and the credentialing system functions as gatekeeper to these positions. In good faith people pursue specialized training and acquire credentials, only to find no room at the top because so many others have done the same. They take jobs for which they are overqualified, thereby raising the formal standards for those positions, and the spiral continues (Burris, 1983).

Standardized testing is the most important of performance proxies, used not only to identify the most qualified job candidates, but also throughout the educational system to identify achievement and aptitude that will admit individuals to privileged educational programs. Standardized tests, it was hoped, would provide the normatively and culturally neutral, objective measures of individual technical or cognitive competence. Standardized tests appear to comply with the requirements of merit evaluation because they are usually procedurally fair. They are blind to race, sex, and ethnicity. They are "objective" in the sense that when they are used to evaluate individuals we can be sure that all have been evaluated according to the same criteria, and in the sense that for a given individual any scorer will come up with the same score. By quantifying test answers and relying on complex statistical techniques, tests also appear able to measure individual skill precisely and to compare and rank individuals, providing an objective assessment of the most and least qualified.

After World War II, and during the 1950s and 1960s, employers increasingly relied on standardized tests as vehicles for awarding positions, promotions, pay increases, and so on. They appeared to do so on the faith that the tests told them who could do the best job, for rarely did employers perform a job analysis to determine the predictive validity of the tests, and rarely did they have empirical evidence that the tests in fact improved their selection process. Often they used generalized intelligence or aptitude tests without making any attempt to correlate them with actual job content (Wigdor, 1982).

A series of court challenges claiming that such use of tests had the effect of excluding people of color and sometimes women led the Equal Employment Opportunity Commission to specify that when test use has a disparate impact on a group, employers must be able to prove that the tests are fair and unbiased measures of job-specific skills. Most employment tests have been unable to meet such stringent guidelines (Fallon, 1980; Wigdor, 1982). Consequently, many employers today rely on tests a great deal less than before. Employer tests that remain, however, for the most part still appear to be developed and used without specific relation to actual job content (Friedman and Williams, 1982). Many employers continue to use "broad-band" tests that cover many generalized skills. The federal government, for example, uses the same test for all its diverse civil service positions (Friedman and Williams, 1982).

If we cannot obtain normatively and culturally neutral assessments of individual performance, then it is not surprising that employers are usually unable to show that tests are job specific. If one cannot measure performance on the job, moreover, then it should be even more difficult to develop demonstrated predictors of such performance.

In the last two decades use of standardized tests for certification purposes and in the educational system has increased. Since the late 1960s the claim of standardized tests to normative and cultural neutrality has been seriously challenged. After two decades of debate, experts seem to agree that the original hope for objective measures of technical and cognitive competence independent of and neutral with respect to values, norms, and culture cannot be sustained. Standardized tests inevitably reflect value choices and cultural meanings (Wigdor, 1982; Shepard, 1982; Tittle, 1982).

For one thing, tests themselves have a culture. Tests reward certain personal or cultural styles, such as competitiveness, the ability to work well alone, the ability to work quickly, and a penchant for abstraction (Wigdor and Garner, 1982, pp. 40, 209–10). Whatever the skills a test is intended to measure, test takers with these test-taking skills and temperament have an advantage.

Whatever their specific content or purpose, most tests draw on a relatively restricted set of aptitudes and skills, notably computation, deductive inference, and analogical reasoning. Many of the skills and achievements that contribute to the ability to learn and perform complicated jobs are simply not amenable to packaging in short questions with yes-or-no answers (Wigdor and Garner, 1982, pp. 209–11; Strenio, 1981, pp. 189–91). The process of test formulation thus reflects a de facto greater valuation of the skills the tests can identify over those they cannot.

Employers and school officials have put so much weight on tests because they seem to offer a means of satisfying two of the requirements of merit evaluation identified in the previous section—a precise measure of the competence of each individual, and a comparison and ranking of all individuals. Tests appear to satisfy the merit principle's demand that persons be rewarded according to their own individual achievement. Because they are universalized and standardized, however, the individuality of test results is illusory. Through the process that Foucault calls normalization, tests produce the reconstituted individuality of a "case" or "score":

> The examination combines the techniques of an observing hierarchy and those of a normalizing judgment. It is a normalizing gaze, a surveillance that makes it possible to quantify, to classify and to punish. It establishes over individuals a visibility through which one differentiates them and judges them. That is why, in all the mechanisms of discipline, the examination is highly ritualized. In it are combined the ceremony of power and the form of the experiment, the deployment of force and the establishment of truth. At the heart of the procedure of discipline, it manifests the subjection of those who are perceived as objects and the objectification of those who are subjected. (Foucault, 1977, pp. 184–85)

The normalizing system of standardized tests reconstitutes individual qualities as instances of abstractly and universally defined attributes (cf. Levontin, Rose, and Kamin, 1984, pp. 92–93). This normalizing process of reducing all individuals to a common measure necessarily reconstructs difference as deviance or devaluation. What in pretested particularity is simply a difference in kind of skill or the mode of its expression becomes the presence of more or less skill when its measurement is standardized according to a single criterion and scale. Since the normalizing measures have most often been constructed by white middle-class men unconsciously operating with white male middle-class styles and meanings as the norm, the skills and competences of women, Blacks, Latinos, and poor and working-class people often show up as lower.

There is little doubt that many tests have exhibited and continue to exhibit results differentiated by class, race, gender, or all three (Strenio, 1981, pp. 9, 37–38; Wigdor and Garner, 1982, pp. 195–96; Shepard, 1982). A recent court case in New York State, for example, found that when Regents scholarships are distributed solely according to SAT scores, females receive a significantly lower proportion than when grades are used as well. In response to criticism that standardized tests have been biased against some groups, test theorists and developers have attempted to arrive at methods of eliminating bias. This research has yielded important and refined methods for identifying the presence of test bias, but researchers have concluded that there is no technical method for preventing bias and for ensuring that a test is fair to all takers. Test development inevitably employs words, phrases, and symbols whose meaning may be understood in culturally varying ways. Test formulation involves a multitude of judgments and choices, any one of which can have culturally specific implications. Students of test bias appear to conclude that test makers and users must recognize the inevitable normative and culture specificity of standarized tests (Shepard, 1982).

Norms, values, and purposes influence decisions about test content, format, the weighting of items and sections, statistical methods used for scoring, and so on. I argue in the next section that this does not necessarily imply that tests are bad methods of evaluation. The important point is that standardized tests cannot be said to provide precise quantitative individual measures of technical or cognitive competence independent of and neutral with respect to values and culture.

THE POLITICS OF QUALIFICATIONS

Merit distribution of positions of reward and privilege can legitimate a social hierarchy only if criteria for determining people's qualifications assess their skills and competences and not whether they belong to a certain group, behave in certain ways, or conform to the evaluator's preferences and purposes. I have argued, however, that in fact the criteria used for evaluating and ranking individual qualifications are usually value-laden, as well as normatively and culturally specific.

From this argument I draw the conclusion that practices of certifying people's qualifications, and ranking those qualifications, are always *political* (cf. Walzer, 1983, pp. 140–43). As I defined the term in the Introduction, all aspects of institutional structure, public action, social practices and habits, and cultural meanings are political insofar as they are potentially subject to collective discussion and decisionmaking. The rules and policies of any institution serve particular ends, embody particular values and meanings, and have identifiable consequences for the actions and situation of the persons within or related to those institutions. All of these things are open to challenge, and politics is the process of struggle and deliberation about such rules and policies, the ends they serve, and the values they embody. The ideology of merit seeks to depoliticize the establishment of criteria and standards for allocating positions and awarding benefits. Controversy about schooling, credentials, tests, and admissions and employment policies should be sufficient to show that this depoliticizing effort fails. Especially in a society where most people depend on collective institutions to provide them with work and livelihood, the rules and policies that determine and apply qualifications are inevitably political. Once we understand merit evaluation as political, then important questions of justice arise beyond distribution, questions about who should decide on qualifications and by what norms and principles.

Affirmative action and equal opportunity discussion rarely question the justice of current practices in our society which mandate that managers, administrators, social scientific experts, and those who "lead the field" in professions should determine criteria of qualification and who is qualified. And the power of the qualification makers is awesome: they decide the fate of all the less powerful who do not make those decisions, as well as the fate of their professional colleagues. Professions are self-credentialing on grounds of expertise. According to the ideology of merit, the "best" doctors should decide what counts as good doctoring and who meets those standards, because they above all others have the technical competence to define and identify good performance. Because of their expertise managers and administrators should decide the qualifications for entry into and advancement in the hierarchy of jobs under their jurisdiction. Bosses legitimately make criteria and selection decisions because their having attained their positions demonstrates their competence to manage. Safeguards must be put on the bosses, however, to prevent their personal prejudices and preferences from influencing their decisions, and for this reason bosses should consult with appropriate experts in the development of criteria and their application to individuals. These experts are the scientists with the know-how to develop objective, impartial, and standardized criteria for measuring performance and potential performance. This situation illustrates the claim I made in Chapter 4 that the ideal of impartiality legitimates hierarchy. The alleged scientificity of merit evaluation supposedly justifies a hierarchical decisionmaking process; knowledge justifies power.

This justification of hierarchical decisonmaking power is problematic. If cultural and normative criteria differentiate individuals more than objectively measured competence, then their status depends on their pleasing their evaluators, on managing impressions (cf. K. Ferguson, 1984, pp. 106–8). The organization and its managers take as a primary goal the affirmation and reproduction of the organization's social relations and system of power. That is, the system of performance evaluation within such a hierarchy supports and reproduces relations of domination (Offe, 1976, pp. 95–125; Collins, 1979, chap. 2).

In principle this hierarchy and system of domination is little different from the traditional status hierarchies that application of a merit principle was supposed to eliminate. A class of powerful people establishes normative criteria, some of which have the function of affirming its own power and reinforcing the organizational system that makes it possible. To occupy positions within the hierarchy they choose persons who have certain status credentials (instead of coming from the "right" family, they went to the "right" school), and persons who by nature or training exhibit the preferred behavioral and temperamental characteristics.

In contrast to the merit ideology, I claim that decisions that establish and apply criteria of qualification should be made democratically. In Chapter 3 I argued that democratic decisionmaking procedures are a necessary condition of social justice, both as a means to self-development and the minimization of domination and as the best way to arrive at substantively just decisions. Since the filling of jobs and offices fundamentally affects the fate of individuals and societies, democratic decisionmaking about these matters is a crucial condition of social justice.

In Chapter 3 I also acknowledged that democratic procedures alone are often insufficient to ensure just decisions; thus democracy must be constitutional, limited by rules that define basic rights and norms. Democratic decisions about criteria for job qualifications and about who is qualified should be limited by fairness. As I understand it, fairness in such decisions includes the following: (1) Criteria for qualifications should be explicit and public, along with the values and purposes they serve. (2) Criteria should not exclude any social groups from consideration for positions, either explicitly or implicitly. (3) All candidates for positions should be given thorough consideration, according to formal procedures which are publicly announced. (4) People with particular group affinities, social positions, or personal attributes may be preferred, but only to undermine oppression or compensate for disadvantage, and never to reinforce privilege.

Just who should be included in the public entitled to deliberate about and determine the criteria of qualification for particular positions must vary with the kind of position. Later in this chapter I will argue that all major workplace decisions should be made democratically; in accord with such a principle, certainly those who work in an institution should participate in decisions about the criteria of qualification for positions and who is qualified. Does this mean that every employee in a multinational corporation must participate in writing the job description and making the hiring decisions for every other employee in the corporation? Obviously it cannot mean this; principles and procedures of representation must be worked out in this democratic process as in all others, and decisions of general policy are more important than particular applications. It does mean, however, that peers and co-workers should have a significant voice in determining the criteria of qualification for the kinds of jobs they do, and in deciding who their peers and co-workers will be. A primary privilege that now distinguishes professionals from nonprofessionals is that the former often participate in these decisions, while the latter rarely do so. Even many professionals, however, do not have the right to determine the qualifications their co-workers should have; while their job may include defining and evaluating the qualifications of their subordinates, their own qualifications and those of their peers are defined and evaluated by superiors. Where relations of superordination and subordination remain in a democratic workplace, subordinates should also have a voice in determining the qualifications their bosses should have.

In many situations co-workers are not the only persons who should constitute the public that decides on qualifications for hiring, promotion, and so forth. As I will discuss shortly, a democratic workplace should define its general job structure and division of labor with the represented participation of all the workers; this definition would include at least general principles and guidelines for the qualifications of each kind of position.

Workers in the affected workplace, moreover, are not always the only persons who should have a right to participate in defining qualifications for positions. Minimizing domination in such a way as to allow persons to participate in decisions that affect their actions and the conditions of their actions sometimes means others too should have a role in determining qualifications. Consumers or clients particularly affected by the work performed in a position should also have representation. Parents of children who attend a day-care center, for example, or consumer members of a health maintenance organization, should have a voice in determining the qualifications at least of those positions with significant power, authority, or expertise. Occupational positions that involve broad social power and authority, or significant control over important knowledge and expertise, may require that citizens of the general community they serve and affect have a represented voice in determining the criteria for filling them (cf. Green, 1985, pp. 193–99; Gould, 1988, chap. 10).

Finally, in accordance with the principle that all social groups in a society should have the opportunity to participate in all institutions and positions equally, decisionmaking bodies that determine qualifications for positions should also include representatives of groups oppressed or disadvantaged in the society at large, as well as social groups that suffer oppression or disadvantage within the particular institution or profession in which the position is defined.

How should qualifications be defined? Democracy implies that decisionmakers can define qualifications any way they choose, within the constraints of fairness set out above, after serious deliberation and argument, according to whatever values and purposes they deem appropriate. They must, however, make those values and purposes explicit, both to themselves and others, and be able to show how the criteria they arrive at promote them. They may if they choose develop tests or other formalized evaluation procedures for assessing and ranking the qualifications of persons according to those criteria. Presumably in any division of labor some positions will have more applicants than can be accepted. Developing ways of ranking in order to eliminate some applicants is not wrong, as long as the values and purposes of the criteria are explicit, and always open to challenge and revision. Representation of groups who experience cultural imperialism is crucial both in establishing job goals and in establishing evaluation procedures, however, to ensure that their particular experiences, culture, and values are not excluded or disadvantaged. If no normatively and culturally neutral criteria for assessing qualifications exist, such social group representation is the only means of making evaluation fair, because it balances values, priorities, and knowledge.

OPPRESSION AND THE SOCIAL DIVISION OF LABOR

John Livingston (1979, pp. 122–24) argues that in the nineteenth century the doctrine of equal opportunity had a more radical and democratic meaning than it does now. Then it meant that there were no barriers to material and social improvement to those who would work hard and develop their skills. Equal opportunity meant everybody who worked hard could be somebody. Homestead and entrepreneurial opportunities at the time made the claim plausible, at least for white men. Social mobility was not so easy as the Horatio Alger myth portrayed it, but there were multiple avenues for social advancement or at least for establishing a comfortable living.

Today there are few such tracks of mobility, and hopping onto the train has become much more difficult. When the vast majority of people must look to wage or salary employment to obtain a livelihood, getting ahead means getting a high-status job, and moving up a bureaucratically defined career ladder. Today equal opportunity has come to mean only that no one is barred from entering the competition for a relatively few privileged positions. There remains the shadow of a rhetoric which suggests that actual opportunities are available to anyone who works hard, but it does not fully obscure the certainty that most people are bound to be losers.

For the competition is getting stiffer. According to Wagman and Folbre (1988), the proportion of professional and managerial jobs in the total labor force has remained stable at about 30 percent during the last ten years. During the same period levels of education have risen, thus increasing the competition for these jobs. Current social trends, moreover, indicate a decline in the number of low-level professional and high-skilled nonprofessional jobs. Increasingly, job structure in the United States is divided between prestige positions for which certification is difficult and costly to acquire, and a vast array of low-skill, low-wage, low-mobility positions that carry little autonomy and creativity (see Bastian et al., 1986, pp. 52–55).

Assuming a division between scarce highly rewarded positions and more plentiful less desirable positions as given, the merit principle asserts that this division of labor is just when no group receives privileged positions by birth or right, but these positions are instead awarded according to demonstrated individual achievement of technical competence measured by normatively and culturally neutral criteria. If, as I have argued, these positions are not and cannot be awarded in this way, then the legitimacy of a hierarchical division of labor in a society committed to the equal moral worth of all persons comes seriously into question.

Discussions of equal opportunity and affirmative action tend to presume as a social given this hierarchical division of labor in which relatively few are winners and most are losers (see, e.g., Sher, 1988, p. 117). As we saw earlier, these discussions usually assume a distributive paradigm of justice. They ask what principles are appropriate for ensuring fairness in the distribution of positions, where the nature of the positions and their relation to one another is already given. A more radical approach is to ask about the justice of this division of labor itself. Is a division of labor with scarce desirable positions and more plentiful positions of little reward itself just? How should tasks and responsibilities be defined in the social division of labor, and how should positions be related to one another? Who should decide the division of labor, and by what procedures? Decisions about these questions determine a great deal about the distribution of goods in a society. Once the division of labor is in place, enforced and reproduced by authority and credentialing, redistribution of goods does not appreciably alter the process that produces that distributive pattern. Most societies in the world today have a hierarchical division of labor that distinguishes between professional and nonprofessional work, or work that is task defining and work that is task executing. This division is unjust, I shall argue, because it involves both domination and oppression.

First, however, I shall note aspects of the division of labor that I am *not* here criticizing, which most discussions of inequality in the workplace tend to focus on. First, I am not criticizing specialization as such. By specialization I mean the development and consolidation of particular technical, artisan, social, or organizational skills for the accomplishing of specialized ends, and the allocation of such specialized work to persons trained in those skills. Specialization in this sense usually has distinct advantages both for accomplishing collective ends and for the individuals who develop their capacities and exercise these skills. My argument is not against a horizontal division of labor, but against a hierarchical division. But I wish to distinguish the specialization of tasks from the detailed division of labor typical of modern factory production. The latter creates minute and repetitive mini-tasks that require little or no skill, that are not visibly tied to a practical outcome, that are easily monitored and automated, and that do not usually enhance a person's general skills and capacities. I do wish to criticize this detailed division of labor.

Second, my criticism does not extend to all hierarchies of authority in the workplace. Often there are good reasons for establishing supervisory and leadership roles in a collective endeavor, and for coordinating large-scale operations through a chain of authority. My discussion implies that there should be upper and lower limits to such authority, but I do not wish to claim that all supervisory and hierarchical decisionmaking structures are wrong.

Finally, I am not arguing against differential pay. Justice does not require equal income for all workers, and there are often good reasons for paying different workers and different occupations differently. As many people have discussed, these reasons include rewarding hard work and extra effort, compensating the sacrifice that may be involved in acquiring specialized skills, providing incentives to perform otherwise less desirable work, and rewarding better than average productivity. I believe that the huge income differentials typical in American society, especially insofar as they are tied to the structural division between task-defining and task-executing work, are wrong. But my argument about the injustice of this structural division of labor does not imply anything about differential pay per se.

The division with which I am concerned is that between, in Philip Green's words, "those who plan their own or other's work routines, however carried out; and those who follow routines that have been planned for them" (Green, 1985, p. 81). Roberto Unger calls this a distinction between task definition and task execution, "between the jobs that allow for the open exercise of reconstructive practical intelligence and the jobs that are supposed to involve the routinized exercise of a well defined task playing a limited role in a plan that practical intelligence has devised" (Unger,

1987b, p. 76). In many enterprises the division of labor is so constructed that some positions are both these in different respects, while some are only one or the other. The justification for this division between task definition and task execution is that the task designers have an expertise that equips them to design and organize. To a significant degree, then, the distinction between task design and task execution corresponds to the division between professional and nonprofessional workers. In much of the discussion that follows I will refer to the two kinds of divisions interchangeably, but I will also indicate ways in which professional workers sometimes tend to fall on the task-execution side of the division.

The division between professional and nonprofessional workers is a basic class division in advanced industrial societies. To be sure, most professional and managerial workers in capitalist society do not belong to the capitalist class, the major owners of the means of production. Most professional and managerial workers are salaried employees, and to some extent for that reason experience the same structural exploitation as the working class and a similar dependence on the owners' pleasure for a continued livelihood. Ownership of capital, however, is not the only important property right in our society. Professional and managerial workers have a class privilege in the property rights of position.

Control over capital is only a special case of property rights. More broadly, property should be understood as a cluster of entitlements that gives people social power, either as "control over the physical commodities and the material products of labor, command over labor itself, [or] the power to dispose of nonmaterial rights" (Unger, 1987b, p. 131). Task-defining positions tend to be what Walzer (1983, pp. 10–13) calls "dominant" goods; they bring with them entitlements to high income, prestige, access to resources, and authority over and benefit from the labor of task-executing workers.

Though there is a hierarchy of professions, the propertied basis of these positions remains a crucial determinant of class division and class struggle in our society; social conflict to a large degree concerns access to the exclusive professional positions that carry entitlements to goods and social power (cf. Collins, 1979, pp. 53–54). The division between professionals and nonprofessionals should be considered a class division because of several features that make the division systematic, a distinction of social groups reproduced over time. A major structural privilege of the professional class consists in regulating entrance to its ranks, thereby maintaining exclusivity in its knowledge and way of life. For the most part the division between professionals and nonprofessionals is maintained across generations, with the children of professionals having a distinct advantage in admittance to the professional class. Professionals should be considered a structured class, finally, because "the mass of people have effectively removed from the possibility of any rational intervention in the determination of policies affecting the practices of that class" (Green, 1985, pp. 83–84). The division of labor between task division and task execution enacts domination; as exhibited in a social class division between professional and nonprofessional workers, it enacts oppression most particularly in the form of exploitation, powerlessness, and cultural imperialism.

Domination, as I defined it in Chapter 1, consists in persons having to perform actions whose rules and goals they have not participated in determining, under institutionalized conditions they have not had a part in deciding. In the typical hierarchically structured organization, many employees have little or no part in deciding their own responsibilities and the constraints on their action, even when they have a role in deciding the actions of others. Prima facie, justice implies freedom, in the sense of self-determination, the ability of people to decide what they will do and why. In collective activity such freedom cannot be autonomous and self-contained, but rather implies a right of participation in decisionmaking (see Gould, 1988, chap. 4; Young, 1979).

One aspect of the division between task definition and task execution is the organizational tendency to separate major decisionmaking power over the operations of an entire enterprise from all the persons and positions that carry out its ends. Organizations typically have centralized planning operations run by a relatively few individuals in top administrative and managerial positions who decide what will be produced or accomplished, how the organization's division of labor will be structured to accomplish it, how the production process will be structured, and what the pay scales and relations of superiority and subordination will be among the positions. Typically these basic task-defining decisions are executed in a descending chain of command in which those in the middle execute the designs of their superiors but also design plans executed by their subordinates, and those at the bottom only execute tasks designed by their superiors. Such a centralization of basic decisions and strict descending hierarchy of authority means that all but those in the top positions are subject to varying degrees of domination.

In Chapter 2 I defined exploitation broadly as any relationship in which the results of the energies of one group systematically benefit another without reciprocation. The division between professionals and nonprofessionals enacts exploitation in this sense. Premodern laboring classes freed aristocrats for the "higher" pursuits of art, priesthood, literature, and statecraft by providing for all their material wants and needs. In a similar fashion, today's working class augments the luxury and working conditions of professionals. The "material" work of nonprofessionals—taking the tolls, cleaning the office, typing the reports, building the planes—frees the professionals and managers for the "higher" work of thinking, designing and calculating, talking to one another or to clients, making decisions, writing reports, planning, and coordinating and supervising complex productive activities. Professionals are usually the ones who directly benefit from the menial labor which, as I discussed in Chapter 2, tends to be race- and gender-specific. This relationship of professionals to nonprofessionals is exploitative because the professionals usually get paid more, get more recognition, and have greater power and authority, even though the work of some nonprofessionals directly enables their work. Often the work of the nonprofessionals is invisible, and its contribution to enabling the work of the professionals unnoticed.

This class division may also contribute to the exploitation of nonprofessionals in the more restricted Marxist sense of the appropriation of the value of what those nonprofessional workers produce. I do not here wish to enter the controversy about this Marxist theory of exploitation, about how one distinguishes productive from unproductive labor, and so on. So I will only suggest, without defending them, two sorts of claims one might make about how the division between task definition and task execution contributes to working-class exploitation. The job of many professionals and managers is specifically to design production processes and work relations that will maximize the productivity of nonprofessional workers, in the narrow sense of increasing profit (Poulantzas, 1978, pp. 236–41). Removing design decisions and autonomy as much as possible from the work process, making the latter only the execution of tasks directed by others, cheapens labor, makes it amenable to automation, and tightens control over workers—all of which contribute to increased exploitation.

If one accepts the Marxist distinction between productive and unproductive labor, moreover, one can argue that much of the work of professionals and managers is not productive in the sense of contributing directly to new value in the economy. Given that professionals nevertheless are paid more than nonprofessionals whose work is productive in this narrow sense, and receive other material benefits, one can argue that their benefits are the result of an appropriation of the surplus value produced by nonprofessionals (cf. Collins, 1979, pp. 64–70). Defending this claim entails criticizing the dominant belief that professionals receive greater benefits than nonprofessionals because they contribute more to the social product. Higher incomes are due to professionals' social power and cultural value, not usually to their social productivity.

The imperative to deskill labor associated with the division between task-defining and task-executing work produces the oppression of powerlessness in many workers. As I explicated it in Chapter 2, powerlessness is the situation of having little or no authority or autonomy in most aspects of one's life, especially one's work. As a concept, powerlessness overlaps with domination, but is not coextensive with it. All who do not participate in deciding the rules and choosing the authorities that order their actions and the conditions of their actions experience domination. This includes all who are powerless. Many who experience domination nevertheless exercise considerable initiative, authority, and creativity in their work, and this is what distinguishes them from those subject to the oppression of powerlessness.

Work organization divides a manufacturing or service activity into a "professional" aspect, exercising the technical knowledge, creativity, and organizational skill needed for the activity, on the one hand, and routinized operations of execution, on the other. This deskilling process is necessitated by the goal of mechanizing work as much as possible, in order to reduce labor costs, maximize unit productivity, and make monitoring of work performance easier. One of the primary jobs of task-defining organizational professionals becomes figuring out how to structure the routinized automated work using the fewest workers, in a detailed division of unskilled tasks (Braverman, 1974, esp. pts. 1 and 2). As I pointed out earlier, only the most routinized, minute, repetitive jobs are clearly subject to objective, quantifiable, and normatively neutral measures of productivity. This is because the skill, judgment, and creativity the total tasks require have been removed and located in a separate managerial function.

Justice entails that all persons have the opportunity to develop and exercise skills in socially recognized settings. Performing automated, routinized, and detailed specialized tasks, however, does not usually develop a person's capacity much, and sometimes deadens ambition or the ability to develop capacities. Some unskilled jobs allow for mobility into more skilled jobs. Often the more complex job requires special training, however, and builds very little on skills acquired in the previous job. I do not wish to exaggerate the prevalence of unskilled work among nonprofessionals; many nonprofessional occupations involve significant skill and room for developing excellence. As I will discuss shortly, much nonprofessional work that does involve the development and exercise of capacities is nevertheless devalued by cultural norms that value occupations according to the degree that they involve abstract rationality removed from practice. The structural division betweeen task-defining and task-executing work, moreover, puts pressure on these skilled nonprofessional occupations to professionalize—that is, to formalize their skills, create techniques and theories for their dissemination, develop professional schools of certification, and separate off these technical aspects of the work from more routine support tasks.

The deskilling imperative aims to increase the ratio of routinized jobs to the more skilled, creative, and autonomous jobs that come to be defined as professional and reserved for those who have acquired credentials. I pointed out earlier that the job structure of American society is increasingly polarized between such professional work and unskilled, routinized work. The creation of a huge class of unskilled, routinized jobs is unjust, because it condemns a large portion of the population to a situation in which they cannot develop and exercise their capacities. These low-skill jobs tend to be dead-end, offering no paths to advancement and job development. Mobility from the nonprofessional to the professional class is nearly impossible without costly and time-consuming schooling.

Nonprofessionals are also powerless in the sense that they are subordinates and exercise little workplace autonomy and decisionmaking power. Nonprofessionals who execute tasks designed by others are subject to domination by professionals and managers, whose right to rule them is legitimated by the expertise they are claimed to have (Poulantzas, 1978, pp. 240–42). Nonprofessional workers typically must follow orders and have little opportunity to give them. They must do the jobs assigned in the way they are assigned, often at a pace regulated by superiors or machines. If they find the job irrationally defined they usually have little opportunity to complain or suggest changes. As I discussed earlier, many workers have considerable discretion about how and whether to intervene to prevent things from going wrong, but their decisionmaking authority usually extends only to the details of their assigned tasks. As executing tasks designed by others, subject to direct supervision and often personal domination by others, nonprofessionals daily must comport themselves as obedient subordinates, a stance that usually diminishes a sense of self.

The division between professional and nonprofessional labor, finally, enacts a cultural imperialism that posits some kinds of work as intrinsically superior to and more valuable than others. Through the operation of what Alison Jaggar (1983, pp. 40–42) calls "normative dualism," work is valued according to a hierarchy that distinguishes "intelligence" from the body. The dominant culture implicitly operates with a narrow meaning of "intelligence" as the exercise of abstract calculative and verbal technical skills, in discourse and activities removed from the concreteness of sensuous things. Professionalizing an activity means creating a theoretical discipline for the formal expression and rationalization of its procedures. This rationalizing process abstracts from the engaged practice of the activity, and splits off the abstracted formal elements from the material embodied elements.

The norms that measure all work against the narrow standard of calculative and technical rationality locate occupations on a single scale of intelligence. But does it really take more intelligence to be a doctor than a librarian? To be a sales representative than a plumber? The cultural meanings of work unjustly victimize some people because of the work they choose or are tracked into, while they reward others entirely out of proportion to their contribution to the social product. Playing with, disciplining, and teaching young children well certainly requires a subtle intelligence, whose characteristics are very different from those manifested in speculating well on the stock market. Figuring out how to move bulky furniture around corners and down stairs without breaking, denting, or scratching anything often requires admirable ingenuity, but in forms rather different from those exhibited in writing computer programs. This cultural imperialism extends beyond nonprofessionals to some professions. Some professions, which tend to be dominated by women, are considered of lower value by the prevailing standard of intelligence; their work is considered less "scientific," and they are often seen as tied to the body and need: teaching young children, social work, nursing.

The current hierarchical division of labor tends to ignore intelligence and skill that have different and in some ways incomparable forms. Intelligence tests, and most other standardized tests, presume a narrow definition of intelligence as abstract rationality, reducing all skills and cognitive styles to a common measure that devalues some skills which might by another measure be called simply different. Yet the naturalness of a single scale for the assessment of intelligence, and the hierarchical valuation of occupations it implies, goes almost entirely unchallenged.

As I discussed in Chapter 5, this normative hierarchy of occupational intelligence contains a white male bias. The work of abstract rationality is coded as appropriate for white men, while work that involves caring for the body or emotions is coded for women, and the "menial" work of serving and being servile is coded for nonwhites. In this way the cultural imperialisms that structure racism and sexism modulate with a cultural imperialism that structures class difference. Its injustice consists in according high prestige to some work and low prestige to other work. Prestige, which is entirely a cultural and symbolic construct, then permits differential material reward and privilege.

The division between professionals and nonprofessionals leads to a general cultural valuation of some kinds of people as "respectable" because of the kind of work they do, and others as less respectable. The needs, experience, life style, and interests of the class of respectable professionals come to dominate many aspects of social life beyond the workplace—including social policy and media imagery. Newspapers, television, advertising, popular magazines and novels, far more often depict the lives and problems of middle-class professionals than those of working-class nonprofessionals, rendering the powerless invisible and depriving them of a cultural voice.

THE DEMOCRATIC DIVISION OF LABOR

From the discussion in the previous section I draw the conclusion that social justice requires democracy in the workplace and an undermining of the division between task definition and task execution. There are many theories and models of workplace democracy (see, e.g., Schweickart, 1980; Pateman, 1970; Mason, 1982; Bernstein, 1980; Gould, 1988). Though less common, some recent writings, which I have cited in this chapter, give detailed proposals for a structured work life that minimizes a class division between task-defining and task-executing work (see Green, 1985, pp. 79–94; Collins, 1979, 200–210). I shall neither reproduce nor evaluate these theories and models here. Nor will I offer another model of the democratic division of labor. To conclude this chapter I will only note some general parameters for a just workplace organization.

Workplace democracy is a necessary element in just social organization, for the same reasons that government should be democratic (see Gould, chap. 9). As many writers point out, moreover, democratic government and democratic workplaces are mutually reinforcing. Participation in decisionmaking in the workplace contributes to the development of an interest in and capacity for participation in decisionmaking in the city and the state (see, e.g., Pateman, 1970, chap. 3; Mason, chap. 4). Workplace democracy has at least two necessary conditions: (a) employees of an enterprise must participate in the basic decisions of the enterprise as a whole, and (b) they must participate in the specific decisions that concern their immediate work situation. These conditions in turn limit the upper and lower reaches of power. The first condition implies that there are no top executives with initiating and final authority over the operations of the enterprise. Instead, basic decisions about the enterprise should be made by a democratically elected and representative legislature accountable to those who elected them. Such basic decisions might include what will be produced, or what services will be provided; the basic plan and organization of the production or service provision processes, including the basic structure of the division of labor; the basic wage and profit-sharing structure; the capital investment strategy; the establishment of bylaws and basic rights of workers within the enterprise, as well as procedures for protecting those rights and adjudicating disputes; and the basic rules for hiring and promotion, as well as procedures for choosing elected officials. As I noted in Chapter 2, the community in which a workplace is located is directly affected by at least some of its activities, such as its capital reinvestment plans, its discharge of pollution, and even its child-care policy. Thus the community deserves some representation in at least those decisions that significantly affect life outside the enterprise. Where enterprises are not employee-owned, moreover, shareholders also deserve some representation. At the level of the general enterprise-governing body, the principle of group representation I argued for in Chapter 6 should operate. Socially oppressed or disadvantaged groups, such as women, racial minorities, and disabled people, should receive specific representation. In the context of a particular enterprise, moreover, other groups might be potentially disadvantaged—such as entry-level workers, or those doing a particular task.

Workplace democracy is less than complete, however, if it only involves participation in top-level decisions through a system of representation. It is at least as important that workers should participate in decisions about their own immediate work context and environment—their own speciality, department, work team, work site, and so on. This does not rule out managers or supervisors, but it means some decisions must be made jointly by managers and workers, that limits are set on managerial power, and that such power must operate alongside considerable individual and team autonomy.

As I discussed earlier, workers should decide democratically the qualifications for jobs and who is qualified for them. This does not imply that all workers should participate in deciding every appointment. It does mean, however, that as a rule there should be democratically elected "search committees," especially for positions of greater than average pay, power, or expertise.

Even if nothing else in workplace structure and the division of labor changes, workplace democracy along the lines I have described can greatly reduce the oppression of powerlessness that currently results fom the division between professionals who define much about their own and other's work and workers who only execute tasks defined by others. If job definitions were to remain more or less as they are, including a distinction between technical experts and administrators, on the one hand, and less skilled production, clerical, and service workers, on the other, democratic decisionmaking in the workplace would reduce the domination and subordination of the latter. Even if these less skilled workers continued to perform routine and rote tasks, moreover, their having the right and opportunity to participate in major workplace decisions could make their working life more interesting and skill-developing.

The division between task-defining and task-executing work, between a professional and a nonprofessional class, I have argued, itself tends to produce and reproduce oppression. This division is so entrenched in modern industry that even the system of workers' cooperatives widely regarded as the most successful example of workers' democracy in the world—Mondragon, in the Basque region of Spain—retains a solid division between a professional and managerial stratum of experts and nonprofessional workers (see Hacker, 1989, chaps. 5 and 7). As long as such a class division remains, there is an inherent tendency for the professional class to monopolize knowledge, to disempower others by deskilling their work, and to stand in a privileged relation of exploitation and cultural imperialism to the others.

A democratic division of labor need not, and probably should not, eliminate specialization. Undermining the class division between professional and nonprofessional workers thus means the following. First, the special privilege associated with professional work solely on grounds of status or prestige, in the form of pay, autonomy, work rules, or access to resources, is wrong. Second, mobility from less skilled to more skilled work should be available to anyone. There should be no such thing as a "dead-end" job, although remaining in one job should not carry stigma either. Skill development on the job and the opportunity to rise through job levels should be much more widespread than they are in typical work structures in advanced industrial societies. Professional and managerial workers, moreover, should begin their working lives with hands-on experience of line production or service delivery (cf. Collins, 1979, 200–201). Much good might come from assigning professional and managerial workers modest production or maintenance tasks. Where long-term schooling is required to develop specialized skills, such schooling should be available free of charge, and as much as possible should be available to all who want it (cf. Green, 1985, pp. 87–89). Persons with specialized technical skills or specialized forms of knowledge, finally, must be accountable to workers and the community. Specialized knowledge, which experts should present and disseminate, is indispensable for decisionmaking, but experts cannot claim authority to make the decisions on grounds of their expertise (cf. Green, 1985; Gould, 1988, chap. 10). Decisions about the uses of technology, the organization and dissemination of information, the planning of buildings and cities, and so on should be made by democratic heterogeneous publics in workplace, neighborhood, and region. The concluding chapter of this book argues, among other things, for the importance of regional government in promoting justice between workplaces and neighborhoods.

CHAPTER 8

City Life and Difference

> The tolerance, the room for great differences among neigh-
> bors—differences that often go far deeper than differences
> in color—which are possible and normal in intensely urban
> life, but which are so foreign to suburbs and pseudosuburbs,
> are possible and normal only when streets of great cities
> have built-in equipment allowing strangers to dwell in peace
> together on civilized but essentially dignified and reserved
> terms.
>
> —Jane Jacobs

ONE IMPORTANT PURPOSE of critical normative theory is to offer an alternative vision of social relations which, in the words of Marcuse, "conceptualizes the stuff of which the experienced world consists . . . with a view to
its possibilities, in the light of their actual limitation, suppression, and
denial" (Marcuse, 1964, p. 7). Such a positive normative vision can inspire
hope and imagination that motivate action for social change. It also provides some of the reflective distance necessary for the criticism of existing
social circumstances.

Many philosophers and political theorists criticize welfare capitalist society for being atomistic, depoliticized, fostering self-regarding interest-
group pluralism and bureaucratic domination. The most common alternative vision offered by such critics is an ideal of community. Spurred by
appeals to community as an alternative to liberal individualism made by
Michael Sandel, Alasdair MacIntyre, and others, in recent years political
theorists have debated the virtues and vices of communitarianism as opposed to liberalism (Gutmann, 1985; Hirsch, 1986; Wallach, 1987; Buchanan, 1989). Many socialists, anarchists, feminists, and others critical of
welfare capitalist society formulate their vision of a society free from domination and oppression in terms of an ideal of community. Much of this
discussion would lead us to think that liberal individualism and communitarianism exhaust the possibilities for conceiving social relations.

It should be clear from the preceding chapters that I share many of the
communitarian criticisms of welfare capitalist liberal democratic theory
and society. I shall argue in this chapter, however, that the ideal of community fails to offer an appropriate alternative vision of a democratic pol-

ity. The ideal of community exemplifies the logic of identity I analyzed in Chapter 4. This ideal expresses a desire for the fusion of subjects with one another which in practice operates to exclude those with whom the group does not identify. The ideal of community denies and represses social difference, the fact that the polity cannot be thought of as a unity in which all participants share a common experience and common values. In its privileging of face-to-face relations, moreover, the ideal of community denies difference in the form of the temporal and spatial distancing that characterizes social process.

As an alternative to the ideal of community, I develop in this chapter an ideal of city life as a vision of social relations affirming group difference. As a normative ideal, city life instantiates social relations of difference without exclusion. Different groups dwell in the city alongside one another, of necessity interacting in city spaces. If city politics is to be democratic and not dominated by the point of view of one group, it must be a politics that takes account of and provides voice for the different groups that dwell together in the city without forming a community.

City life as an openness to unassimilated otherness, however, represents only an unrealized social ideal. Many social injustices exist in today's cities. Cities and the people in them are relatively powerless before the domination of corporate capital and state bureaucracy. Privatized decisionmaking processes in cities and towns reproduce and exacerbate inequalities and oppressions. They also produce or reinforce segregations and exclusions within cities and between cities and towns, which contribute to exploitation, marginalization, and cultural imperialism.

Many democratic theorists respond to these ills of city life by calls for the creation of decentralized autonomous communities where people exercise local control over their lives and neighborhoods on a human scale. Such calls for local autonomy, I argue in conclusion, reproduce the problems of exclusion that the ideal of community poses. I offer a conceptual distinction between autonomy and empowerment, and sketch out some parameters of democratic empowerment in large-scale regional government.

THE OPPOSITION BETWEEN INDIVIDUALISM AND COMMUNITY

Critics of liberalism frequently invoke a conception of community as an alternative to the individualism and abstract formalism they attribute to liberalism (cf. Wolff, 1968, chap. 5; Bay, 1981, chap. 5). They reject the image of persons as separate and self-contained atoms, each with the same formal rights, rights to keep others out, separate. For such writers, the ideal of community evokes the absence of the self-interested competitiveness of modern society. In this ideal, critics of liberalism find an alternative to the abstract, formal methodology of liberalism. Existing in community with others entails more than merely respecting their rights; it entails attending to and sharing in the particularity of their needs and interests.

In his rightly celebrated critique of Rawls, for example, Michael Sandel (1982) argues that liberalism's emphasis on the primacy of justice presupposes a conception of the self as an antecedent unity existing prior to its desires and goals, whole unto itself, separated and bounded. This is an unreal and incoherent conception of the self, he argues. It would be better replaced by a conception of the self as the product of an identity it shares with others, of values and goals that are not external and willed, as liberalism would have it, but constitutive of the self. This constitutive conception of the self is expressed by the concept of community.

Benjamin Barber (1984) also uses the idea of community to evoke a vision of social life that does not conceive the person as an atomistic, separated individual. Liberal political theory represents individuals as occupying private and separate spaces, as propelled only by their own private desires. This is a consumer-oriented conception of human nature, in which social and political relations can be understood only as goods instrumental to the achievement of individual desires, and not as intrinsic goods. This atomistic conception generates a political theory that presumes conflict and competition as characteristic modes of interaction. Like Sandel, Barber appeals to an ideal of community to invoke a conception of the person as socially constituted, actively oriented toward affirming relations of mutuality, rather than oriented solely toward satisfying private needs and desires (cf. Ackelsberg, 1988).

As earlier chapters in this book indicate, I share these critiques of liberalism. Liberal social ontology, I have argued, has no place for a concept of social groups. I have characterized a social group as the relational outcome of interactions, meanings, and affinities according to which people identify one another. The self is indeed a product of social relations in profound and often contradictory ways. A person's social group identities, moreover, are in some meaningful sense shared with others of the group.

I have also criticized liberalism's consumer-oriented presuppositions about human nature, and agree with Barber that these lead to an instrumentalist understanding of the function of politics. With Barber and other new republican theorists, I too reject the privatization of politics in liberal pluralist processes, and call for the institution of democratic publics. I think, however, that all these criticisms of liberalism can and should be made without embracing community as a political ideal.

Too often contemporary discussion of these issues sets up an exhaustive dichotomy between individualism and community. Community appears in the oppositions individualism/community, separated self/shared self, private/public. But like most such terms, individualism and community have a common logic underlying their polarity, which makes it possible for them to define each other negatively. Each entails a denial of difference and a desire to bring multiplicity and heterogeneity into unity, though in opposing ways. Liberal individualism denies difference by positing the self as a solid, self-sufficient unity, not defined by anything or anyone other than itself. Its formalistic ethic of rights also denies difference by bringing all such separated individuals under a common measure of rights. Proponents of community, on the other hand, deny difference by positing fusion rather than separation as the social ideal. They conceive the social subject as a relation of unity or mutuality composed by identification and symmetry among individuals within a totality. Communitarianism represents an urge to see persons in unity with one another in a shared whole.

For many writers, the rejection of individualism logically entails the assertion of community, and conversely any rejection of community entails that one necessarily supports individualism. In their discussion of a debate between Jean Elshtain and Barbara Ehrenreich, for example, Harry Boyte and Sara Evans (1984) claim that Ehrenreich promotes individualism because she rejects the appeal to community that Elshtain makes. Recent accounts of the debate among political theorists generated by communitarian critiques of Rawls all couch that debate in terms of a dichotomy between liberal individualism and community, suggesting that these two categories are indeed mutually exclusive and exhaust all possible social ontologies and conceptions of the self (see Hirsch, 1986; Wallach, 1987; Cornell, 1987). Thus even when the discussants recognize the totalizing and circular character of this debate, and seek to take a position outside its terms, they tend to slide into affirming one or the other "side" of the dichotomy because that dichotomy, like the dichotomy a/not-a, is conceived as exhausting all logical possibilities.

THE ROUSSEAUIST DREAM

The ideal of community submits to the logic of identity I discussed in Chapter 4. It expresses an urge to unity, the unity of subjects with one another. The ideal of community expresses a longing for harmony among persons, for consensus and mutual understanding, for what Foucault calls the Rousseauist dream of

> a transparent society, visible and legible in each of its parts, the dream of there no longer existing any zones of darkness, zones established by the privileges of royal power or the prerogative of some corporation, zones of disorder. It was the dream that each individual, whatever position he occupied, might be able to see the whole of society, that men's hearts should communicate, their vision be unobstructed by obstacles, and that the opinion of all reign over each. (Foucault, 1980, p. 152)

Whether expressed as shared subjectivity or common consciousness, on
the one hand, or as relations of mutuality and reciprocity, the ideal of
community denies, devalues, or represses the ontological difference of
subjects, and seeks to dissolve social inexhaustibility into the comfort of a
self-enclosed whole.

Sandel is explicit about defining community as shared subjectivity. The
difference between his own constitutive meaning of community and the
instrumental and sentimental meanings he finds in Rawls is precisely that
in constitutive community subjects share a common self-understanding
(Sandel, 1982, pp. 62–63, 173). He is also explicit about social transparency as the meaning and goal of community:

> And in so far as our constitutive self-understandings comprehend a wider sub-
> ject than the individual alone, whether a family or tribe or city or class or nation
> or people, to this extent they define a community in the constitutive sense. And
> what marks such a community is not merely a spirit of benevolence, or the
> prevalence of communitarian values, or even certain 'shared final ends' alone,
> but a common vocabulary of discourse and a background of implicit practices
> and understandings within which the opacity of the participants is reduced if
> never finally dissolved. In so far as justice depends for its pre-eminence on the
> separatedness or boundedness of persons in the cognitive sense, its priority
> would diminish as that opacity faded and this community deepened. (Sandel,
> 1982, pp. 172–73)

Barber also takes shared subjectivity as the meaning of community.
Through political participation individuals confront one another and adjust their wants and desires, creating a "common ordering of individual
needs and wants into a single vision of the future in which all can share."
Strong democracy seeks to reach a "creative consensus" which through
common talk and common work creates a "common consciousness and
political judgment" (Barber, 1984, p. 224).

Some theorists of community, on the other hand, replace commonness
in the meaning of community with mutuality and reciprocity, the recognition by each individual of the individuality of all the others (see Cornell,
1987). Seyla Benhabib, for example, regards a standpoint that emphasizes
the commonness of persons as that of an ethic of rights and justice of the
sort that Rawls represents, which she calls the standpoint of the "generalized other." Moral theory must also express a complementary point of
view which Benhabib calls the standpoint of the "concrete other." Benhabib refers to this as a vision of a community of needs and solidarity, in contrast to the community of rights and entitlements envisaged by liberalism:

> The standpoint of the "concrete other," by contrast, requires us to view each
> and every rational being as an individual with a concrete history, identity, and
> affective-emotional constitution. In assuming this standpoint, we abstract from

what constitutes our commonality and seek to understand the distinctiveness of the other. We seek to comprehend the needs of the other, their motivations, what they search for, and what they desire. Our relation to the other is governed by the norm of *complementary reciprocity*: each is entitled to expect and to assume from the other forms of behavior through which the other feels recognized and confirmed as a concrete, individual being with specific needs, talents, and capacities. . . . The moral categories that accompany such interactions are those of responsibility, bonding, and sharing. The corresponding moral feelings are those of love, care, sympathy, and solidarity, and the vision of community is one of needs and solidarity. (Benhabib, 1986, p. 341)

Despite the apparent divergence of Sandel's and Barber's language of shared subjectivity and Benhabib's language of complementary reciprocity, I think all three express a similar ideal of social relations as the *copresence of subjects* (cf. Derrida, 1976, pp. 137–39). Whether expressed as common consciousness or as mutual understanding, the ideal is one of the transparency of subjects to one another. In this ideal each understands the others and recognizes the others in the same way that they understand themselves, and all recognize that the others understand them as they understand themselves. This ideal thus submits to what Derrida calls the metaphysics of presence, which seeks to collapse the temporal difference inherent in language and experience into a totality that can be comprehended in one view. This ideal of community denies the ontological difference within and between subjects.

In community persons cease to be other, opaque, not understood, and instead become mutually sympathetic, understanding one another as they understand themselves, fused. Such an ideal of the transparency of subjects to one another denies the difference, or basic asymmetry, of subjects. As Hegel first brought out and Sartre's analysis deepened, persons necessarily transcend one another because subjectivity is negativity. The regard of the other is always objectifying. Other persons never see the world from my perspective, and in witnessing the other's objective grasp of my body, actions, and words, I am always faced with an experience of myself different from the one I have.

This mutual intersubjective transcendence, of course, makes sharing between us possible, a fact that Sartre notices less than Hegel. The sharing, however, is never complete mutual understanding and reciprocity. Sharing, moreover, is fragile. At the next moment the other person may understand my words differently from the way I meant them, or carry my actions to consequences I do not intend. The same difference that makes sharing between us possible also makes misunderstanding, rejection, withdrawal, and conflict always possible conditions of social being.

Because the subject is not a unity, it cannot be present to itself, know itself. I do not always know what I mean, need, want, desire, because meanings, needs, and desires do not arise from an origin in some transparent ego. Often I express my desire in gesture or tone of voice, without meaning to do so. Consciousness, speech, expressiveness, are possible only if the subject always surpasses itself, and is thus necessarily unable to comprehend itself. Subjects all have multiple desires that do not cohere; they attach layers of meanings to objects without always being aware of each layer or the connections between them. Consequently, any individual subject is a play of difference that cannot be completely comprehended.

If the subject is heterogeneous process, never fully present to itself, then it follows that subjects cannot make themselves transparent, wholly present to one another. Consequently the subject also eludes sympathetic comprehension by others. I cannot understand others as they understand themselves, because they do not completely understand themselves. Indeed, because the meanings and desires they express may outrun their own awareness or intention, I may understand their words or actions more fully than they.

The ideal of community expresses a desire for social wholeness, symmetry, a security and solid identity which is objectified because affirmed by others unambiguously. This is an understandable dream, but a dream nevertheless, and, as I shall now argue, one with serious political consequences.

PRIVILEGING FACE-TO-FACE RELATIONS

The ideal of community as a pure copresence of subjects to one another receives political expression in a vision of political life that privileges local face-to-face direct democracy. Critics of welfare capitalist society repeatedly invoke such a model of small group relations as a political ideal. The anarchist tradition expresses these values most systematically, but they retain their form in other political soils as well. This model of politics as founded in face-to-face relations poses as the alternative to the impersonality, alienation, commodification, and bureaucratization of governance in existing mass societies:

> The incarnation of this project is the immediate, indeed unmediated, community that enters so profoundly into the fashioning of our humanity. This is the community in which we genuinely encounter each other, the public world that is only a bare step above our private world, in short, our towns, neighborhoods, and municipalities. (Bookchin, 1982, p. 267; cf. Manicas, 1974, pp. 246–50; Bay, 1981, chaps. 5 and 6; Taylor, 1982, pp. 27–28)

Several problems arise when a community that privileges face-to-face relations is taken as the ideal of the polity. The ideal presumes a myth of

unmediated social relations, and wrongly identifies mediation with alienation. It denies difference in the sense of temporal and spatial distancing.
It implies a model of the good society as consisting of decentralized small
units which is both unrealistic and politically undesirable, and which
avoids the political question of just relations among such decentralized
communities.

As the above quotation indicates, theorists of community privilege face-
to-face relations because they conceive them as *immediate*. Immediacy is
better than mediation because immediate relations have the purity and
security longed for in the Rousseauist dream: we are transparent to one
another, purely copresent in the same time and space, close enough to
touch, and nothing comes between us to obstruct our vision of one another.

This ideal of the immediate copresence of subjects, however, is a metaphysical illusion. Even a face-to-face relation between two people is mediated by voice and gesture, spacing and temporality. As soon as a third
person enters the interaction the possibility arises of the relation between
the first two being mediated through the third, and so on. The mediation
of relations among persons by the speech and actions of other persons is a
fundamental condition of sociality. The richness, creativity, diversity, and
potential of a society expand with growth in the scope and means of its
media, linking persons across time and distance. The greater the time and
distance, however, the greater the number of persons who stand between
other persons.

I am not arguing that there is no difference between small groups in
which persons relate to one another face-to-face and other social relations,
nor am I denying a unique value to such face-to-face groups. Just as the
intimacy of living with a few others in the same household has unique
dimensions that are humanly valuable, so existing with others in communities of mutual regard has specific characteristics of warmth and sharing
that are humanly valuable. There is no question either that bureaucratized capitalist patriarchal society discourages and destroys such communities of mutual friendship, just as it pressures and fragments families. A
vision of the good society surely should include institutional arrangements
that nurture the specific experience of mutual friendship which only relatively small groups interacting in a plurality of contexts can produce. But
recognizing the value and specificity of such face-to-face relations is different from privileging them and positing them as a model for the institutional relations of a whole society.

In my view, a model of the good society as composed of decentralized,
economically self-sufficient face-to-face communities functioning as autonomous political entities does not purify politics, as its proponents
think, but rather avoids politics. First, it is wildly utopian. To bring it into

being would require dismantling the urban character of modern society, a gargantuan overhaul of living space, workplaces, places of trade and commerce. A model of a transformed society must begin from the material structures that are given to us at this time in history, and in the United States those are large-scale industry and urban centers.

More important, however, this model of the good society as usually articulated leaves completely unaddressed the question of how such small communities relate to one another. Frequently the ideal projects a level of self-sufficiency and decentralization which suggests that proponents envision few relations among these communities except occasional friendly visits. Surely it is unrealistic, however, to assume that such decentralized communities need not engage in extensive relations of exchange of resources, goods, and culture.

Proponents frequently privilege face-to-face relations in reaction to the alienation and domination produced by huge, faceless bureaucracies and corporations, whose actions and decisions affect most people, but are out of their control. Appeals to community envision more local and direct control. A more participatory democratic society should indeed encourage active publics at the local levels of neighborhood and workplace. But the important political question is how relations among these locales can be organized so as to foster justice and minimize domination and oppression. Invoking a mystical ideal of community does not address this question, but rather obscures it. Politics must be conceived as a relationship of strangers who do not understand one another in a subjective and immediate sense, relating across time and distance.

UNDESIRABLE POLITICAL CONSEQUENCES OF THE IDEAL OF COMMUNITY

I have argued that the ideal of community denies the difference between subjects and the social differentiation of temporal and spatial distancing. The most serious political consequence of the desire for community, or for copresence and mutual identification with others, is that it often operates to exclude or oppress those experienced as different. Commitment to an ideal of community tends to value and enforce homogeneity (cf. Hirsch, 1986).

In ordinary speech in the United States, the term community refers to the people with whom one identifies in a specific locale. It refers to neighborhood, church, schools. It also carries connotations of ethnicity, race, and other group identifications. For most people, insofar as they consider themselves members of communities at all, a community is a group that shares a specific heritage, a common self-identification, a common culture and set of norms. As I argued in Chapter 5, self-identification as a member of such a community also often occurs as an oppositional differentiation from other groups, who are feared, despised, or at best devalued. Persons feel a sense of mutual identification only with some persons, feel in community only with those, and fear the difference others confront them with because they identify with a different culture, history, and point of view on the world. The ideal of community, I suggest, validates and reinforces the fear and aversion some social groups exhibit toward others. If community is a positive norm, that is, if existing together with others in relations of mutual understanding and reciprocity is the goal, then it is understandable that we exclude and avoid those with whom we do not or cannot identify.

Richard Sennett (1970, chap. 2) discusses how a "myth of community" operates perpetually in American society to produce and implicitly legitimate racist and classist behavior and policy. In many towns, suburbs, and neighborhoods people do have an image of their locale as one in which people all know one another, have the same values and life style, and relate with feelings of mutuality and love. In modern American society such an image is almost always false; while there may be a dominant group with a distinct set of values and life style, within any locale one can usually find deviant individuals and groups. Yet the myth of community operates strongly to produce defensive exclusionary behavior: pressuring the Black family that buys a house on the block to leave, beating up the Black youths who come into "our" neighborhood, zoning against the construction of multiunit dwellings.

The exclusionary consequences of valuing community, moreover, are not restricted to bigots and conservatives. Many radical political organizations founder on the desire for community. Too often people in groups working for social change take mutual friendship to be a goal of the group, and thus judge themselves wanting as a group when they do not achieve such commonality (see Mansbridge, 1980, chap. 21; Breines, 1982, esp. chap. 4). Such a desire for community often channels energy away from the political goals of the group, and also produces a clique atmosphere which keeps groups small and turns potential members away. Mutual identification as an implicit group ideal can reproduce a homogeneity that usually conflicts with the organization's stated commitment to diversity. In recent years most socialist and feminist organizations, for example, have taken racial, class, age, and sexual diversity as an important criterion according to which the success of political organizations should be evaluated. To the degree that they take mutual understanding and identification as a goal, they may be deflected from this goal of diversity.

The exclusionary implications of a desire for face-to-face relations of mutual identification and sharing present a problem for movements asserting positive group difference, which I described in Chapter 6. I argued there that the effort of oppressed groups to reclaim their group identity, and to form with one another bonds of positive cultural affirmation around their group specificity, constitutes an important resistance to the oppression of cultural imperialism. It shifts the meaning of difference from otherness and exclusion to variation and specificity, and forces dominant groups to acknowledge their own group specificity. But does not such affirmation of group identity itself express an ideal of community, and is it not subject to exclusionary impulses?

Some social movements asserting positive group difference have found through painful confrontation that an urge to unity and mutual identification does indeed have exclusionary implications. Feminist efforts to create women's spaces and women's culture, for example, have often assumed the perspective of only a particular subgroup of women—white, or middle class, or lesbian, or straight—thus implicitly excluding or rendering invisible those women among them with differing identifications and experiences (Spelman, 1988; Phelan, 1987). Similar problems arise for any movement of group identification, because in our society most people have multiple group identifications, and thus group differences cut across every social group.

These arguments against community are not arguments against the political project of constructing and affirming a positive group identity and relations of group solidarity, as a means of confronting cultural imperialism and discovering things about oneself and others with whom one feels affinity. Critique of the ideal of community, however, reveals that even in such group-specific contexts affinity cannot mean the transparency of selves to one another. If in their zeal to affirm a positive meaning of group specificity people seek or try to enforce a strong sense of mutual identification, they are likely to reproduce exclusions similar to those they confront. Those affirming the specificity of a group affinity should at the same time recognize and affirm the group and individual differences within the group.

City Life as a Normative Ideal

Appeals to community are usually antiurban. Much sociological literature diagnoses modern history as a movement to the dangerous bureaucratized *Gesellschaft* from the manageable and safe *Gemeinschaft*, nostalgically reconstructed as a world of lost origins (Stein, 1960; Nisbet, 1953). Many others follow Rousseau in romanticizing the ancient *polis* and the medieval Swiss *Bürger*, deploring the commerce, disorder, and unmanageable mass character of the modern city (Ellison, 1985; cf. Sennett, 1974, chaps. 7–10). Throughout the modern period, the city has often been decried as embodying immorality, artificiality, disorder, and danger—as the site of treasonous conspiracies, illicit sex, crime, deviance, and disease (Mosse, 1985, pp. 32–33, 137–38; Gilman, 1985, p. 214). The typical image of the modern city finds it expressing all the disvalues that a reinstantiation of community would eliminate.

Yet urbanity is the horizon of the modern, not to mention the postmodern, condition. Contemporary political theory must accept urbanity as a material given for those who live in advanced industrial societies. Urban relations define the lives not only of those who live in the huge metropolises, but also of those who live in suburbs and large towns. Our social life is structured by vast networks of temporal and spatial mediation among persons, so that nearly everyone depends on the activities of seen and unseen strangers who mediate between oneself and one's associates, between oneself and one's objects of desire. Urbanites find themselves relating geographically to increasingly large regions, thinking little of traveling seventy miles to work or an hour's drive for an evening's entertainment. Most people frequently and casually encounter strangers in their daily activities. The material surroundings and structures available to us define and presuppose urban relationships. The very size of populations in our society and most other nations of the world, coupled with a continuing sense of national or ethnic identity with millions of other people, supports the conclusion that a vision of dismantling the city is hopelessly utopian.

Starting from the given of modern urban life is not simply necessary, moreover; it is desirable. Even for many of those who decry the alienation, bureaucratization, and mass character of capitalist patriarchal society, city life exerts a powerful attraction. Modern literature, art, and film have celebrated city life, its energy, cultural diversity, technological complexity, and the multiplicity of its activities. Even many of the most staunch proponents of decentralized community love to show visiting friends around the Boston or San Francisco or New York in or near which they live, climbing up towers to see the glitter of lights and sampling the fare at the best ethnic restaurants.

I propose to construct a normative ideal of city life as an alternative to both the ideal of community and the liberal individualism it criticizes as asocial. By "city life" I mean a form of social relations which I define as the being together of strangers. In the city persons and groups interact within spaces and institutions they all experience themselves as belonging to, but without those interactions dissolving into unity or commonness. City life is composed of clusters of people with affinities—families, social group networks, voluntary associations, neighborhood networks, a vast array of small "communities." City dwellers frequently venture beyond such familiar enclaves, however, to the more open public of politics, commerce, and festival, where strangers meet and interact (cf. Lofland, 1973). City dwelling situates one's own identity and activity in relation to a horizon of a vast variety of other activity, and the awareness that this unknown, unfamiliar activity affects the conditions of one's own.

City life is a vast, even infinite, economic network of production, distribution, transportation, exchange, communication, service provision, and amusement. City dwellers depend on the mediation of thousands of other people and vast organizational resources in order to accomplish their individual ends. City dwellers are thus together, bound to one another, in what should be and sometimes is a single polity. Their being together entails some common problems and common interests, but they do not create a community of shared final ends, of mutual identification and reciprocity.

A normative ideal of city life must begin with our given experience of cities, and look there for the virtues of this form of social relations. Defining an ideal as unrealized possibilities of the actual, I extrapolate from that experience four such virtues.

(1) *Social differentiation without exclusion.* City life in urban mass society is not inconsistent with supportive social networks and subcultural communities. Indeed, for many it is their necessary condition. In the city social group differences flourish. Modernization theory predicted a decline in local, ethnic, and other group affiliations as universalist state institutions touch people's lives more directly and as people encounter many others with identifications and life styles different from their own. There is considerable evidence, however, that group differences are often reinforced by city life, and that the city even encourages the formation of new social group affinities (Fischer, 1982, pp. 206–30; Rothschild, 1981). Deviant or minority groups find in the city both a cover of anonymity and a critical mass unavailable in the smaller town. It is hard to imagine the formation of gay or lesbian group affinities, for example, without the conditions of the modern city (D'Emilio, 1983). While city dwelling as opposed to rural life has changed the lives and self-concepts of Chicanos, to take another example, city life encourages group identification and a desire for cultural nationalism at the same time that it may dissolve some traditional practices or promote assimilation to Anglo language and values (Jankowski, 1986). In actual cities many people express violent aversions to members of groups with which they do not identify. More than those who live in small towns, however, they tend to recognize social group difference as a given, something they must live with (Fischer, 1982, pp. 206–40).

In the ideal of city life freedom leads to group differentiation, to the formation of affinity groups, but this social and spatial differentiation of groups is without exclusion. The urban ideal expresses difference as I defined it in Chapter 6, a side-by-side particularity neither reducible to identity nor completely other. In this ideal groups do not stand in relations of inclusion and exclusion, but overlap and intermingle without becoming homogeneous. Though city life as we now experience it has many borders and exclusions, even our actual experience of the city also gives hints of what differentiation without exclusion can be. Many city neighborhoods have a distinct ethnic identity, but members of other groups also dwell in them. In the good city one crosses from one distinct neighborhood to another without knowing precisely where one ended and the other began. In the normative ideal of city life, borders are open and undecidable.

(2) *Variety*. The interfusion of groups in the city occurs partly because of the multiuse differentiation of social space. What makes urban spaces interesting, draws people out in public to them, gives people pleasure and excitement, is the diversity of activities they support. When stores, restaurants, bars, clubs, parks, and offices are sprinkled among residences, people have a neighborly feeling about their neighborhood, they go out and encounter one another on the streets and chat. They have a sense of their neighborhood as a "spot" or "place," because of that bar's distinctive clientele, or the citywide reputation of the pizza at that restaurant. Both business people and residents tend to have more commitment to and care for such neighborhoods than they do for single-use neighborhoods. Multifunctional streets, parks, and neighborhoods are also much safer than single-use functionalized spaces because people are out on the streets during most hours, and have commitment to the place (Jacobs, 1961, chap. 8; Sennett, 1970, chap. 4; cf. Whyte, 1988, chaps. 9, 22–25).

(3) *Eroticism*. City life also instantiates difference as the erotic, in the wide sense of an attraction to the other, the pleasure and excitement of being drawn out of one's secure routine to encounter the novel, strange, and surprising (cf. Barthes, 1986). The erotic dimension of the city has always been an aspect of its fearfulness, for it holds out the possibility that one will lose one's identity, will fall. But we also take pleasure in being open to and interested in people we experience as different. We spend a Sunday afternoon walking through Chinatown, or checking out this week's eccentric players in the park. We look for restaurants, stores, and clubs with something new for us, a new ethnic food, a different atmosphere, a different crowd of people. We walk through sections of the city that we experience as having unique characters which are not ours, where people from diverse places mingle and then go home.

The erotic attraction here is precisely the obverse of community. In the ideal of community people feel affirmed because those with whom they share experiences, perceptions, and goals recognize and are recognized by them; one sees oneself reflected in the others. There is another kind of pleasure, however, in coming to encounter a subjectivity, a set of meanings, that is different, unfamiliar. One takes pleasure in being drawn out of oneself to understand that there are other meanings, practices, perspectives on the city, and that one could learn or experience something more and different by interacting with them.

The city's eroticism also derives from the aesthetics of its material being: the bright and colored lights, the grandeur of its buildings, the juxtaposition of architecture of different times, styles, and purposes. City space offers delights and surprises. Walk around the corner, or over a few blocks, and you encounter a different spatial mood, a new play of sight and sound, and new interactive movement. The erotic meaning of the city arises from its social and spatial inexhaustibility. A place of many places, the city folds over on itself in so many layers and relationships that it is incomprehensible. One cannot "take it in," one never feels as though there is nothing new and interesting to explore, no new and interesting people to meet.

(4) *Publicity.* Political theorists who extol the value of community often construe the public as a realm of unity and mutual understanding, but this does not cohere with our actual experience of public spaces. Because by definition a public space is a place accessible to anyone, where anyone can participate and witness, in entering the public one always risks encounter with those who are different, those who identify with different groups and have different opinions or different forms of life. The group diversity of the city is most often apparent in public spaces. This helps account for their vitality and excitement. Cities provide important public spaces— streets, parks, and plazas—where people stand and sit together, interact and mingle, or simply witness one another, without becoming unified in a community of "shared final ends."

Politics, the critical activity of raising issues and deciding how institutional and social relations should be organized, crucially depends on the existence of spaces and forums to which everyone has access. In such public spaces people encounter other people, meanings, expressions, issues, which they may not understand or with which they do not identify. The force of public demonstrations, for example, often consists in bringing to people who pass through public spaces those issues, demands, and people they might otherwise avoid. As a normative ideal city life provides public places and forums where anyone can speak and anyone can listen.

Because city life is a being together of strangers, diverse and overlapping neighbors, social justice cannot issue from the institution of an Enlightenment universal public. On the contrary, social justice in the city requires the realization of a politics of difference. This politics lays down institutional and ideological means for recognizing and affirming diverse social groups by giving political representation to these groups, and celebrating their distinctive characteristics and cultures. In the unoppressive city people open to unassimilated otherness. We all have our familiar relations and affinities, the people to whom we feel close and with whom we share daily life. These familial and social groups open onto a public in which all participate, and that public must be open and accessible to all. Contrary to the communitarian tradition, however, that public cannot be conceived as a unity transcending group differences, nor as entailing complete mutual understanding. In public life the differences remain unassimilated, but each participating group acknowledges and is open to listening to the others. The public is heterogeneous, plural, and playful, a place where people witness and appreciate diverse cultural expressions that they do not share and do not fully understand.

Cities and Social Injustice

An ideal can inspire action for social change only if it arises from possibilities suggested by actual experience. The ideals of city life I have proposed are realized incidentally and intermittently in some cities today. There is no doubt, however, that many large cities in the United States today are sites of decay, poverty, and crime. There is just as little doubt that the smaller towns and suburbs to which many people escape from these ills are strung along congested highways, are homogeneous, segregated, and privatized. In either case, an ideal of city life as eroticized public vitality where differences are affirmed in openness might seem laughably utopian. For on city streets today the depth of social injustice is apparent: homeless people lying in doorways, rape in parks, and cold-blooded racist murder are the realities of city life.

In Chapter 1 I argued that a critical theory of social justice must consider not only distributive patterns, but also the processes and relationships that produce and reproduce those patterns. While issues of the distribution of goods and resources are central to reflections on social justice, issues of decisionmaking power and processes, the division of labor, and culture are just as important. Nowhere is this argument better illustrated than in the context of social injustice in the city. Inequalities of distribution can be read on the face of buildings, neighborhoods, and towns. Most cities have too many places where everyone would agree no one should have to live. These may be a stone's throw from opulent corporate headquarters or luxury condominiums. The correct principles and methods of distribution may be a subject of controversy, but as they wander through American city streets few would deny that something is wrong with existing distributions.

The social structures, processes, and relationships that produce and reproduce these distributions, however, are not so visible on the surface of our cities. Yet normative theory must identify and evaluate them as well as their outcomes. In this section I shall discuss three aspects of these processes that contribute to domination and oppression: (a) centralized corporate and bureaucratic domination of cities; (b) decisionmaking structures in municipalities and their hidden mechanisms of redistribution; and (c) processes of segregation and exclusion, both within cities and between cities and suburbs.

(a) Corporate and city power once coincided. Firms started in a city and exploited the labor of the city's population, and the city grew and prospered with the success of its major firms. Industrial magnates ruled the cities, either directly as city officials, or more indirectly as behind-the-scenes framers of city policy. Having a self-serving paternal attitude toward these cities, the ruling families engaged in philanthropic projects, building museums, libraries, parks, plazas, and statues as gifts to the public and monuments to their wealth and entrepreneurial ingenuity. The captains of industry often ruled ruthlessly, keeping the majority of people in squalor and ignorance, but they had a sense of place, were tied economically, socially, and politically to one or a few cities.

Today corporate capital is homeless. The enterprises that rule the world economy are larger than many cities, some larger than many nations, with branches dotting the globe, and no center. Mergers, interlocking directorships, holding companies, and the dispersion of ownership through securities and stock market speculation mean that political and economic power is dislodged from place. Fast as a satellite signal, capital travels from one end of a continent to the other, from one end of the world to the other. Its direction depends on the pull of profit, and its directors rarely consider how its movement may affect local economies.

Municipalities are dependent on this flighty capital for the health of their economic infrastructure. They must sell bonds on the open market to raise funds for public works. Because there are no national or state policies for encouraging investment in particular cities or regions that need resources and industry for their economic health, cities must compete with one another to provide an attractive "investment climate" (cf. Elkin, 1987, pp. 30–31). They depend on private capital for housing, office, and commercial space, production facilities, public works, and with all this, of course, jobs. Their public funds depend on taxing the private investors doing business within their borders. Where cities once at least could hold the carrot of lordly power and prestige before corporate decisionmakers, today cities are reduced to lowly supplicants, with little leverage for bargaining.

Cities are also relatively powerless before the state. Gerald Frug (1980) relates how American liberalism has always been hostile to a distinct and independent legal status for cities, and how gradually the law has removed most of the powers cities once had. Cities today have only those powers delegated to them by state governments, and these are usually rigorously limited by judicial interpretation. What decisionmaking authority cities have is restricted to matters deemed entirely local, and these are increasingly few. State laws not only regulate the kind and amount of taxes cities can levy, they also restrict the powers of cities to borrow money. Cities are limited in the kind of laws they can pass, which are generally restricted to "welfare improving regulatory services" (cf. Elkin, 1987, pp. 21–31).

Not only are city legal powers restricted and regulated by the state, but cities have become increasingly dependent on state and federal government for operating funds to provide their services, and increasingly come under the authority of state and federal government in the administration of services. Health, housing, and welfare services administered at the city level are usually regulated by state and federal bureaucracies, and cities depend on state and federal grants for their continued operation. Many local services, "such as education, transportation and health care, are provided not by cities but by special districts or public authorities organized to cut across city boundaries and over which cities have no control" (Frug, 1980, p. 1065). The "new federalism" of the past decade has not significantly altered the city's financial dependence on larger bureaucratic entities. It has somewhat increased cities' administrative responsibilities, often while reducing the resources with which they can administer.

The domination of centralized bureaucracies, whether public or private, over municipal economies tends to dissociate lived or experienced space from the commodified space of abstract planning and calculation (Gottdinger, 1985, pp. 290–97; Castells, 1983, chap. 31). Capitalist bureaucratic rationality fosters bird's-eye planning which encompasses vast regions including huge metropolitan areas, or even several states together. From this skytop vision, investors and planning bureaucrats determine the placement and design of highways, factories, shopping facilities, offices, and parks. They decide the most rational and efficient investment from the point of view of their portfolio and their centralized office operations, but not necessarily from the point of view of the locales in which they invest. Too often this bureaucratic rationality and efficiency results in a deadening separation of functions, with oppressive consequences that I will discuss shortly. It also often results in abrupt disinvestment in one region and massive disruptive speculation in another, each with significant consequences for the welfare of people in those locales.

The realization of the designers' plans creates an abstract space of efficiency and Cartesian rationality that often comes to dominate and displace the lived space of human movement and interaction:

What tends to disappear is the meaning of places for people. Each place, each city, will receive its social meaning from its location in the hierarchy of a network whose control and rhythm will escape from each place and, even more, from the people in each place. Furthermore, people will be shifted according to the continuous restructuring of an increasingly specialized space. . . . The new space of a world capitalist system, combining the informational and the industrial modes of development, is a space of variable geometry, formed by locations hierarchically ordered in a continuously changing network of flows: flows of capital, labor, elements of production, commodities, information, decisions, and signals. The new urban meaning of the dominant class is the absence of any meaning based on experience. The abstraction of production tends to become total. The new source of power relies on the control of the entire network of information. Space is dissolved into flows: cities become shadows that explode and disappear according to decisions that their dwellers will always ignore. The outer experience is cut off from the inner experience. The new tendential urban meaning is the spatial and cultural separation of people from their production and from their history. (Castells, 1983, p. 314)

(b) Though city and town governments are seriously constrained by the domination of state and corporate imperatives, they nevertheless do make decisions, especially about land use and zoning. Decisionmaking structures and processes at the local level, however, often tend to create and exacerbate injustice.

In Chapter 3 I discussed how policy formation in welfare capitalist society tends to be depoliticized and operates through a relatively closed club of interest-group bargainers. Such depoliticization is perhaps even more typical at the municipal level than at state or national levels. Stephen Elkin argues that in most cities land use decisions, the local decisions that most affect the spatial environment of the city and its economic life, are a semiprivate process involving a triangle of capitalist developers, city bureaucrats, and elected city officials. The assumptions and interests of these groups set the basic parameters for such decisions, which are routine, usually unquestioned and rarely publicly discussed. This routine framework, Elkin argues, is usually biased toward growth and downtown development, emphasizing big, flashy, visible projects. The empirical record shows, however, that land use decisionmaking biased in these ways contributes to increasing inequalities (see Elkin, 1987, chap. 5; cf. Logan and Molotch, 1987, chaps. 3 and 4).

With the basic resources and institutional structure already given, interest groups in the city vie for and bargain over the distributive effects of city projects. Because some interests are better able to organize than others, have easier access to the major decisionmakers and their information, and so on, this political process usually either reproduces initial distributions or increases inequalities (Harvey, 1973, pp. 73–79; Elkin, 1987, pp. 93–102).

The framework of privatized land use decisionmaking according to unquestioned routines, coupled with interest-group bargaining over the consequences of applying the framework, illustrates one of several "hidden mechanisms" that David Harvey (1973, esp. chap. 3) argues produce and reproduce social inequalities and oppression in cities. Policies to improve the lives and opportunities of the poor, the marginalized, or those otherwise disadvantaged will have little effect unless these hidden mechanisms are understood and restructured. Two other such mechanisms that Harvey cites are location and adaptability.

The location of land use projects often has serious redistributional impact on residents of a city. Some, usually the poor and unorganized, are displaced by projects. The location of production facilities, public services, transportation facilities, housing, and shopping areas affects different sectors of the population differently. Proximity to one facility may benefit some, by giving them easier or less costly access to a good or activity. Proximity to another kind of facility, on the other hand, may disadvantage some by imposing inconveniences such as dirt, noise, or environmental danger. Although a person's own material situation may remain constant, his or her life opportunities may nevertheless change significantly because of surrounding changes (Harvey, 1973, pp. 56–63). The losses caused by urban changes may involve not only monetary burdens, inconvenience, and loss of access to resources and services, but also the loss of the very environment that helps define a person's sense of self or a group's space and culture (Elkin, 1987, p. 90).

Another hidden mechanism of redistribution, according to Harvey, is the different adaptability of groups: some groups are better able than others to adjust to change in the urban environment. Thus one group's adjustment often lags behind another's, usually increasing inequality between them. Sometimes the disparity is caused by differences in initial levels of material resources. Just as often, however, the differences in ability to adjust have their sources in culture or life style (Harvey, 1973, pp. 62–64). Poverty, exploitation, marginalization, and cultural imperialism often determine that those less able to adapt to urban changes are more often required to do so (Elkin, 1987, p. 86).

(c) I have already noted how bureaucratic rationality imposes an abstract space of order and function over the lived space of multiuse interaction. The twentieth century has seen a steady increase in the functionalization and segregation of urban space. The earliest separation was the creation of residential districts spatially separated from manufacturing, retail, entertainment, commerce, and government. Recent decades, however, have seen a rapid increase in the spatial segregation of each of these other functions from one another. Each sort of activity occurs in its own walled enclaves, distinctly cut off from the others.

The separation of functions in urban space reduces the vitality of cities, making city life more boring, meaningless, and dangerous. Downtown districts bustling with people in the day hours become eerily deserted at night, when people swarm to the indoor shopping mall, which, despite the best efforts of designers, is boring and frenetic. Residential neighborhoods find few people on the streets either day or night, because there is nowhere to go and not much to look at without appearing to encroach on the privacy of others.

This separation of functions augments oppression and domination in several ways. The territorial separation of workplaces from residential communities divides the interest of working people between the shop floor, on the one hand, and consumer and neighborhood concerns, on the other. While corporate and state bureaucrats construct their bird's-eye view of cities and regions, citizens are unable to engage in significant collective action on the same scale, because the separation of home and work prevents them from constructing a larger pattern.

Territorial separation of residences from shopping centers, manufacturing, public plazas, and so on has specific damaging consequences for the lives of women, especially mothers. A full-time homemaker and mother who lives in a central city apartment within walking distance of stores, restaurants, offices, parks, and social services has a life very different from that of the woman who spends her day in a suburban house surrounded for miles by only houses and schools. The separation of urban functions forces homemaking women into isolation and boredom. It also makes their work—shopping, occupying children, taking them to activities, going to doctors, dentists, insurance agents, and so on—more difficult and time consuming. To the degree that they retain primary responsibility for children and other dependent family members, working women too suffer from the spatial separation of urban functions, which often limits their work opportunities to the few usually low-paying clerical and service jobs close to residential locations, or else forces them to traverse large spans of city space each day in a triangle or square, from home to child care to work to grocery store to child care to home (Hayden, 1983, pp. 49–59). The separation of functions and the consequent need for transportation to get to jobs and services also contributes directly to the increased marginality of old people, poor people, disabled people, and others who because of life situation as well as limited access to resources are less able to move independently in wide areas.

One aspect of the normative ideal of city life, I have said, is a social differentiation without exclusion. Groups will differentiate by affinities, but the borders will be undecidable, and there will be much overlap and intermingling. One of the most disturbing aspects of contemporary urban life is the depth and frequency of aversive behavior which occurs within it. Group segregation is produced by aversive perceptions that deprecate some groups, defining them as entirely other, to be shunned and avoided. Banks, real estate firms, city officials, newspapers, and residents all promote an image of neighborhoods as places where only certain kinds of people belong and others do not, deeply reinforcing aversive racism and the mechanism by which some groups are constructed as the depised Others. Zoning regulation enforces class segregation, and to a large degree racial segregation as well, by, for example, excluding multifamily dwellings from prosperous neighborhoods and even from entire municipalities. These group exclusions produce the conditions for harrassment of or violence against any persons found where they do not "belong." The myth of neighborhood community, of common values and life style, I have argued, fuels such exclusions.

The separation perhaps most far reaching in its effect on social justice is the legal separation of municipalities themselves. While social and economic processes have nearly obliterated any distinction between urban and rural life, and corporate and bureaucratic planning encompasses huge metropolitan regions, these same regions include scores of legally distinct municipalities, with their own local governments, ordinances, and public services. To avoid the ugliness, complexity, and dangers of contemporary city life, and often to avoid having to interact with certain kinds of people, many people seek community in the suburbs and small towns outside the city. The town's smallness and the fact that it is legally autonomous to make its own ordinances within the limits of state and federal regulation produce the illusion of local control. In fact the separation of towns renders them powerless against corporate and bureaucratic domination.

The legal and social separation of city and suburbs, moreover, contributes to social injustice. A direct relation of exploitation exists between most large American cities and their suburbs. Residents of the suburbs work in the city, use the city's services, and enjoy its life but, except in those rare cases where there is a city income or sales tax, pay no taxes to the city. Suburban municipalities usually benefit from their proximity to the city, but their legal autonomy ensures that they pay little or nothing for these benefits (Lowi, 1969, p. 197; Harvey, 1973, p. 94).

By means of their legal autonomy, some municipalities exclude certain kinds of people and certain kinds of activities from their borders. Because local governments generate funds to pay for local services by taxing residents, some towns and cities have far better schools and services than others. Because each municipality runs its own schools, police, fire department, and other public services, there is often an unjust and inefficient imbalance in the density and quality of services among different areas.

In the context of a large-scale and interdependent economic system under the control of private capital, "autonomy becomes a lead weight for the majority of cities, with only the most affluent towns able to create privilege from their formal independence. The political autonomy of places, as well as the planning power this entails, reproduces and exaggerates the inequalities between places rather than leveling them" (Logan and Molotch, 1987, p. 152).

These injustices have their primary source in the structural organization of decisionmaking. While all of the problems of city life I have discussed in this section involve distributive issues, the full extent of oppression and domination they involve can be understood only by considering culture and decisionmaking structures as they affect city geography, activities, and distributions.

EMPOWERMENT WITHOUT AUTONOMY

I have agreed with many participatory democratic theorists that democratization of governmental and corporate decisionmaking is necessary to undermine domination and oppression. Many theorists of participatory democracy identify such democratization with the decentralization of urban decisionmaking and the creation of small autonomous local communities. In this concluding section I shall challenge this model of democracy, and argue instead that social justice involving equality among groups who recognize and affirm one another in their specificity can best be realized in our society through large regional governments with mechanisms for representing immediate neighborhoods and towns.

To solve the problems of the domination of cities by state and corporate bureaucracies, Gerald Frug (1980) recommends legal, economic, and social reforms that would vest in municipalities autonomous local control over most of the activity within their borders. Decentralizing power and giving real power to cities requires, in his view, the municipalization of control over economic enterprise; the split between private and public corporate power should be transcended, and cities should have real autonomous control over the major productive, financial, and commercial entities within their borders. As a first step, Frug recommends that control over banking and insurance institutions be turned over to cities, which thereby would gain real power over investment decisions and the direction of building and development, as well as revenue sources in profit-making institutions. The purpose of such economic control, however, is to decentralize state power, and create autonomous political entities intermediate between the individual and the state, which provide individuals the opportunity for genuine participation and self-determination.

Murray Bookchin, to take another example, also calls for the municipalization of economic activity and the creation of small, decentralized, autonomous local communities, where people experience the rewards of citizenship through face-to-face interaction, discussion, and decisionmaking. The tendency toward urban sprawl, corporate internationalism, and political centralization and bureaucratization should be reversed. Municipal power should be institutionalized in a system of small-scale organic communities linked only by confederative agreements, over which no central state power is sovereign (Bookchin, 1987, pp. 245–70). Some other writers do not call for completely abolishing the state, but nevertheless take decentralized local autonomy as a priority (e.g., Sunstein, 1989, pp. 24–26; Elkin, 1987, chap. 7).

There is much compelling about such visions, which are common among democratic theorists critical of the hierarchy, expertism, and bureaucracy of contemporary advanced industrial society. Democratization requires the development of grass-roots institutions of local discussion and decisionmaking. Such democratization is meaningless unless the decisions include participation in economic power. Investment and land use will often cause or reinforce oppression when they are dominated by private corporate interests (see Elkin, 1987, pp. 174–80). Nevertheless, I wish to question the common identification of democracy with decentralized power vested in autonomous local communities. It is necessary to distinguish local empowerment from local autonomy.

Writers who call for the creation of decentralized municipal units with legal and economic autonomy rarely define precisely what they mean by autonomy. For the sake of this discussion I will give it the following strong meaning: An agent, whether individual or collective, is autonomous to the degree that it has sole and final authority to decide on specific issues and actions, and no other agent has the right to interfere. Autonomy implies sovereignty. A vision of decentralized democracy composed of small municipalities exercising autonomous local control, then, would mean at least prima facie that citizens in each municipality decide their form of government, what their rules and laws are, how their land and economic resources will be used and invested, the character and extent of their public services, and so on.

There are serious problems, however, with this vision of decentralized democracy, which engage the deepest issues of social justice. I have already discussed how the existing autonomy of municipal zoning functions in many municipalities to exclude low-income people as well as the jobs they might wish to have close to home. The autonomous choice by many municipalities not to run public transportation systems also excludes or

isolates poor and old people. The autonomous choices of suburban communities allow those communities to exploit the benefits of the city without providing anything in return.

If the whole society were to be organized as a confederation of autonomous municipalities, what would prevent the development of large-scale
inequality and injustice among communities, and thereby the oppression
of individuals who do not live in the more privileged or more powerful
communities? Can an adequate level of social and welfare services be
guaranteed for all individuals, for example, if one increases local autonomy (cf. Frankel, 1987, pp. 34–49)? Greater local autonomy would be
likely to produce even more exaggerated forms of the inequities that current decentralization produces: the concentration of needy people in
those locales that provide the more extensive social and welfare services,
putting an increased burden on them which their productive and resource
base cannot meet, while other municipalities turn their backs on what
they do not consider their problem. What, moreover, is to prevent the
economic exploitation of one municipality by another? If one municipality has a large source of water in an otherwise arid farming district, and
the others have nothing that municipality wants in return for use of the
water, they are likely to pay dearly, both in money and in political independence.

The problems of atomism are the same whether the atoms are individuals, households, or cities. At least since Hobbes it has been clear that
without a sovereign authority to mediate and regulate relations between
agents, there is nothing to prevent domination, exploitation, and oppression. Bookchin's suggestion that a set of marketlike contracts or confederative agreements can prevent such domination and oppression presumes
something even less true of municipalities than of individuals: that they
are equal in power, capacity, and resources. Where there are diverse and
unequal neighborhoods, towns, and cities, whose residents move in and
out of one another's locales and interact in complex webs of exchange,
only a sovereign authority whose jurisdiction includes them all can mediate their relations justly.

I do not mean to suggest that there is no room at all for local autonomy
as I have defined it. Certainly there is reason for a wide latitude of individual autonomy—a sphere of decisions which individuals have the sole right
to make, without interference from other agents, including state authority. There is also reason for collectivities to have such autonomy over a
certain range of decisions and activities. Clubs, production facilities,
stores, political parties, neighborhood committees, and towns all should
have autonomy over certain actions. For both individuals and collectivities one should apply a modified Millian test. Agents, whether individual
or collective, have the right to sole authority over their actions only if the

actions and their consequences (a) do not harm others, (b) do not inhibit the ability of individuals to develop and exercise their capacities within the limits of mutual respect and cooperation, and (c) do not determine conditions under which other agents are compelled to act. These conditions make the limits of autonomy narrow indeed—narrower, I suggest, for collectivities than for individuals. For the actions of collective agents are more likely to affect other agents in these ways than are the actions of individuals.

The range of autonomous action defined by these conditions is necessarily much narrower than the range our current legal system grants to private corporations and municipalities. It is also much narrower than that recommended or implied by most theorists of decentralized democracy. Such limitation of autonomy need not be a limitation of freedom or power, however, provided the bodies regulating the actions of individuals and collectivities are democratic and participatory. The principle is simple: wherever actions affect a plurality of agents in the ways I have specified, all those agents should participate in deciding the actions and their conditions.

The writers I have referred to call for decentralization and local autonomy as a means of counteracting hierarchical domination, alienation, and powerlessness. But it is democratization that confronts those problems, and democratization does not entail decentralization into small units of autonomous local control. Governmental authority should become more empowering but also more encompassing than municipal government is now.

Autonomy is a closed concept, which emphasizes primarily exclusion, the right to keep others out and to prevent them from interfering in decisions and actions. Autonomy refers to *privacy*, in just the sense that corporations are private in our current legal system. It should be distinguished from *empowerment*, which I define as participation of an agent in decisionmaking through an effective voice and vote. Justice requires that each person should have the institutionalized means to participate effectively in the decisions that affect her or his action and the conditions of that action. Empowerment is an open concept, a concept of publicity rather than privacy. Agents who are empowered with a voice to discuss ends and means of collective life, and who have institutionalized means of participating in those decisions, whether directly or through representatives, open together onto a set of publics where none has autonomy.

Empowerment means, at minimum, expanding the range of decisions that are made through democratic processes. Even if nothing else changed about the American political system, for example, extensive democratization would occur if the regulations and policies currently made by executive governmental authority were opened to democratic participation. If the use of major capital resources, to take a different example, were decided through discussion and democratic decisionmaking, this would represent a major change in power relations.

Dismantling the bureaucratic hierarchies of governmental and corporate power and bringing decisions such as these under democratic control, however, does also mean that participation must become more immediate, accessible, and local. Theorists of decentralized local democracy are right in their conviction that democratic participation means that authority cannot be concentrated in a center, far away from the majority of people who are affected by it. It does mean that there must be local institutions, right where people live and work, through which they participate in the making of regulations. Thus, along with many other theorists of participatory democracy, I imagine neighborhood assemblies as a basic unit of democratic participation (cf. Elkin, 1987, p. 176; Bay, 1981, pp. 152–60; Jacobs, chap. 21), which might be composed of representatives from workplaces, block councils, local churches and clubs, and so on as well as individuals. Despite my earlier criticism of his communitarianism, I find Barber's proposals about the role and functioning of such assemblies very good (Barber, 1984, pp. 269–72). Their purpose is to determine local priorities and policy opinions which their representatives should voice and defend in regional assemblies. The jurisdiction of neighborhood assemblies might correspond to existing municipalities, and there might be several in large metropolitan areas. But in such a scheme of restructured democracy municipalities as we now know them would cease to have sovereign authority.

In order to solve the problems of cities I identified in the previous section, the lowest level of governmental power should be regional (Lowi, 1969, chaps. 9 and 10; Harvey, 1973, pp. 110–11). I conceive a region as both an economic unit and a territory that people identify as their living space. A region is the space across which people commonly travel to work, shop, play, visit their friends, and take the children on errands, the span of a day trip. It is the range of television and radio transmission. The expanse of a region thus varies with culture, geography, economic base, and primary modes of transportation. Regions usually have a city or cluster of cities as a focus of their activity and identity, but include less densely populated suburban and rural areas. While hardly economically self-sufficient, regions nevertheless count as units of economic interdependence, the geographical territory in which people both live and work, in which major distribution occurs, much of it of products made in the region.

Not even regional governments should have complete autonomy, but their power would be extensive, matching or exceeding the present powers of local municipalities: powers of legislation, regulation, and taxation, significant control over land use and capital investment, and control over the design and administration of public services. Such regional government should be composed of representatives from neighborhood assemblies, which hold those representatives accountable. Neighborhoods and workplaces would have considerable powers of implementing regional policy and administering public services. At the level of regional government, finally, the system of representation for oppressed groups that I recommended in Chapter 7 would operate. Workplaces, neighborhood assemblies, and other collectives might choose to have group-based caucuses, but at the regional level group representation would be guaranteed by right. These provisions of local participation in the discussion and implementation of policy would empower individuals and social groups at the same time that policy would regulate perhaps millions of people in a wide jurisdiction.

This discussion of the levels and forms of government raises the question of whether state and federal government as they currently exist in the United States are appropriate forms. Many metropolitan regions now spill into several states, and the fact that a region is ruled by different state laws often leads to contradiction and irrationality. It would take us too far afield to consider this question of the role or appropriateness of state and national government. The arguments I have made about the dangers of autonomy would seem to indicate, however, that several levels of government are necessary to coordinate social relations and promote justice. Nevertheless, justice might require a fundamental reorganization of state and national government.

Besides making rules and laws, the primary functions of regional government would be planning and the provision of services. Only regionally scaled planning and service provision can solve the problems of domination and oppression which typify urban life today.

Democratized regional-level investment decisionmaking would end corporate monopoly of the productive capital of the region. With control over many investment decisions, regions could plan to meet their industrial, commercial, housing, transportation, and recreational development needs, not with an eye to private profit for absentee owners, but with an eye to what is needed and useful. In democratized regional planning many disagreements and conflicts would often no doubt occur among diverse sectors, groups, and interests about how best to use large capital resources, and the decisions would perhaps not always be the wisest or most rational. But it is unlikely that when a region already has five huge shopping malls, a democratic public would decide to construct another right across the highway from one of them, with the primary purpose of drawing business away from it. Nor would democratic investment planning be likely to result in the construction of additional luxury office space in a city

with a surplus of offices. Broad democratic planning is more likely to result in rational and just distributive decisions, that is, than hundreds of
autonomous public and private units attempting to maximize their perceived interests.

Regional-level service provision can solve many of the problems of injustice that I have identified as currently endemic to urban life. A primary
task of regional government would be to provide regionally (and perhaps
nationally) standardized services many of which are now paid for and run
by individual municipalities: schools, libraries, fire and police protection,
health and welfare services, highways, transportation, sanitation, and so
on. As I mentioned earlier, while standards and policy would be regionally based, they would be administered locally. Regional standardization
of services would build on a trend already exemplified in our society by
public transportation systems and health maintenance organizations. Regionally run public services maximize efficiency in those systems. It is
silly and artificial for fifteen small municipalities to maintain their own fire
departments when each uses its three trucks only twice a year. But the
major benefit of regionally based public services is that they best promote
justice. Regionally standardized and regionally financed schools, for example, would reduce the motivation for "white flight" and the resultant
degradation of schools in the inner city. Such regionally administered
schools should go together with school councils that seriously empower
parents and teachers to make policy for their own schools (see Bastian et
al., 1986, chap. 6). Regional democratically developed and administered
transportation services would reduce the isolation of certain populations,
and thereby reduce their marginalization.

Regional planning and service provision would have to attend to the
problems of structural injustice that Harvey (1973) discusses: the fact that
the location of facilities and services can advantage some and disadvantage
others; the fact that some groups may be better able to adapt to urban
change than others; and the fact that some groups may have more power
and influence than others. With traditional forms of interest-group bargaining and brokering there is no reason to think that regional policies
would fare any better in countering structural injustices than current city
policies. But with restructured processes of democratic participation that
include provision for the effective and specific representation of oppressed and disadvantaged groups, such injustices would be much less
likely to be reproduced as a matter of course.

To conclude, consider some principles that regional representatives
ought to follow. First, regions should promote liberty. Major capital investment decisions, development, construction, and planning decisions,
I have said, should be public, democratic, participatory, and regional in
scope. This does not preclude any and all manner of "private enter-

prise"—individuals and collectives engaging in a diversity of activities of their choosing for ends they privately determine. Government at whatever level—whether regional, state, or national—should protect and encourage the liberty of individuals and collectives to do what they choose within the limits of regulation and planning decisions. Individuals and collectives should not only be able to do what they want, but they should be able to do it *where* they want, as long as their activity does not harm other agents or inhibit their ability to develop and exercise their capacities. This means a reformation in the meaning and function of zoning (cf. Hayden, 1983, pp. 177–82; Sennett, 1970, chap. 4). The ideal of differentiated city life means in principle that people should not have power or authority to exclude persons or activities from public territory. People should be able to set up a store or a restaurant, build whatever dwelling they wish, set up a production facility, make a park, operate a religious center or counseling service for any population, without zoning regulations that limit their location choices. Potential neighbors must be free to discourage them, but they must not have the authority of law to exclude unwanted activities or constructions.

Second, as a matter of principle, regional planning decisions should be aimed at minimizing segregation and functionalization, and fostering a diversity of groups and activities alongside of and interspersed with one another. Fostering multiuse neighborhoods maximizes convenient access to goods, services, and public spaces for residents, and thereby minimizes some of the oppressions of marginalization. Fostering diversity of space and land use, moreover, rather than the functionalization of space, tends to make any facility more attractive and human. A production facility situated near residences, a day-care center, and a public park is more likely to regulate its polluting effects and make its building moderately attractive than one out of sight in a suburban industrial park, which invisibly endangers the health of nearby residents.

Regionally based public policy, planning, and service provision, finally, should be committed to fostering public spaces—assembly halls, indoor and outdoor plazas, wide sidewalks, recreation facilities and parks. Such spaces should be open to all activities, except perhaps selling things, and closed to vehicular traffic. There must be easy access to their use, with permits required only for the sake of safety and fairness, so that, for example, one group does not dominate a whole park or plaza day after day. Speechmaking, sign-carrying, and other modes of expression should be possible at any time, without a permit, as should the assembly of small groups.

In this chapter I have criticized a predominant tendency in participatory democratic theory to deny or think away social difference by appeal to an ideal of community. I have tried to fill out the implications of a politics of difference by envisioning an ideal of city life as a being together of strangers in openness to group difference. This ideal cannot be implemented as such. Social change arises from politics, not philosophy. Ideals are a crucial step in emancipatory politics, however, because they dislodge our assumption that what is given is necessary. They offer standpoints from which to criticize the given, and inspiration for imagining alternatives.

International Justice

I SHALL CLOSE with an opening.

Because I conceive critical theory as historically and socially situated, I have restricted discussion of social justice in this book to Western welfare capitalist societies, particularly the United States. Precisely the position of the United States in relation to the rest of the world, however, obliges any theorist of social justice to ask about justice in the rest of the world, both between and within countries. For the United States occupies a position of privilege in relation to much oppression in the world, and actions originating with state or private institutions in the United States contribute to much of that oppression.

The principles, categories, and arguments I have developed in the preceding chapters cannot be simply extended or applied to the context of international relations, or to issues of justice within many countries of the Southern or Eastern Hemispheres. Many of these principles, categories, and arguments, however, are also not irrelevant to understanding social justice in these parts of the world. Issues similar to those I have discussed in the context of the United States arise in other parts of the world, within and between nations. Treating them appropriately in relation to those other contexts might require modifications in the formulation of the issues, principles, categories, or arguments. In these few closing pages I explore ways in which the issues of this book may be extended to an international context, and to contexts of justice in societies other than Western welfare capitalist societies. Once again, this is meant as an opening, to raise questions for further research, rather than any definitive statement about international justice.

Normative theorizing about international justice is in its infancy, at least among Anglo-American writers. The literature on international justice that has emerged so far, however, tends to fall within the distributive paradigm of justice. In his excellent book on international morality, for example, Charles Beitz (1979) concentrates most of his discussion of justice on issues of the distribution of wealth and resources among nations, and particularly whether redistribution of resources from rich to poor nations is morally required. Distributive issues are perhaps even more important in a world context than in the context of single societies, especially relatively affluent Western welfare states. The vast inequalities in living standards between nations, owing to unequal access to resources, the legacy of colonialism, and the current ravages of international trade, finance, and exploitative investment, represent a gross distributive injustice.

The criticism I have voiced of a focus on distributive issues, however, applies with perhaps more force in this context. Without analysis of the institutional relations that structure the decisionmaking power behind distributions, and without an evaluation of the justice of those decision-making structures, moral theorists fail to touch important issues of international justice. The division of labor and culture also supply important categories for conceptualizing relations among nations in terms of justice that cannot be reduced to distribution.

My claim that injustice should be understood in terms of the categories of domination and oppression holds, I think, for any social context in the world today, as well as for relations among nations or states. Domination as I have defined it, as a lack of participation in determining one's actions and the conditions of one's actions, applies as well to Western Europe and North America as to the rest of the world. But the context-bound character of the theorizing in this book begins to emerge when we inquire about oppression in contexts other than Western societies. The five criteria of oppression that I have developed may be useful starting points for asking what oppression means in Asia, Latin America, or Africa, but serious revision of some of these criteria, or even their wholesale replacement, may be required. The categories of exploitation and cultural imperialism may stand more or less as I have defined them. But marginalization, power-lessness, and violence must be rethought, and perhaps recombined. There may be need for additional categories to describe oppression in these contexts.

In Chapter 2 I claimed that oppression in the United States is structural and systemic, and that the model of an identifiable oppressor group corresponding to each oppressed group does not hold. While oppression in other parts of the world is also structural and systemic, in many societies it is easier to identify oppressor groups. This fact alone alters the meaning of oppression in those contexts, and may require changing the categories of oppression and their relationships. The social group structures in such societies also produce specific social relationships that require their own analysis in terms of oppression. The criteria I have developed by thinking through the experience of oppressed groups in the United States have no reference, for example, to the specific experience of peasants, a major and usually oppressed social group in the Southern Hemisphere.

The five faces of oppression I have explicated may apply more easily to relations among nations in the total world context, and especially relations between advanced industrial societies and the rest of the world.

My discussion in Chapter 3 of the depoliticization of policy in welfare capitalist society is certainly the most context-bound in the book. For me it nevertheless raises interesting questions about justice, politics, and social movements in the international context. Is there an analogue to welfarism in the international context, which focuses people's efforts on redistribution while leaving the basic structures untouched? To me the answer is fairly clear. The system of "foreign aid" by which rich countries grant resources to poorer countries serves just this function. Does the international political and economic system depoliticize conflict, try to contain it within such distributive issues, and make policy formation the province of experts? While I am inclined to think that international relations are more politicized than the normal workings of state policy formation in welfare capitalist societies, state officials the world over exhibit a clear tendency to look on international conflict as something to be "managed" in private closed-door negotiations. Is there, then, in international politics something like an international civil society that repoliticizes public life outside or at the margins of these official state activities? I think there is, and that investigation of marginal international economic networks, the international peace movement, international people-to-people organizations of material and cultural solidarity, and international movements of women, people of color, and other groups can reveal a promising underside to the future of international relations.

The issues of the politics of difference I have analyzed are certainly important in contexts other than Western welfare capitalism. Working through social and political relations that affirm a positive sense of group difference and give specific representation to oppressed groups may be the most important political agendum in the world today.

Western welfare capitalist societies are by no means the only societies that have promoted an ideal of universal citizenship that transcends group differences. State socialist societies have a long tradition of this unifying urge, as do many other nation-states in Asia, Africa, and Latin America. In most cases this universalist ideal allows some groups to define the norm and appear neutral; that is, in most cases the ideal of social unity transcending differences reproduces cultural imperialist relations of privilege and oppression, and other relations of oppression as well. Social movements all over the world increasingly challenge this unifying standard, asserting positive images of group specificity (Rothschild, 1981; Ross, 1980). Movements of ethnic minorities in the Soviet Union, Yugoslavia, Spain, and India, just to mention a few, expose the ideal of a neutral citizenship transcending difference as naive at best. Women's movements all over the world also challenge the assumption of a gender-neutral citizenship. We are witnessing the worldwide breakup of such nationalist and state-fostered unities.

At the same time, major movements are underway toward greater international federation, breaking down the exclusions and separations that hitherto have defined state sovereignty and autonomy. The pan-African movement has taken steps toward greater economic interaction and cooperation among African states under a common governance structure. The European Economic Community is on the brink of a historical breakdown of the separation of twelve European states.

Group difference is the source of some of the most violent conflict and repression in the world today. An essentialist and absolutist understanding of social group difference is often more pronounced and deadly in places outside of relatively tolerant Western capitalist societies. Sexual, ethnic, and national groups are often understood as entirely other and opposed, sharing no attributes with the defining group, locked in despised bodies and fixed natures. World historical and economic conditions at the same time bring these groups into necessary interaction. Presently in many parts of the world this combination of necessary interaction and absolute opposition fuels horrible violence. I cannot pretend to understand the complexities of the causes of such violence and conflict in Lebanon, India, Indonesia, and many other places. Certainly these situations are tied up with issues of economic domination and exploitation, both within and between states.

I have mentioned three kinds of social and political situations involving difference in various parts of the world. First, there is the resurgence of ethnicity within states that had claimed to transcend such differences as politically irrelevant. Second, separate nations and states are creating institutions that bring them into greater contact and interaction, without giving up their differences. Third, in many places in the world group difference continues to be understood as absolute otherness, with domination and violence the result. An ideal of politics as deliberation in a heterogeneous public which affirms group differences and gives specific representation to oppressed groups is, I believe, immediately relevant to each of these situations. An ideal of community as shared final ends and mutual identification is even more absurd in these contexts than in the context of any city in the United States. At the same time, the interfusion and interdependence of groups is too thorough to make separation and complete group autonomy a realistic option. Only psychological dispositions, cultural expressions, and political institutions able to loosen but not dissolve borders, make them permeable and undecidable, at the same time that they create guarantees of group self-definition and representation in the public, can hold the hope of a more peaceful and just future for the world.

References

Ackelsberg, Martha. 1988. "Communities, Resistance and Women's Activism." In Ann Bookman and Sandra Morgen, eds., *Women and the Politics of Empowerment*. Philadelphia: Temple University Press.

Ackerman, Bruce. 1980. *Social Justice and the Liberal State*. New Haven: Yale University Press.

Adams, Robert. 1985. "Involuntary Sins." *Philosophical Review* 94 (January): 3–31.

Adorno, Theodor. 1973. *Negative Dialectics*. New York: Continuum.

Alexander, David. 1987. "Gendered Job Traits and Women's Occupations." Ph.D. dissertation, Economics, University of Massachusetts.

Altman, Dennis. 1982. *The Homosexualization of American Society*. Boston: Beacon.

Anderson, Benedict. 1983. *Imagined Communities: Reflections on the Origin and Spread of Nationalism*. London: New Left Books.

Arato, Andrew and Jean Cohen. 1984. "Social Movements, Civil Society, and the Problem of Sovereignty." *Praxis International* 4 (October): 266–83.

Arendt, Hannah. 1958. *The Human Condition*. Chicago: University of Chicago Press.

Arthur, John and William Shaw, eds. 1978. *Justice and Economic Distribution*. Englewood Cliffs, N.J.: Prentice-Hall.

Bachrach, Peter and Morton Baratz. 1969. "Two Faces of Power." In Roderick Bell, David Edwards, and Harrison Wagner, eds., *Political Power*. New York: Free Press.

Barber, Benjamin. 1984. *Strong Democracy*. Berkeley and Los Angeles: University of California Press.

Barthes, Roland. 1986. "Semiology and the Urban." In M. Gottdiener and Alexandros P. Lagopoulos, eds. *The City and the Sign: An Introduction to Urban Semiotics*. New York: Columbia University Press.

Bastian, Ann, Norm Fruchter, Marilyn Gittell, Colin Greer, and Kenneth Haskins. 1986. *Choosing Equality: The Case for Democratic Schooling*. Philadelphia: Temple University Press.

Bay, Christian. 1981. *Strategies for Political Emancipation*. Notre Dame: University of Notre Dame Press.

Bayes, Jane H. 1982. *Minority Politics and Ideologies in the United States*. Novato, Calif: Chandler and Sharp.

Beatty, Richard W. and James R. Beatty. 1981. "Some Problems with Contemporary Job Evaluation Systems." In Helen Remick, ed., *Comparable Worth and Wage Discrimination: Technical Possibilities and Political Realities*. Philadelphia: Temple University Press.

Beetham, David. 1985: *Max Weber and the Theory of Modern Politics*. Oxford: Polity.

Beitz, Charles. 1979. *Political Theory and International Relations*. Princeton: Princeton University Press.

———. 1988. "Equal Opportunity in Political Representation." In Norman Bowie, ed., *Equal Opportunity*. Boulder: Westview.

Bell, Derek. 1987. *And We Are Not Saved: The Elusive Quest for Racial Justice*. New York: Basic.

Benhabib, Seyla. 1986. *Critique, Norm and Utopia*. New York: Columbia University Press.

Berman, Marshall. 1982. *All That Is Solid Melts into Air*. New York: Simon and Schuster.

Bernstein, Paul. 1980. *Workplace Democratization: Its Internal Dynamics*. New Brunswick: Transaction.

Blum, Lawrence. 1980. *Friendship, Altruism and Morality*. London: Routledge and Kegan Paul.

———. 1988. "Gilligan and Kohlberg: Implications for Moral Theory." *Ethics* 97 (April): 472–91.

Blumfield, Warren S. 1976. *Development and Evaluation of Job Performance Criteria*. Athens, Ga.: Georgia State University Publishing Services.

Boggs, Carl. 1987. *Social Movements and Political Power*. Philadelphia: Temple University Press.

Bookchin, Murray. 1987. *The Rise of Urbanization and the Decline of Citizenship*. San Francisco: Sierra Club Books.

Boris, Ellen and Peter Bardaglio. 1983. "The Transformation of Patriarchy: The Historic Role of the State." In Irene Diamond, ed., *Families, Politics and Public Policy*. New York: Longman.

Bourdieu, Pierre. 1977. *Outline of a Theory of Practice*. Cambridge: Cambridge University Press.

Bowles, Samuel and Herbert Gintis. 1982. "Crisis of Liberal Democratic Capitalism: The Case of the United States." *Politics and Society* 11:51–94.

———. 1986. *Democracy and Capitalism*. New York: Basic.

Boxill, Bernard. 1984. *Blacks and Social Justice*. Totowa, N.J.: Rowman and Allanheld.

Boyte, Harry. 1984. *Community Is Possible*. New York: Harper and Row.

——— and Sara M. Evans. 1984. "Strategies in Search of America: Cultural Radicalism, Populism, and Democratic Culture." *Socialist Review*, May–August, pp. 73–100.

——— and Frank Reissman, eds. 1986. *New Populism: The Politics of Empowerment*. Philadelphia: Temple University Press.

Braverman, Harry. 1974. *Labor and Monopoly Capital*. New York: Monthly Review Press.

Breines, Wini. 1982. *Community and Organization in the New Left: 1962–68*. South Hadley, Mass.: Bergin.

Brittan, Arthur and Mary Maynard. 1984. *Sexism, Racism and Oppression*. Oxford: Blackwell.

Brown, Carol. 1981. "Mothers, Fathers and Children: From Private to Public Patriarchy." In Lydia Sargent, ed., *Women and Revolution*. Boston: South End.

Buchanan, Allen. 1982. *Marx and Justice*. Totowa, N.J.: Rowman and Allanheld.
———. 1989. "Assessing the Communitarian Critique of Liberalism." *Ethics* 99 (July): 852–82.
Bulkin, Elly, Minnie Bruce Pratt, and Barbara Smith. 1984. *Yours in Struggle: Three Feminist Perspectives on Anti-Semitism and Racism*. New York: Long Haul.
Burris, Beverly H. 1983. *No Room at the Top: Under-Employment and Alienation in the Corporation*. New York: Praeger.
Calhoun, Cheshire. 1989. "Responsibility and Reproach." *Ethics* 99 (January): 389–406.
Canter, Norma V. 1987. "Testimony from Mexican American Legal Defense and Education Fund." *Congressional Digest* (March).
Card, Claudia. 1989. "Responsibility and Moral Luck: Resisting Oppression and Abuse." Paper presented at the American Philosophical Association Eastern Division meeting, Atlanta, December.
Carmichael, Stokley and Charles Hamilton. 1967. *Black Power*. New York: Random House.
Castells, Manuel. 1983. *The City and the Grass Roots*. Berkeley and Los Angeles: University of California Press.
Cerroni, Umberto. 1983. "The Problem of Democracy in Mass Society." *Praxis International* 3 (April): 34–53.
Chodorow, Nancy. 1978. *The Reproduction of Mothering*. Berkeley and Los Angeles: University of California Press.
Clavel, Pierre. 1986. *The Progressive City: Planning and Participation, 1969–1984*. New Brunswick: Rutgers University Press.
Cliff, Michelle. 1980. *Reclaiming the Identity They Taught Me to Despise*. Watertown, Mass.: Persephone.
Cohen, Jean. 1985. "Strategy or Identity: New Theoretical Paradigms and Contemporary Social Movements." *Social Research* 52 (Winter): 663–716.
Cohen, Joshua and Joel Rogers. 1983. *On Democracy*. New York: Penguin.
Cole, Thomas R. 1986. "Putting Off the Old: Middle Class Morality, Antebellum Protestantism, and the Origins of Ageism." In David Van Tassel and Peter N. Stearns, eds., *Old Age in a Bureaucratic Society*. New York: Greenwood.
Colker, Ruth. 1986. "Anti-Subordination Above All: Sex, Race, and Equal Protection." *New York University Law Review* 61 (December): 1003–66.
Collins, Sheila. 1986. *The Rainbow Challenge: The Jackson Campaign and the Future of U.S. Politics*. New York: Monthly Review Press.
Collins, Randall. 1979. *The Credential Society: A Historical Sociology of Education and Stratification*. New York: Academic.
Connolly, William. 1983. *The Terms of Political Discourse*. 2d ed. Princeton: Princeton University Press.
Cornell, Drucilla. 1987. "Two Lectures on the Normative Dimensions of Community in the Law." *Tennessee Law Review* 54 (Winter): 327–43.
Cornell, Stephen. 1988. *The Return of the Native: American Indian Political Resurgence*. New York: Oxford University Press.
Coward, Rosalind and John Ellis. 1977. *Language and Materialism*. London: Routledge and Kegan Paul.

Cruse, Harold. 1987. *Plural but Equal: Blacks and Minorities and America's Plural Society*. New York: Morrow.

Cunningham, Frank. 1987. *Democratic Theory and Socialism*. Cambridge: Cambridge University Press.

Dallmayr, Fred. 1981. *Twilight of Subjectivity: Contributions to a Post-Structuralist Theory of Politics*. Amherst: University of Massachusetts Press.

Daniels, Norman. 1978. "Merit and Meritocracy." *Philosophy and Public Affairs* 7 (Spring): 206–23.

———. 1985. *Just Health Care*. Cambridge: Cambridge University Press.

Darwall, Stephen. 1983. *Impartial Reason*. Ithaca: Cornell University Press.

Davidson, Kenneth. 1976. "Preferential Treatment and Equal Opportunity." *Oregon Law Review* 55:53–83.

Deloria, Vine and Clifford Lytle. 1984. *The Nations Within*. New York: Pantheon.

Delphy, Christine. 1984. *Close to Home: A Materialist Analysis of Women's Oppression*. Amherst: University of Massachusetts Press.

D'Emilio, Joseph. 1983. *Sexual Politics, Sexual Communities*. Chicago: University of Chicago Press.

Derrida, Jacques. 1976. *Of Grammatology*. Baltimore: Johns Hopkins University Press.

———. 1978. "Violence and Metaphysics: An Essay on the Thought of Emmanuel Levinas." In *Writing and Difference*. Chicago: University of Chicago Press.

Devries, Davis L., Ann M. Morrison, Sandra L. Shullman, and Michael L. Gerlach. 1980. *Performance Appraisal on the Line*. New York: Wiley.

Doppelt, Gerald. 1987. "Technology and the Humanization of Work." In Gertrude Ezorsky, ed., *Moral Rights in the Workplace*. Albany: State University of New York Press.

Dreier, Peter. 1987. "Community Based Housing: A Progressive Approach to a New Federal Policy." *Social Policy* 18 (Fall): 18–22.

Du Bois, W. E. B. 1969 [1903]. *The Souls of Black Folk*. New York: New American Library.

Dworkin, Ronald. 1981. "What Is Equality? Part I." *Philosophy and Public Affairs* 10 (Summer): 185–246.

Easton, Barbara. 1978. "Feminism and the Contemporary Family." *Socialist Review* 39 (May/June): 11–36.

Edley, Christopher. 1986. "Affirmative Action and the Rights Rhetoric Trap." In Robert Fullinwider and Claudia Mills, eds. *The Moral Foundations of Civil Rights*. Totowa, N.J.: Rowman and Littlefield.

Eisenstein, Zillah. 1979. *The Radical Future of Liberal Feminism*. New York: Longman.

Elkin, Stephen L. 1987. *City and Regime in the American Republic*. Chicago: University of Chicago Press.

Ellison, Charles. 1985. "Rousseau and the Modern City: The Politics of Speech and Dress." *Political Theory* 13 (November): 497–534.

Elshtain, Jean. 1981. *Public Man, Private Woman*. Princeton: Princeton University Press.

Epstein, Steven. 1987. "Gay Politics, Ethnic Identity: The Limits of Social Constructionism." *Socialist Review* 17 (May–August) 9–54.

Fallon, Richard H. 1980. "To Each According to His Ability, From None According to His Race: The Concept of Merit in the Law of Antidiscrimination." *Boston
University Law Review* 60 (November): 815–77.

Fanon, Frantz. 1967. *Black Skin, White Masks*. New York: Grove.

Ferguson, Ann. 1984. "On Conceiving Motherhood and Sexuality: A Feminist
Materialist Approach." In Joyce Trebilcot, ed., *Mothering: Essays in Feminist
Theory*. Totowa, N.J.: Rowman and Allanheld.

———. 1989. *Blood at the Root*. London: Pandora.

Ferguson, Kathy. 1984. *The Feminist Case against Bureaucracy*. Philadelphia:
Temple University Press.

Fischer, Claude. 1982. *To Dwell among Friends: Personal Networks in Town and
City*. Chicago: University of Chicago Press.

Fishkin, James. 1983. *Justice, Equal Opportunity, and the Family*. New Haven:
Yale University Press.

Fisk, Milton. 1980. *Ethics and Society*. New York: New York University Press.

Fiss, Owen. 1976. "Groups and the Equal Protection Clause." *Philosophy and
Public Affairs* 5 (Winter): 107–76.

Fitzpatrick, Peter. 1987. "Racism and the Innocence of Law." *Journal of Law and
Society* 14 (Spring): 119–32.

Foucault, Michel. 1970. *The Order of Things*. New York: Random House.

———. 1977. *Discipline and Punish*. New York: Pantheon.

———. 1980. *Power/Knowledge*. New York: Pantheon.

Frankel, Boris. 1987. *The Post Industrial Utopians*. Madison: University of Wisconsin Press.

Fraser, Nancy. 1987a. "Women, Welfare, and the Politics of Need Interpretation." *Hypatia: A Journal of Feminist Philosophy* 2 (Winter): 103–22.

———. 1987b. "Social Movements vs. Disciplinary Bureaucracies: The Discourse
of Social Needs." CHS Occasional Paper No. 8. Center for Humanistic Studies,
University of Minnesota.

——— and Linda Nicholson. 1988. "Social Criticism without Philosophy: An Encounter between Feminism and Postmodernism." In Andrew Ross, ed., *Universal Abandon? The Politics of Postmodernism*. Minneapolis: University of
Minnesota Press.

Freeman, Alan D. 1982. "Antidiscrimination Law: A Critical Review." In David
Karys, ed., *The Politics of Law: A Progressive Critique*. New York: Pantheon.

French, Peter. 1975. "Types of Collectivities and Blame." *The Personalist* 56
(Spring): 160–69.

Friedman, Marilyn. 1985. "Care and Context in Moral Reasoning." In Carol Har-
ding, ed., *Moral Dilemmas: Philosophical and Psychological Issues in the Development of Moral Reasoning*. Chicago: Precedent.

———. 1987. "Beyond Caring: The De-Moralization of Gender." In Marsha
Hanen and Kai Nielsen, eds. *Science, Morality and Feminist Theory*. Calgary:
University of Calgary Press.

———. 1989. "Impracticality of Impartiality." *Journal of Philosophy* 86 (November): 645–56.

——— and Larry May. 1985. "Harming Women as a Group." *Social Theory and
Practice* 11 (Summer): 297–34.

Friedman, Toby and E. Belvin Williams. 1982. "Current Use of Tests for Employment." In Alexandra Wigdor and Wendell Garner, eds., *Ability Testing: Uses, Consequences, and Controversies, Part II*. Washington, D.C.: National Academy Press.

Frug, Gerald. 1980. "The City as a Legal Concept." *Harvard Law Review* 93 (April): 1059–1154.

Frye, Marilyn. 1983a. "Oppression." In *The Politics of Reality*. Trumansburg, N.Y.: Crossing.

———. 1983b. "On Being White: Toward a Feminist Understanding of Race Supremacy." In *The Politics of Reality*. Trumansburg, N.Y.: Crossing.

Fullinwider, Robert. 1980. *The Reverse Discrimination Controversy*. Totowa, N.J.: Rowman and Allanheld.

———. 1986. "Reverse Discrimination and Equal Opportunity." In Joseph DiMarco and Richard Fox, eds., *New Directions in Ethics*. London: Routledge and Kegan Paul.

Galston, William. 1980. *Justice and the Human Good*. Chicago: University of Chicago Press.

Giddens, Anthony. 1976. *Central Problems of Social Theory*. Berkeley: University of California Press.

———. 1981. *A Contemporary Critique of Historical Materialism*. Berkeley and Los Angeles: University of California Press.

———. 1984. *The Constitution of Society*. Berkeley and Los Angeles: University of California Press.

Gilligan, Carol. 1982. *In a Different Voice*. Cambridge: Harvard University Press.

Gilman, Sander L. 1985. *Difference and Pathology: Stereotypes of Sexuality, Race and Madness*. Ithaca: Cornell University Press.

Gintis, Herbert and Samuel Bowles. 1986. *Capitalism and Democracy*. New York: Basic.

Glennon, Lynda. 1979. *Women and Dualism*. New York: Longman.

Gottdiener, Mark. 1985. *The Social Production of Urban Space*. Austin: University of Texas Press.

Gottlieb, Rhonda. 1984. "The Political Economy of Sexuality." *Review of Radical Political Economy* 16 (Spring): 143–65.

Gottlieb, Roger. 1987. *History and Subjectivity*. Philadelphia: Temple University Press.

Gough, Ian. 1979. *The Political Economy of the Welfare State*. London: Macmillan.

Gould, Carol. 1988. *Rethinking Democracy: Freedom and Political Cooperation in Politics, Economics, and Society*. Cambridge: Cambridge University Press.

Green, Philip. 1985. *Retrieving Democracy*. Totowa, N.J.: Rowman and Allanheld.

Gutmann, Amy. 1980. *Liberal Equality*. Cambridge: Cambridge University Press.

———. 1985. "Communitarian Critics of Liberalism." *Philosophy and Public Affairs* 14 (Summer): 308–22.

Habermas, Jürgen. 1973. *Theory and Practice*. Boston: Beacon.

———. 1974. "The Public Sphere: An Encyclopedia Article." *New German Critique* 1 (Fall): 49–55.

———. 1975. *Legitimation Crisis*. Boston: Beacon.

———. 1981. "New Social Movements." *Telos* 49 (Fall): 33–37.

———. 1983. *The Theory of Communicative Competence*. Vol. 1: *Reason and the Rationalization of Society*. Boston: Beacon.

———. 1987. *The Theory of Communicative Competence*. Vol. 2: *Lifeworld and System*. Boston: Beacon.

Hacker, Sally. 1988. *Pleasure, Power and Technology*. London: Allen and Unwin.

Haraway, Donna. 1985. "Manifesto for Cyborgs." *Socialist Review* 80 (March/April): 65–107.

Hartsock, Nancy. 1983. *Money, Sex and Power*. New York: Longman.

Harvey, David. 1973. *Social Justice and the City*. Baltimore: Johns Hopkins University Press.

Hawkesworth, Mary E. 1984. "The Affirmative Action Debate and Conflicting Conceptions of Individuality." *Women's Studies International Forum* 7:335–47.

Hayden, Delores. 1983. *Redesigning the American Dream*. New York: Norton.

Heidegger, Martin. 1962. *Being and Time*. New York: Harper and Row.

Held, Virginia. 1987a. "Feminism and Moral Theory." In Eva Kittay and Diana Meyers, eds., *Women and Moral Theory*. Totowa, N.J.: Rowman and Littlefield.

———. 1987b. "A Non-Contractual Society." In Marsha Hanen and Kai Nielsen, eds., *Science, Morality and Feminist Theory*. Calgary: University of Calgary Press.

Heller, Agnes, 1987. *Beyond Justice*. New York: Basic.

Herzog, Don. 1986. "Some Questions for Republicans." *Political Theory* 14 (August): 473–93.

Hirsch, H. N. 1986. "The Threnody of Liberalism: Constitutional Liberty and the Renewal of Community." *Political Theory* 14 (August): 423–49.

Hochschild, Jennifer. 1988. "Race, Class, Power, and Equal Opportunity." In Norman Bowie, ed., *Equal Opportunity*. Boulder: Westview.

Holmstrom, Nancy. 1977. "Exploitation." *Canadian Journal of Philosophy* 7 (June): 353–69.

Howard, Michael. 1985. "Worker Control, Self-Respect, and Self-Esteem." *Philosophy Research Archives* 10:455–72.

Howe, Irving. 1982. Introduction to Irving Howe, ed., *Beyond the Welfare State*. New York: Schocken.

Husani, Ziyad. 1980. "Marx on Distributive Justice." In Marshall Cohen et al., eds., *Marx, Justice, and History*. Princeton: Princeton University Press.

Irigaray, Luce. 1985. *Speculum of the Other Woman*. Ithaca: Cornell University Press.

Jacobs, Jane. 1961. *The Death and Life of Great American Cities*. New York: Random House.

Jaggar, Alison. 1983. *Feminist Politics and Human Nature*. Totowa, N.J.: Rowman and Allanheld.

Jankowski, Martin Sanchez. 1986. *City Bound: Urban Life and Political Attitudes among Chicano Youth*. Albuquerque: University of New Mexico Press.

Janowitz, Morris. 1976. *Social Control of the Welfare State*. New York: Elsevier.

Karst, Kenneth. 1986. "Paths to Belonging: The Constitution and Cultural Identity." *North Carolina Law Review* 64 (January): 303–77.

Katznelson, Ira. 1980. *City Trenches*. New York: Pantheon.

Keane, John. 1984. *Public Life in Late Capitalism*. Cambridge: Cambridge University Press.

———. 1988. *Democracy and Civil Society*. London: Verso.

Keller, Evelyn Fox. 1986. *Reflections on Gender and Science*. New Haven: Yale University Press.

Kleven, Thomas. 1988. "Cultural Bias and the Issue of Bilingual Education." *Social Policy* 19 (Summer): 9–12.

Kovel, Joel. 1984. *White Racism: A Psychohistory*. 2d ed. New York: Columbia University Press.

Kristeva, Julia. 1977. "Le Sujet en Procès." In *Polylogue*. Paris: Editions du Seuil.

———. 1982. *Powers of Horror: An Essay in Abjection*. New York: Columbia University Press.

Laclau, Ernesto and Chantal Mouffe. 1985. *Hegemony and Socialist Strategy*. London: Verso.

Lader, Laurence. 1979. *Power on the Left*. New York: Norton.

Landes, Joan. 1988. *Women and the Public Sphere in the Age of the French Revolution*. Ithaca: Cornell University Press.

Lange, Lynda. 1979. "Rousseau: Women and the General Will." In Lynda Lange and Lorenne M.G. Clark, eds., *The Sexism of Social and Political Theory*. Toronto: University of Toronto Press.

Lawrence, Charles R. 1987. "The Id, the Ego, and Equal Protection: Reckoning with Unconscious Racism." *Stanford Law Review* 39 (January): 317–88.

Lefort, Claude. 1986. "What Is Bureaucracy?" In *The Political Forms of Modern Society*. London: Polity.

Levinas, Emmanuel. 1969. *Totality and Infinity*. Pittsburgh: Duquesne University Press.

Levontin, R. C., Steven Rose, and Leon Kamin. 1984. *Not in Our Genes: Biology, Ideology and Human Nature*. New York: Pantheon.

Littleton, Christine. 1987. "Reconstructing Sexual Equality." *California Law Review* 75 (July): 1279–1337.

Livingston, John C. 1979. *Fair Game? Inequality and Affirmative Action*. San Francisco: Freeman.

Lloyd, Genevieve. 1984. *The Man of Reason: "Male" and "Female" in Western Philosophy*. Minneapolis: University of Minnesota Press.

Lofland, Lyn H. 1973. *A World of Strangers: Order and Action in Urban Public Space*. New York: Basic.

Logan, John R. and Harvey L. Molotch. 1987. *Urban Fortunes: The Political Economy of Place*. Berkeley and Los Angeles: University of California Press.

Lowi, Theodore. 1969. *The End of Liberalism*. New York: Norton.

Lugones, Maria C. and Elizabeth V. Spelman. 1983. "Have We Got a Theory for You! Feminist Theory, Cultural Imperialism and the Demand for 'the Woman's Voice.' " *Women's Studies International Forum* 6:573–81.

Luke, Timothy. 1987. "Power and Resistance in Post-Industrial Society." Paper presented at the Third International Social Philosophy Conference, Charlotte, N.C., June.

Lyotard, Jean-François. 1984. *The Postmodern Condition*. Minneapolis: University of Minnesota Press.

———. and Jean-Loup Thébaud. 1985. *Just Gaming*. Minneapolis: University of Minnesota Press.

MacIntyre, Alasdair. 1981. *After Virtue*. Notre Dame: University of Notre Dame Press.

Macpherson, C. B. 1962. *The Political Theory of Possessive Individualism*. Oxford: Oxford University Press.

———. 1973. *Democratic Theory: Essays in Retrieval*. Oxford: Oxford University Press.

Manicas, Peter. 1974. *The Death of the State*. New York: Putnam.

Mansbridge, Jane. 1980. *Beyond Adversarial Democracy*. New York: Basic.

Marable, Manning. 1984. *Race, Reform and Rebellion: The Second Reconstruction in Black America, 1945–82*. Jackson: University Press of Mississippi.

Marcuse, Herbert. 1964. *One-Dimensional Man*. Boston: Beacon.

Markus, Maria. 1986. "Women, Success, and Civil Society: Submission to or Subversion of the Achievement Principle." *Praxis International* 5 (January): 430–42.

Mason, Ronald. 1982. *Participatory and Workplace Democracy*. Carbondale: Southern Illinois University Press.

May, Larry. 1987. *The Morality of Groups: Collective Responsibility, Group-Based Harm, and Corporate Rights*. Notre Dame: Notre Dame University Press.

———. 1990. "Insensitivity and Moral Responsibility." *Journal of Value Inquiry*, in press.

McConohay, John. 1986. "Modern Racism, Ambivalence, and the Modern Racism Scale." In John Davidio and Sam Gaetner, eds., *Prejudice, Discrimination and Racism*. New York: Academic.

McGary, Howard. 1983. "Racial Integration and Racial Separatism: Conceptual Clarifications." In Leonard Harris, ed., *Philosophy Born of Struggle*. Dubuque, Iowa: Hunt.

Merchant, Carolyn. 1978. *The Death of Nature*. New York: Harper and Row.

Michelman, Frank. 1986. "Traces of Self-Government." *Harvard Law Review* 100 (November): 4–77.

Miles, Angela. 1985. "Feminist Radicalism in the 1980's." *Canadian Journal of Political and Social Theory* 9:16–39.

Miller, David. 1976. *Social Justice*. Oxford: Clarendon Press.

Miller, Richard. 1984. *Analyzing Marx*. Princeton: Princeton University Press.

Minow, Martha. 1985. "Learning to Live with the Dilemma of Difference: Bilingual and Special Education." *Law and Contemporary Problems* 48 (Spring): 157–211.

———. 1987. "Justice Engendered." *Harvard Law Review* 101 (November): 11–95.

———. 1990. *Making All the Difference*. Ithaca: Cornell University Press.

Mosse, George. 1985. *Nationalism and Sexuality*. New York: Fertig.

Murphy, Raymond. 1985. "Exploitation or Exclusion?" *Sociology* 19 (May): 225–43.

Nagel, Thomas. 1986. *The View from Nowhere*. Oxford: Oxford University Press.

Nell, Edward and Onora O'Neill. 1980. "Justice under Socialism." In James Sterba, ed., *Justice: Alternative Political Perspectives*. Belmont, Calif.: Wadsworth.

Nicholson, Linda. 1986. *Gender and History*. New York: Columbia University Press.

Nickel, James. 1988. "Equal Opportunity in a Pluralistic Society." In Ellen Frankel Paul, Fred D. Miller, Jeffrey Paul, and John Ahrens, eds., *Equal Opportunity*. Oxford: Blackwell.

Nielsen, Kai. 1978. "Class and Justice." In John Arthur and William Shaw, eds., *Justice and Economic Distribution*. Englewood Cliffs, N.J.: Prentice-Hall.

———. 1979. "Radical Egalitarian Justice: Justice as Equality." *Social Theory and Practice* 5 (Spring): 209–26.

———. 1985. *Liberty and Equality*. Totowa, N.J.: Rowman and Allanheld.

Nisbet, Robert A. 1953. *The Quest for Community*. New York: Oxford University Press.

Noedlinger, 1981. *On the Autonomy of the Democratic State*. Cambridge: Harvard University Press.

Nozick, Robert. 1974. *Anarchy, State, and Utopia*. New York: Basic.

O'Connor, James. 1973. *The Fiscal Crisis of the State*. New York: St. Martin's.

Offe, Claus. 1976. *Industry and Inequality: The Achievement Principle in Work and Social Status*. New York: St. Martin's.

———. 1984. *Contradictions of the Welfare State*. Cambridge: MIT Press.

———. 1985. *Disorganized Capitalism*. Cambridge: MIT Press.

Okin, Susan. 1978. *Women in Western Political Thought*. Princeton: Princeton University Press.

———. 1982. "Women and the Making of the Sentimental Family." *Philosophy and Public Affairs* 11 (Winter): 65–88.

———. 1986. "Are Our Theories of Justice Gender-Neutral?" In Robert Fullinwider and Claudia Mills, eds., *The Moral Foundations of Civil Rights*. Totowa, N.J.: Rowman and Littlefield.

———. 1989. "Reason and Feeling in Thinking about Justice." *Ethics* 99 (January): 229–49.

Omi, Michael and Howard Winant. 1983. "By the Rivers of Babylon: Race in the United States, Part I and II." *Socialist Review* 71 (September–October): 31–66; 72 (November–December): 35–70.

———. 1986. *Racial Formation in the United States*. New York: Routledge and Kegan Paul.

Orr, Eleanor Wilson. 1987. *Twice as Less: Black English and the Performance of Black Students in Mathematics and Science*. New York: Norton.

Ortiz, Roxanne Dunbar. 1984. *Indians of the Americas*. New York: Praeger.

Pateman, Carole, 1970. *Participation and Democratic Theory*. Cambridge: Cambridge University Press.

———. 1979. *Political Obligation*.

———. 1986. "Feminism and Participatory Democracy: Some Reflections on Sexual Difference and Citizenship." Paper presented at the American Philosophical Association Western Division meeting, St. Louis, April.

———. 1988. *The Sexual Contract*. Stanford: Stanford University Press.

Pelczynski, Z. A. 1971. "The Hegelian Conception of the State." In Z. A. Pelczynski, ed., *Hegel's Political Philosophy: Problems and Perspectives*. Cambridge: Cambridge University Press.

Pevar, Stephen L. 1983. *The Rights of Indians and Tribes*. New York: Bantam.

Piper, Adrian. 1988. "Higher-Order Discrimination." Paper presented at the Conference on Moral Character, Radcliffe College, April.

Pitkin, Hannah. 1981. "Justice: On Relating Public and Private." *Political Theory* 9 (August): 327–52.

Piven, Frances Fox and Richard Cloward. 1982. *The New Class War*. New York: Pantheon.

Poulantzas, Nicos. 1978. *Classes in Contemporary Capitalism*. London: Verso.

Rawls, John. 1971. *A Theory of Justice*. Cambridge: Harvard University Press.

Reich, Michael. 1981. *Racial Inequality*. Princeton: Princeton University Press.

Reiman, Jeffrey. 1987. "Exploitation, Force, and the Moral Assessment of Capitalism: Thoughts on Roemer and Cohen." *Philosophy and Public Affairs* 16 (Winter): 3–41.

Reynolds, William Bradford. 1986. "*Stotts*: Equal Opportunity, Not Equal Results." In Robert Fullinwider and Claudia Mills, eds., *The Moral Foundations of Civil Rights*. Totowa, N.J.: Rowman and Littlefield.

Rhode, Deborah L. 1988. "Occupational Inequality." *Duke Law Journal* 1988 (December): 1207–41.

———. 1989. *Justice and Gender*. Cambridge: Harvard University Press.

Roemer, John. 1982. *A General Theory of Exploitation and Class*. Cambridge: Harvard University Press.

Ross, Jeffrey. 1980. Introduction to Jeffrey Ross and Ann Baker Cottrell, eds., *The Mobilization of Collective Identity*. Lanham, Md.: University Press of America.

Rothschild, Joseph. 1981. *Ethnopolitics*. New York: Columbia University Press.

Ruchwarger, Gary. 1987. *People in Power: Forging a Grassroots Democracy in Nicaragua*. South Hadley, Mass.: Bergin and Garvey.

Ruddick, Sara. 1984. "Maternal Thinking." In Joyce Trebilcot, ed., *Mothering: Essays in Feminist Theory*. Totowa, N.J.: Rowman and Allanheld.

Runciman, W. G. 1978. "Processes, End States and Social Justice." *Philosophical Quarterly* 28 (January): 37–45.

Ryan, Michael. 1982. *Marxism and Deconstruction*. Baltimore: Johns Hopkins University Press.

Said, Edward. 1978. *Orientalism*. New York: Pantheon.

Sandel, Michael. 1982. *Liberalism and the Limits of Justice*. Cambridge: Cambridge University Press.

Sartre, Jean-Paul. 1948. *Anti-Semite and Jew*. New York: Schocken.

Sawicki, Jana. 1986. "Foucault and Feminism: Toward a Politics of Difference." *Hypatia: A Journal of Feminist Philosophy* 1 (Summer): 23–36.

Scales, Ann. 1981. "Towards a Feminist Jurisprudence." *Indiana Law Journal* 56 (Spring): 375–444.

Schmitt, Eric. 1989. "As the Suburbs Speak More Spanish, English Becomes a Cause." *New York Times*, 26 February.

Schweickart, David. 1980. *Capitalism or Worker Control?* New York: Praeger.

———. 1984. "Plant Relocations: A Philosophical Reflection." *Review of Radical Political Economics* 16 (Winter): 32–51.

Scott, Joan. 1988. "Deconstructing Equality-versus-Difference: Or the Uses of Post-Structuralist Theory for Feminism." *Feminist Studies* 14 (Spring): 33–50.

Sears, David O. and Leonie Huddy. 1987. "Bilingual Education: Symbolic Meaning and Support among Non-Hispanics." Paper presented at the annual meeting of the American Political Science Association, Chicago, September.

Sennett, Richard, 1974. *The Fall of Public Man*. New York: Random House.

———. and Jonathan Cobb. 1972. *The Hidden Injuries of Class*. New York: Vintage.

Shepard, Orrie. 1982. "Definitions of Bias." In Ronald A. Berk, ed., *Handbook of Methods for Detecting Test Bias*. Baltimore: Johns Hopkins University Press.

Sher, George. 1987a. "Groups and the Constitution." In Gertrude Ezorsky, ed., *Moral Rights in the Workplace*. Albany: State University of New York Press.

———. 1987b. "Predicting Performance." In Ellen Frankel Paul, Fred D. Miller, Jeffrey Paul, and John Ahrens, eds., *Equal Opportunity*. Oxford: Blackwell.

———. 1988. "Qualifications, Fairness, and Desert." In Norman Bowie, ed., *Equal Opportunity*. Boulder: Westview.

Shklar, Judith. 1969. *Men and Citizens*. Cambridge: Cambridge University Press.

Simon, Robert. 1984. "Troubled Waters: Global Justice and Ocean Resources." In Tom Regan, ed., *Earthbound*. New York: Random House.

Simpson, Evan. 1980. "The Subject of Justice." *Ethics* 90 (July): 490–501.

Slaughter, Thomas F. 1982. "Epidermalizing the World: A Basic Mode of Being Black." In Leonard Harris, ed., *Philosophy Born of Struggle*. Dubuque, Iowa: Hunt.

Smart, Barry. 1983. *Foucault, Marxism, and Critique*. London: Routledge and Kegan Paul.

Smith, Michael and Dennis R. Judd. 1984. "American Cities: The Production of Ideology." In Michael P. Smith, ed., *Cities in Transformation*. Berkeley: Sage.

Smith, Paul. 1988. *Discerning the Subject*. Minneapolis: University of Minnesota Press.

Spelman, Elizabeth V. 1989. *The Inessential Woman*. Boston: Beacon.

Spraegens, Thomas. 1981. *The Irony of Liberal Reason*. Chicago: University of Chicago Press.

Stein, Maurice. 1960. *The Eclipse of Community*. Princeton: Princeton University Press.

Sterba, James. 1980. *The Demands of Justice*. Notre Dame: University of Notre Dame Press.

Strenio, Andrew J., Jr. 1981. *The Testing Trap*. New York: Rawson, Wade.

Sumner, L. W. 1987. "Positive Sexism." In Ellen Frankel Paul, Fred D. Miller, Jeffrey Paul, and John Ahrens, eds., *Equal Opportunity*. Oxford: Blackwell.

Sunstein, Cass R. 1988. "Beyond the Republican Revival." *Yale Law Journal* 97 (July): 1539–90.

Symanski, Al. 1985. "The Structure of Race." *Review of Radical Political Economy* 17 (Winter): 106–20.

Takaki, Ronald. 1979. *Iron Cages: Race and Culture in Nineteenth Century America*. New York: Knopf.

Taub, Nadine and Wendy Williams. 1985. "Will Equality Require More than Assimilation, Accommodation or Separation from the Existing Social Structure?" *Rutgers Law Review* 37 (Summer): 825–44.

Taylor, Charles. 1985. "The Nature and Scope of Distributive Justice." In *Philosophy and the Human Sciences*. Cambridge: Cambridge University Press.

Treiman, Donald J. and Heidi I. Hartman. 1981. *Women, Work and Wages*. Washington, D.C.: National Academy Press.

Turner, John C., Michael A. Hogg, Penelope V. Oakes, Stephen D. Rucher, and Margaret S. Wethrell. 1987. *Rediscovering the Social Group: A Self-Categorization Theory*. Oxford: Blackwell.

Unger, Roberto. 1974. *Knowledge and Politics*. New York: Free Press.

———. 1987a. *Social Theory: Its Situation and Its Task*. Cambridge: Cambridge University Press.

———. 1987b. *False Necessity: Anti-Necessitarian Social Theory in the Service of Radical Democracy*. Cambridge: Cambridge University Press.

Vesperi, Maria D. 1985. *City of Green Benches: Growing Old in a New Downtown*. Ithaca: Cornell University Press.

Vogel, Lisa. 1990. "Debating Difference: The Problem of Special Treatment of Pregnancy in the Workplace." *Feminist Studies*, in press.

Wagman, Bainat and Nancy Folbre. 1988. "The Feminization of Inequality: Some New Patterns." *Challenge* 31 (November/December): 56–59.

Walton, Anthony. 1983. "Public and Private Interests: Hegel on Civil Society and the State." In S. Benn and G. Gause, eds., *Public and Private in Social Life*. New York: St. Martin's.

Walzer, Michael. 1982. "Politics in the Welfare State: Concerning the Role of American Radicals." In Irving Howe, ed., *Beyond the Welfare State*. New York: Schocken.

———. 1983. *Spheres of Justice*. New York: Basic.

———. 1987. *Interpretation and Social Criticism*. Cambridge: Harvard University Press.

Wartenburg, Thomas E. 1989. *The Forms of Power: An Essay in Social Ontology*. Philadelphia: Temple University Press.

Wasserstrom, Richard. 1980a. "On Racism and Sexism." In *Philosophy and Social Issues*. Notre Dame: Notre Dame University Press.

———. 1980b. "On Preferential Treatment." In *Philosophy and Social Issues*. Notre Dame: Notre Dame University Press.

West, Cornel. 1982. *Prophesy Deliverance! An Afro-American Revolutionary Christianity*. Philadelphia: Westminster.

White, Kirby et al. 1982. *The Community Land Trust Handbook*. Emmaus, Pa.: Doale.

Whyte, William. 1988. *City: Rediscovering the Center*. New York: Doubleday.

Wigdor, Alexandra. 1982. "Psychological Testing and the Law of Employment Discrimination." In Alexandra Wigdor and Wendell Garner, eds., *Ability Testing: Uses, Consequences, and Controversies, Part II*. Washington, D.C.: National Academy Press.

——— and Wendell Garner, eds. 1982. *Ability Testing: Uses, Consequences, and Controversies, Part I*. Washington, D.C.: National Academy Press.

Williams, Bernard. 1985. *Ethics and the Limits of Philosophy*. Cambridge: Harvard University Press.

Williams, Robert A. 1986. "The Algebra of Federal Indian Law: The Hard Trail of Decolonizing and Americanizing the White Man's Indian Jurisprudence." *Wisconsin Law Review*, pp. 219–99.

Williams, Wendy. 1983. "Equality's Riddle: Pregnancy and the Equal Treatment/Special Treatment Debate." *New York University Review of Law and Social Change* 13:325–80.

Wilson, William J. 1978. *The Declining Significance of Race*. Chicago: University of Chicago Press.

Withorn, Ann. 1984. *Serving the People: Social Services and Social Change*. New York: Columbia University Press.

Wolfe, Alan. 1977. *The Limits of Legitimacy: Political Contradictions of Contemporary Capitalism*. New York: Free Press.

Wolff, Robert Paul. 1968. *The Poverty of Liberalism*. Boston: Beacon.

———. 1977. *Understanding Rawls*. Princeton: Princeton University Press.

———. 1984. *Understanding Marx*. Princeton: Princeton University Press.

Wolgast, Elizabeth. 1980. *Equality and the Rights of Women*. Ithaca: Cornell University Press.

Wood, Allen. 1972. "The Marxian Critique of Justice." *Philosophy and Public Affairs* 1 (Spring): 244–82.

Young, Iris. 1979. "Self-Determination as a Principle of Justice." *Philosophical Forum* 11 (Fall): 172–82.

———. 1981. "Toward a Critical Theory of Justice." *Social Theory and Practice* 7 (Fall): 279–302.

———. 1983. "Justice and Hazardous Waste." In Michael Bradie, ed., *The Applied Turn in Contemporary Philosophy*. Bowling Green, Ohio: Applied Philosophy Program, Bowling Green State University.

———. 1985. "Humanism, Gynocentrism and Feminist Politics." *Women's Studies International Forum* 8:173–83.

———. 1987. "Impartiality and the Civic Public: Some Implications of Feminist

Critiques of Moral and Political Theory." In Seyla Benhabib and Drucilla Cornell, eds., *Feminism as Critique*. Oxford/Minneapolis: Polity/University of Minnesota Press.

———. 1989. "Polity and Group Difference: A Critique of the Ideal of Universal Citizenship." *Ethics* 99 (January): 250–74.

Zola, Irving Kenneth. 1987. "The Politicization of the Self-Help Movement." *Social Policy* 18 (Fall): 32–33.

Index

Abject, category of, 124
Abjection, and border anxiety: defined, 124; prejudice and, 141–48; theory of, 11
Ableism, abjection and, 147–48
Acceptance, consciousness of, 130–36
Ackerman, Bruce, 17, 52, 103–4
Adams, Robert, 150
Administered society, domination in, 76–81
Aesthetic judgment, cultural bias and, 152
Affectivity: discursive consciousness and, 134–36; impartiality and, 100; reason and, 118–19. *See also* Subjectivity
Affinity: insurgency and, 84; politics of difference and, 172–73
Affirmative action: assimilationist ideal and, 173–74; as compensation, 194; distributive paradigm and, 12, 198–200; hierarchical division of labor and, 215–16; liberal equality and, 192–93; nondiscrimination principle and, 193–98; politics of qualifications and, 211–12; social groups and, 9–10; unconscious racism/sexism and, 135
Afro-American culture, emergence of, 159–60
Ageism, abjection and, 147–48; scaling of bodies and, 129–30
Aggregate model of groups, 43–48
Alexander, David, 51
Ambiguity, abjection and, 145–46
American Indian Movement (AIM), 160
American Indians, 160, 181–83
Anti-nuclear power movement: group differences in, 188; as insurgency, 83–84
Arendt, Hannah, 119–20
Assimilation: American Indian Movement and, 182–83; behavioral norms of respectability and, 140–41; cultural pluralism and, 177–81; equal treatment and, 195–96; ideal of, 158–63, 168–69; politics of difference and, 157–58, 164–66; role of, in policy making, 173–74
Association model of groups, 43–48

Authority, ideal of impartiality and, 115–16
Autonomy: empowerment of city life and, 248–55; impartiality and, 112–16; insurgency and, 83–84, 88; marginalization and, 54–55; politics of difference and, 167–68; professionalization of work and, 221
Aversion: cultural imperialism and, 123–24; myth of merit and, 206; oppression and, 142; unconscious, 130–36, 148–49
Aversive racism, 141–42

Barber, Benjamin, 117–18, 228, 230
"Basic security system:" defined, 131–32; prejudices and, 133, 138–39
Beauty, white bourgeois ideal of, 128–30
Behavior: exclusionary, 235–36, 238–39; norms of respectability and, 136–41; professional standards of, 139–41
Beitz, Charles, 257–58
Benhabib, Seyla, 35, 106–7, 230–31
Bilingual-bicultural maintenance programs, 181
Bilingual Education Act, 180
Bilingualism, unity vs. pluralism in, 178–81
Black English, legitimation of, 160, 207
Black liberation movement, 89–90
Black Power movement, 159–60
Blame, vs. responsiblity, 151
Blaming the victim syndrome, myth of merit and, 196
Bodies, scaling of, 11; abjection and, 144–48; conscious acceptance/unconscious aversion, 130–36; cultural revolution and, 152–55; dichotomy with reason and, 139–41; discursive consciousness and, 134–36; ideal of civic public and, 111; insurgency movements and, 87–88; modern context of, 124–30; norms of respectability and, 137–41; politics of identity and, 122–55; professionalization of work and, 139–40, 221–22; white bourgeois bias in, 127–30
Bookchin, Murray, 249–50

Bourgeois bias: ideal of civic public and, 110–11; norms of respectability and, 137–41; scaling of bodies and, 127–30; sexuality and, 138–39

Boxill, Bernard, 169

"Broad-band testing," limits of, 208

Brown, Carol, 51

Bureaucracy: democratization of, 252–55; distributive paradigm of justice and, 22; domination of, in administered society, 76–81; ideal of impartiality in, 113–16; impact of, on city life, 243–44; insurgency against, 81–88; in welfare capitalist society, 69–70

Bureau of Indian Affairs, 160

Capital accumulation: as goal of welfare capitalist society, 68–69; insurgency and, 81–82; professionalization of work and, 217–18

Capitalism. See also Welfare capitalist society

Care, justice and, 97

Careerism, 80–81

Castells, Manuel, 90

Central America solidarity movements, 84–85

Central planning, decisionmaking power and, 67–68, 218

Chastity: enforcement of, on women, 109–10; white bourgeois ideal of, 128–30

Citizenship: duality of, for American Indians, 183; ideal of civic public and, 110–11, 120–21; ideal of impartiality and, 97; international aspects of, 259; justice and, 33–34; marginalization and, 54–55; participatory democracy and, 117–18

City life: ideal of, 13; civic public ideal and, 108; defined, 237; difference and, 226–56; empowerment without autonomy in, 248–55; eroticism in, 239–40; exclusion lacking in, 238–39; necessity of, 237–38; as normative ideal, 236–41; power of state and, 242–43; publicity in, 240–41; social injustice and, 241–48; variety in, 239

Civic public, ideal of, 10–11; ideal of impartiality and, 96–121; insurgency and, 82–83; logic of identity and, 107–11; participatory democracy and decisionmaking, 117–21

Civil Rights Act, 159

Class structure: distributive paradigm of justice and, 20–21; exploitation and, 48–53, 49–50; history of, 156–57; institutionalization of, 70–71; marginalization and, 53–55; oppression and, 42; powerlessness and, 56–58; professionalization of work and, 217–22; scaling of bodies and, 126–27

Cole, Thomas, 147

Collective action, domination in administered society and, 77–81

"Common good," myth of, 118–19

Communicative ethics: democracy and, 92–94; ideal of impartiality and, 106–7; justice and, 33–34; participatory democracy and, 117–18; theory of, 45–46

Community, ideal of, 12–13, 226–27; individualism and, 227–29; international aspects of, 260; mutuality and reciprocity in, 230–31; political consequences of, 233–36; privileging of face-to-face relations, 232–34; Rousseauist dream of, 229–32. See also City life, ideal of

Community control of schools, 93–95

Comparable worth policies, gender neutrality vs. group consciousness in, 177–78

"Concrete other," 106–7

Confederative agreements, 250–51

Connolly, William, 30–31

Consciousness raising, 11; cultural revolution and, 153–55

Constitutionality of democracy, 92–93

Consumer: ideal of community and, 228–29; marginalization and, 54–55; role of in welfare capitalist society, 71–72

Contract model of social relations, 44–45

Copresence of subjects, ideal of community and, 231, 233–34

Corporations, rootlessness of, 242–43

Credential inflation, 207–8

Critical theory, 5–8

Cultural identity: distributive paradigm of justice and, 23–24; educational attainment and, 207–8; emergence of, 157; insurgency and, 83–84; justice and, 152–55; and oppression, 11; pluralism vs. unity in, 163–68, 178–81; politicization of, 86–88, 153–55; revitalization through, 166–67

Cultural imperialism: abjection and, 147–48; dynamics of aversion and, 123–24; oppression and, 58–61, 64; politics of difference and, 165–68, 172–73; professionalization of work and, 140–41, 221–22; racism and, 122–23; standardized testing as, 209; unintended action and, 148–51; violence and, 63

Darwall, Stephen, 102
Decisionmaking: in administered society, 78–81; affirmative action and, 194–95; cultural, 11; democratization of, 91–95, 116–21, 248–55; distributive paradigm of justice and, 10, 19–20, 22–23; impartiality and, 112–16; insurgency and, 83–84; interest-group structure of, 72–74; as nonmaterial good, 24; oppressed group representation in, 184–91; politics of qualifications and, 213–14; power of city life and, 243–45; professionalization of work and, 213–14, 218, 221; regionalization of government and, 254–55; task definition and execution classification, 218
Deconstruction, impossiblity of impartiality and, 102
Delphy, Christine, 50
Democracy: as condition for social justice, 91–95; cultural pluralism in, 163–68; in division of labor, 222–25; heterogeneity and, 116–21; intrinsic value of, 92–95; justice and, 190–91; vs. recontainment, 88–91
Democratic Party, group representation in, 189
Dependency, marginalization and, 54–55
Depoliticization, 70, 80
Deskillinization, professionalization of work and, 219–21
Dialogic reason, 107
Dichotomy, impossibility of impartiality and, 102–3
Difference, politics of, 13–14; city life and, 226–56; critical theory and, 7–8; denial of, 10, 99–102; emancipation through, 163–68; gender polarization and, 137–38; Giddens' three-level strategy and, 133–36; groups and, 47–48; ideal of community and, 235–36; vs. impartiality, 99–107; international aspects of, 259; justice and, 3–5; logic of identity and, 98–99;

medicalization of, 129–30; participatory democracy and, 118–19; positive images of, 11, 185–86; reclaiming meaning of, 168–73; role of, in policy making, 173–83; social movements and, 156–91; stereotypes and, 197; vs. unity, 97
Discursive consciousness: defined, 131; of oppressed groups, 133–34; prejudice and, 132; unintended action and, 150–51; xenophobia and, 145–46
"Disparate impact" doctrine, 196
Displacement, policy making and, 134–35
Distributive paradigm of justice, 15–38; affirmative action and, 198–200; city life and, 241–48; defined, 16–18; depoliticization process and, 70–71; domination and oppression as injustice, 33–38; ideological function of, 74–76; institutional context of, 18–24; limits of, 8–9, 24–30; power distribution and, 30–33
Diversity, ideal of, 158–63. See also Difference, politics of
Division of labor: affirmative action and, 199–200; democratic division, 222–25; depoliticization of, 70–71; distributive paradigm of justice and, 20–24; myth of merit and, 203–4; oppression and, 214–22; professional/nonprofessional, 57–58; reason and sentiment and, 110–11; sexual and racial exploitation in, 50–53. See also Professionalization of work; Task definition and execution
Dominant goods, 217
Domination: in administered society, 76–81; defined, 38; democratic decisionmaking and, 91–95; distribution of power and, 31–33, 56–58; injustice as, 9–10, 33–38; institutional context of, 38; insurgency as response to, 82–83; politics of qualifications and, 212–13; professionalization of work and, 218
Dominative racism, 141–42
Double consciousness: abjection and, 148; cultural imperialism and, 60–61; politics of difference and, 165–66
Du Bois, W.E.B., 60, 169
Dworkin, Ronald, 30
Dyadic modeling of power, 31

Economic activity: educational opportunity and, 207; international aspects of, 259–

Economic activity (*cont*.):
60; municipalization of, 249; planning of, in welfare capitalist society, 67–68

Education: equal opportunity as distributive justice, 26; as performance proxy, 206–10; privilege and, 154. *See also* Credential inflation

Ehrenreich, Barbara, 229

Elderly, marginalization of, 53–55

Elkin, Stephen, 244–45

Elshtain, Jean, 229

Emancipation through difference, 163–68

Employment testing, 208. *See also* Standardized testing

Empowerment, autonomy without, 248–55

Enablement, opportunity as, 26

End-state patterns of distributive paradigm, 28–29, 32

English as Second Language (ESL), 180–81

Enlightenment: history of, 156–57; impartial moral reason and, 97; racist consequences of, 130–31

Entitlement, 68–69; property as, 217

Environmental movements, 83

Epstein, Stephen, 45

Equal Employment Opportunity Commission, 208

Equality: acceptance model of, 176–78; vs. affirmative action, 195–96; discursive consciousness and, 132; politics of difference and, 11–12, 173–74; in welfare capitalist society, 69–70

Equal opportunity: affirmative action and, 192–93; distributive paradigm and, 25–26; hierarchical division of labor and, 215–16; history of, 214–15; politics of qualifications and, 211–12. *See also* Social mobility

Eroticism, in city life, 239–40

"Ethic of rights," 96–97

Ethnicity, resurgence of, 260

Ethnopolitics, development of, 88

Etiquette, discursive consciousness and, 132

European Economic Community, 260

Exclusionary behavior: ideal of community and, 235–36; lack of, in city life, 238–39

Expertism: foreign policy and, 84; politics of qualifications and, 211–12; in welfare capitalist society, 80–81. *See also* Credential inflation; Professionalization of work

Exploitation: distributive paradigm of justice and, 23; local government control and, 94–95; as oppression, 48–53; professionalization of work and, 218–19; segregation of city and suburbs and, 247–48

Face-to-face relations, in community, 232–34

Family structure, distributive paradigm of justice and, 21

Fault, discrimination as, 196. *See also* Blame

Feeling, vs. reason, 102–3

Femininity, bourgeois norms of respectability and, 137–38

Feminism: critical theory and, 8; cultural imperialism and, 58–61; cultural specificity and, 87–88, 161–62; gender neutral vs. group conscious policy making and, 175–78; ideal of civic public, 109–10; marginalization theory and, 55; oppression and, 13; paradigm of moral reasoning and, 96–97; "personal is political" slogan, 120–21; as politicized self-help, 85–86; racism and, 154–55. *See also* Sexism; Women

Feminist separatism, 161–62

Ferguson, Ann, 50–51

Fishkin, James, 201

Foreign aid, depoliticization of, 259

Foreign policy, expertism and, 84

Foucault, Michel, 32, 229–30

Freudian analysis, critics of, 143

Frug, Gerald, 242–43, 248–55

Frye, Marilyn, 41

Fullinwider, Robert, 194–95

Functions, separation of, in city life, 244–48

Galston, William, 17, 24, 27

Gay movement. *See* Homosexuality; Lesbianism

Gender-neutral vs. group conscious policy making, 175–78

Gender socialization, 50–51

"Generalized other", 106–7

Giddens, Anthony, 28, 131–32

Goods, allocation of: distributive paradigm and, 15–16; justice theories focused on, 19; marginal deprivation of, 53–55

Government institutions: corporate aspects of, 67–68; distributive paradigm of justice and, 22; economic regulation by, 67–70; gender exploitation and, 51–52; group representation in, 189–90; ideal of impartiality in, 113–16; impact on city life of, 242–43; regionalization of, 252–55. *See also* Local government

Gramm-Rudman bill, 68

Grass-roots institutions: decisionmaking by, 92–93; economic empowerment and, 249

Green, Philip, 216

Groups: affinity in, 46–48; affirmative action and, 9–10; consciousness of, in policy making, 173–83; cultural revolution and, 153–55; defined, 186; heterogeneous public and, 183–91; ideal of community and, 235–36; ideal of impartiality and, 115–16; liberal humanism and, 168–69; oppression and, 3–5, 42–48; positivity of, 165–67; representation of, in policy making, 185–91; social groups vs. interest or ideological groups, 186–87; specificity of, 157–58, 182–83; violence towards, 62–63

Gutmann, Amy, 93–95, 184

Gynocentric feminism, 161–62

Habermas, Jurgen, 7–8; civic public ideal and, 117–18; colonization of the life world concept, 79; communicative ethics of, 33–34, 45–46, 92–94; on ideal of impartiality, 106–7

Harvey, David, 245

Health, white bourgeois bias towards, 127–30

Hegel, Georg Freidrich, 113, 231

Heidegger, Martin, 46

Heller, Agnes, 33

Heterogeneity: of feeling, impartiality and, 100; group representation and, 183–91; ideal of, 179–81; participatory democracy and, 116–21 subjectivity and, 231–32

"Hidden mechanisms" of redistribution, 244–45

Hierarchical organization: affirmative action and, 193; decisionmaking in, 56–58, 112–16; domination of, in administered society, 78–81; in education, 206–7; impartiality and, 112–16; increased competition

in, 215–16; myth of merit and, 203–6; politics of qualifications and, 212–13; powerlessness and, 56–58

Higher-order discrimination, 135

Hispanic minorities: bilingual policy making and, 177–81; cultural specificity of, 160

Homoeroticism, in bourgeois respectability, 138–39

Homophobia: abjection and, 146–47; consciousness raising about, 154–55

Homosexuality: abjection and, 146–47; consciousness raising about, 154–55; cultural specificity of, 160–61

Human nature, justice and, 35–37

Ideals, genesis of, 6–8

Identity, logic of: civic public ideal and, 107–11; group differences and, 43–46, 160–73; ideal of community and, 229–32; impartiality and, 97; postmodernist critique of, 98–99; scaling of bodies and, 122–55

Ideological group, defined, 186

Ideology: defined, 112–16; distributive paradigm and, 74–76; ideal of impartiality and, 111–16

Immersion language programs, 180–81

Impartiality, ideal of, 10–11; civic public and, 96–121; denial of difference and, 99–102; ideological function of, 111–16; impossibility of, 102–7; myth of merit and, 12, 205–6

Income distribution: distributive paradigm of justice and, 19–22; division of labor and oppression linked to, 216–17. *See also* Goods allocation of; Wealth, distribution of

Income supports, in welfare capitalist society, 70

Indian Reorganization Act, 182

Individualism: affirmative action and, 192–93; distributive paradigm of justice and, 35–36, 74–76; groups and, 45–48; ideal of community and, 226–29; myth of merit and, 200–206; politics of difference and, 166–67

Injustice: in city life, 241–48; domination and oppression defined as, 33–40; segregation of city and suburbs and, 247–48; violence as, 61–62

Institutional context: affirmative action and, 197–98; distributive paradigm of justice and, 18–24, 34–35

Insurgency: recontainment and, 90–91; repoliticization with, 81–88

Intelligence tests: cultural biases in, 126–27; testing for, normative biases in, 222

Interest groups: defined, 186; ideology and distributive paradigm, 75–76; participatory democracy and, 118–19; regionalization of government and, 254–55; role of, in welfare capitalist society, 72–74

Irrationality of violence, 62–63

Jensen's theory of IQ differential, 133

Jewish Americans, cultural specificity of, 160

Job allocation: distributive paradigm of justice and, 22; gender neutral vs. group conscious policies and, 177–78; myth of merit and, 12, 201–3. *See also* Task definition and execution

Justice: care and, 97; cultural revolution and, 152–55; democratic decisionmaking and, 91–95, 190–91; ethico-political concept of, 33–34; international aspects of, 257–58; politics of, 9–10; theory of, 3–5; transfer of power and, 49–50; unintended action and, 149–51. *See also* Distributive paradigm of justice; Injustice

Karst, Kenneth, 173–74

Katznelson, Ira, 89

Kirkpatrick, Jean, 84

Knowledge, visual metaphors for, 125–30

Kovel, Joel, 141–48

Kristeva, Julia, 142–48, 152–53

Labor theory of value, exploitation and, 48–49

Labor unions, depoliticization of, 70–71

Land use policies: American Indians and, 182; in city life, 244–45

Language support programs, 180–81

Lawrence, Charles, 135, 150–51

Legal theory, unintended action and, 150–51

Lesbianism: cultural expression and, 160–61; homophobia and, 146, 154–55, 164; repoliticization and, 87–88; separatist impulse and, 162–63

Liberal humanism, politics of difference and, 166–67

Liberalism, individualism and, 228

Liberation, paradigms of, 158–63

Liberty, regionalization of government and, 254–55

Littleton, Christine, 176–78

Livingston, John, 214

Local government: autonomy in, 227; democracy and, 94–95; insurgency against, 84; minority representation in, 183. *See also* Government institutions

Locke, John, 113

Lowi, Theodore, 74

Lyotard, Jean-François, 3–4

Macpherson, C. B., 36, 49

Managerial work: increased competition for, 215–16; task analysis and, 203–6

Mansbridge, Jane, 184

Marcuse, Herbert, 6–8, 89

Marginalization: as criterion for oppression, 64; distributive paradigm of justice and, 23; as oppression, 53–55

Markus, Maria, 82

Marriage, exploitation in, 50

Marxism: distributive paradigm of justice and, 20–21; exploitation and, 48–53; professionalization of work and, 219

Masculinity, norms of respectability and, 137–38

Mass media, racism and sexism in, 135–36; stereotyping by, 20

Mathematics, gender/racial bias in, 207

May, Larry, 150

Menial labor, exploitation and, 52

Mental balance, white bourgeois bias towards, 127–30

Merit, myth of, 200–206; expertism and, 80–81; ideal of impartiality and, 12; oppression and division of labor, 214–22; politics of qualifications and, 210–14; value-neutral evaluation and, 193

Metaracism, 141–42

Mill, John Stuart, 92

Miller, David, 17, 24, 30

Minorities: cultural politics in, 85–86, 88; ideal of civic public and, 111; importance of, in city life, 238–39; oppression of, 40; scaling of bodies and, 129–30. *See also* *specific minorities*

Minow, Martha, 169
Modernism, critical theory and, 8. *See also* Postmodernism
Moral judgments: higher-order discrimination and, 134–35; impartiality and, 105–6; logic of identity and, 100–102; paradigm of, 96–97; unintended action and, 148–51; white bourgeois bias towards, 127–30
"Moral point of view," 100–102, 106
Mosse, George, 136

Nagel, Thomas, 102–3
Nationalism, cultural aspects of, 138
National Women's Studies Association, 188
Needs assessment, in welfare capitalist society, 67–70
Neighborhoods, 90–91; empowerment of, 252; variety in, 239
Nell, Edward, 17
Nickel, James, 26
Nielsen, Kai, 17
Nondiscrimination, affirmative action and, 193–98
Nonmaterial goods, distributive paradigm of justice and, 24–30
Normalization of testing, 209–10
Normative concepts: behavior and respectability, 136–41; city life and, 236–41; of culture, 59–61; distributive paradigm and, 24–30; ideal of civic public and, 111; of justice, 4–5, 34–35; moral responsibility and unintended action, 149–51; reflection, 5–6; scaling of bodies and, 11, 125–30; of welfare capitalist society, 67–70
"Normative dualism," professionalization of work and, 221
Nozick, Robert, 28

Oedipal psyche, racism and, 142
Offe, Claus, 74
Okin, Susan, 105
O'Neill, Onora, 17
Oppression: affirmative action and, 197–99; assimilation and, 159–63, 166; aversion and, 142; criteria for, 63–64; cultural imperialism and, 58–61; discrimination and, 195–96; defined, 38; division of labor and, 214–22; exploitation and, 48–53; group differences and, 160–71, 186–91; heterogeneous public and, 184; homogeneity as, 179–81; as injustice, 33–38; institutional context of, 38; international aspects of, 258–60; marginalization as, 53–55; political context of, 39–42; as powerlessness, 56–58; privilege and, 127–28; scaling of bodies and, 123–24; social groups and, 9–10, 42–48; task definition and execution as, 224–25; unintended action and, 148–51; violence and, 61–63. *See also* Domination
Otherness: aversion and, 143–44; cultural imperialism and, 60–61; group difference and, 160–71; ideal of impartiality and, 106–7; international aspects of, 260. *See also* Difference, politics of

Pan-African movement, 260
Paradigm: defined, 16; of liberation, 158–63
"Paradox of democracy," 92–93
Participation, in decisionmaking, 91–95, 248–55; marginalization and, 54–55; repoliticization and, 83;
Participatory democracy, 117–21; justice of, 92–93, 190–91
Particularist affiliation, emergence of, 163–64; vs. impartiality, 103–5
"Path to belonging" of assimilation, 159
Pay scales, division of labor and, 216
Peace movement, 84–85
Peer review, politics of qualifications and, 213
Performance evaluation: educational attainment and, 207–8; myth of merit and, 203–5
Performance proxies, education and testing as, 206–10
"Philosophy of consciousness," 45–46
Phobia, abjection and aversion and, 144–45
Piper, Adrian, 135
Pitkin, Hannah, 9, 107, 185–86
Platonic theory of justice, 33, 35–36
Pluralism: ideal of impartiality and, 114–16; of self, 101–2
Policy making: affirmative action and, 197–98; depoliticization of, 10, 258–59; difference and, 173–83; powerlessness and, 56–58; power of cities in, 244–45

Politics: city life and, 240–41; culture and, 86; defined, 9–10; group representation and, 190–91; ideal of, 12–13; ideal of community and, 233–36; justice and, 9–10; moral responsibility and unintended action, 149–51; scope of justice and, 34–35

Positivism, political theory and, 3

Postmodernism: critical theory and, 8; logic of identity and, 98–99; scaling of bodies and, 124–30; theory of justice and, 35–36

Power: in administered society, 76–81; in city life, 248–55; distributive paradigm of justice and, 30–33; of expertism, 80–81; exploitation and, 49; insurgency and, 83–84; oppression and, 41–42; politics of qualifications and, 211–12; recontainment vs. democracy and, 89–91

Powerlessness: of cities, 242–43; oppression and, 56–58; professionalization of work and, 219–20; respectability and, 139–40

Powers of Horror, 143

Practical consciousness: abjection and, 146; defined, 131; prejudice and, 133, 138–39

Pregnancy and childbirth rights, gender neutral vs. group conscious policy making and, 175–78

Prejudice, history of, 156–57

Privacy: autonomy as, 251; morality and, 137; participatory democracy and, 119–20

Privilege: heterogeneous public and, 184; schooling and, 154; structuring of, 127–28

Procedural fairness, myth of merit and, 201–2

Production: marginalization and, 54–55; private ownership of, 49; sex-affective, 50–51

Professionalization of work: behavioral norms of respectability and, 139–40; class structure and, 217; domination of, in administered society, 77–81; increased competition in, 215–16; politics of qualifications and, 211–12; powerlessness and, 56–58; task analysis and, 203–6

Profit, exploitation and, 48–49

Property, as entitlement, 217

Proportional representation, 187–88

Public, defined, 119–20

Publicity, in city life, 240–41

Public life, repoliticization of, 81–88

Public patriarchy, 51

Public space, in city life, 240–41

Qualifications: defined, 201; merit and, 204–5; peer review of, 224–25; politics of, 210–14

Racism: abjection and, 141–48; cultural imperialism and, 58–61; discursive consciousness and, 132–33; exploitation and, 50–53; professionalism and, 57–58; role of in policy making, 135; violence and, 61–62; in welfare capitalist society, 122–23. *See also* Aversive racism; Dominative racism; Metaracism

Rainbow Coalition, 188–89

Rationality, cultural biases in, 126–27. *See also* Reason

Rawls, John: distributive paradigm of justice and, 16–17, 20–21; on impartiality, 104; "rights and duties" concept, 24–25; on self-respect, 27; on utilitarianism, 101–2

Reason: behavioral norms of respectability and, 136–41; scaling of bodies and, 124–30, 139–41

Reciprocity, ideal of community and, 230–31

Recontainment vs. democracy, 88–91

Red Power (American Indian Movement), 160

Reductionism, political theory and, 3

Regional government, importance of, 252–55

Reiman, Jeffrey, 52–53

Relational understanding of difference, 171–73

Representation, equality of, with heterogenous groups, 185–91

Respectability: behavioral norms of, 136–41; ideal of, 136; oppression and, 57–58; powerlessness and, 139–40

Responsibility vs. blame, 151

Rightful possession, justice as, 17

Rights: distributive paradigm and, 25; ethic of, 96–97; marginalization and, 54–55; tribal rights of American Indians, 183

Roemer, John, 49, 52

Rousseau, Jean-Jacques, 92, 108–9, 229–32
Runciman, W. G., 16–17

Sandel, Michael, 35, 228, 230
Sartre, Jean-Paul, 231
Science, gender/racial bias in, 207
Segregated residential patterns, 57, 245–48
Self, plurality of, 101–2
Self-determination: of American Indians, 183; democratic decisionmaking and, 91–95; ideal of community and, 234–36; separation and, 143–44
Self-esteem: distributive paradigm of justice and, 26–27; politics of difference and, 165–66
Self-organization: by groups, 184; heterogenous public and, 190–91; politicization of, 85–86; politics of difference and, 159–60, 167–68
Semiotic capacity, 143
Sennett, Richard, 108, 235
Services: exploitation and, 52–53; regionalization of, 253–55
Sexism: discursive consciousness and, 132–33; exploitation and, 50–51; professionalization of work and, 57–58; role of in policy making, 135; violence and, 61–62
Sexuality, repression of, in bourgeois mentality, 138–39
Sharing, community as, 231–32
Situation, particularlity of, 100
Social cooperation, domination of, in welfare capitalist society, 78–81
Social groups. See Groups
Social justice. See Justice
Social mobility: division of labor and, 214–15; professionalization of work and, 221
Social movements of 1960s and 1970s: concept of oppression in, 7, 41–42; as insurgency, 82–83; group specificity and, 162–63
Social ontology, 45
Social reality, critical theory and, 6
Social relations: group dynamics and, 42–48; ideal of, 12–13; power and, 31
Social theory: defined, 5; distributive paradigm of justice and, 28–30
Sovereignty: individualism and, 107–8; oppression and, 41–42
Spatial segregation and functionalization, urban, 245–48

Specialization, division of labor and, 216, 225
Specificity, meaning of difference and, 171–73
Sports, gender neutral vs. group conscious policy making and, 178
Standardized testing, myth of merit and, 207–10
Stereotypes: cultural imperialism and, 59–61; distributive paradigm of justice and, 20
Subjectivity: community as shared, 230–32; cultural imperialism and, 124; impartiality and, 100–101; scaling of bodies and, 125–30; three-level theory of, 131–36
Supervisory roles, division of labor and, 216
Symbolic capacity, 143
Systemic aspects of oppression, 41–42
Systemic violence, 62

Task analysis: of managerial and professional work, 203–6; myth of merit, 201–2; task definition and execution, 12, 193, 216–22, 224–25; task design, myth of merit and, 193
Task discontinuous hierarchies, 203
Taube, Nadine, 175
Tax policy, 68–69
Taylor, Charles, 18–19, 34–35
Tenant organizations, 86
Terms of Political Discourse, 30–31
Testing, as performance proxy, 206–10
"Throwness," 46
Transitional bilingual programs, 180–81

Unger, Roberto, 9, 216–17
Unintended action, moral responsibility and, 148–51
Unity: vs. cultural identity, 178–81; vs. difference, 97; group specificity and, 162; impartiality and, 100–101; logic of identity and, 99
Universality: of civic public, 10–11; of cultural norms, 59–61; domination of, in administered society, 77–81; ideal of impartiality and, 100–102; participatory democracy and, 118–19; vs. particularity, 103–5; politics of difference and, 165–68; of theory of justice, 4–5

Urban social movements, 84; recontainment vs. democracy in, 89. *See also* City life
Utilitarianism, impartiality and, 101–2
Utopianism, of impartiality, 103–4

Value-neutral evaluation and myth of merit, 202
Value systems, distributive paradigm of justice and, 37–38
Variety, of city life, 239
Violence: oppression as, 61–64; racism and, 122–23
Voting Rights Act, 159

Walzer, Michael, 6–7, 17–18, 81
Wartenburg, Thomas, 32
Wasserstrom, Richard, 158–59, 198–99
Wealth, distribution of: democratic decisionmaking and, 94–95; distributive paradigm of justice and, 19–22
Welfare capitalist society: depoliticization of, 70–74; distributive paradigm of justice and, 66–67; domination in, 76–81; exploitation and, 48–49; insurgency and repoliticization in, 81–88; marginalization and, 53–55; normative principles of, 67–70; recontainment vs. democracy in, 88–91
West, Cornel, 130–31
Williams, Bernard, 104–5
Williams, Wendy, 175
Women: exclusion of, from civic public ideal, 109–10; oppression of, 50–51; spatial separation and functionalization and, 246; white bourgeois ideal of, 129–30. *See also* Feminism
Wood, Allen, 20
Worker discretion, negative and positive roles in, 202–3
Workplace democracy: division of labor and, 223–25; gender neutral vs. group conscious policy making in, 175–76; myth of merit and, 193; politics of qualifications and, 212–13; powerlessness and, 56–58

Xenophobia, as abjection, 141–48

Zoning: autonomy of, 249–50; group segregation with, 246–47; impact on city life of, 244–45